Palgrave Studies in Prisons and Penology

This is a unique and innovative series, the first of its kind dedicated entirely to prison scholarship. At a historical point in which the prison population has reached an all-time high, the series seeks to analyse the form, nature and consequences of incarceration and related forms of punishment. Palgrave Studies in Prisons and Penology provides an important forum for burgeoning prison research across the world.

More information about this series at
http://www.palgrave.com/gp/series/14596

Sacha Darke • Chris Garces
Luis Duno-Gottberg • Andrés Antillano
Editors

Carceral Communities in Latin America

Troubling Prison Worlds in the 21st Century

palgrave
macmillan

Editors
Sacha Darke
School of Social Sciences
University of Westminster
London, UK

Luis Duno-Gottberg
Rice University
Houston, TX, USA

Chris Garces
Universidad San Francisco de Quito
Cumbaya, Ecuador

Andrés Antillano
Central University of Venezuela
Caracas, Miranda, Venezuela

Palgrave Studies in Prisons and Penology
ISBN 978-3-030-61498-0   ISBN 978-3-030-61499-7 (eBook)
https://doi.org/10.1007/978-3-030-61499-7

This Palgrave Macmillan imprint is published by the registered company Springer Nature Switzerland AG.
The registered company address is: Gewerbestrasse 11, 6330 Cham, Switzerland

Contents

Notes on Contributors

Andrés Antillano is Professor and Chair of Criminology at the Escuela de Derecho and researcher at the Institute of Criminal Sciences of the Universidad Central de Venezuela. He has written several articles and book chapters about prisons, police, violence, and gangs.

Libardo José Ariza is an associate professor at the School of Law of Universidad de los Andes (Bogotá-Colombia) and is currently co-director of the Prisons Group (a legal clinic). His research and academic interests focus on Criminology, Sociology of Punishment, Sociology of Law, Criminal Law, and Constitutional Law.

Karina Biondi holds a doctoral degree in Social Anthropology from the Federal University of São Carlos (UFSCar). She is professor at the State University of Maranhão (UEMA), where she coordinates the Laboratory of Studies in Political Anthropology. Biondi's research interests include prisoners, criminals, and technologies of crime control and punishment. She is author of *Sharing This Walk: An Ethnography of Prison Life PCC in Brazil* (winner of the APLA 2017 Book Prize) and *Proibido Roubar na Quebrada: Território, Lei e Hierarquia no PCC* (winner of the LASA Brazil Section Book Prize 2019).

Jon Horne Carter is a sociocultural anthropologist who writes about criminality, aesthetics, and sovereignty. He is Assistant Professor of

Anthropology at Appalachian State University and co-director of the AppState Ethnography Lab. He has been working in Honduras since 1997.

Francesca Cerbini is a senior researcher at the Center for Research in Anthropology (CRIA), University of Minho (UMinho). She carried out ethnographic fieldwork mainly in Bolivia, concerning the everyday life within the self-governed male prison of San Pedro (La Paz), and in Brazil, on the dengue epidemic and the local community engagement in public health related issues. At CRIA-UMinho, she is currently involved in a long-term ethnography on religious pluralism within Portuguese prisons.

Sacha Darke is Senior Lecturer in Criminology at the University of Westminster, Visiting Lecturer in Law at the University of São Paulo, and Affiliate at King's Brazil Institute, King's College London. His interests include Brazilian prison order and prison higher education. He is a founding member of British Convict Criminology, and author of *Conviviality and Survival: Co-Producing Brazilian Prison Order* (2018).

Kristen Drybread is a cultural anthropologist based at the University of Colorado, Boulder. She has written on prison rapes and murders, political corruption, and the meanings of unremarked graves. Her current project examines relationships between citizenship and violence in Brazil.

Luis Duno-Gottberg is a Professor at Rice University. He specializes in nineteenth-, twentieth-, and twenty-first-century Caribbean culture, with emphasis on race and ethnicity, politics, violence, and visual culture. His book project, *Dangerous People: Hegemony, Representation and Culture in Contemporary Venezuela*, explores the relationship between popular mobilization, radical politics, and culture. Duno-Gottberg taught at Universidad Simón Bolívar in Caracas, Venezuela, and Florida Atlantic University in Boca Raton. He was director of Caribbean and Latin American Studies while at FAU, where he also directed the MA in Comparative Literatures.

Cory Fischer-Hoffman is Visiting Assistant Professor of International Affairs at Lafayette College. She completed her PhD in Latin American, Caribbean and US Latino Studies from the University of Albany in 2016 with her dissertation focused on prison regime formation in Venezuela. Her work as a journalist, radio producer, and oral historian shapes her research on prison media and the gendered reproductive labor of prison visits in Venezuela. After moving to Bethlehem, Pennsylvania, for a post-doctoral fellowship in Digital Humanities at Lehigh University, she commenced her next big project: tracing the history of the Bethlehem Steel Corporation's iron mining operations in Latin America.

Chris Garces teaches at the Universidad San Francisco de Quito (USFQ) as Research Professor of Anthropology. His ethnographic interests range from the study of politics and religion—or contemporary political theologies—to the unchecked global development of penal state politics and the history of Catholic humanitarian interventions in Latin America.

Manuel Iturralde is an associate professor at the School of Law of Universidad de los Andes (Bogotá-Colombia) and is currently co-director of the Prisons Group (a legal clinic). His research and academic interests focus on Criminology, Sociology of Punishment, Sociology of Law, and Criminal Law.

Fiona Macaulay's is Associate Professor in the department of Peace Studies and International Development at the University of Bradford. She previously worked for Amnesty International as their Brazil researcher and her research interests focus on criminal justice system reform, human rights, and on gender, violence and security issues in Latin America, especially Brazil. Ongoing research projects include the transformation of state responses to feminicide and the involvement of police officers in politics in Brazil.

Hollis Moore is an assistant professor in the Department of Law and Legal Studies at Carleton University. She holds a PhD in Socio-Cultural Anthropology from the University of Toronto (2017). Her academic interests include the intersection between political and legal anthropology, urban ethnography, and the study of gender and family life. She has conducted extensive ethnographic fieldwork in and around prisons in Northeast Brazil. At its core, her research examines the sociality of uneven carceral expansion. She is currently conducting a longitudinal study of the trajectories of young Brazilians who have experienced the incarceration of a parent. This project focuses on the (re)production of marginalization through criminal law, policing, and imprisonment as well as intergenerational processes of care and (de)criminalization.

Caroline Mary Parker is a presidential postdoctoral fellow of Medical Anthropology in the Department of Social Anthropology, University of Manchester. Her work combines approaches in cultural and medical anthropology and public health with a geographical focus on the Caribbean and the urban United States. Her anthropological work engages questions of social suffering, poverty, and inequality; addiction therapeutics, labor, and the carceral state, and liberalism, boredom, and temporality. Her work has been published in *Culture, Medicine and Psychiatry*, *Medical Anthropology Quarterly*, *Culture, Health and Sexuality*, and the *New England Journal of Medicine*. Her first book project, *Carceral Livelihoods in Puerto Rico*, examines the use of unpaid labor as a treatment for drug addiction in Puerto Rican therapeutic communities.

Jennifer Peirce is a doctoral candidate in criminology at John Jay College and the CUNY Graduate Center. Her dissertation research on the Dominican prison reform experience was funded in part by the Pierre Elliott Trudeau Foundation and the Social Sciences and Humanities Research Council (Canada). She works on research and policy focused on reducing incarceration in Latin America, the Caribbean, and North America.

Iván Pojomovsky is a PhD candidate from the Sociology Program of the Universidade Federal de Pernambuco, in Recife, Brazil. He has conducted ethnographic work on police accountability, violence, and participation mechanisms, all in urban popular contexts in Venezuela. He is researching on a comparative perspective on different forms of inmate self-government in Venezuela and Brazil.

Chelina Sepúlveda Is an MSc in Social Anthropology and Ethnology from the École des Hautes Études en Sciences Sociales (Paris), a professor in the Sociology Department of Universidad Central de Venezuela (UCV), and researcher of Instituto de Estudios Avanzados (IDEA). Her research interests center around ethnography of the popular classes. In this perspective, she has approached the subject of violence and social conflict as related to exclusion processes from the viewpoint of the transformation in the relationship between the state and poor communities. She has developed ethnographic work in penitentiary institution and urban poor contexts.

Loïc Wacquant is Professor of Sociology at the University of California, Berkeley, and researcher at the Centre de sociologie européenne, Paris. His interests include urban marginality, penality, carnality, and social theory. He is the author of the trilogy *Urban Outcasts* (2008), *Punishing the Poor* (2009) and *Deadly Symbiosis: Race and the Rise of the Penal State* (forthcoming).

Julienne Weegels is Assistant Professor of Latin American Studies at the Centre for Latin American Research and Documentation (CEDLA), University of Amsterdam. She has conducted extensive multi-sited ethnographic research inside and around Nicaragua's prison system. Her research focuses on (former) prisoners' experiences of imprisonment and the state, violence, and the politics of (dis)order.

List of Images

1

Ethnographic Reflexivity and Ethics of Community in the New Mass Carceral Zone

Chris Garces and Sacha Darke

Whatever one might argue about prisons in Latin America or the Caribbean today, cross-regional booms in prison construction signal an immediate, pressing need for new kinds of study and critical diagnostics—and a revisiting of the ethics of community. The Western Hemisphere beyond North America occupies a key role in any study of the last quarter century of globalized carceral accelerationism. Almost all countrywide prison populations have doubled or tripled in size since the mid-to-late 1990s: national numbers approached, and sometimes surpassed, 300

Sacha Darke would like to acknowledge the support of the Leverhulme Trust. He is currently a Leverhulme Trust Research Fellow (award RF-2020-373\8). His research focuses on community self-governance in Brazilian former-prisoner-led voluntary sector NGO prisons.

C. Garces (✉)
Universidad San Francisco de Quito, Cumbaya, Ecuador

S. Darke (✉)
School of Social Sciences, University of Westminster, London, UK

S. Darke et al. (eds.), *Carceral Communities in Latin America*, Palgrave Studies in Prisons and Penology, https://doi.org/10.1007/978-3-030-61499-7_1

locked-up individuals per hundred-thousand national population. Indeed, the ranks of the incarcerated grew in Latin and Central America more than in any other global region, from approximately 650,000 in 2000 to 1.5 million in 2014 (Walmsley 2018). Every Latin American country has a prison population far above the global average, and subjects more people to living in cages than they did in 2000 (ibid). Moreover, in most territories, the rise in prison population has far exceeded police recorded increase in serious violent crime. This global trend quietly generates ethical imbroglios and practical stresses in any number of national contexts, particularly when incarceration rates have grown proportionally faster than the curve of national population—most troublesomely, in nominally democratic states—with multiple ill-understood collateral consequences and ramifying political economic effects.

Brute nationwide numbers place this trend in broader relief. Among the countries covered in this volume, for example, Nicaragua's prison rate reached 278 per 100,000 in 2017, up from 128 in 2000; that countrywide figure now stands at 332. In the same year, Venezuela's prison rate reached 178 (up from 58 in 2000). The *Observatorio Venezolano de Prisiones* has recognized the existence of 57,096 state prisoners, but also estimates that 32,000 prisoners were being held in police station jails—which brings Venezuela's nationwide number more accurately closer to 276. Ecuador had 64 prisoners per 100,000 in 2000, but that number has jumped to 224 only two decades later. In the meantime, Honduras stands at 237 as of September 2019. Populous Brazil of course remains the region's leading incarcerator. At 759,518 adult prisoners as of June 2020, Brazil's official prison population had increased by more than 2000 percent from December 1984, when only 37,071 adults were imprisoned (Pavarini and Giamberardino 2011); the number of Brazilian prisoners per 100,000 currently stands at some 357 souls. The situation is equally stark across the Caribbean; among territories/nations explored in this volume, Puerto Rico had approximately 313 per 100,000 in July 2017, and the Dominican Republic was at 243 as of September 2019. Other Caribbean islands we do not explore here are equally or far more troubled: Trinidad and Tobago (292), Cuba (510), the U.S. Virgin Islands (412), Guadeloupe (814), and Barbados (874), to name but a few. Although generally smaller in population, the problem of carcerality across the Greater Antilles rivals only that of the United States which resides at 665 per hundred thousand (figures provided by World Prison Brief, accessed 30 August 2020).

Ethnographic research on prisons and carcerality in South America and the Caribbean demonstrate how the condemning/caging of human beings can indeed be "normalizing" in practice, but never in any case quite "normal." For starters, national figures are usually higher than reports would suggest. States are incentivized to publicize "incarceration rate" numbers favorable to instrumental government interests, and local or international watchdog groups observe what they can during their occasional, indispensable, short-term prison visits. Slipping through the cracks of such formal tallies are shadow prisoners, temporarily detained subjects, illegal immigrants, adolescents held in administrative detention, and people held under house arrest and the special category of dangerous inmates being held virtually incommunicado in supermaximum security cellblocks; such individuals, typically un(der)counted in citywide or federal statistics, only add to the state's de facto labyrinthine concentration and "public disappearance" of criminally stigmatized, sentenced, or unruly populations.

This volume brings forward a powerfully representative sample of ethnographic research exploring the multifaceted practical and ethical problems of regional carceral acceleration. For every newly imprisoned Latin American subject, volume contributors observe that a myriad of civilians' everyday lives and futures have been interrupted or jarringly altered by prison population expansion—starting, of course, with prisoners and their loved ones. Our work as a whole is dedicated to them and to their configurations of care and collective lines of flight from abject forms of domination; or, more specifically, to a better understanding of Latin American prisoners' modalities of survival; to the untold numbers of civilians who traverse the space of the prison or protect prisoners against penal state abuses; or to those for whom prisoners of state remain stubbornly un-subtractable from one's family or broader community. This is the work of prison ethnography. On the one hand, our volume brings together empirically grounded, theoretically innovative research and interdisciplinary activist pushback against the disintegrative social forces of contemporary carcerality—probing and exposing its visible and invisible apparatuses. On the other hand, each of these studies, informed by long-term prison fieldwork in men's prisons, highlights the ethical dynamics and problems involved when carceral communities quietly organize and attempt to navigate regimes of punitive enclosure.

Through years of collaborative research with people who inhabit prison facilities, ethnographers understand intuitively that carceral communities quite often exist to defy the "names" (or material-symbolic destinies) bestowed on them by non-incarcerated prison specialists. In contrast to economic game theories, abstract archetypal systems, and cognitive behaviorist understandings of prisoners' motives, activist and self-reflexive ethnographic models help to comprehend prison dynamics, system-wide problems, and the unintentional harms of living in cages from the perspectives of prisoners themselves. Ethnographic research today may have its empirical strengths and limitations and tendencies toward exploration of "the dark sides" of contemporary life (Ortner 2016), but long-term, first-person, theoretically informed fieldwork—carried out inside prison facilities—brings forward unusual insights into what goes without saying across the grotesque task of storing away human beings in states of punitive custody. The prison ethnographer's mode of bearing "secondary witness" (cf. LaCapra 2011) to a problematic "ethics of captivity" (cf. Gruen 2014), we submit, offers untold humanizing perspectives into the formation of communities largely invisible or misrecognized by the state in its unstinting obsessions with policing sovereign violence and control (Blom and Stepputat 2006). It is to the study of this most curious blind spot in research on prison worlds that volume contributors, from a variety of different disciplinary backgrounds, direct their ethnographic fieldwork, subtle policy insights, and personal concerns. In this introductory chapter, we therefore put forward a theory of carceral community and demonstrate how reflexive ethnographic fieldwork allows for extraordinary depth of inquiry into these infra-political formations, along with how they pose a direct challenge to common theoretical understandings of biopolitics, sovereignty, and the invisibilized influence of carcerality on other communities and broader national publics.

Carceral Communities

By personal choice, ethnographers place their own bodies into often-uncomfortably situated problem areas in order to gain better, previously unacknowledged insight into this "new mass carceral zone" (Darke and

Garces 2017: 2). Unlike other forms of scholarship, however, we generally stop at nothing to privilege the knowledge, experiences, and desires of prisoners themselves, a process we define below and our contributors explore in greater detail across the volume as a whole. Prison ethnographers are typically drawn to interpret the vital material importance of collectivism, taking into account the multiple "worlds," "networks," "relations," or human-material "affordances" that comprise life inside contemporary prison estates. We actively track the ways in which prisoners suffer and seek delimited enjoyments, being subject to deliberate state-imposed deprivations, while attempting to make contingent peace with, or to short-circuit modalities of dehumanizing social engineering. Each volume contributor demonstrates how different modalities of prison communitarianism well up organically in men's prisons, if not always consciously or instrumentally, in response to serialized civil dispossession, or the deracinated prison-absence of loved ones, friends, colleagues, or neighbors. Their being thrown into the penal complex, new relationships and elective affinities quickly become paramount to one's survival. As a result, prisons themselves become what might be called community-generating machines, whether or not prison staff, state actors, and popular or social media are willing to recognize this entrenched side-effect of carcerality as such. It is precisely for this reason why our volume could just as easily have been called *Anticarceral Communities*.

The intrinsic desire to survive imprisonment, or to embrace delimited modes of carceral flourishing, generates novel and typically misunderstood varieties of *communitas*, ritualized forces of effervescent togetherness operating inside as well as at maximal remove from "the state"—or at least at an extreme distance from assorted, self-denominated experts who attempt to see the prison "like a state" (cf. Scott 1998). Those who bear witness to self-governing Latin American and Caribbean prison communities are all too often tainted by the Western, Occidentalist tendency to assume other countries or regions are "like our own" (cf. Coronil 1996, 2004). Such ethnocentric assumptions are not only largely misplaced, but are also remarkably dangerous. They can make us blind to regionally grounded, alternately cosmopolitan, ethnic, or cultural differences, and have been the cause of many a failed, one-size-fits-all prison policy being imported into the region that ultimately ended up doing more harm than good. More generally, they divert our gaze away from 'ideas and theory rooted in the history and experience of societies of the [Global] South' (Carrington et al. 2016: 2).

Carceral communities develop across Latin American and Caribbean men's prisons as collectives or subcultures on cellblock wings; foreign-national or regionally distinct affinity groups; ad hoc therapeutic sodalities; prisoner leadership councils; infra-political blocs of violent entrepreneurs; or simply as groups of friends—in addition, at times, to being de facto extensions of legitimate or outlawed political parties; local or international gangs; paramilitary or guerillas; multinational drug cartels; and even incarcerated former members of state military or police forces. Carceral communities therefore spring up intra-, inter-, or even extra-institutionally vis-à-vis any prison complex. The deep ethnographic study of carceral community permits a better understanding of how—in addition to being a poorly understood though central bureaucratic field of the contemporary state (Wacquant 2003, 2005, 2008)—the prison itself has morphed into a largely disavowed, non- or para-state project of community outgrowth. And yet, the full extent to which prisons turn unconsciously into vectors of and for "community development" has been systematically, and oftentimes tragically, unacknowledged.

Prisons exert "force at a distance" both inside and outside their physical-material constraints. Consider for instance the prison's exteriorizing/demonizing role—perhaps the best-known reactionary and negative manifestation of public responses to carceral communities. Especially in Latin America and the Caribbean, where law is unashamedly used and barely disguised as a motivated tool of injustice and repression (e.g. Castro 1987; Zaffaroni 1989; Aguirre and Salvatore 2001). National publics who advocate for zero tolerance policing and prosecutorial efforts, along with the criminalization of certain urban subjects—poor and working class youths of color, and, increasingly, economic refugees—celebrate how prisons, or their ominous concrete action at a distance, inoculate civilians against *felt*, imminent threats to one's personal, family-oriented, and/or private economic security. The prison turns into a concrete reminder of how penal policy efforts tacitly exercise psychological and ontological influence across the state. The Latin American carceral complex becomes inseparable from modern understandings of citizen-being and its variety of others. Witness a flagrant crime, then throw any offender(s) across the legal-physical threshold of the society-versus-prison divide.

In the name of defending "citizens security," for example, entire urban districts have recently seen their architectural and public cultures transformed in tandem to provide physical barriers and psychological buffers against crime and carceral community. Common manifestations of this development include the building of commercial security corridors through the policing of "urban renewal" (Garces 2004; Gandolfo 2009; Collins 2015); the territorial expansion of private gated communities and the barred window-front, protective walling-in of poor and middle class households (Caldeira 2000; Andrade 2007); and vertical or "Narcotectura" developments such as high-rise buildings and high-tech apartment compounds, technologically beyond the reach of the streets across "insecure urban areas" (O'Neill and Fogarty-Valenzuela 2013; O'Neill 2016). Meanwhile, political parties actively bolster such private and collective material responses to fear of criminality, feeding into public demand for *mano dura* policing and perpetual prison construction—complex psychological and socio-political processes entirely dependent on carcerality, rather conveniently labeled "penal populism" (Sozzo 2007). Popular civilian understandings of community, in any case, have been actively retooled, not merely "in the shadows" or "far away" from prisons, but rather propagating cybernetically in lock-step with their monstrous and seemingly limitless material potential for concentrating-segregating and caging criminalized subjects (Müller 2013; Carter 2014; Garces 2014a; Hathazy and Müller 2016).

Most influential Latin American research on carcerality to date has focused on the centrifugal function of neoliberal and postneoliberal state policing. The prison has indeed quietly shifted its role in state-organized society, from being institutions of social rehabilitation, to an interiorized dumping grounds for the mass warehousing or "internment" of criminal subjects (Birkbeck 2011) or the (il)logical neoliberal end-point of an increasingly militarized "penalization of poverty" (Wacquant 2003). Building on these foundational frameworks, our volume is among the first collective works to systematically, comparatively explore the multiple ways in which disavowed non-state kernels of community-building potential develop behind the edifice of prison walls, allowing for illicit circulation within, across, and beyond different penal institutions. If there are historical intellectual precedents to viewing carceral community as such, they would include Durkheimian sociology and its successive interdisciplinary interlocutors. In this trajectory of sociological thought, different forms of organic solidarity and the maintenance of *conscience collective* always require a material, performative manifestation of "community" as a proxy for localized "international relations," subtly requiring the exercise of soft power (ritual and liaisonship) as well as hard power (taboo expulsion/abandonment) in any active community-building process (2014[1893], 2008[1912]).

As Andrés Antillano, Sacha Darke, Kristen Drybread, Jennifer Peirce, Jon Horne Carter, and Cory Fischer-Hoffman demonstrate in the opening chapters of the volume, in the contexts of Venezuela, Brazil, Honduras, and the Dominican Republic, Latin American men's prisons inmates are more than often left by prison administrators to manage everyday routines and order in the cellblocks. In Brazil, Darke illustrates, newly arrived detainees often receive no more than the briefest registration and most cursory of health checks, and within 24 hours delivered straight to "inmate leaders" or "inmate representatives" for their triage, instruction, and care. In Venezuela, Fischer-Hoffman emphasizes, inmate bosses further utilize their authority to mobilize and tax prison labor. Across central and south America, even the power to discipline is displaced, and in some prisons formally delegated, to inmates. In effect, penal state "order" becomes a matter of negotiation between selected prisoners and the titular prison administration, while the majority rarely have need or reason to deal with prison staff. Any study of Latin American prison order, as Antillano insists, should start from the "bottom up." This arguably continues to be the case in even the most "modern" of prison units, including the Dominican Republic, where authorities have made concerted efforts to build new international human-rights-compliant facilities, and to recruit extra staff. Peirce explains that Dominican Republican prisoners have had difficulty adjusting to the attempted formalizing of everyday discipline and order in the country's much lauded "new prison" system. As Drybread emphatically reminds us, absence of formal, top-down order is also important to understanding the plight of prison inmates—in this case, those arrested for rape—whose crimes cause them to be ostracized and themselves violated by other prisoners, with the knowledge and tacit facilitation of prison staff.

Symptomatically, most regional ethnographers follow the carceral traffic in bodies, goods, technologies, relations of love, and feelings of belonging which transcend or criminally trespass what prison walls attempt to keep uncivilly segregated and apart. The oft-stated anthropological insight into state carcerality's innermost failures, that is, the so-called porosity of the prison, described most carefully by Cunha (2014), is therefore nothing if not a mirror reflecting clandestine mobilizations of carceral communities themselves. Furtive compacts about "permissible illicit trafficking" help to facilitate the prison's informal living networks, relations, and affordances—temporary escape routes, both into and out of the penal complex, undermining the prison-institution's inherent world-destroying capabilities (Martin and Chantraine 2018). These simultaneously centrifugal *and* centripetal forces effectively blur any singular point of origin of and for the omnipresent traffic increasingly generated by systems of hyperincarceration. Ethnographic fieldworkers trace these furtive movements in practice and show how they reaffirm the integral problem of maintaining bonds of relationality over time within the space of the prison itself. Here, the ethnographer's task becomes that of showing how the prison becomes an active, albeit deeply fraught and problematically dissociative institution. In a word, we materially humanize a system programmed to dehumanize. Ethnographers explore these multifarious, oftentimes illicit pathways toward prisoners' psychological re-integration and the mitigated enjoyment of common pleasures, without cartographically drawing crime maps of consequential "threats," "risks," or "blame" for non-incarcerated others to exoticize, demonize, or prosecute. At the same time, we throw a far-reaching, skeptical spotlight onto other scholars' policy-minded research when such modes of inquiry fail to take prisoners' safety and living forms of relationality to heart.

As in all labor-intensive, large-scale infrastructural projects, the "smooth functioning" of an expanding penal state architecture—that is, jails, penitentiaries, rehabilitation centers, maximum security sites, and detention facilities—typically requires permanent and credit relationships between prisoners (or prisoners and select administrative staff), the development of symbolic or literal debt accumulation, and tacit social pacts largely ignored in broader civilian life. Again, this point is particularly poignant in Central and South America, where one of the major consequences of rising prison populations has been an equally dramatic and consequential decrease in the proportion of staff to inmates. At the end of the twentieth century, Latin American prison historians called attention to research on secretive "pacts" being fundamental to any understanding of prison life-worlds—both in the past and present alike (Aguirre and Salvatore 2001; Salvatore and Aguirre 2010). This volume will serve as a direct response, update, and extension of their provocation. Most citizens only rarely gain access to the day-to-day work of survival or the strange dehumanizing affordances that are part and parcel of living and working inside a prison complex. As Carter illustrates in this volume, so-called breakdowns in prison order, such as fires, strikes, escapes, riots, or disease outbreaks (e.g. HIV/AIDS, tuberculosis, and Covid-19), bring this curious contemporary institution temporarily back into public media and civil discourse. During these extraordinary periods, carceral communities are typically demonized as the source of penal state malfunction, and this, despite the penal state's glaring Achilles Heel that carceral communities are always indispensable to proxy administrative management of the wings, or the ways in which any prisoner's day-to-day life becomes minimally tolerable. When "emergency" becomes restored to so-called normalcy, such carceral communities (glossed over by media, prison staff, or state functionaries as "mafias," "gangs," or "cartels") are subsequently marched back inside the complex and out of public view, their largely invisible, hub-like "pluri-relational" role in prison governance having been restored to its proper place. The responses to the 2013 and 2014 fires in La Ceiba and San Pedro Sula prisons, Honduras, allegedly instigated by anti-gang security forces, are instructive. Despite the national outrage caused by the 197 official death count, Carter explains that for the ordinary MS-13 or Barrio 18 inmate, life immediately went back to normal. Prison gangs locked themselves back up in their self-governed barracks, from where prison staff rarely heard a word.

Events in Mexico over the last 20 years draw particular attention to the way in which "emergency periods" in the federal prison system (CEFERESO) belie deeper understandings of the largely unconscious operations of carceral community. During the rise of internecine warfare between drug Cartels, which involved killings of rival groups within and between cellblocks, CEFERESO prison ministry officials developed whole stand-alone prisons in order to shelter and demobilize Cartels, whether the Zetas, for example, or the Sinaloa Cartel, and others. Carceral communities proved to be so intransigent, and dangerous to rivals, that state officials preferred housing them in separate facilities. When Cartels openly defy CEFERESO orders, say, by releasing an inmate from prison to carry out a nighttime "hit" and to subsequently return to the facility under cover of darkness, or when Cartel leaders, such as Joaquin Guzmán "El Chapo" Loera, could effectively enjoy negotiated sovereign privileges over a whole CEFERESO supermaximum prison and stage his own escape twice, this does not necessarily speak to any anomalous, emergency period power-sharing between carceral communities and their titular prison administrations (although it potentially could). It rather more precisely demonstrates the deeply embedded, implacable role that carceral communities simultaneously play on the insides of all prison facilities, between their facilities, and on the outsides of facilities themselves (Garces 2018). To fail to pay attention to carceral communities and their interests has been all-too common and, in the end, ultimately a grave mistake.

The prison may thus, again, be understood as a strange kind of dissociative institution, as any number of theorists in other contexts have argued—highlighting how imprisonment feeds into modes of individual alienation, estrangement, existential vertigo, and psychoses of corporeal disintegration or comprehensive feelings of being conspiratorially subject to state and non-state terror (Rhodes 2004; Guenther 2013; Reiter 2016). Prisons give civilian publics a most curious license, or prerogative, to turn their backs on individuals and ostracized communities tainted with the brush of criminality and relegated to spatial/physical separation from the *polis* at large. Only, from the perspective of those who are imprisoned, including their loved ones and associates, the prison oftentimes rather cruelly becomes the concrete material manifestation *of the polis itself.* Our authors ingeniously lay out how and why carceral communities thus spring into existence against broader society's unrelenting sovereign, "democratic" demand to imprison more and more subjects.

Ethnographic Reflexivity

Latin American carceral regimes may have become the material-and-symbolic grounds for untold experiments on human beings' punitive enclosure or civil abandonment; for the ad hoc managerial tinkering with the limits of human custody; and for the outsourcing of justice, as when prison management becomes too financially burdensome, and the state devolves its custodial responsibilities to private agents and individuals—delegating penal tasks to "model inmates" themselves, as in the curious figure of the prisoner "*trustee*." Most, but not all, forms of punitive enclosure maintain criminalized populations physically segregated from civilians at large. Yet it would be a categorical error to understand Latin American jails, detention centers and prisons as isolated institutions. Prison ethnography focuses by contrast on the prison as a multiplex, easily misrecognized bundle of interpersonal movement and long-lasting community bonds. In her chapter, for example, Hollis Moore explores how the *Mata Oscura* neighborhood in Northeast Brazil grew up alongside the state's largest penal compound. Further sharpening new ethnographic work on the intimate relationship between "the prison" and "the street," which look to the prison's urban ecologies of exclusion as an interface of deep urban circuitry, cross-cutting movement, and ceaseless exchange (Weegels et al. 2020), Moore shows us how material and symbolic flows across Mata Oscura's prison threshold evidence the literal co-development of a stigmatized yet inseparable "prison-neighborhood nexus."

Similarly, prison ethnographers demonstrate how shifting norms of carcerality doubly shape the lives of criminalized populations *and* their imprisoned neighbors alike. Although typically working within national academies, particular disciplines, and local contexts, ethnographers figure mainly as *outsiders* who tend to play an outsized institutional role in documenting the continent-wide rise of penal state expansionism and theorizing its modes of governance, interpersonal life-worlds, and/or hidden political economies. Book-length ethnographic works by Cerbini (2012), Biondi (2016), Darke (2018), and Weegels (2018) stand as testimonies to deep study of the inner worlds of the prison and public misinformation about the stigmatized denizens of these institutions. Such ethnographic works not only "broaden," comparatively, but also "deepen," across sustained in-person and theoretically informed fieldwork, the traditional study of prison worlds, querying what might be called "ethnographic first questions" such as how incarceration most curiously remains a universalized mode of punishment—but they also explore what carcerality effectively means and does in practice to individuals and groups of human beings.

Prison religion is an increasingly important area of ethnographic investigation in Latin America and in other parts of the world. The very history of the prison derives in large part from the secularization of religious concepts such as "guilt," "punishment," "penitence," and a host of other keywords whose meanings unmoored themselves and remade cultural life in their transit from premodern to modern bureaucratic worlds. Latin American Catholic and Protestant traditions greatly influence the idea of the prison as space for controlling political as well as moral sovereignty over "Fallen" populations (O'Neill 2010). Prisons themselves become staging grounds for religious movements of personal spiritual flight and revitalization (Macaulay 2014; Garces 2019), or therapeutic recovery of drug-addicted individuals (Garcia and Anderson 2016, Parker, this volume), or "reclamation" from a life of criminal activity and family disintegration (Darke 2014, this volume; O'Neill 2016). Still other religious movements are remarkably particular and derive in large part from local, hybridized Christian and indigenous practices. In this volume, Francesca Cerbini adds a considerable new chapter to the study of Andean religion in her Bolivian ethnographic fieldwork in La Paz's San Pedro Prison. Inside one of the most classic examples of a Latin American "prisoner-run prison," Cerbini analyzes how in carceral spaces governed largely by prisoners themselves, requiring constant renegotiation and exchange, "legitimation" potentially turns into a fraught matter of contested authority and debate. Andean ritual complexes involving the expert use of magic and witchcraft, which anthropologists have long demonstrated inspire fear and control across the Andes, are here recast as a mode of community regulation, at once stable but always potentially marked by the personal threat of black magic—in Cerbini's words, "where different powers are set against each other to create or destroy likewise."

Similarly, carceral communities oftentimes reframe, navigate, and reorder the space of the prison as a religious territorial zone. Many ethnographers develop friendships and collaborative modes of research that openly participate "deeply," or perhaps complicitly, in this popular carceral symbolic-material "transubstantiation." Speaking to a hard-nosed, field-leading lawyer in the International Commission on Human Rights, one of us was struck when she responded to our query, "what would you do if you were sentenced to time in a Latin American prison?"[;] she immediately and without hesitation responded, "I'd join the first Evangelical prison community I could find." The reason, she said, was that they protected one another and against the typical kinds of blackmail, physical extortion, and modes of domination that prevail in many, if not all, penal complexes. The full ethical entailments of such religious pursuits, be they quasi-secularized, sincere yet instrumentalized, or even perhaps simple protection rackets, may not always be fully understood by the researcher, but their religious participatory relationship often becomes the immediate entry point of one's access to carceral community. Ethnographers in tandem draw reflexively upon how prison religion alters one's relationship to the wages of punishment and appeal to sovereign power wrought by the spiritualization of responses to national hyperincarceration (Garces 2010).

Importantly, ethnographic research on prisons as an outsider to the prison system as a whole *demands* a fair measure of reflexivity. Ethnographic reflexivity may be said to originate in the disciplinary history of professional cultural anthropology, whereby the researcher was (stereo-)typically asked to eschew his or her own cultural value system in the act of researching other peoples' life-worlds. Ethnography's historic reliance on this kind of "cultural relativism" is often highly misunderstood, as early ethnographic theorists such as Boas, Mead, Bateson, and others, rarely considered the possibility of the individual researcher's capacity to fully bracket or entirely ignore their own forms of cultural reasoning—subtly nationalized Western values in studying "non-Western cultures." Rather, ethnography's pioneers were influenced by speculative reasoning in the European natural field sciences and in particular by German theorists in the exact sciences such as Heisenberg and Einstein, whose "field challenging" concepts of relativism had deeply problematized fidelity even to modest, rational-empirical scientific observations. Much like these scientists, the Boasian ethnographic tradition viewed field research as a mode of empirical inquiry in which research observations built up knowledge that undermines the inherent prejudice of one's own perspective, or Heisenberg's "observer's effect," which allows people principally to see what they look for (Darnell 2001). Ethnographic reflexivity gains empirical value by demonstrating *precisely* how prejudices, psychological projections, and preconceived understandings of the prison prove wrong.

There are plenty of reasons why most ethnographic researchers of prisons in Latin America and the Caribbean have been outsider figures. Ethnographic training has become central to "minor knowledge" formations across a variety of academic fields: anthropology, sociology, criminology, legal studies, geography, political science, peace and conflict studies, cultural studies, gender studies—to name only the disciplines to which our volume ethnographers contribute. But ethnography is only a dominant methodology within anthropology. Therefore, a majority of ethnographic researchers hail from countries with strong anthropological academic traditions, which actively carry over into other fields. The ethnographic prison specialist hailing from abroad, or from powerful national universities, maps uncomfortably onto what Fischer-Hoffman (this volume), following Quijano, has called the "coloniality of power." They often arrive to their ethnographic destinations with their research already partly or fully funded, and carry out fieldwork other scholars might never consider, much less pursue.

"Northern experts" are a problematic category in the states of the Global South, perhaps especially experts in crime and justice. Since its disciplinary inception, Bowling explains, "criminology has sought to develop general theories of crime causation and control that can be applied far beyond the cultural context and empirical data from which they were first conceived" (2011: 362). Yet most "established" criminological (and other social science) theories were originally developed in north America and western Europe, and more particularly still the United States and United Kingdom, which between them account for less than 10 percent of the global population. Fully nine in ten published social science articles are written by academics working in northern America and western European universities (Aas 2012), most from just the two aforementioned countries (Carrington et al. 2019). Latin American university-based ethnographers—with their research directed to national and international currents—are often viewed as "outsiders" even inside their home countries. Meanwhile, ministries of justice and prison wardens often find themselves embattled within their own institutions, navigating multiple problems wrought by hyperincarceration itself. Some look to outsider-ethnographers as potential allies in the "neutral" gathering of information that could prove useful. Others would rather just completely ignore them and their work.

At times, ethnographers are practically recruited into their research fields, though heavy securitization of certain carceral sectors, such as maximum security wings or gang prisons, has generally made them harder to access. In the meantime, other advocacy communities, such as prisoner support groups, humanitarian NGOs, human rights organizations, prison chaplains, and their religious communities (among other interested parties), often seek to pair with ethnographers in order to gain access to prisons or legitimize their authority to establish regular contact with prisoners. In any event, ethnographers typically require self-reflexive analysis of their institutional "arrival" in any research site, probing how their research depends on situated forms of knowledge inherent to carceral communities, including both incarcerated and non-incarcerated members. The omnipresent possibility of one's own ethical "complicity" or collusion with these institutions and/or specific communities can, and should, be reflexively explored and described in one's ethnographic account—leading to a depth of engagement that allows readers of one's work to understand that ethnographers always remain "positioned" vis-à-vis carceral communities. Caroline Parker's study of recovering Puerto Rican drug offenders' search for employment (this volume), and how their plight involves the struggle to align with newly emerging "entrepreneurial" discourses integral to neoliberal carceral governing strategy, is a case in point. Her ethnographic essay, tracking informants' narratives of becoming the prized governmental category of "certified re-educated ex-addict," demonstrates the processual, slow-going characteristics of ethnographic reflexivity as a vehicle for generating uncommonly insightful knowledge.

Ethnographers look first and foremost to personal, lived experiences, testimonies, case studies, and even the revelatory counterintuitive anecdote—in all their integral complexity (e.g. Fassin 2017). Untethered, then, from the public "academic" demand to classify imprisoned populations—or to burden theorization by making it exclusively, diagnostically beholden to test criminogenic paradigms—prison ethnographers study what some might call "tangential" phenomena: for example, topics such as prison food and its consumption, the continued existence of romantic love, the (inter)personal management of addiction, fear of ghosts and other specters, the affective state of being forced into cages, and how living without civil (or human) rights changes human corporeality and sociality itself, among other topics. Ethnographic insight is produced orthogonally vis-à-vis the traditional goals of socio-legal, criminological, and penological sciences—informed primarily by the concerns of offender rehabilitation, inmate threat-neutralization, or just application of the rule of law. The ethnographer's reflexivity, or deep study of the subjectivities and life-worlds produced by punitive enclosure, nevertheless proves increasingly important to any understanding of carceral reform, not to mention commonplace yet problematic practices of state penality, such as (super)maximum security custody. Thanks to ethnographers' openness to diverse theoretical inquiries, or dependence on qualitative research designs that rely on the researchers lived, inductive experiences, extreme carceral measures such as supermaximum security isolation, and the "*prisión-depósito*" have been more comprehensively described and understood for what they are, as analogues of state torture (Sozzo 2007; O'Day and O'Connor 2013; Garces 2014b), ultimately exposing such practices to policy discussions around human rights.

Latin American prison ethnography also points out the abundance of undocumented captive populations. Consider, for example, the rapid "in and out" of prisoners relegated to short-term detention; or detainees "caught in the act" and held illegally by the police until remand prison spaces become available; or punitive/bureaucratic transit of "troublesome inmates" from one facility to another; or individuals whom judges have discreetly ordered into private lock-down drug rehabilitation centers; or the indefinite detention of deportees increasingly being repatriated from points of origin in the United States; or children whom the courts frequently order to accompany their incarcerated mothers; or what some scholars call "secondary prisonization," whereby families of the incarcerated get caught up in penal bureaucracies' multiple labyrinths (physical, legal, emotional) while attempting to support their loved ones. The full scope of prison expansionism tends to adjust more clearly into focus when ethnography takes these secondary, extralegal, or informal carceral dynamics into account. But ethnographers may also more directly confront regimes of prison governance, particularly when they have a strong fieldwork background and the ear of Ministries of Justice and assorted state officials.

Volume chapters by Loïc Wacquant and Fiona Macaulay demonstrate the challenges and necessity of describing actually existing modalities of prison regulation as well as their potential futures. Both note that the space of the prison itself is the site of multiple actors' open contests over carceral authority, which demonstrate how the protection of carceral community may bring professional prison experts into alliance, if not necessarily accord, with supporters of different prison-regulatory regimes. Wacquant's chapter, a public talk to Chilean authorities which meditated on his field research and conversations with prison governors, outlines the importance of human rights discourse and implementation given that they serve as a counterbalance to more punitive measures. His lecture's casting of human rights as "the feminine left hand of the state" subtly points to how not just masculinized *mano dura* regulations, but also human rights themselves (based more on feminized systems of protection and care) are the twinned-symmetrical forces that have accompanied the rise of mass incarceration. For Wacquant, despite the fact that human rights often derive from "elite" quarters and may even veil the quotidian, non-exceptional horrors of mass detention in Latin America, they can also, he suggests, be supported to help governments remediate certain remediable socio-bureaucratic and infrastructural ills (e.g. prison overcrowding, physical deterioration of facilities, lack of access to public services, improving staff training, etc.). They also form an immediately actionable, supra-legal justification for moving responsibility for prisons to a Ministry of Social Development. All rather practical, ethnographically informed guidelines toward improving the futures of prisoners and carceral communities themselves.

Macaulay, one of the most respected policy-minded ethnographic researchers within Brazil, looks to prison governance, in her words, "from the outside-in": challenging how "how extra-mural criminal justice institutions have created and sustained such an enormous prison population." The prison becomes a key site of tension within the state precisely because different judges, public defenders, prosecutors, government councils, in addition to carceral community leaders, usually tussle over the gatekeeping powers to determine prison regimes. The various institutional motives of these different actors involve "rent-seeking," "moral/philosophical," and "territorial" penal strategies. Not only does Macaulay's essay draw legal attention to how Brazil presently countenances the region's largest diversity of penal institutions, her work also demonstrates the extent to which top-down penal juridical machinery articulates with carceral community regulation, forming tensions that produce tacit alliances and pushback, all the way up and down the hierarchical legal structure of the Brazilian state.

Since their nineteenth century origins, Latin American prisons have deployed multiple rationales and alternating disciplinary regimes, from positivism, to racial eugenics and hygienist paradigms, to multiple social rehabilitation or therapeutic programs, and ideologies of threat neutralization. In global historical terms, the prison-institution arrived comparatively late on the scene in these regional projects of carceral state development—abiding the dominant Creole interests of elite-controlled capital and moral prestige—, a process intimately interwoven across the rise of the new nineteenth and early twentieth century Republics (see especially, Aguirre and Salvatore 2001). For each emerging state or *patria chica* (minor territorially circumscribed or imagined homeland), the birth of the prison materially manifested ideologies of citizenship and the politico-moral needs of the small minorities of privileged, male, creole, rights-bearing subjects. Indeed, the relationship between carceral development and national "first modernities," along with their aftermaths, has grown increasingly well-documented in historical, literary, and socio-legal studies (e.g. Piccato 2001; Kingman 2006; Maia et al. 2009). Our volume adds new dimensions and a sense of urgency to the study of contemporary prison worlds and their tucked-away centrality to the maintenance of law-preserving violence.

Meanwhile, prisons (whether slowly, or quickly) ultimately beget more prisons—a legacy of public desire for containment and confinement that continues largely unabated. This growth of the penal state nevertheless (cf. Sozzo Ed. 2017) does not necessarily obey a singular political economic logic. Ethnographers since the beginning of the twenty-first century, for example, have explored how most South American countries shifted models of governance from neoliberal to neosocialist political economies, and back again. What remained nearly constant has been a steady rise in national incarceration rates and the ways in which racial policing or majoritarian political influence affects emerging carceral trends. The prosecutory *raison d'etre* of different carceral regimes, as ethnographers know, may shift from one political administration to another over time (Antillano, this volume, Ariza and Iturralde, this volume), but prison infrastructure usually accommodates to changing statist demands. Ecuador's partial decriminalization of petty drug trafficking after Rafael Correa took office in 2007 ultimately decarcerated several thousand *mulas* ("drug mules"), but his government also worked assiduously to build up penal supports for a new "state institutionality," punishing more kinds of offences and effectively tripling the general population of prisoners over his decade in office (Garces 2014a). In Venezuela, Chávez's egalitarian measures likewise quickly decarcerated the prison sector, but urban security forces increasingly policed dissidence among the lumpen youth in marginalized urban *colonias*, and by the time Maduro had succeeded him, the country's prison population had similarly swollen to explosive new breaking points (Antillano et al. 2016).

In Colombia, Libardo José Ariza and Manuel Iturralde (this volume) explore how in Bogotá's "Prisión Modelo" the internal war between Columbian military, guerrilla, and paramilitary forces, encompassing multiple generations, saw the facility as a staging grounds for pitched internecine battles between guerillas and the paramilitary—the memory of which remained quite alive as the country transitioned toward a neoliberal penal model. In these authors' ethnographic perspective, Colombia's fractured penal past literally haunts its present and recently broke through into an ignominious and some would say still-unresolved future. Without realizing it at first, Ariza and Iturralde's fieldwork analyzed a major human rights violation before it was publicly revealed: the clandestine burial of masses of individuals killed during intra-prison skirmishes. Their extraordinary research, however, demonstrated how the traces of civil war, symbolically framed by the bullet holes wedged into the windows of the prison's external security checkpoint, did not stop there. Prisoners worried about the ominous, spectral fear of the abandoned cellblock wing where it was later confirmed that bodies were stuffed into the sewage canals directly underneath. Prison ethnography demonstrates how carceral communities shift and realign with broader political bodies, including in moments of extreme division, civil war, and unrest. But doing so also reveals the lived, psychological space in which carceral communities may experience external division and warfare, projected inwards and across facility grounds.

Not all prison fieldwork is similarly riven with such genocidal civil war trauma. The ordinary technocratic managerial, day-to-day problem of administrating over-filled, under-subsidized and *ipso facto* "unruly" facilities has been addressed, of course, not by implementing a new modality of social rehabilitation, but rather by the building of extra facilities, additional prison beds, and even greater temporary detention capacity; or by internal measures of threat neutralization, whereby local or national governments implement maximum security regimes; or lastly, by outsourcing custodianship to select NGOs and religious groups who manage "therapeutic prisons," and selectively recruit prisoners into their projects of "reeducation" or "recovery." The consequences of perpetual prison expansion, however, are stunningly ad hoc and largely managed vis-à-vis informal governance, and tensions wrought by this transition have been explored at length in other publications (Macaulay 2013, 2014, 2017; Darke and Karam 2016; Antillano 2017; Darke and Garces 2017; Fischer-Hoffman 2020). Latin America and the Caribbean now preside over the second highest rate of imprisonment on a global-continental scale—falling immediately behind the United States. In this quickly emerging context, ethnographic scholarship has documented the metastasis of the prison-institution across the political body of the state, along with its hidden roles and micro-dynamics in everyday life.

Meanwhile, prison managerialism continually shifts its objects of control to meet internal and external challenges to penal state order. To keep up with carceral transformation requires sustained, on-the-ground investigation, and perpetual retheorization of carceral dynamics. However, Latin American prison ethnographers increasingly contribute to post-Foucauldian debates over the *dispositive* of how prisons technocratically vest some peoples and strip others of civil and human rights, and materialize new forms racialized, necropolitical social abandonment, or tacit penal management of the "color line" (Alves 2018; Weegels 2020)—regardless of their "disciplinary context." Such critics insightfully argue that the acceleration of penality as a generative form of dissociative belonging actively feeds into the further racialization and extension of ethno-racial frontiers, demonstrating how a largely disavowed racial calculus informs both "disciplinary" and "post-disciplinary" penal state institutions—the alpha and omega of emerging ethnographic researchers' frame-shifting critical carceral focus.

"Dangerous Subjects" and Biopolitical Inversion

Our volume addresses these and other troubling issues related to the contemporaneity of penality across Latin America and the Caribbean. Each of our chapters concerns themselves with specific, commonplace topics in prison life, such as inmate self-governance; conjugal prison visits; new technocratic models for control or rehabilitation; the impact of drug wars on internal prison dynamics; the aftermath of fires and mass-killings on the cellblocks; the lingering effects of civil war on prison life; pitched struggles between incarcerated para-state actors; and the co-development of prisons and the neighborhoods that surround them—among other salient research rubrics. Ordinarily, Latin American cellblocks are not as disorderly or their systems of community governance as illegitimate as they tend to be depicted (cf. Peirce and Fondevila 2020). Altogether, our contributors show how the prison-institution has buttressed and reinforced the psychic architecture of citizen life. Regional similarities and differences abound in the study of these carceral phenomena. Community governance is also prevalent in many African (Jefferson and Martin 2014, 2016) and Asian prisons (Bandyopadhyay 2016). What appears to separate Latin American prisons from those in other southern global regions is the incredible diversity of informal arrangements for delimited prisoner autonomy exercised by prisoner collectives. In the absence of legitimate and effective state governance, inmate and staff-inmate pacts are shaped by a plurality of institutional relationships and practices that ultimately vary from one cellblock, let alone prison, to another (cf. Aguirre 2005; Biondi, this volume).

Sustained fieldwork inside and around particular facilities ultimately leads to a re-theorization of penal state order and breakdown. As we signaled above, Latin American prisons play host to quietly negotiated practices of accountability-to-the-state in which prisoners themselves play a curiously large role. Most live under conditions of acute institutional abandonment whereby "penal order" is shaped more by systematic state undersubsidization and neglect than by the vaunted ideals of capital-intensive "penitentiary reform." Incarcerated populations in these contexts—typically more concerned with survival—turn to behind-the-scenes negotiations between inmate blocs and the titular prison administration. Our contributors generally reject the public recourse to labeling such carceral communities "prison gangs" or "mafias" of any kind. While violence is an everyday part of prison life in many parts of the region, prisoners do not survive and organize their communities through recourse to violence and violence alone. Viewing them as such would present a true limit case for "blaming the victim." Though all contributors recognize that prisoner-on-prisoner violence must remain a key problem in carceral studies, most would agree with Fanon's assertion that such dissociative violence only psychologically masks and telescopes inwards the ravages of (neo)colonial state domination within carceral settings (2007, 2008). Instead, individual chapters prefer to explore in greater ethnographic detail prisoners' ad hoc arrangements of power-sharing, hierarchies, and semi-autonomous modes of governing on the insides of the facilities which house them. The volume's over-arching focus on criminalized subjects and their incarcerated neighbors opens up a more realistic and less defamatory perspective on what we have taken to call "carceral community."

Carceral communities are nonetheless remarkably active, infra-political agents. For quite some time, ethnographic students of carcerality in most parts of the world have drawn on theories of abandonment, civil dispossession, and susceptibility to premature death. Among the more influential treatments of these problems include works by Italian biopolitical theorists Giorgio Agamben (1998) and Roberto Esposito (2011). Both draw upon a particular genealogical line of inquiry into "sovereignty" within the West to frame how extreme forms of subjugation, such as, for example, concentration camps and purges of unwanted subjects, are not only exceptional but also *de regueur* across sovereign historical formations. The originary capacity of the state to "banish" individuals, making unwanted beings into a living exception (Agamben), or the capacity of emerging community to "inoculate" itself vis-à-vis processes of relational excision and active disregard (Esposito): such theoretical treatments of the manifestation of sovereignty fit almost perfectly into any understanding of today's global carceral emergency. But, we suggest, only to an extent. Importantly, for Agamben, the dangerous limit point of such sovereign configurations can be detected when extreme subjection generates entire populations, not unlike concentration or labor camp detainees, systematically overworked, underfed, beaten down, subjected to dissociative violence, or mistreated to such a degree that they can barely, if at all, speak. In Agamben's view, this "sacred man"/*homo sacer*, who, in his curious formulation, "can be killed without being sacrificed," is also the paradigmatic figure from whom political speech cannot issue forth (Agamben 1999). It is quite tempting indeed to make use of such "Italian biopolitical" lenses on so-called bare life in reconsidering the deepest horrors of civil divestment, being stripped of one's rights and protections and subjected to arbitrary "punishments within punishment," wrought by the new mass carceral zone. The first thing most ethnographers who do any research in Latin American or Caribbean prisons usually hear from their interlocutors is that the prison is a space where no civil or even human rights are being observed. Criminalized populations are serially tossed away by civil society on the outsides of prison facilities (cf. Biehl 2005), and on the insides are typically left to their own devices, or subjected the strategic enrollment within rival carceral communities, without basic guarantees of medical care or administrative protection. But ethnographic research on carceral communities also, at times, turns the so-called bare life hypothesis squarely on its head.

Three contributions to our volume, by Julienne Weegels, by Luis Duno-Gottberg, and by Chelina Sepúlveda and Iván Pomojovky, explore in great ethnographic detail the everyday dynamics of prison life, violence, and order—vis-a-vis different prisons' *ethical and esthetic* regimes. Each explores to some degree the remarkable abjection of subjects shorn of their civil rights in Nicaraguan or Venezuelan prison, but each also probes counter-intuitive, delimited forms of stylized pleasure, or forms of the ethical recovery of self, wrought by participating in the choreographed *performances* of carceral community.

Weegels's ethnography offers one of the most remarkable holistic analyses of the prisoners' felt dispossession of one's own body, being thrown into to what she calls the "cemetery of the living." However, her entry point into a Nicaraguan prison as part of a therapeutically oriented theater community also showed, across the prisoners' staging of theatrical performances, how prisoners problematize their institutional disposal through, in her language, "parallel performances of violence and change." Duno-Gottberg contribution similarly probes the esthetics of prison violence. Inside the Venezuelan Parahuachón prison complex, his ethnographic work explored how tacit state devolution of authority to prisoners led to a modality of prison government deeply informed by Evangelical prison leaders. This strange religious "state-within-a-state," which Duno-Gottberg assiduously documents in his photographic essay, thrived on the reframing of violent prisoner-on-prisoner enforcement of convict codes though recourse to biblical language and mythicized moral foundations. Here, religious structures consolidated power and regulated life-taking potential among the most potentially malevolent subjects (*malandros*). Importantly, through recourse to such religious re-figurings, prisoners found ways to arrogate, reorganize, and delegate the pleasures of justice within their own community. Lastly, Sepúlveda and Pomojovky, working in the same prison, developed an ethnographic film about the "*rutina*" or "daily self-rule" activities set up by the carceral community leadership. Roughly analogous to "action anthropology," or the therapeutic role-playing of cultural problems in order to help communities grapple with their constructed social orders and identities, the filming process demonstrated the differentially experienced values of *rutina* by powerful inmates "who approved and shaped the film's content" and those who served the production, including screen writers, producers, and actors. The collaborative exploration of the staging of punishments for breaks in convict code unnervingly reaffirmed the hierarchical character of the facility as governed by carceral community. In each of these ethnographies, in other words, the vitalistic ethical character and esthetics of carceral community play out against the backdrop of radical dispossession and the need for inmates to navigate internal prison hierarchies.

Carceral communities, as these ethnographies demonstrate, form out of the state's aggregation of individuals who find themselves *already* socially abandoned by the state—but such subjects *become* carceral communities through performed, everyday projects that reframe the mythic re-attributions of prisoners from dehumanized to humanized subjects. The specter of the state's mythic, foundational violence shadows these prisoners in their acts and programs of self-recovery. As the volume contributors make clear, carceral communities indicate a strange kind of relation to the imposition of civil death by sovereign state order. For it is rather *precisely* the fact that carceral communities can *also* exercise countervailing, mythmaking power and influence—both within the complex and, as evidenced by prison ethnography, projecting their interests beyond the physical space of the prison itself—that makes them so indispensable to ordinary prison governance. And so frightening a public specter, when unaligned with prison administrations. Or pitched in conflict against one another. Unlike the figure from whom political speech cannot issue forth, the influential member of a carceral community plainly exhibits speech always capable *in potentia* of challenging, upturning, or partly refashioning carceral order.

Symptomatically, the so-called gang leader, typically being held in a supermaximum security cell, is detained under conditions of radical isolation *precisely* because a single word from him—a mere gesture—can set in motion a chain of events that undermines prison security and penal state control as such. True, Latin American and Caribbean gang leaders may wield extortive or deadly violence; they are often quickly relegated to the most dehumanizing forms of isolation custody at the mere hint of being involved in violence on the blocks (or outside the prison itself). Prison scholarship as a whole is categorically riven by the penal state's inherent vulnerability, or custodial handling at loggerheads with prison gangs, in the face of such episodes (cf. Lessing 2016). But to clarify once more. Prison ethnographers categorically do not seek to adumbrate or in any event defend the exercise of gang or prisoner violence wherever it arises. Nor does ethnographic research engage in the whitewashing of gang violence, turning it into something it is not, when documenting the active humanizing role of "carceral communities" and their disavowal by the state. Rather, we propose to all prison scholarship and international schools of criminology that we should *also* consider the ethical matter of carceral communities' humanizing affordances, or simply declare as a matter of fact *something which already exists*. And move forward from this basic understanding.

In Brazil, prison gangs explicitly aim to increase inmate solidarity and collective action, through "raising their consciousness" (about injustice and oppression) and "unifying" the country's existing system of "postcode gangs" (created by allocating people from different areas to different wings or corridors) under the banner of one prison, state, even nationwide collective. These ideals have been corrupted to an extent by illicit markets, but they are far from irrelevant, at least in the eyes of ordinary prisoners who expect them to be delivered. Stand-alone prisons dedicated to housing gangs such as the Mara Salvatrucha in Honduras, or the Primeiro Comando do Capital in Brazil, for example, are concentrated together—uniformly and inevitably—not just because of their potential to assassinate rival gang members, but also because of their inherent capacity to influence, recruit, and extend their para-state or non-state zone of influence and control. In Ecuador, David Brotherton and Rafael Gude have researched corollary social policies set in motion during Rafael Correa's administration (2008–16) to "legalize" the Latin Kings transnational gang, which turned into a lightning rod of criticism, as the political Right and reactionary civilians inured to citizens security viewed such decriminalizing efforts as an abandonment of the values of civil society. These ethnographic researchers nevertheless discovered, working in tandem with governmental advisors, police leaders, and other state actors that such measures led in part to a generalized decrease in gang-related homicides over the duration of the policy (2020). Ethnographic studies of these kinds demonstrate how carceral machinery for "publicly disappearing" gang-members ultimately turns into quicksilver for the acceleration of already deadly "gang violence," distracting from carceral communities' more latent agendas oriented toward ethics of co-governance and survival.

That is to say, once prison infrastructure has been built up, the perceived dangerousness and influence of "gangs" not only exists a priori to the state's sovereign command… but the mapping of individuals and populations subjected to the worst kinds of radical dehumanization and civil divestment, which biopolitical theorists conflate with the evacuation of political speech, turns out to map *one-to-one* onto the "dangerous speech" of carceral communities. And this kind of speech can be segregated and isolated, but never fully extinguished. With regard to prison worlds at least, the bare life hypothesis indeed ought to be inverted. The full problem of carcerality in the service of sovereignty is not only the fateful absence of prisoner political speech, but also its inverse: carcerality's excessive capacity for producing transgressive, non-state influence—ironically emitting as it does from the "deepest" zones of sovereign state custody and punishment.

At the same time, it is important not to lose sight of the fact that Latin American "prison gangs" operate fundamentally as ideals as much as physical realities. They are best regarded, ethnographers attest, as organizations of the criminally stigmatized and convicted, rather than as criminal organizations per se. In Brazil, gang leadership regularly changes hands as individuals lose their peers' confidence in their ability to represent them. Some prison wings even operate under gang rules despite none of their occupants being gang members (Biondi 2016, this volume). Prison administrators and the few guards that work in the region's cellblocks continue to have a say in which inmates they deal with, that is, whomever assumes the "gang side" of any negotiating "link" between the politicized prisoner collective and the titular prison administration (Darke 2018, this volume).

Much like Brotherton and Gude's work (discussed above), Karina Biondi (this volume) has dedicated much of her ethnographic research not only to studying the infamous Primeiro Comando do Capital gang (PCC) both "outside-in" and "inside-out" of PCC prisons; she also has demonstrated how citywide homicide rates decreased in tandem with ascending power and influence of this particular carceral community. Inside and outside prison, Biondi keenly recalls how developing a more reflexive, ethnographic understanding of PCC individuals, and their projects of becoming PCC, required stripping away the lenses provided by non-incarcerated Brazilian "gang experts," so-called specialists in extralegal violence, whose terms of analysis displace community members' intentions and ultimately estrange PCC from commonalities that would render their lives more legible and less publicly demonized. Given the complexity of this massive carceral community—spanning multiple prisons and regions—Biondi argues that studying the PCC requires *looking first at its community origins in prisons*, and also taking its multiple (ultimately non-reducible) positionalities into account. If the so-called "gang" functions more like a social movement (in all its internal complexity), in Biondi's view, the PCC should rather be understood as something more akin to an inter-carceral "movement of movements". Once again, the study of carceral community becomes paramount to any reflexive ethnographic comprehension of "gang life," and analyzing the PCC's dangerous speech (or actions) looks first and foremost to the ethics that allow such diversities of criminalized communities to sublate personal interests toward a common good and to coordinate their activities.

Carcerality—the expertly managed practices of caging human beings, and their ramifying impact within normalizing functions of the state—may once have occupied a somewhat peripheral location within Latin American study. However, such age-old intellectual arrangements of complicity with penal power no longer hold. Carceral community, and its misread "dangerous subjects," often troubles the dark heart of national-sovereign political order. Latin American countries today may be the product of widely varying postcolonial struggles, Cold War influence over state or regional power, and spasms of civil warfare burnt into collective memory, in addition to neoliberal and neosocialist scrambles over the trajectories or spoils of national political economy. Today, however, the roll call of "classic topics" in Latin American study would indeed be impossible to imagine, much less to investigate systematically, without articulating the increasing prominence and invidious "productivity" of carceral order in all sectors of Latin American and Caribbean societies.

To research and write about prisons is always to enter a field of multifold contestation. Out of meticulously detailed ethnographic works on prison life in specific prison facilities, a number of empirically documented trends openly trouble commonplace understandings of crime and punishment. Our collective wager is that Latin America's quickly rising tide of imprisonment can be held out as a mirror for what presently ails broader "state" or "social" questions, along with the latent influence of carceral communities. The effects of state criminalization must be studied from within penal facilities, as well as on the outside, in order to gain a clearer picture.

Our contributors may variously analyze prison worlds from the perspectives of prison-neighborhood dynamics, gender relations, the politics of religious belief and practice, the psychological causes and aftermaths of "prison riots," the ethics *and* esthetics of the convict code, the intimate and poorly understood internal institution of conjugal visits, largely failed attempts to implement human rights, and a myriad of other relational perspectives—normally considered "secondary," or merely "externalities," within the criminological discourses that dominate penological study. We nonetheless hold that such matters of "minor detail" within prisoners' lived experiences are critical to understanding the monster that has been unleashed by the statist and public demand for carceral solutions to nearly all deep-seated cultural and political economic problems. However, an abiding concern with the ethics of carceral community thematically ties forward thinking ethnographic research together—and points in new directions for future study and much-needed institutional critique.

References

Aas, K. F. (2012). The earth is one but the world is not: Criminological theory and its geopolitical divisions. *Theoretical Criminology, 16*(1), 5–20.

Agamben, G. (1998). *Homo sacer: Sovereign power and bare life*. Palo Alto: Stanford University Press.

Agamben, G. (1999). *Remnants of Auschwitz: The witness and the archive.* New York: Zone books.

Aguirre, C. (2005). *The criminals of Lima and their worlds: The prison experience, 1850–1935*. Durham: Duke University.

Aguirre, C., & Salvatore, R. D. (2001). Writing the history of law, crime, and punishment in Latin America. In R. D. Salvatore et al. (Eds.), *Crime and punishment in Latin America*. Durham: Duke University Press.

Alves, J. A. (2018). *The anti-black city: Police terror and black urban life in Brazil.* Minneapolis: University of Minnesota.

Andrade, X. (2007). "Mas ciudad", menos ciudadania: Renovación urbana y aniquilación del espacio público en Guayaquil. *Ecuador Debate, 68*, 161–197.

Antillano, A. (2017). When prisoners make the prison: Self-rule in Venezuelan prisons. *Prison Service Journal, 229*, 26–30.

Antillano, A., Pojomovsky, I., Zubillaga, V., Sepúlveda, C., & Hanson, R. (2016). The Venezuelan prison: From neoliberalism to the Bolivarian revolution. *Crime, Law and Social Change, 65*(3), 195–211.

Bandyopadhyay, M. (2016). Asian prisons: Colonial pasts, neo-liberal futures and subversive sites. In Y. Jewkes et al. (Eds.), *Handbook on prisons* (2nd ed.). Abington: Routledge.

Biehl, J. (2005). *Vita: Life in a zone of social abandonment.* Berkeley: University of California Press.

Biondi, Karina. (2016). *Sharing this walk: An ethnography of prison life and the PCC in Brazil.* (trans: Jon F. Collins). Chapel Hill: University of North Carolina Press.

Birkbeck, C. (2011). Imprisonment and internment: Comparing penal institutions north and south. *Punishment & Society, 13*(3), 307–332.

Blom Hansen, T., & Stepputat, F. (2006). Sovereignty revisited. *Annual Review of Anthropology, 35*, 295–315.

Bowling, B. (2011). Transnational criminology and the globalization of harm production. In M. Bosworth & C. Hoyle (Eds.), *What is criminology?* Oxford: Oxford University Press.

Brotherton, D. C., & Gude, R. (2020). Social control and the gang: Lessons from the legalization of street gangs in Ecuador. *Critical Criminology*. https://doi.org/10.1007/s10612-020-09505-5.

Caldeira, T. P. R. (2000). *City of walls: Crime, segregation and citizenship in São Paulo.* Berkley: University of California.

Carrington, K., Hogg, R., Scott, J., & Sozzo, M. (2016). Southern criminology. *British Journal of Criminology, 56*(1), 1–20.

Carrington, K., Hogg, R., Scott, J., Sozzo, M., & Walters, R. (2019). *Southern criminology.* London: Routledge.

Carter, J. H. (2014). Gothic sovereignty: Gangs and criminal community in a Honduran prison. *South Atlantic Quarterly, 113*(3), 475–502.

Castro, L. A. (1987). *Criminologia de la liberacion.* Maracalbo: Universidad del Zulia.

Cerbini, F. (2012). *La casa de Jabón: Etnografía de una cárcel Boliviana.* Barcelona: Edicions Bellaterra.

Collins, J. F. (2015). *Revolt of the saints: Memory and redemption in the twilight of Brazilian racial democracy*. Durham: Duke University Press.
Coronil, F. (1996). Beyond Occidentalism: Toward nonimperial geohistorical categories. *Cultural Anthropology, 11*(1), 51–87.
Coronil, F. (2004). Latin American postcolonial studies and global decolonization. In N. Lazarus (Ed.), *The Cambridge companion to postcolonial literary studies*. New York: Cambridge University.
Cunha, M. (2014). The ethnography of prisons and penal confinement. *Annual Review of Anthropology, 43*, 217–233.
Darke, S. (2014). Recoverers helping recoverers: Discipline and peer-facilitated reform in Brazilian faith-based prisons. In *Transnational penal cultures: New perspectives on discipline, punishment and desistance*. New York: Routledge.
Darke, S. (2018). *Conviviality and survival: Co-producing Brazilian prison order*. London: Springer.
Darke, S., & Garces, C. (2017). Surviving in the new mass carceral zone. *Prison Service Journal, 229*, 2–9.
Darke, S., & Karam, M. L. (2016). Latin American prisons. In Y. Jewkes et al. (Eds.), *Handbook on prisons* (2nd ed.). Abington: Routledge.
Darnell, R. (2001). *Invisible genealogies: A history of Americanist anthropology* (Vol. 1). Lincoln: University of Nebraska Press.
Durkheim, E. (2008). *The elementary forms of the religious life*. New York: Courier Corporation.
Durkheim, E. (2014). *The division of labor in society*. New York: Simon and Schuster.
Esposito, R. (2011). *Immunitas: The protection and negation of life*. London: Polity.
Fanon, F. (2007). *The wretched of the earth*. New York: Grove/Atlantic.
Fanon, F. (2008). *Black skin, white masks*. New York: Grove Press.
Fassin, D. (2017). *Prison worlds: An ethnography of the carceral condition*. New York: John Wiley & Sons.
Fischer-Hoffman, C. (2020). Rival carceralities: Legitimising discourses of prison regime formations in Bolivarian Venezuela. *Journal of Latin American Studies, 52*(2), 373–397.
Gandolfo, D. (2009). *The city at its limits: Taboo, transgression, and urban renewal in Lima*. Chicago: University of Chicago Press.
Garces, C. (2004). Exclusión constitutiva: las organizaciones pantalla y lo antisocial en la renovación urbana de Guayaquil. *Íconos, 20*, 53–63.
Garces, C. (2010). The cross politics of Ecuador's penal state. *Cultural Anthropology, 25*(3), 459–496.

Garces, C. (2014a). Denuding surveillance at the carceral boundary. *South Atlantic Quarterly, 113*(3), 447–473.

Garces, C. (2014b). Ecuador's "black site": On prison securitization and its zones of legal silence. *Focaal, 68*, 18–34.

Garces, C. (2018). Narco-capitalism and carceral marronage in northern Mexico: What La Flaquita knows. In T. Martin & G. Chantraine (Eds.), *Prison breaks: Toward a sociology of escape*. London: Palgrave Macmillan.

Garces, C. (2019). Prisons of charity: Christian exceptionality and decarceration in Ecuador's penal state. In E. C. James (Ed.), *Governing gifts: Faith, charity, and the security state*. Albuquerque: University of New Mexico Press.

Garcia, A., & Anderson, B. (2016). Violence, addiction, recovery: An anthropological study of Mexico's *anexos*. *Transcultural Psychiatry, 53*(4), 445–464.

Gruen, L. (2014). *The ethics of captivity*. Oxford: Oxford University Press.

Guenther, L. (2013). *Solitary confinement: Social death and its afterlives*. Minneapolis: University of Minnesota Press.

Hathazy, P., & Müller, M.-M. (2016). The rebirth of the prison in Latin America: Determinants, regimes and social effects. *Crime, Law and Social Change, 65*(3), 113–135.

Jefferson, A. M., & Martin, T. M. (2014). Everyday prison governance in Africa. *Prison Service Journal*, 202.

Jefferson, A. M., & Martin, T. M. (2016). Prisons in Africa. In Y. Jewkes et al. (Eds.), *Handbook on prisons* (2nd ed.). Abington: Routledge.

Kingman, E. (2006). *La ciudad y los otros. Quito 1860–1940: higienismo, ornato y policía*. Quito: FLACSO.

LaCapra, D. (2011). *History and its limits: Human, animal, violence*. Ithaca: Cornell University Press.

Lessing, B. (2016). *Inside out: The challenge of prison-based criminal organizations*. Washington, DC: The Brookings Institution.

Macaulay, F. (2013). Modes of prison administration, control and governmentality in Latin America: Adoption, adaptation and hybridity. *Conflict, Security and Development, 13*(4), 361–392.

Macaulay, F. (2014). Whose prisons are these anyway? Church, state and society partnerships and co-production of offender 'resocialization' in Brazil. In V. Miller & J. Campbell (Eds.), *Translating penal cultures: New perspectives on discipline, punishment and desistance*. London: Routledge.

Macaulay, F. (2017). The policy challenges of informal prisoner governance. *Prison Service Journal, 229*, 51–56.

Maia, C. N., Veto, F. S., Costa, M., & Bretas, M. L. (Eds.). (2009). *História das prisões no Brasil.* Rio de Janeiro: Rocco.
Martin, T., & Chantraine, G. (2018). *Prison breaks: Toward a sociology of escape.* London: Palgrave Macmillan.
Müller, M.-M. (2013). Penal statecraft in the Latin American city: Assessing Mexico City's punitive urban democracy. *Social & Legal Studies, 1*(13), 1–23.
O'Day, P., & O'Connor, T. (2013). Supermaxes south of the border. In J. I. Ross (Ed.), *The globalization of supermax prisons.* New Brunswick: Rutgers University Press.
O'Neill, K. L. (2010). The Reckless Will: Prison Chaplaincy and the Problem of Mara Salvatrucha. *Public Culture, 22*(1), 67–88.
O'Neill, K. L. (2016). Narcotecture. *Environment and Planning D: Society and Space, 34*(4), 672–688.
O'Neill, K. L., & Fogarty-Valenzuela, B. (2013). Verticality. *Journal of the Royal Anthropological Institute, 19*(2), 378–389.
Ortner, S. B. (2016). Dark anthropology and its others: Theory since the eighties. *HAU: Journal of Ethnographic Theory, 6*(1), 47–73.
Pavarini, M., & Giamberardino, A. (2011). *Teoria da pena e execução penal: Uma introdução crítica.* Rio de Janeiro: Lumen Juris.
Peirce, J., & Fondevila, G. (2020). Concentrated violence: The influence of criminal activity and governance on prison violence in Latin America. *International Criminal Justice Review, 30*(1), 99–30.
Piccato, P. (2001). *City of suspects: Crime in Mexico City, 1900–1931.* Durham: Duke University Press.
Reiter, K. (2016). *23/7: Pelican Bay prison and the rise of long-term solitary confinement.* New Haven: Yale University Press.
Rhodes, L. A. (2004). *Total confinement: Madness and reason in the maximum security prison.* Berkeley: University of California Press.
Salvatore, R. D., & Aguirre, C. (Eds.). (2010). *The birth of the penitentiary in Latin America: Essays on criminology, prison reform, and social control, 1830–1940.* New Haven: University of Texas Press.
Scott, J. C. (1998). *Seeing like a state: How certain schemes to improve the human condition have failed.* New Haven: Yale University Press.
Sozzo, M. (2007). ¿Metamorfosis de la prisión? Proyecto normalizador, populismo punitivo y "*prisión-depósito*" en Argentina. *URVIO. Revista Latinoamericana de Estudios de Seguridad, 1*, 88–116.

Sozzo, M. (Ed. 2017). *Pós-neoliberalismo e penalidade na américa do sul.* São Paulo: Fundação Perseu Abramo.

Wacquant, L. (2003). Towards a dictatorship over the poor: Notes on the penalization of poverty in Brazil. *Punishment & Society, 5*, 197–205.

Wacquant, L. (2005). Castigar a los parias urbanos. *Comunicacion y Violencia Año XI, 17*, 10–14.

Wacquant, L. (2008). The militarization of urban marginality: Lessons from the Brazilian metropolis. *International Political Sociology, 2*, 56–74.

Walmsley, R. (2018). *World prison population list* (12th ed.). London: International Centre for Prison Studies.

Weegels, J. (2018). *Performing prison: Power, agency and co-governance in Nicaraguan prisons*. Amsterdam: Universiteit van Amsterdam.

Weegels, J. (2020). From *pinta* to changed man: Performing reinsertion and escaping color at the Nicaraguan margins. *Latin American and Caribbean Ethnic Studies, 15*(3), 309–224.

Weegels, J., Jefferson, A. M., & Martin, T. M. (2020). Confinement beyond site: Connecting urban and prison ethnographies. *The Cambridge Journal of Anthropology, 38*(1), 1–14.

Zaffaroni, E. R. (1989). *En busca de las penas perdidas*. Buenos Aires: Editar Sociedad Anónima.

Part I

Carceral Communities

2

When to Punish Is Not to Discipline

Andrés Antillano

Foucault in Peonía

I don't know if Dante was the first to describe hell as concentric circles, but this seems to be the appropriate way to represent a territory governed by desperation and atonement: a ferocious and inexorable center, radiating outward into darker regions, ordered according to degrees of gravity (both the offense being punished and the punishment itself). Within the infernal complex, one cannot turn back the clock and escape from suffering; this territory remains defined by a categorical separation from the world; on the inside, in other words, no hope remains. What similarly best represents the prison is not so much the segregation from the world outside, but enclosure in a regulated, suppressed, and codified order. In one of its most famous utopias, the Panopticon, the prison manifests in

This work is part of a research conducted together with Iván Pojomovsky, Verónica Zubillaga, Chelina Sepúlveda, Alberto Alvarado, and Amarilis Hidalgo. I thank Yana Stainova and Rebecca Hanson for the translation and suggestions.

A. Antillano (✉)
Central University of Venezuela, Caracas, Venezuela

S. Darke et al. (eds.), *Carceral Communities in Latin America*, Palgrave Studies in Prisons and Penology, https://doi.org/10.1007/978-3-030-61499-7_2

the form of concentric circles in whose all-seeing center lies a power that, as it observes, punishes. The punishment operates vis-à-vis an imposed order, and a central gaze that disciplines. The prison: an institution that separates as it includes, that condemns with the same gesture with which it offers salvation. Whoever crosses its threshold not only leaves the world behind but enters into a dense and relentless social order; no space is left untouched by the disciplining power. There is no "outside" in the prison, just as there was no hope in Dante's inferno.

Until We Found Out About Peonía.[1]

In order to enter Peonía, we had to pass through rigorous checks, a verification of documents, and exhaustive inspections. We then passed through a type of no man's land in which prisoners circulated and wandered freely. We left behind a line of abandoned installations, which once contained administrative offices; now there was only a dilapidated doctor's office.

Upon entering the courtyard, a clashing and surprising sight meets the eye. The prisoners walk around at all times without restrictions, far from the control and vigilance of those in charge of watching over the prison. Some prisoners offer a variety of goods and services: food, clothes, pirated copies of films, liquor made within the prison itself, tattoos, hair-cutting, internet, and telephone calls, all the items necessary for daily life. In both the open air and in improvised spaces such as cells converted into stores, they sell cigarettes, coffee, handicrafts, and various drugs placed on top of plastic tables… Almost anything you can imagine. Armed prisoners with rifles and pistols patrol different areas of the prison and control the access points; they monitor the movements of the guards as well as the neighboring prison (with which they maintain a long and bloody war) from the rooftops or behind their fortified parapets. They also monitor what is happening in the prison yard. Others dedicate themselves to the necessary labor of maintaining the jail itself: they collect the trash, fix any damage done to the facilities, or repair appliances in bad shape; they cook the communal meal for the prisoners who cannot pay for their own food; they build houses of wood and metal sheets that serve as their own commercial spaces; they haul construction materials and merchandise. Some pass the time in their small artisanal workshops, making local *vodka* from the fermentation of rice or packaging cocaine in thin straws. Other groups of prisoners relax in hammocks which they have made themselves, on cardboard thrown on the floor, or under a roof that protects them from the harsh sun. They play cards, video games, and *parqué* (a game appropriate for the prison atmosphere, very similar to "Parcheesi"); they practice boxing or basketball or get together to watch a movie or chit chat. If it were not for the conspicuous presence of drugs and weapons, and the fact that it is a world of only men, the picture wouldn't look any different from a day at the market or the street of a poor barrio.

Nevertheless, all of this is happening beyond the surveillance and control of those in charge of guarding the prison. Rather than a hell of organized and connected concentric circles, Peonía looks more like a walled precinct where Alexander the Great confined the people of Gog and Magog, the frightening towns that announced the apocalypse, constructing an impassable wall around them. The row of abandoned buildings, tucked inside the walls of the perimeter, barely masks these outlawed people. Though the complex's outward appearance conveys that all is hidden and out of view, this is only an appearance, a courtesy, or rule of etiquette, because from the high watchtowers, located along the entire perimeter of the prison, armed guards oversee, at least to some degree, the fugitive world.

Those in charge of the administration and guarding the prison never, except in exceptional circumstances, dare intrude upon this territory. Only a few activities controlled by the institution take place within these facilities, namely those that are of use to the prisoners: the coordination of culture and education (which allows prisoners to accumulate hours of study in order to reduce their sentence), medical services, and sports. Otherwise, the entrance of corrections officers or authorities is sporadic and always coordinated with the leaders of the *Carro*, the group that runs life inside of the prison. When corrections officers do enter, a half-hearted attempt at concealment means that heavy weaponry and pistols slip beneath clothing—half visible in their barely disguised menace.

In Peonía, the prison authorities either do not see, do not want to see, or pretend not to see what is happening inside. The inspections that *do* take place are few, and armed officials, whether soldiers from the National Guard or civilian security guards, rarely enter the space of the prison itself. In the two-plus years we regularly visited Peonía, armed guards had entered only twice. During one visit, this involved "checking the numbers," a supposedly routine head-counting activity (which takes place twice a day as a measure of security and control in other prisons) that hardly ever takes place in Peonía. This visit was coordinated with the prisoners, and a group of them escorted a commission of around 20 guards around the prison, making cautious stops before entering a new area, so that the residents could "prepare." In fact, the watchmen never entered many of the cellblocks and had to be content with the information provided by prisoners who served as their guides.

Months after this initial visit, however, there was an inspection of the prison, this time an exhaustive and thorough one, which lasted two days. But it only took place after an intense armed confrontation between the prisoners and the National Guard, a hunger strike that lasted a week, and arduous negotiations, as a result of which the prisoners agreed to an inspection of the complex. Nevertheless, the prison "bosses" determined the specific day and conditions under which the inspection would take place. Being able to determine the time gave prisoners advanced warning to hide drugs and weapons. When we asked one of the prison bosses what risks an inspection presented, he responded like a good sport and with a touch of stoicism: "They have to look and we have to hide. If they find it, we lose. If not, they lose." This phrase also contained a taste of cynicism: possibly, some of the guards in charge of the inspection were those who allow the selling of drugs and guns to the prisoners, or even sell these items themselves.

In this article, we discuss our fieldwork in a prison in which the state has relinquished its traditional functions for control and discipline, the mutations in the punishment of the poor, and the duplication of the penal experience by the experience of exclusion. The old disciplinary prison, the total institution, has given way to new and surprising forms of self-government by the prisoners themselves. Although Peonía can be seen as an extreme and solitary case, it should not be understood as an exceptional one.[2] The displacement of the state and its substitution by the government of prisoners is repeated, in different ways and intensities, in different prisons in Latin America. We suggest, finally, that in this interval defined by the desertion of the state, which makes the prison a mechanism of pure exclusion, and with the appearance of forms of domination over prisoners by prisoners, the prison has acquired a new position and meaning.

More than 40 years ago, the publication of *Discipline and Punish* shook the foundations of contemporary thinking and marked the emergence of a new canonical work for studying the prison. Foucault distanced himself from grand theories which explained the prison through its social function or general changes in societal sensibilities, instead looking at modest deployments of its techniques, procedures, and rationalities. The prison would be a result of the invention and adjustment of a combination of technologies of security (individualization, distribution of bodies, codification of space, control of activities), technologies of surveillance (hierarchical inspection, permanent, and generalized vigilance), and technologies of normalization (exams, normalizing sanctions) (Foucault 1978). More than the refinement of criminal justice mechanisms, at issue is a transition from a criminal justice system that exerts itself on the marked body, as the surface where power and truth express themselves, to a system that inscribes the body of the prisoner, as a surface remade by power and truth. The punishment no longer lies in the suffering that marks the body but in the submission to an extensive and regulatory control, an uninterrupted mode of surveillance, to an enclosed moral order without emptiness or unutilized space.

Without a doubt, Foucault's thesis has been vehemently challenged from different sides. The veracity of his findings and the universality of his conclusions have been put in doubt (see, among others, Garland 1993; Alford 2000; Ignatieff 1978; Perrot 1980; Rothman 1990; Fernández Liria 1992). In the case of Latin America, much critical discussion has addressed whether the disciplining order so described in the book has reached our shores and whether it has been applied across our prisons (see Salvatore and Aguirre 1996; Bohoslavsky 2005; Bohoslavsky and Di Liscia 2005; Caimiri 2005). Foucault himself clarified that his research was based in specific time and place: France between the end of the XVIII and the beginning of the XIX centuries (Foucault 1991). One could justifiably accuse him of according too little to the practices of resistance, in spite of his own militant activity in support of prisoners' demands and insistence in this work, as well as others, that power generates from below and that forms of resistance from below influence, neutralize, or lend support to relations of power (Foucault 1978, 1991). But what interested Foucault here was not so much the processes of fighting and resistance, the "clamor of the fight," but describing the prison as a "dispositif" (Foucault 1978; Deleuze 1990), as a program and technology of power, rather than its tangible effects.[3]

But this simultaneously global and capillary functioning of control within the prison seems to have eroded in recent years, alongside mass incarceration and a decline of the ideal of rehabilitation. The trend combines a progressive moving of North American prisons to warehouses (Irwin and Owen 2004),[4] an abandonment of treatment and a relaxation of the standards of living and individual control (even when the means of physical security and general coercion are intensified). The absence of effective surveillance in the interior of the prison, such as predicted by Alford (even though he considers it a general argument against Foucault's thesis), suggests significant changes in the functioning of the prison as a disciplinary mechanism (2000).

In Latin America, where the prison more clearly resembles a warehouse (Birkbeck 2010), the combination between an accelerated growth of the incarcerated population (a result of the increase in poverty and exclusion from years of neoliberal hegemony, and draconian drug laws), together with fiscal crises that impoverished the state and made it difficult to sustain the ostentatious penitentiary system, has driven state power within the prison to despair and has led to a decline in its capacity to surveil and control life between the prison walls. In response, various forms of co-responsibility (Garland 1996) have appeared, within which the state transfers responsibilities to non-state actors, such as civic organizations (see Macaulay 2014), and even prisoner trustees (see Birkbeck 2010; Darke 2013). These tasks typically belong to the penitentiary organization and were once monopolized by government authorities. But efforts of the prisoners to dismantle the timid power of the carceral state have also intensified, disputing the state's zones of control, interrupting its forms of surveillance, and escaping its dominion (Pérez Guadalupe 2000; Nuñez 2007; Biondi 2010; Cerbini 2012).

In the case of Venezuela, the disproportionate growth of the prison population and the gradual loss of control by the State have posed a serious challenge to the prison as a disciplinary mechanism or total institution. The prison population has spiked since the 80s. In 1980, there were 12,000 prisoners, while by the late 80s, this number had increased to 29,000. In the mid-90s, the number of the incarcerated exceeded 30,000 for the first time. With arrival of Chavez's government in 1999 and his leftist conviction and discourse initially contrary to the politics of repression against popular sectors, the population decreased to 12,000, the lowest in almost three decades; but in a short time, it rose again to reach its historical maximum. Today there are more than 50,000 individuals locked up inside Venezuelan prisons (Provea 1999–2013).

Different authors have insisted on a correspondence between social and political changes in Western nations in the past decade (neoliberal governments, dismantling the welfare state, flexible accumulation) and massive imprisonment (see, for instance, De Giorgi 2007; Wacquant 2003, 2010). From this perspective, the prison substitutes social policies for regulation of subaltern sectors and currently operates as a mechanism of surplus labor population control in the context of a shortage of work.

This correlation between systematic labor exclusion and a rise in the prison population has been closely observed in Venezuela. In the 80s, the growing incarcerated population did not correlate with a rise in the crime rate, which was relatively stable, but with changes in the labor market and increased poverty. In the 90s, even though the crime rate rose, possibly as a result of neoliberal policies of dispossession, the number of people in prison paralleled the deterioration of the situation of underprivileged sectors.

The relationship between social policies, poverty, and imprisonment has not been quite so clear since 1999, the beginning of the Chavez government. After a significant fall, the number of prisoners spiked to historic highs, despite redistributive policies that managed to improve social indicators, at least until 2015. Unemployment fell from 19% to 8%; inequality fell from a Gini coefficient of 0.5 to 0.38; and poverty fell from 68% to 27%. I argue that this paradoxical relationship between redistributive policies and social inclusion, on the one hand, and a rise in the prison population, on the other, clearly points to the difficulty in making these policies universal, which could alter the structural conditions that produce exclusion. The obstacles to universalizing these policies, in practice, lead to a significant group of people still excluded from employment but also from redistributive policies. From this view, penal punishment complements social policies by acting upon this surplus population. The prison operates by controlling those who could not be incorporated by social policies set in place during Chavez's administration.

Coextensive with spiking incarceration, the capacity of the state to control and regulate populations of the unwanted diminishes. There are insufficient funds for maintaining and securing the prisons, the places to house prisoners are limited, there is a deficit of guards and technical personnel, and there are gaps in the supplies and in the resources for maintaining and controlling prisoners. In 1993, the number of security personnel in the entire prison system was 800 guards for more than 25,000 prisoners (Rosales 1997). In 2015, there were around 2000 for 50,000 inmates, which constitutes a deficit of 11,000 guards, according to reports administrated by penitentiary authorities. In Peonía, 20 watchmen had to guard more than 5000 prisoners in the complex.

Secondly, there is a move away from rehabilitation as an aim. Even though legislation defines rehabilitation as the aim of the prison sentence, in practice rehabilitation programs were disbanded long ago, leaving behind a chronic deficit of professionals in this area. Peonía, for example, does not rely on specialized personnel; the few times that technical teams have visited the prison, they do so to carry out social and psychological evaluations for anticipated release dates. Educational and labor programs, which are intended to reduce one's sentence, and psychosocial evaluations operate as institutional rituals and serve as a strategy to relieve an overburdened and explosive penitentiary system. This is not to say that rehabilitation has had any effect in the past, but only that "treatment" inside the prison largely served as a mechanism of control and production of docile incarcerated bodies, while it gave sense and purpose to the functioning of the prison itself. When people are stuffed into prison as never before, the institution and its cultural protocols increasingly reveal their cynicism and senselessness.

The prison's ungovernable nature is evidenced by the rise of violence within it. In 1993, there were 151 violent deaths in prisons throughout Venezuela. Just two years later, in 1995, this number had risen to 276. In 2003, 402 inmates were killed (Provea 1996, 1999, 2004). *Cocopelao*, the prisoner who had served the most time in Peonía, remembers how in the beginning of his sentence, the violence and abuse between the prisoners were spreading: "We were all Indians and there were no chiefs... Each one had to have a knife to fight against all the rest. People killed one another, the prisoners were robbing other prisoners or their visitors. They were raping the other prisoners as well as the women who came to visit. It was the time of *villaneo* (prisoners′ acts of abuse and violence against other prisoners and their families). It was horrifying." Meanwhile, the guards did take notice, but they stayed on the margins, seemingly helpless. Episodes of mass violence likewise arose, with groups of prisoners involved in pitched and bloody battles. The most dramatic case was in 1994 in the Prison Sabaneta, in the West, where 108 prisoners were killed by their inmates before the apathetic gaze of their watchmen. Even though these are scandalous numbers, they happened with macabre regularity during the 90s.

At the same time that state power was retreating, it was also intensifying and becoming more violent (Rosales 1997). Reports of mistreatment, brutal guard-on-prisoner violence, massacres, and torture all increased. In 1992, soldiers from the National Guard and Metropolitan policeman shot more than 60 prisoners in Catia prison, inside the capital of the country. In 1996, a fire caused by bombs thrown by security personnel caused the death of 24 inmates in La Planta prison, likewise in Caracas. *Popeye*, one of the bosses of the prisoners, alluded to the habitual practice of abuse on the part of the authorities when the state attempted to re-take control over the prison: "They just want us to wear yellow (the color of the uniforms worn by inmates in prisons controlled by the state, where cases of mistreatment and abuse of prisoners are frequent) and [to] fight amongst ourselves all day."

The state has also increasingly lost the capacity to guarantee minimum requirements for life. For the past few decades, a shortage of goods, medical attention, medication, and space have plagued carceral facilities. Images of overpopulated prisons, with people sleeping one on top of the other or out in the open, or episodes of famine within the prison, frequently shake public opinion.

The state is proving to be ever more incompetent and impotent in governing the prisons and controlling their population. This could indicate a break in the disciplinary model or could even represent an inability to govern, through previous mechanisms, control of the ultramarginalized. In the United States, this deficit of governmentality has occurred alongside an increase in mass control, normalized legal coercion, institutional violence, and the adoption of militarized methods. In Latin America, where there are fewer available resources, a more obvious retreat of the state has taken place within the prisons—an abandonment of prisoners to whatever may befall them. Counter-intuitively, "not to see," or "not to control," seems to be the new insignia of institutional power.

Within Peonía, prisoners seem free: they are free, at least, from inspections, vigilance, institutional norms, iron-clad discipline, being locked up in cells, strict hours and routines imposed by the administration, punishment and abuse by the guards, and the ritualized practices of the humiliating and debasing total institution. But at the same time, prisoners are unprotected and defenseless from the abuse of other inmates, subject to the invasive vigilance of the groups that do control the prison, subject to the draconian informal norms that exist within them, exposed to continuous uncertainty—elaborate and cruel forms of violence, extortion, and an oppression among so-called equals. "This is like Paradise," one prisoner told us, celebrating the relaxed life outside the *enmaximado* regimen of discipline in other prisons controlled by the state. "This is hell," lamented another, tired of punishment and abuse that the other prisoners imposed. This dual nature, ambivalent and paradoxical, emancipated from institutional control but at the same time unprotected by it; one is "free" from being a prisoner of the state, but is abandoned while in custody; this marks a novel relationship between prisoners and the state. This new nature of punishment does not operate to discipline or to force prisoners to give up control; but neither is there possibility for redemption.

The prison has ceased to function as an establishment for discipline, normalization, and control. In a post-industrial and post-salary world (even more so in Latin America, subjected to an aggressive process of reprimarization of its economy and deeper dependence on the exploitation of its natural commodities), where there are limited job opportunities, the prison no longer serves the purpose of disciplining the labor force and regulating the reserve army, nor does it duplicate the effects of welfare, nor is it a privileged locus of social discipline in an ever more unregulated society. The prison is content to reinforce social exclusion and contain the surplus population, with no intervention or forms of care beyond their stripped-down mechanisms of containment. Whereas before the prison operated as an "inside" in an attempt to normalize, it now exists as an "outside" that mirrors, replicates, and intensifies exclusion of the socially undesirable. At the same time, this social exclusion is doubled and prolonged, as is the case in many Latin American prisons, through institutional abandonment. This power can still lock up and keep locked up, but it is unable to govern what happens inside. Punishment becomes exile in confinement. In Peonía, people are locked up in an outside.

The Carceral Brave New World

There is no need to see emptiness in this. The movement that ends surveillance and control is not extinguished in its negativity. An "absence" does not follow from the withdrawal of institutional power: a complete and ferocious new order, this time produced and sustained by prisoners themselves, takes up the state's vacated place.

Sociological work carried out in the social order within the prison, which had its apogee in the middle of the last century in the United States, generally describes informal tactics of the prisoners as ones of defense, resistance, cooperation, and in all cases adaptation to institutional mechanisms of control and their variety of social effects (Clemmer 1958; Morris and Morris 1963; Sykes 1974; Goffman 2001). But what happens when the institution no longer governs prisoners? The informal social order inside Peonía is no longer understood as a response to institutional control, but its substitute. As state control diminishes, different forms of self-regulation take place, through patterns of conduct and norms that regulate the interaction between the prisoners and prison life, forms of self-government that preserve an internal order and protect at least some of the population from "external" threats, and strategies for self-sustainment that guarantee modes of subsistence and funds to reproduce a functioning social order (Antillano 2015; Antillano et al. 2016).

Life in a prison controlled by the prisoners is full of rules that regulate even the most miniscule and intimate aspects of life. Rule violations now bring on implacable sentences, corporal punishment, and sometimes even summary execution. Despite their severity, their purpose is to maintain order and decrease violence between the prisoners, banishing unsanctioned kinds of interpersonal violence, outlawing situations that provoke conflict, and reinforcing values and norms that give the group cohesion (Antillano 2015). They protect the honor of prisoners, the goods inside the prison; the prisoners' visitors—especially the women—are prohibited from collaboration with authorities and thereby strengthen incarcerated groups.

Despite the harshness and extravagance, the norms that rule the prisoners adhere to conventional morality, one that can even be seen as conservative and prudish. Homosexuality is severely punished, and any act that can be interpreted as sexually ambiguous (to shave one's legs or any affectation) is repressed. This includes the church,[5] where the Evangelicals have a prisoner who monitors the bathrooms to avoid homosexual contact or masturbation. Speech is cleansed of any double meanings, substituted by a new language, many times difficult to understand and one that every prisoner needs to learn the minute they enter in order to be able to survive. *Candelaria* remembers how in his first days in the prison he had to walk around with a notebook, where he wrote down all the strange names assigned to all kinds of objects, as if learning a new language.

Women, including officers but especially visitors, are treated according to an etiquette similar to the gallant rules of court life; this stands in stark contrast to the sexually overcharged and aggressive machismo that marks relations between genders in Venezuelan popular society. One should not walk topless in front of them, nor ogle them, or disrespect them, or make improper insinuations. One can't even run into them or wear dark glasses, as these might allow for concealed glances. Among Evangelicals, conjugal visits are only allowed for well-established married couples, which leads to the newly baptized being married by the local pastor to bring their relationships in line with such informal norms.

Respect for property is also resolute. The worst crime within the prison, perhaps on par with abuse of a family member, is stealing. To take something from someone, even when it is later found, is subject to the most severe punishment, generally death, or if not execution, then subjugation to a type of slavery to the prison bosses. Equally important is to repay debts and honor commitments that are taken on. In Peonía, the prisoners who do not pay their debts (accrued through drugs, games, favors or acquired goods, or the obligatory weekly taxes that everyone has to pay) might receive a *cachazo* (a blow with the handle of a weapon) to the head or be taken to the "prison" that the prisoners themselves have to punish those that behave poorly. They are held until they are able to pay the money they owe.

Similarly, prisoners have been assigned certain tasks: to do *garita* (working as guard in sensitive locations); to pay *causa* (weekly tax paid to the bosses of the prison); to comply with the rules within the prison, without complaining; to be ready to confront rival gangs or the National Guard in case of armed confrontations; to carry out hunger strikes; to carry out any tasks, no matter how dangerous or unpleasant they may be, once they are ordered to do so by the bosses.

The *Carro* (the car)[6] is the clearly delineated political formation that is in charge of making sure prisoners comply with norms inside the prison; they also evaluate and punish violations and resolve conflicts. The *Carro* is in charge of defending the prisoners and guaranteeing certain aspects of everyday life, from food provision to hosting the parties that frequently take place.

The members of the *Carro* carry firearms, which they ostentatiously display. They control different spaces of the prison and continuously watch over what happens, inside and out. Armed prisoners stationed in different pavilions—the entrance, the roof, the communal areas, behind fortified barricades, in strategic points—are accountable to the bosses for everything that happens on a regular basis. Immediately upon entering Peonía, you can hear the *luces*, the words of the *gariteros* (guards that watch over different parts of the prison) about what is happening: who goes in and where they walk, what the guards are doing, the prisoners in the neighboring prison, if there is a situation that is out of the ordinary or an *atmosfera*. The *principales* (the bosses of the *Carro*) are informed by the prisoners who bring news of things that are going on. While reporting or "rolling" on prison bosses is considered an unforgivable crime that leads inexorably to a death sentence, to report on fellow inmates to the bosses is considered an obligation. A dense and fluid network of vigilance keeps the *principales* informed about new happenings about the complex, about the prisoners' states of mind, what they do, their faults, and neglects. When we accompanied *Popeye* throughout his day—eating lunch with him, following him in his daily activities, conversing in a corner of the prison—we frequently saw his subordinates come closer or simply members of the prison population to inform him of abnormal situations, conflicts or disputes, or about the inappropriate behavior of one of the prisoners. "The *principal* is like a god: he knows everything" is how one of the prisoners described this omniscient power. If, according to Foucault, the modern prison system substituted people as the spectators of a theater of torture to the discreet and efficient bureaucratic power, in Peonía, the surveillance of the prisoners and their hierarchy replaces the myopic gaze of the institution.

Prisoners submissively obey the orders given by the members of the *Carro* and submit to their orders of punishment, including death[7]; indeed, these sentences are carried out without questioning, at least openly. On one occasion, a prisoner complained about a boss's decision in front of us. His friends, who were there at the same time, abruptly told him to shut up so that indiscreet ears would not hear and result in harsh punishment. The bosses are enveloped by an almost sacred aura of authority and admiration by the rest of the prison community. The *principales* cannot be referred to directly, or in the first person, and when the other prisoners pass by them, they frequently turn to them with genuflections and other shows of reverential respect.

The *Carro*'s organization emulates the structure of the state. It has policemen who control the entire territory under their control; there is a tribunal that judges violations and, in the case of Peonía, there is a "rehabilitation center" (Antillano 2015) where *chocones*, that is, those that do not respect the norms, are sent. Those punished might have their hair shaved off or can be required to pray several times a day at a center run by Evangelicals. Or, they might be punished with physical labor in the service of the *Carro*.

Ironically, the prison order that emerges from the withdrawal of institutional control is not so different, at least in its forms, from the functioning of the institution. It is a surprising restitution of the *total institution* but this time reproduced from below, by the prisoners themselves. The grueling rules, which leave barely any detail out of sight, must be complied with. They impose implacable punishments (Goffman reminds us that to follow detailed rules and to be punished for not performing them reduces prisoners to the level of children or mentally disabled people); a prudish and conservative morality is enforced, which maintains conventional values (extreme heterosexuality, respect for property, care in dealing with the opposite gender, the imperative to respect and obey authority, honor debt and commitments). Prisoners are subjected to a hierarchical yet diffuse system of authority (from the *principal* to the last pawn of the *Carro*, the structure of the group may impose harsh sanctions on prisoners); surveillance is capillary and extended, discipline uninterrupted, with continuous supervision; there is judgment of and sanctions placed upon deviations, even those that might seem miniscule or trivial. In an unexpected twist, the prison copies itself, a prison within the prison. Excised from the state's institutional control, left behind in a generalized state of abandonment, the prison does not become an emancipated space but one wherein oppression can be observed to amplify, increase, and intensify.

This most curious total institution from below, the self-government of the abandoned, may also exceed institutional models. A control that nothing escapes, that permeates all spheres of life, governs language, metaphors, sexuality, gestures, looks... A vigilance that operates through those who are governed. And, above all, an active and choreographed expression of compliance, subjugation with consent. Even when harsh punishment is applied to the stubborn or handed down to disobedient subjects, the majority of the prisoners who submit to this order find it a source of honor and respect.

Inside/Outside

There is no clear separation between the state, its institutional power, and the power exercised by the prisoners themselves. It is not only a question of signature forms that emulate the state and its modes within the prison system fostered by the prisoners themselves or the policies of mass incarceration and a decline of institutional resources that erode state power. State actors have an impact on the modes of domination, even if indirectly, over what happens within the prison.

Despite the loss of internal power within the prison, state workers continue to control the external perimeter, regulating who and what enters or leaves. This apparently precarious resource, the final stronghold of state sovereignty over the prison, is also the source of its power: people, arms, drugs, and goods pass through the hands of those in charge of guarding the external perimeter, while they maintain the prisoners confined to the institutional complex. The strategic management of the tension between inside and outside, because of the confinement of the prisoners, as well as the flow of people and goods, allows them to govern what is happening on the inside at a remove. Additionally, there is the omnipresent risk that the state could take back control of the prison at any moment if certain boundaries are overstepped.

The self-governing of the prisoners represents certain advantages for those responsible for the prison. On the one hand, most of the key resources that allow for extortion and illegal markets are in the hands of state agents: the guards and watchmen, in charge of directly administering the prison, in addition to lawyers, district attorneys, judges, and prison employees. On the other hand, the self-government guarantees order and a form of governmentality unobtainable through regular means, that the administration depends upon; the state in turn benefits from the *Carro*'s enforcement of rules, allowing for the control of disorder which reduces excessive violence and nearly eliminates acts of direct coercion against state authorities.

The social exclusion that reinforces the prison, in other words, does not suppose a definitive rupture with the outside social order. Possibly more than ever there are multiple ties connecting the inside of the prison with the outside, which permits the massive consumption of goods associated with the rough prison world.[8] An illicit economy that passes through the prison and its operations has risen in scale, offering future careers to criminals once they are free; and prisons' form of criminal sovereignty has been imported to poor communities. The prison itself feeds criminal networks and legal activities, criminal transactions between police and prisoners, political relations of patronage, that leap over the prison's confines and blur the limits between what happens in the prison and broader society.

From the captives' exclusion from the social order, to the new connections with the outside world, the relationships between formal and informal power, between social order and prison order, do not exist in a simple opposition or in mutual exclusion. Power obtains economic and political returns from the prisoners' self-rule. Inside/outside, exclusion/inclusion, center/periphery: as on the surface of a pond, these concentric circles move in different directions, all of them interdependent.

Notes

1. In November 2012, we entered for the first time into the prison Peonía (fictional name) located in the center of the country with a population of 5000 prisoners. We visited the prison regularly, one or two times a week, until the beginning of 2015. Since then, even though we continued going to the prison, we did not do so with the same frequency. Peonía forms part of a penitentiary complex together with other confinement centers, two of which are controlled by prisoners, and a third under the control of the authorities.
2. In Venezuela, there are 35 prisons, with the majority under the control of the federal government. Only a small number of ten penitentiaries (though they are the most populous) are governed by prisoners. Nevertheless, only a few years ago practically all of the prisons in the country were in this situation. The recovery of state authority was the result of military siege of the rebel prisons combined with negotiations with the prison gangs. This recently recovered and precarious order is sought to be maintained through a rigorous disciplinary regime and "harsh" treatment programs (military-inspired, and strongly ideologized).

But the continuous increase of the population and the lag in the available resources for the control and maintenance of the inmates produce frequent cases of riots, mistreatment, and even slaughter. A strategy of the prison authorities to avoid the erosion of their control over these retaken establishments has been to decrease the flow of new inmates, which has displaced the problems of overcrowding toward police detention centers. Even so, in many cases the institutional order breaks down and the previous forms of self-government reemerge.

3. There are other works of different origins which offer different perspectives, many times without a connection to Foucault's work, and give an account of the prison's fascination with controlling everything, the stubbornness to govern the most intimate forms, the most minuscule activities, the lives of all the inmates (see, among others, Melossi and Pavarini 1980; Goffman 2001). When talking about total institutions, from the point of view of the sociology of organization, Goffman notes how the bureaucratic management of needs and different aspects of communal life of the interns requires authoritarian modes of government, exhaustive control, and sustained supervision on the part of the administration.
4. While conducting research in a prison in California, Irwin evidences changes that operate inside the prison as adaptations to mass imprisonment: decreasing access to adequate services, the dismantling or restriction of treatment programs, and the harshening of mechanisms of control and administration of the incarcerated population. Even though the context is different and with opposite results, the changes highlighted by Irwin (and Owen in the case of incarcerated women) coincide rather well with the recent mutations in distinct prisons in Latin America where, facing a dramatic growth in the incarcerated population, the administration fails to attend to basic living conditions and abandons any concept of treatment (see Birkbeck 2010).
5. The church is the space separated from the rest of the prison in which the Evangelical prisoners, controlled by a pastor (also a prisoner), subject to its own rules and instances of power. On this subject, see Duno (this volume).
6. The term *Carro*, which designates the organization of the recluses that govern the carceral order, alludes to the idea of *driving, taking the wheel* (bosses are referred to as drivers). All of the vocabulary reinforces the metaphor that carries ideas of circulation, speed, and driving. The bosses take the wheel, they know how to "drive the car," prisoners should not "run the

red light" or "crash the car" (break the rules), those who repeatedly break the rules are called "wreckers" (*chocones*), things occur at a determined "speed," and so on. The metaphor also alludes to the machine-like character, mechanical and automatic, of the carceral order. As the bosses should drive the car, all the parts should function fluidly, without disorder and without falling behind.

7. Even though during the time that we were visiting the prison we were not aware of any executions, the use of different corporal punishments was relatively frequent, including the shooting of hands and feet or pistol-whips to the head. Prisoners talked to us about these episodes; even the bosses referred to these as a demonstration of the softening of the punishments that are applied to those responsible for serious offenses, which in another time would have resulted in capital punishment applied to their own companions in reclusion. In another instance, we saw a prisoner walking around with a cracked skull, the result of a one of the bosses hitting him with his gun as a sanction on bad behavior.
8. During the last few years, the circulation and consumption of videos, songs, and graphic products, which allude to the violence and the prison mafias, have risen. We ourselves participated in the taping of a fictional series in which some prisoners, excited by the illusion of an imminent success, represent the cruel battles for control over the prison (see Sepúlveda and Pojomovski, this volume). A cartoon series about life within Venezuelan prisons, "Cárcel o Infierno," became a viral phenomenon and was seen by millions on the web: https://www.youtube.com/watch?v=rhmM_mqKBbk

References

Alford, A. (2000). What would it matter if everything Foucault said about prison were wrong? Discipline and punish after twenty years. *Theory and Society, 29*(1), 125–146.

Antillano, A. (2015) Cuando los presos mandan. Control informal dentro de una cárcel venezolana. Espacio Abierto, 24, 4: 16–39.

Antillano, A., Pojomovsky, I., Zubillaga, V., Sepúlveda, C., & Hanson, R. (2016). The Venezuela prison: From neoliberalism to the Bolivarian revolution. *Crime, Law and Social Change, 65*(3), 195–211.

Biondi, K. (2010). *Junto e misturado: Uma etnografia do PCC*. Sao Paulo: Terceiro Nome.

Birkbeck, C. (2010). Prisiones en Internados: Una comparación de los establecimientos penales entre América del Norte y América Latina. *Caderno CRH, 23*(58), 129–149.

Bohoslavsky, E. (2005). Uso (y abuso) de Foucault para mirar las instituciones de castigo en Argentina, 1890–1930. *Cyber Humanitatis, 35*.

Bohoslavsky, E., & Di Liscia, M. L. (2005). *Instituciones y formas de control en América Latina (1840–1940)* (Una revisión ed.). Buenos Aires: Prometeo.

Caimiri, L. (2005). Usos de Foucault en la investigación histórica. *Documento de Trabajo*, 18. Escuela de Eucación, Universidad de San Andrés, Buenos Aires.

Cerbini, F. (2012). *La casa de jabón. Etnografía de una cárcel boliviana*. Barcelona: Edicions Bellaterra.

Clemmer, D. (1958). *The prison community*. New York: Rinehart.

Darke, S. (2013). Inmate governance in Brazilian prisons. *The Howard Journal of Criminal Justice, 52*(3), 272–284.

De Giorgi, A. (2007). Toward a political economy of post-Fordist punishment. *Critical Criminology, 15*, 243–265.

Deleuze, G. (1990). ¿Qué es un dispositivo? In VVAA (Ed.), *Michel Foucault Filósofo*. Barcelona: Gedisa.

Fernández Liria, C. (1992). *Sin vigilancia y sin castigo. Una discusión con Michel Foucault*. Madrid: Libertarias.

Foucault, M. (1978). *Vigilar y Castigar: Nacimiento de la prisión*. Madrid: Siglo XXI.

Foucault, M. (1991). *Saber y Verdad*. Madrid: Ediciones la Piqueta.

Garland, D. (1993). *Punishment and modern society*. A study in social theory: University of Chicago Press, Chicago.

Garland, D. (1996). The limits of the sovereign state. *The British Journal of Criminology, 36*, 4.

Goffman, E. (2001). *Internados*. Barcelona: Amorrortu.

Ignatieff, M. (1978). *A just measure of pain: The penitentiary in the industrial revolution, 1750–1850*. New York: Pantheon Books.

Irwin, J., & Owen, B. (2004). *The warehouse prison: Disposal of the new dangerous class*. Oxford: Oxford University Press.

Macaulay, F. (2014). Whose prisoners are these anyway? Church, state and society partnerships and co-production of offender 'resocialisation' in Brazil. In V. Miller & J. Campbell (Eds.), *Translating penal cultures: New perspectives on discipline, punishment and desistance* (pp. 202–2016). London, Routledge.

Melossi, D., & Pavarini, M. (1980). *Cárcel y fábrica: Los orígenes del sistema penitenciario.* Siglos XVI–XIX. Siglo XXI Mexico.
Morris, T., & Morris, P. (1963). Pentonville. In *A sociological study of an English prison.* London: Routledge & K. Paul.
Nuñez, J. (2007). Las cárceles en la época del narcotráfico: una mirada etnográfica. *Nueva sociedad, 208,* 103–117.
Pérez Guadalupe, J. L. (2000). *La construcción social de la realidad carcelaria: Los alcances de la organización informal en cinco cárceles latinoamericana: Perú, Chile, Argentina, Brasil y Bolivia.* Lima: Fondo Editorial de la Pontificia Universidad Católica de Perú.
Perrot, M. (Ed.) (1980). L'impossible Prison. In *Recherches sur le système pénitentiaire au XIXe siecle.* Paris: Edition du Seuil.
Provea. (1999). Derecho a los privados de libertad. In *Situación de los derechos humanos en Venezuela.* Caracas: Provea.
Provea. (2000). Derecho a los privados de libertad. In *Situación de los derechos humanos en Venezuela.* Caracas: Provea.
Provea. (2001). Derecho a los privados de libertad. In *Situación de los derechos humanos en Venezuela.* Caracas: Provea.
Provea. (2002). Derecho a los privados de libertad. In *Situación de los derechos humanos en Venezuela.* Caracas: Provea.
Provea. (2003). Derecho a los privados de libertad. In *Situación de los derechos humanos en Venezuela.* Caracas: Provea.
Provea. (2004). Derecho a los privados de libertad. In *Situación de los derechos humanos en Venezuela.* Caracas: Provea.
Provea. (2005). Derecho a los privados de libertad. In *Situación de los derechos humanos en Venezuela.* Caracas: Provea.
Provea. (2006). Derecho a los privados de libertad. In *Situación de los derechos humanos en Venezuela.* Caracas: Provea.
Provea. (2007). Derecho a los privados de libertad. In *Situación de los derechos humanos en Venezuela.* Caracas: Provea.
Provea. (2008). Derecho a los privados de libertad. In *Situación de los derechos humanos en Venezuela.* Caracas: Provea.
Provea. (2009). Derecho a los privados de libertad. In *Situación de los derechos humanos en Venezuela.* Caracas: Provea.
Provea. (2010). Derecho a los privados de libertad. In *Situación de los derechos humanos en Venezuela.* Caracas: Provea.
Provea. (2011). Derecho a los privados de libertad. In *Situación de los derechos humanos en Venezuela.* Caracas: Provea.

Provea. (2012). Derecho a los privados de libertad. In *Situación de los derechos humanos en Venezuela*. Caracas: Provea.
Provea. (2013). Derecho a los privados de libertad. In *Situación de los derechos humanos en Venezuela*. Caracas: Provea.
Rosales, E. (1997). Cárcel y violencia (Una aproximación sociojurídica a la violencia penitenciaria en Venezuela). *Capítulo Criminológico, 25*(2), 49–88.
Rothman, D. (1990). *The discovery of asylum: Social order and disorder in the New Republic*. New York: Aldine de Gruyter.
Salvatore, R., & Aguirre, C. (Eds.). (1996). *The birth of the penitentiary in Latin American. Essays on criminology, prison reform and social control, 1830–1940*. Austin: University of Texas Press.
Sykes, G. (1974). *The society of captives: A study of a maximum security prison*. New Jersey: Princeton University Press.
Wacquant, L. (2003). Toward a dictatorship over the poor? Notes on the penalization of poverty in Brazil. *Punishment & Society, 5*(2), 197–205.
Wacquant, L. (2010). *Castigar a los pobres*. Barcelona: Gedisa.

3

Self-Governing Prison Communities

Sacha Darke

Things were clearly going wrong in *pavilhão cinco* (pavilion five or cell block five) of Carandiru. When Jocimar, who headed the cell block *faxina* (literally, cleaning, in Brazilian prison slang also meaning cleaning team or, as in the context here, cell block housekeepers), was confronted by the head of security, Luis, over rumors members of his team were abusing their position and collecting drugs debts and protection money directly from prisoners' families, the best explanation he could provide was that it was not possible for him to control everything that happened under his command. By refusing to take responsibility for a matter that went to the heart of inmate relations at the men's prison—*"só pode se dirigir a um familiar do outro se convidado a fazê-lo"* ("never approach another prisoner's family/acquaintance unless he asks you") (Varella 1999: 164)—Jocimar

This chapter was originally published in longer version as chapter one of Darke, S. (2018) *Conviviality and Survival: Co-producing Brazilian Prison Order*, London: Palgrave Macmillan. Portuguese version (2019): *Convívio e Sobrevivência: Ordem Prisional em Cogovernança* (trans: Karam, M.L.), Belo Horizonte: D'Placido.

S. Darke (✉)
School of Social Sciences, University of Westminster, London, UK

S. Darke et al. (eds.), *Carceral Communities in Latin America*, Palgrave Studies in Prisons and Penology, https://doi.org/10.1007/978-3-030-61499-7_3

must have known he was treading on thin ground. Luis had every right to warn him of the consequences of not restoring order as quickly as possible. A few evenings later, the status quo in the cell block was completely shattered, when the six guards on duty were taken hostage by the occupants of one of the cells set aside for members of the *faxina* on the second floor. Landing staff had been held hostage many times before, but what was unusual this time was that the inmates assaulted one of the officers in a bid to hasten their transfer out of the prison. Luis resisted demands from other guards to allow them to retaliate to such a clear breach of trust by beating up the hostage takers once they had reached the apparent safety of the police van and released their captives. However, any informal agreements they had with prisoners not to *reagir* (react) in hostage situations did not apply to the police that transported them.

Luis was faced with a dilemma. Transferring Jocimar was the easy part. Having overseen the extortion of prisoners' families and the humiliation of guards, Jocimar was also guilty of failing to enforce codes relating to inmate solidarity and dealings with prison staff. He would not be missed on the wings. Removing the other 200 inmates that made up the current cell block hierarchy would be far more risky and certainly controversial. Running a leaderless cell block of 1500 inmates was not an option with the handful of guards Luis had at his disposal; and a cell block *faxina* seen to be put in place by the prison management would never gain the confidence of other inmates. In a successful Machiavellian maneuver, Luis approached Pirulão, a powerful prisoner he knew he could trust on pain of exposing him to other inmates as a previous police informant and now prison snitch. Within a few days, Pirulão had gathered a group of more than 300 disgruntled prisoners. Shortly after lockdown, they removed the old cell block *faxina* cell by cell, masked and armed with sticks and knives, before beating them and handing them over to officers to distribute them to the segregation unit in cell block four.

I return to the significance of this episode, narrated by Drauzio Varella (1999) in the book *Estação Carandiru* (*Carandiru Station*), in a moment. Varella worked voluntarily as a doctor at the prison for more than 10 years, from 1989 to 2001. Estação Carandiru was later adapted for the award winning film *Carandiru* (Babenco and Kramer 2003).

Managing in Prison

Carandiru made international headlines on 2 October 1992, when 300 shock troops, many armed with machine guns, entered cell block nine in response to a dispute among rival groups of prisoners. Within 30 minutes, at least 111 prisoners were dead or mortally injured (Veja, 14 October 1992).[1] Most prisoners died at the hands of the equally infamous military police unit Rondas Ostensivas Tobias de Aguiar (ROTA) (Folha de São Paulo, 21 June 2001), whose 700 officers were responsible for a large proportion of the 1470 citizens killed by São Paulo state police that year (Caldeira 2000), and continued to be responsible for up to one in five police killings in the state in the 2000s and into the 2010s (Veja São Paulo, 11 August 2010; Folha de São Paulo, 28 January 2012). As the police entered the cell block, television reporters read out the names and death records of their commanders, including Captain Wanderley Mascarenhas, 5 of whose 34 previous victims had died at the same prison 10 years earlier (Ramos 2003). Guards, prisoners, and police that witnessed the killings give varying descriptions of the source of the dispute that led to the tragic police incursion, from unpaid debts, the results of a game of soccer, an accusation of sleeping with a sex offender, to someone's space being taken on a washing line. What is clear is that the *faxina* running the cell block failed to prevent what had started out as a relatively minor, everyday dispute from escalating out of control. Varella depicts the riot as an illogical, chaotic affair, and is quick to point out that cell block nine was populated by first time prisoners, who not surprisingly were renowned for being undisciplined and volatile. They also made the mistake of allowing the guards on duty to leave the cell block rather than take them as hostages (Mendes 2009; Varella 2012). Tragically, and in complete contrast to the inexperience demonstrated by these prisoners, Varella (1999) laments, ROTA's response was unleashed with military precision.

Aware inmates across the prison were in fear of their lives, the officer in charge of the neighboring cell block eight convinced its 1700 prisoners to return with their weapons to their cells, with the promise he would leave the keys to the cells in the hands of the cell block *faxina* in case the shock troops did not stop at cell block nine (Varella 2012). Explanations for why the police took control of cell block nine with such deadly force also vary, from public expectation (ROTA, for instance, could count on the support of the majority of the São Paulo public, despite its reputation for summary executions), prisoners threatening to attack officers with knives covered in HIV-contaminated blood, to a systematic attempt to rid the cell block of its inmate hierarchy. What is broadly agreed is that most of the killings occurred on the *faxina*-occupied second floor, and that by the time ROTA reached this floor, prisoners had, like those in cell block eight, discarded their weapons and fled to the nearest cells. Survivors claim officers fired their machine guns into many cells, in some cases through the service hatches (e.g. Ramos 2003; Rap and Zeni 2002). The police forensics team that examined the crime scene concluded a number of prisoners had also been shot while kneeling or lying down. Of the 397 bullets that reached their target, 126 were to the head (Justiça Global 2001). Carandiru did not recover from the controversy surrounding the operation and was eventually deactivated in September 2002. Two months later, three cell blocks, including cell blocks eight and nine, were imploded live on television. Paradoxically, the final victims of the Carandiru massacre, as the event came to be known, were the director of the prison, José Ismael Pedrosa, and the head of the São Paulo state military police, who commanded the operation, Ubiratan Guimarães. Pedrosa was assassinated in 2005 on the orders of the Primeiro Comando da Capital (First Command of the Capital: PCC), a gang formed in the aftermath of the massacre with the explicit aim to protect prisoners from such a tragedy being repeated. Today the PCC operates in over 90 percent of São Paulo prisons and is Latin America's largest criminal organization. Guimarães was sentenced to 632 years' imprisonment in 2001, only to escape punishment by being elected onto the São Paulo state legislature before winning an appeal against his conviction in 2006. Seven months later, he was shot dead in as yet unexplained circumstances.

I visited the empty Carandiru with my Brazilian brother-in-law shortly before its remaining cell blocks were demolished in 2005. I knew of the massacre, but not the depth inmates participated in governing the prison. As I sifted through a pile of rubble just inside the outer wall of the prison compound that contained the remains of cell blocks eight and nine, I remained in my comfort zone. A law graduate versed in the language of human rights and prison abolition, I contemplated the degrading treatment Carandiru's prisoners must have experienced. The security guard on duty at a gap in the wall we had entered hesitated to allow us to go any further into the compound, but as Brazilians are fond of saying, *sempre tem um jeito* (there is always a way) or *a gente pode dar um jeito* (we can find a way). This was the first of many occasions when the word *jeito*, or the diminutive *jeitinho*, would come to the aid of my research and analysis. It is a word I find increasingly important to understanding the flexible and clientelistic characteristics of everyday political and social interactions in Brazil.

When the security guard eventually agreed to let us in, we walked through the compound to what I later discovered to have been cell block four. Wary of the security guard getting into trouble if anyone else showed up, we spent a few frantic minutes taking photos of the yard, corridors, and cells, before crossing over the ruins of cell block six to take more photos in cell block two. On the way into and back out of the prison compound, we passed by cell block five, scene of the breakdown of governance at the prison described above, and then in the early stages of preparation for the filming of the part fact, part fictional television series, *Carandiru: Outras Histórias* (Babenco et al. 2005). Besides the utter physical disrepair of the prison, what caught our attention in each of the cell blocks were the murals and scribbled writing left behind by prisoners in almost every cell and communal area. A few of these referred to the PCC. Others depicted religious scenes or artifacts, most Christian, some spiritualist or demonic. The majority were more mundane—emblems of São Paulo's major soccer clubs; messages of love for those on the outside; and messages of support for those on the inside.

Opened in 1952, the Casa de Detenção de São Paulo (São Paulo House of Detention: Carandiru prison) remains the largest ever or at least most populous self-contained prison in Latin America. In 1992, it held 7000 prisoners, three times the number for which it had been built. Since the massacre, numerous first-hand accounts of life in Carandiru have been published, including Luiz Alberto Mendes (2005, 2009, 2012, 2015); Drauzio Varella (1999, 2012); Luiz Wolfmann (2000); and André du Rap (Rap and Zeni 2002), and also a quite remarkable documentary film, *O Prisioneiro da Grade de Ferro* (Steinberg and Sacramento 2004), shot by prisoners over seven months the year before the prison was deactivated.

The Carandiru massacre highlighted two aspects of life behind bars in Brazil. The first, and the basis of most academic and governmental literature, concerns the appalling conditions in which prisoners find themselves, from severe staff shortage and overcrowding to wholly inadequate facilities, legal and medical cover. Varella (1999) devotes several chapters to prisoners' health, outlining among other things the devastatingly high levels of drug abuse and serious illness such as tuberculosis, leprosy, and HIV Aids. The second aspect of Brazilian prison life highlighted by the massacre, and the main focus of my research, concerns the means by which Brazilian prison managers, staff, and inmates manage to get by in spite of such adversity and state neglect. This, we will see, is due in part to the amount of time the majority of inmates spent outside their cells, often from sunrise to sunset, mixing freely in the cell block corridors and exercise yards. It is also part due to prison work. At Carandiru, most prisoners had some form of paid activity to occupy their time. Some were employed by private contractors, not always officially, manufacturing items such as toys, umbrellas, soccer balls, or greetings cards. The prison even had a bakery and ice-cream factory. As in other prisons in the country, these inmates gained up to—although usually far less than—three-quarters of the national minimum wage; the prison administration kept the rest of their wages. Inmates also got by through participating in the prison's thriving informal economy in drugs, alcohol, pornography, sex, and even clothing repairs. A further 1000 inmates affiliated to the prison's Assembléia de Deus (Assembly of God) spent five to six hours a day in prayer or religious learning. As many as 3000 family visitors filled the cell block yards each weekend, 20,000–25,000 at Christmas, Easter, or on mothers' day (Varella 2012). Two thousand prisoners' wives or girlfriends were registered for intimate visits. Sexual services were also provided by prisoners housed on the Street of Flowers or Paris, a corridor that in the past had housed female prisoners and by the 1970s had become perhaps one of the first spaces in a prison anywhere in the world to be reserved for transvestite prisoners.

What continues to fascinate me most about Carandiru is how the prison operated despite employing very few staff, in particular the roles played by inmates in running the prison, and the formal and (mostly) informal relations they maintained with prison staff. At the time of the massacre, Carandiru's main cell blocks (five, eight, and nine) each held up to 2000 prisoners, guarded by 5 or 6 officers during the day, even fewer during the night time (Varella 2012). In order to govern the prison, staff relied on its inmates.

Varella's (1999) interest in inmate participation is made clear from the first few pages, where he describes the work carried out by prisoners loading and unloading vans used to transport prisoners, food, and building materials. He goes on to explain that some 1700 of the prison's 7000 inmates worked alongside or in the place of staff in the 1990s, up to 1000 officially as trusty prisoners, for instance as porters, couriers, cooks, cleaners, laundry washers, tailors, hairdressers, or clerks. Like other prisoners formally employed by private contractors, trusty prisoners gained a day's remission of sentence for every three days worked. Most were held separately in cell block two, but carried passes that allowed them access to other parts of the prison. It is Varella's first impression of the prison that sets the central theme and my interest in the book: how inmates are formally recruited to work as janitors and administrators, and how prisoners organize themselves to provide security, discipline, and material support on the wings. While much has been written about the rise of major gangs like the PCC since the 1980s and 1990s, few studies have provided more than a partial picture of the nature of inmate involvement in running Brazilian prisons, or the complexity of relations between inmates and prison staff.

Having outlined the functions played by trusty prisoners, whose work was restricted to the communal areas of the prison, Varella (1999) moves on to explore the work of prisoners who worked unofficially in the remaining cell blocks, 150 to 200 in each of cell blocks five, eight, and nine, and 20 to 30 in cell blocks four, six, and seven. In total around 700 prisoners were integrated into these cell block *faxina*, most of who we have seen accommodated in cells on the second floor.[2] Each cell block had its own inmate hierarchy. In addition to performing domestic tasks such as sweeping corridors, mopping, cooking, and distributing meals, these *faxineiros* (cleaners)—or the grammatically incorrect but more commonly used word in Brazilian prison slang, *faxinas*, or as a collective noun, *faxina*—acted as cell block leaders and representatives and maintained order through enforcing inmate codes and, as we saw in Varella's account of the changing of the *faxina* in cell block five, tacit agreements with prison staff. Through enforcing the decisions of ad hoc quasi-legal debates when prisoners are accused of breaking inmate codes (which at Carandiru, as elsewhere, included averting your eyes from others' visitors, remaining in your cell and not using the bathroom during mealtimes, maintaining silence during sleeping hours, not getting into debt, not resorting to violence without permission, and sharing food, toiletries, and clothing brought in by your family), the cell block *faxina* set the *ritmo* (rhythm) of the prison. Carandiru guards did not interfere with the organization of the *faxina*, nor with its management of the wings unless prisoners were severely beaten, though even an execution would more often than not be settled by a *laranja* (orange or scapegoat), typically an indebted crack addict, stepping forward to falsely confess to the crime. Moreover, guards would consult senior *faxina* before making their own decisions as to when and how to discipline wayward prisoners.

Compared to the relatively well-resourced prisons of the postindustrial world, the average Brazilian prison is remarkably overcrowded and unhealthy. My point is simply that to understand what it is like inside Brazilian prisons, it is also important to study the means and extent to which they continue to operate and the ordinary inmate and staff member get along in spite of their poor conditions of work and incarceration:

to study everyday matters of prison management and situational adjustments as much as deprivations, staff shortages, and the need for decarceration. In my experience, Brazilian prisons are as striking for the fact they continue to exhibit complex social orders as the fact they are effectively abandoned by state authorities. Central to my analysis is that the daily lives of frontline prison workers and inmates are entangled to an extent that would be hard to imagine in the West of Europe or North of America. Not only do prison inmates rely on each other as much as they do on prison staff, but prison staff also rely on the cooperation and support of prisoners. Prison staff also experience diminishing levels of everyday authority, as cell block, prison, city, state, and even nation-wide inmate collectives, including self-proclaimed criminal gangs such as the PCC, increasingly step in to occupy historical voids in state responsibility and governance. At the same time, prison staff rely on prisoners' families and local volunteers to make up for shortfalls in state provision, including bedding, clothing, pharmaceuticals, food, cigarettes, legal, and medical services. As a result, the barriers between prison and community life are generally more permeable than they are in, for instance, the United States, the United Kingdom, or Norway. Prison life in Brazil, therefore, is shaped as much by attachments as detachments, between inmates and staff, and also between prisons and the localities in which they are situated. Under such conditions, shared-, or my preferred term, co-governance, is a social (or institutional) fact of increasing importance in Brazil. Human rights abuses tell one side of the story of what it means to live or work in a Brazilian prison; co-governance tells the other. Remarkably, at the time of the Carandiru massacre, prison staffing levels were significantly higher than they are today. In São Paulo, for instance, the official number of inmates per member of prison staff has risen from around two to one in the early 1990s to eight to one today. Once shift patterns, staff roles, and absence through sickness are taken into account, it is quite normal to find one officer on duty per 100, even 200 prisoners (Karam and Saraiva 2017; Salla 2017). To make up for staff shortages, not only are as many as one in ten prisoners officially employed by prison authorities in trusty positions (henceforth referred to as trusty *faxina*), but thousands more prisoners work informally on the wings, usually with the implicit or explicit support of prison staff, as was the case in Carandiru. As for situational adjustments to the deprivations of prison, at the weekends the number of visitors sometimes exceeds the number of inmates. Families start queuing up outside prisons with their *jumbos* (bags of food and other basic goods—toiletries, confectionaries, cigarettes, clothing, and so on—they are allowed to take for those they are visiting) from well before dawn.

Indeed, accounts of Brazilian prison life point toward an everyday reality in which inmates and staff are often able to create and maintain relationships of accommodation and trust in even the most despairing of settings. Similar to the ways in which alternative systems of governance have filled the gap left by ineffective state governance in the country's urban slums (see, inter alia, Biondi 2018; Feltran 2020), most Brazilian prisons continue to operate under normative, if generally "thin and multilayered" (Darke 2014: 65) and "forced" (Darke 2013: 280) reciprocal and customary orders, based not upon the democratic rule of law or bureaucratic regulations, but on organically produced *regras de procedimento* (rules of procedure) (Varella 1999: 100) or *regras de convivência* (rules of conviviality) (Marques 2010: 318). As Arruda (2015) and Human Rights Watch (2015) demonstrate in the case of the Curado complex in the north-eastern state of Pernambuco, in some prisons officers have gone so far as to delegate even their most basic of tasks—security and discipline—to inmates. Pernambuco has the highest level of prison overcrowding and lowest staff–inmate ratio of the 27 states in the country. A Brazilian parliamentary report found an average of just five guards on duty in the complex, which at the time was holding 4200 inmates (Câmara dos Deputados 2008). To make up for these shortfalls, prison directors rely on police to secure the spaces between the three prisons in the complex, and on *chaveiros* (key holders) to manage the spaces within its 17 cell blocks. At another prison highlighted in Câmara dos Deputados (2008), Penitenciária Lemos de Brito, in the central-eastern state of Bahia, the parliamentary investigators found the head inmate leader had a key to his own cell. When the discovery was reported to the press and police officers subsequently arrived to transfer the prisoner, the director of the prison had to knock on his door (ibid). Sensationalism aside, the fact is it is not so unusual in Brazil for prisoners to be entrusted with keys. In some cases, this may mean no more than having a key to a room in which they work, for instance, a kitchen or library. In other cases, prisoners may be given keys to allow them access to individual prison wings, for instance to distribute meals. Besides the Curado complex, inmates are also employed and entrusted with keys to control access to and from the wings in at least two other major prisons in Brazil, Cadeia Pública de Porto Alegre (Porto Alegre Public Prison; more commonly referred to by its previous name, Central Prison) in the southern state of Rio Grande do Sul (Bassani 2016), and Alcaçuz prison complex in the northern state of Rio Grande do Norte (Madeiro 2017). During my 12 years of fieldwork, I have also learnt of inmates being entrusted with keys to the cell blocks at *carceragens* (police lockups) in São Paulo in the 2000s and at a remand prison in Rio de Janeiro today; and of prisons in Bahia and Mato Grosso where officers pass keys to gang leaders to lock the cells on their wing at the end of the day. Inmates also control the wing entrances in dozens of community prisons across the country, nine of which I have visited in the states of Minas Gerais and São Paulo. I introduce Rio de Janeiro's pre-trial system, and Minas Gerais and São Paulo's community prison systems below.

Moreover, Brazilian prisons do not inevitably become violent and disorderly or their governance illegitimate when the power to maintain order and security is delegated to prisoners. This does not signify that certain aspects of co-governance should be adopted as prison policy in Brazil or anywhere else, but that in many cases, prison inmates and staff are simply better off with than without it.

Getting By

Compare my reflections on my initial impressions of Carandiru, and Varella's description of the changing of the *faxina* in cell block five, with my field notes of my first visit to a *carceragem*, in Rio de Janeiro in 2010, where I returned in September the same year to complete the first of two fieldwork prison studies. I was accompanied on this initial visit by Judge

Maria Lúcia Karam and Orlando Zaccone, a senior civil police officer. Zaccone coordinated the state's 16 *carceragens* from 2009 until he succeeded in closing them down in the early 2010s:

Orlando picked us up soon after 1 pm. As we drove to Polinter, he explained that with a current population of around 650 inmates, the *carceragem* was the largest in the state. Prisoners stayed on average six months while they waited for spaces to become available in remand prisons, when by law the police were only allowed to hold them for 24 hours. Many chose to stay there until they were tried and sentenced, so as to stay closer to their families, who were treated with as much dignity as possible when they visited. The officers that worked there received no resources to run the *carceragem* apart from the delivery of prison meals. Converted from police horse stables, there were no outdoor spaces to allow prisoners their legal right to a minimum of two hours unlock a day, but the police had been able to open up a corridor that ran along across the front of the cells. Orlando assured us relations were good between officers and the Comando Vermelho (CV), Rio's largest and Brazil's second largest "criminal" gang after the PCC, that ran one of the two wings at the *carceragem,* and the Povo de Israel, made up of prisoners that were not accepted or not interested in gang membership, that ran the other, the *seguro* (vulnerable persons unit). Importantly, Orlando had managed to put an end to police violence. He had also ended the strip-searching of prisoners' families and made sure the family of every prisoner was able to visit almost any day of the week. In response, the CV and Povo de Israel leadership assured the safety of the police and trusty prisoners, and discipline and order in the cell block. They had also agreed to ban weapons and hard drugs from entering.

When we arrived, it was immediately apparent that Polinter was far from large physically. With the use of Google satellite images, I later discovered the single-storey *carceragem* occupied a space of no more than 1200 m^2. A whiteboard in the office showed there to be currently 603 inmates, around 550 of which were being held across nine cells, or rather caged former animal stalls, which I subsequently estimated to be an average of 25 m^2. When I returned to the *carceragem* to conduct fieldwork six months later, a prisoner told me that a year earlier he had shared one of the cells with over 100 people.

Orlando took us straight to the office where, besides two of only three officers working that afternoon (the other was stationed at the entrance to the *carceragem*), we met the first of perhaps 50 *colaboradores* (collaborators: Rio de Janeiro prison workers' preferred term for trusty prisoners) at the *carceragem*, who worked as clerks. Alongside the police, they were dealing with a group of newly arrived prisoners, represented by a current prisoner who I was soon to realize to be the leader of the *carceragem*'s CV. Sitting down for coffee after the new prisoners had been registered and taken to the cell block, one of the officers explained the police could not run the *carceragem* without their *colaboradores*, and that at night there was sometimes only one officer on duty. (I later discovered it was actually unusual to have more than one officer on duty overnight). At these times he slept with his mobile phone by his bed, not as I inquired because of the risk of escape or rebellion, but in case a prisoner was taken ill and had to be rushed to hospital. Clearly appreciating the effect this would have on me, he broke into a grin. It wouldn't look good if there were only prisoners left in charge, he added. I only understood the full irony of this otherwise throwaway comment when I returned to start research. When I arrived on the first day, the director was away. While I waited for him to return, I was left in the hands of two former police officers, now prisoners and chief *colaboradores*. Together with the director, these two *colaboradores* were referred to by other inmates as Polinter's administration. Both carried mobile phones and keys. These included keys to an unstaffed back gate, which was used as a trade entrance, and also keys to the cell block.

After coffee, Orlando took Maria Lúcia and me onto the CV wing to explain my plans for research. Crossing the few meters of the yard to the cell block, a group of prisoners on the *seguro* shouted out to Orlando, *"tu vai ser o novo presidente!"* ("you're going to be the next president!"), in reference to nationwide elections that were due to take place later in the year. As *colaboradores* opened the gate to the CV wing, inmates on the other side noticed Maria Lúcia's presence and the word was spread that a woman was entering. In spite of the cramped conditions and searing heat (Orlando instructed me to put my hand up to a grill to the outside, where the 30 degree centigrade air coming through felt as cool as if it were emerging from an air conditioning unit), the 250 or so prisoners quickly put on immaculately clean and pressed white T-shirts (each of the cells had a stove, which allowed them to boil water for washing and filling two-liter plastic soft drinks bottles for ironing). We squeezed along the wing corridor to speak with the CV leader I had seen in the office, who greeted Orlando and, encircled by his entourage, agreed to my research schedule. On the way back to the town center, Orlando remarked that he was quite sure he was the only police officer the CV shook hands with. I wondered whether I was the first prison researcher they had given permission to conduct ethnographic research on their organization and structure.

If Varella's accounts of disorder at Carandiru help introduce the reader to the realities of co-governance as a means of negotiating personal safety (of resolving conflicts, and allowing prison inmates to keep their heads down and do their time safe in the knowledge that to do so will not be interpreted as a sign of weakness), my intention in focusing on my first impressions of Polinter is to emphasize the broader importance of co-governance in enabling prison staff and inmates to get by. Without the support of prisoners and their survival "know how", it would not have been possible for the police to do any more at the *carceragem* than patrol the perimeter walls and deliver food to the entrances to the cell block, even had there always been two officers on duty. Not only would escapes have been more likely, and disputes between and among prisoners and staff more difficult to resolve, as already noted, but who for example would have distributed the food to the cells? Subsequently collected the empty food containers? Swept the floors? Organized cell rotas for the use of corridors during unlock, and in-cell rotas for the 40–50 prisoners who had to share each shower and toilet? Attended to prisoners with ailments? Regulated their medication? Registered and seen to the needs of visitors? Checked that the *jumbos* brought in by visitors did not contain weapons or drugs? Made sure prisoners stood out of the way and averted their eyes from each other's families during visiting hours, and kept their voices down in the evening so others could get to sleep? Dealt with lawyers, court, and prison service officials? Represented the *coletivo* (collective or inmate body) in dealings with *colaboradores* and police? Mended the showers, water taps, and fans that prevented the temperature from rising to life-threatening levels such as the 56.7 degrees centigrade recorded at the *carceragem* shortly after Zaccone took over (Globo, 11 February

2010)? Of course, all of this does not happen in every Brazilian prison. It is also true that under Zaccone's oversight, Polinter was also going through extraordinary times. But it is equally true that hunger and sickness are no more in the interest of those who live and work in any Brazilian prison as are conflict and disorder; nor the ill-treatment of prisoners' families, without whom prisoners would have to go without some of the most essential of items. To the extent prison staff and inmates want routines to run smoothly, and for neither to be damaged by their prison experience, they likewise have to negotiate. In most prisons, staff and inmates cobble together ways to co-produce everyday matters of survival as well as personal safety. Many of the practices I observed at Polinter are common to prisons of all types across Rio de Janeiro and the remainder of the country. The pertinent question is not why, but under what conditions they manage to do so.

More generally, I make use of this narrative of my first visit to the *carceragem* in order to highlight three areas in which my analysis departs from much of the existing literature on Brazilian prisons alluded to in this chapter.

First, Brazilian prisons are not necessarily as disorderly or violent as they are often depicted. In most Brazilian states, homicide rates are not significantly higher in prison than on the outside, and in many cases are lower than homicide rates among young men in the areas prisoners come from. This includes Pernambuco. It included Carandiru, and also Rio de Janeiro's police *carceragens*, where no prisoner was killed during Zaccone's three-year tenure. Similarly, while it is arguably mistaken to regard the gangs that increasingly monopolize networks of co-governance as having "pacified" the prison system (Dias 2013), it is equally important not to underestimate the role prison gangs play in supporting systems of mutual aid and protection.

Second, in Brazil prison governance is a largely temporal and localized matter that varies from one context to another. This remains the case despite the rise of prison gangs and is the main reason I have adopted the term prison communities in the title to this chapter (the other reason being entanglements between individual prisons and the localities in which they are situated). Further, while many of these practices may have been absorbed and formalized by local prison authorities and prison gangs, in most places co-governance continues to be more fluid and customary than bureaucratic and prescriptive, and grounded as much in interpersonal and social interactions and everyday interdependencies and accommodations, what Garces and I refer to as informal prison dynamics (Darke and Garces 2017), as hierarchies and impositions of formal rules. In this sense, prison governance is made up of informal practices that are not so much shared, as if they were the result of calculated policies, as co-produced from convergences in everyday practices of co-existence, which will be different in one context to another. Some prison researchers in Brazil argue, convincingly in my view, that co-governance is less hierarchical as habitual even in the PCC prisons of São Paulo. This can be noted in the position occupied by the PCC leadership. Important decisions are collectively made among affiliated gang members, and most roles are interchangeable (Dias 2013). Moreover, local gang members are typically chosen among those considered to have good skills of negotiation and control over their emotions and impulses (ibid), *humilde* (humble) (Biondi 2010), and committed to *igualdade* (equality) and *paz entre ladrões* (peace among thieves) (Marques 2014) rather than their depth of involvement in crime. All prisoners participate in the PCC's quasi-legal processes of adjudication. In some prisons, PCC codes of conduct are enforced even in the complete absence of gang leaders. PCC-affiliated prisoners do not feel obliged to take orders from gang members that vary from the codes to which they are accustomed. At the same time, inmate codes of conduct vary with the *ritmo* of one PCC prison to another (see Biondi, this volume).

Finally, and closely related to this methodologically, is the importance, first and foremost, of studying places (in this case Brazilian prisons) in their own terms. As they are tested and revised over time, theories of crime and justice become academic common sense. Yet, as postcolonial theorists such as Said (1978) and more recently Connell (2007), and de Souza Santos (Santos 2007) observe in their analysis of the historical and continuing global dominance of Western thought, few social science theories have been adequately put to the test beyond the global North, yet many are presented as if they are of universal application. At the same time, too many social scientists in the South continue to privilege the standpoints and knowledge of Northern experts and to rely on utilizing

Northern concepts and theories in contexts that are often very different to those upon which they were developed. This is certainly the case in Latin America (Castro 1987; Olmo 1981; Sozzo 2017).

With this epistemological position in mind, a major aim of my research has been to question the extent to which our established (Northern) understanding of prisons is useful in Brazil. Throughout the research process, it has also been necessary for me to critically reflect on the presumed standpoints and knowledge I have developed through my own academic training in England, as well as the privileged position I have enjoyed in Brazil as a researcher from the North. Moreover, I am constantly reminded of the dangers highlighted by Cain (2000), Cohen (1988), Jefferson and Jensen (Eds. 2009), and others that even the most benign transfer of criminal justice theories and practices developed in one part of the world to another may do more harm than good. This Northern occidentalist mindset (Cain 2000: 257) is at the center of much that is wrong with international prison reform. After three-week participant observation, I came to the conclusion it would have been potentially disastrous if prison staff were not allowed to co-govern Polinter with its prisoners on the assumption inmate and staff-inmate relations are inherently predatory and conflictual in overcrowded, under-resourced prisons. I could not help but be troubled by many of the practices I observed—prisoners handcuffing and strip-searching other prisoners; prisoners being entrusted with weapons; officers turning a blind eye to minor assaults; prisoners deciding who was allowed to talk with officers; prisoners being required to share food brought in by their families with their less fortunate cellmates—but I knew I had to set aside my cultural sensibilities and academic training to evaluate these practices objectively.

Equally concerning is the opposing tendency—emerging from an orientalist mindset (ibid)—for criminal justice policies to be tainted by underlying assumptions that certain aspects of Southern cultures and everyday realities are quite different to those in the occidental North. In Brazil, perceived differences map on to a long colonial and postcolonial history of social and political divisions and take on radical class, gender, and racial identities. We will see some of the discourses employed by advocates of penal reform in Brazil inadvertently shift attention beyond the toxic nature of poor prison conditions toward popularized notions of the dangerous, irrecoverable prisoner. If my work is to inform prisons policy in Brazil, and as a research activist my ultimate goal is indeed to make a positive difference, however small, to the lives of those caught up in prison, it is paramount I remain committed to exploring the local conditions under which international penal and human rights norms might be implemented.

Mutual Aid

Counter-intuitively perhaps, Brazilian inmates do not leave prison any more harmed socially and psychologically than prisoners in the United States or England and Wales. Prison guards likewise appear to suffer no more than their Northern American or Western European counterparts. Where it is able to take root, it appears inmate conviviality provides support networks and a sense of togetherness that shield the average prison inmate from some of the most debilitating pains of imprisonment and institutional processes of mortification. The chances of a Brazilian prisoner dying or being maimed by accidents or preventable illnesses or disease are relatively high. Overcrowding also has negative psychological as well as physical effects. On the other hand, fewer experience the pains of isolation, and fewer live in fear of being humiliated or bullied by disciplinarian or sadistic prison guards. As previously stated, most enter a climate of violence that is little if any more intense than they experience outside. Finally, their families will have suffered, and they will face the stigma of having been imprisoned, but most former prisoners will soon find work, at least in the informal economy (see Madeira 2008). A survey of prisoners in São Paulo in the 1980s found only one in a hundred had never worked (see Goifman 2002). Nor does prison have quite the same impact on people's social stability as it does in many Northern countries. Seventeen in 20 male prisoners maintain regular contact with their families throughout their sentence (Câmara dos Deputados 2008).

None of this means people exactly flourish in Brazilian prisons. It is simply to state that the more prison authorities fail in their responsibilities toward prisoners, the more they are replaced by alternative, informal systems of governance. As anyone else, most prisoners need systems of collective responsibility to help them cope with the uncertainties of their social/institutional selves, and to enable them to make better use of their time. It also means going to prison in Brazil may not interrupt the processes by which most young people eventually leave crime behind to the extent it does in the North. I will explain what I mean by this in a little more detail in a moment. First I present one more narrative of prison co-governance, this time taken from my field notes regarding an incident I witnessed in 2012, at a faith-based, voluntary sector prison:

When I arrived back at the semi-open unit of Franz de Castro prison, after a day out visiting another prison in the area, a scuffle broke out in the workshop. A prisoner from the Conselho de Sinceridade e Solidariedade (Sincerity and Solidarity Council: the CSS) had just approached another prisoner to escort him back to the cell block after work as punishment for refusing to stand up during morning prayers earlier that day. Both had to be physically restrained by other prisoners. Once CSS members had taken the two culprits to their cells, the president of the council immediately called for a disciplinary hearing, where it was informally agreed that the second prisoner, who had picked up a metal instrument, was mostly to blame. When the president told others on the council the director's initial reaction to the incident had been to suggest both inmates return to the closed unit, they complained the director was also partly to blame, having only that morning overridden a decision they had made following the first incident not to allow the second prisoner to lose both an evening's association and a day of work. While the CSS was solely responsible for dealing with breaches of low-level offences, the director had been right to insist prison rules did not allow for the offender to lose his right to work. Nonetheless, some members of the council insisted it was still a decision that was theirs to make, and the director had not understood that the culprit, a known troublemaker from since their school days, was bound to use the fact he had worked all day as an excuse for argument. Since arriving at the prison two weeks earlier, I had already formed the opinion the director exercised limited authority at the prison, and that this was partly due to him being the first director in the prison's by then 17-year history not to have previously served time there himself. The last two directors had both risen through the CSS ranks at Franz de Castro to become directors of the prison on release. In a clear show of defiance, when it came to recording their testimonies, each witness, including several council members, downplayed the entire incident, now "officially" telling the president they had not seen any weapons being raised at all. Still, at the end of the meeting the president explained to the director that the council would be recommending the second prisoner return to the closed unit, but that the first prisoner receive no more than a few days' loss of association. When the prison's disciplinary committee received the CSS's formal report on the incident, it agreed to their suggestion.

To enforce the first prisoner's punishment (I shall call him Robson), the CSS temporarily moved the tuck shop he ran in the evenings into the cell block. In the immediate days after he had completed his punishment, Robson was given the responsibility to sleep on a sofa in a corridor of the administrative block to care to the needs of Mário Ottoboni, the elderly founder of the APAC (Associação de Proteção e Assistência ao Condenado: Association for the Protection and Assistance of the Convict) movement, who was staying for a few days during the movement's 40th anniversary celebrations. I was also staying in the administrative block, and was quite annoyed at having lost the sofa, which I had been sleeping on for two weeks due to sharing a room with another guest who snored profusely (I also found it difficult to take my mind off the fact the room had in the recent past been used for intimate visits). One late evening Robson told me he was ashamed of himself for rising to the provocation, and that he still had much to learn before he was released. Over breakfast one morning, Mário told me the story of one of the first APAC prisoners, a particularly troublesome young man who eventually went on to help develop the APAC methodology. Mário claimed to have finally turned him around following a similar violent incidence by giving him money and sending him to the shops to buy some prison supplies. Sometime after I finished my research at Franz de Castro, Robson became president of the CSS on the prison's semi-open unit. Like many CSS presidents before him, after he is released he may return to the prison to work as a volunteer or paid guard. From the number of times he has appeared in news items on the Fraternidade Brasileira de Assistência aos Condenados (Brazilian Fraternity for the Assistance of Convicts: FBAC)'s website and

Facebook page, I expect he has already been identified as a potential APAC prison director.

The title APAC is associated with a Catholic Cursillo group that in the early 1970s opened Brazil's first voluntary sector prison wing at Humaitá, São José dos Campos, São Paulo, before taking full control of the prison in 1984. In 1985, the group established a second non-profit legal entity to inaugurate a new APAC prison, Franz de Castro, in Itaúna, Minas Gerais, and a regulatory body, FBAC, to oversee the two. Only a handful of APAC prisons opened over the next 20 years. However, the movement advanced considerably from the mid-2000s, principally in Minas Gerais. In 2006, state legislation came into effect that authorized prison authorities to enter into formal agreements to fund the building and maintenance of APAC prisons irrespective of the fact they operated without state employees, including police or prison officers. In the past decade, the APAC movement has spread to other parts of Brazil, for instance Maranhão (which opened its first APAC prison in 2008), and Paraná (which opened its first APAC prison in 2013). One hundred forty-seven voluntary sector organizations had registered with FBAC by the time I visited Franz de Castro for the first time in 2012, although the majority had not yet secured permission or funding to start building. Forty-one APAC prisons were in operation by the end of 2013, 35 of which in Minas Gerais. My introduction to this alternative prison system came in 2010 when I visited APAC de Nova Lima and encountered a prisoner working at the front gate. In 2012, I visited a further six APAC prisons, including Franz de Castro, where I stayed for the next three weeks. FBAC no longer regulates Humaitá (since renamed São José dos Campos) or other prisons in São Paulo. A further 21 voluntary sector prisons were eventually opened in São Paulo following the introduction of government funding in 1996, many by groups that were likewise originally constituted under the title APAC. However, in contrast to the situation in Minas Gerais, these CR (Centro de Ressocialização: Resocialization Centre) prisons were administered in partnership with state authorities. While voluntary sector non-governmental organizations managed the inside of the prisons, state penitentiary guards retained control over the outer walls. After a major rebellion across São Paulo's prison system in 2006, guards were stationed inside CR prisons as well. Many CR prisons managed to retain their ethos of rehabilitation and regimes of full-time, purposeful activity (Macaulay 2014). Still, many voluntary sector services were replaced with private sector provision.

APAC prisons operate strict but active regimes. They boast a reconviction rate of less than 10 percent (Ferreira 2016). However, it was not the religious or disciplinary elements of APAC regimes that originally drew me to study Franz de Castro, nor their broader focus on humanity and therapy, but the fact they are deliberately designed to operate with minimal interference from state authorities and prisoners deliberately put into positions of authority. APAC prisons are administered according to a methodology that takes state abandonment of prisoners and the failure of the prison system as its starting point (ibid). The APAC vision, FBAC explains in its rules and regulations (Fraternidade Brasileira de Assistência aos Condenados 2014), is of community and peer-facilitated reintegration rather than state-led exclusion. At the entrance to every APAC prison is written the message, *aqui entra o homem, o delito fica lá fora* (here enters the man, his offence stays outside). Under the headings of *aprendendo a viver em comunidade* (learning to live communally) and *aprendendo a servir* (learning to serve), inmates are required to be centrally involved in all aspects of prison community life, including religious services, group therapy, cleaning and (for women prisoners) cooking, representing their cellmates, participating in family days and local events, assisting guards, of which there is usually just one on duty, and through their participation in inmate councils, whose membership rotates every six months, adjudicating on breaches of APAC prison rules and implementing punishments. APAC prisoners also develop their own "house rules", much in the same way as (to use FBAC terminology) any responsible person living with others would do on the outside. One house rule I had explained to me by inmates at a women's APAC prison was not to leave your wet towel on your bed. Failure to do so could mean a day's loss of association, which in the APAC vision of rehabilitation is the equivalent of a child being grounded or sent to bed early.

As such, APAC prisons are relevant to my study of co-governed prison order for the extent they depart from certain aspects of the common Brazilian prison system (its abandoning of prisons and prisoners), but comply with others (its reliance on prisons and prisoners self-governing and collaborating with staff). In the words of Ottoboni (2006: 30), what the APAC methodology rejects is the view prisoners are "beyond recovery, social rubbish". What it embraces, though for very different reasons (rehabilitation rather than order), is the need to maintain prisoners' connections to their community, and for prisoners, as people who have lost sight of what it means to be part of the community, to learn to be responsible (to lead and care for) one another. APAC prisons are therefore co-governed in three ways. First and most obviously, like Carandiru, Polinter, and prisons across the country, APAC prisons are co-governed in the sense staff run them in partnership with inmates, and with the local community. Here the APAC methodology embraces the collective nature of Brazilian prison life, and the consequent entanglements between inmates and staff, prisons and communities, and on purpose, not by default. Second, in order for the APAC vision of staff–inmate–community co-governance to work in practice, FBAC rules require all inmates and staff come from within a short distance of the prison. Moreover, FBAC draws little distinction between prison staff and inmates, both of who are ultimately tasked with setting good examples to one another and behaving as mentors and substitute families. A special case is made for inmates' families, whose presence as volunteers is seen as the best means to prepare prisoners for release, and also for former APAC inmates, many of whom, as I noted in the narrative above, are encouraged to stay on at the prison in which they served their sentence. Indeed, most volunteers and FBAC employees, including prison guards and directors, are former APAC prisoners. One prison director and one senior FBAC manager I met in 2012 were still on conditional release.

Finally, APAC prisons are co-governed in the sense prisoners and volunteers jointly administer them in order to promote a version of rehabilitation premised in philosophies of mutual aid and self-help. Similar to the methods utilized by therapeutic community prisons such as HMP Grendon in the United Kingdom, and peer-support groups like Alcoholic Anonymous and Narcotics Anonymous, APAC prisons treat desistance as a personal journey that is best undertaken with fellow recoverers. APAC prisons have clearly been instrumental in helping some people turn their backs on their criminal lifestyles, or perhaps more accurately, not damaging people as much as they might do. But in the refusal of some APAC prison managers not to go beyond FBAC prison rules and take seriously, for instance, issues of trauma, substance abuse, education, and training, they have failed many others. In contrast to wider developments in the peer-support/therapeutic community movements, FBAC's methods are based less on the ideal of mutual aid as mutual control.

Notes

1. 111 is the number officially recorded as having been killed. It is likely that at least twice this number died. Survivors of the massacre claim the official body count was made only after truckloads of corpses had left the prison (Biondi 2010) and did not include over 100 wounded prisoners that later died in hospital (Varella 1999). Milton Marques Viana, for example, claimed that while he was recovering in the hospital wing of the prison a few days after the killings, other hospitalized survivors spoke of more than 150 dead and 400 wounded (Ramos 2001).
2. Carandiru's main blocks each had five floors. The first floors were used for communal activities and included exercise yards. The majority of the *faxina* were housed on the second floor. The remaining *faxina* occupied the first cells after the entrances to the three floors above.

References

Arruda, R. F. (2015). *Geografia do cárcere: Territorialidades na vida cotidiana carcerária no sistena prisional de Pernambuco,* PhD thesis, University of São Paulo. https://teses.usp.br/index.php?option=com_jumi&fileid=12&Itemid=77&lang=pt-br&filtro=Arruda&pagina=4. Last accessed 23 July 2020.

Babenco, H., & Kramer, O. (2003). *Carandiru.* Film, Rio de Janeiro: Globo Filmes.

Babenco, H., Carvalho, W., Gervitz, R., & Faria, M. (2005). *Carandiru: Outros historias.* Television series, Rio de Janeiro: Rede Globo.

Bassani, F. (2016). *Visita íntima: Sexo, crime e negócios nas prisões.* Porto Alegre: Bestiário.

Biondi, K. (2010). *Junto e misturado: Uma etnografia do PCC*. São Paulo: Teirciero Nome. English version: Biondi, K. (2016). *Sharing this walk: An ethnography of prison life and the PCC in Brazil* (trans: Collins, J. F.). Chapel Hill: University of North Carolina.

Biondi, K. (2018). *Proibido roubar na quebrada: Território, hierarquia e lei no PCC*. São Paulo: Terceiro Nome.

Cain, M. (2000). Orientalism, occidentalism and the sociology of crime. *British Journal of Criminology, 40*, 239–260.

Caldeira, T. (2000). *City of walls: Crime, segregation and citizenship in São Paulo*. Berkley: University of California.

Castro, L. A. (1987). *Criminologia de la liberacion*. Maracalbo: Universidad del Zulia. Portuguese version: Castro, L. A. (2005). *Criminologia da libertação* (trans: Moretzsohn, S.). Rio de Janeiro: Revan.

Cohen, S. (1988). *Against criminology*. New Brunswick: Transaction.

Connell, R. (2007). *Southern theory: The global dynamics of knowledge in social sciences*. Cambridge: Polity.

Darke, S. (2013). Inmate governance in Brazilian prisons. *Howard Journal of Criminal Justice, 52*(3), 272–284.

Darke, S. (2014). Managing without guards in a Brazilian police lockup. *Focaal, 68*, 55–67.

Darke, S., & Garces, C. (2017). Surviving in the new mass carceral zone. *Prison Service Journal, 229*, 2–9.

Dias, C. N. (2013). *PCC: Hegemonia nas prisões e monopólio da violência*. São Paulo: Saraiva.

dos Deputados, Câmara. (2008). No title, resource document. http://www1.folha.uol.com.br/folha/cotidiano/20060708-marcos_camacho.pdf. Last accessed 23 July 2020.

Feltran, G. (2020). *Irmãos: Uma história do PCC*. São Paulo: Companhia das Letras.

Ferreira, V. A. (2016). *Juntando cacos, resgatando vidas: Valorização humana – base do método APAC e a viagem ao mundo interior do prisioneiro – psicologia do preso*. Belo Horizonte: Gráfica o Lutador.

Fraternidade Brasileira de Assistência aos Condenados. (2014). Regulamento Disciplinar APAC, resource document. http://www.criminal.mppr.mp.br/arquivos/File/ExecucaoPenal/Mateiral_de_Apoio/APAC/Regulamento_Disciplinar_APACs.pdf. Last accessed 23 July 2020.

Goifman, K. (2002). Killing time in the Brazilian slammer. *Ethnography, 3*(4), 435–441.

Human Rights Watch. (2015). *The state let evil take over: The prison crisis in the Brazilian state of Pernambuco*. New York: Human Rights Watch.

Jefferson, A. M., & Jensen, S. (Eds.). (2009). *State violence and human rights: State officials in the south*. Abingdon: Routledge-Cavendish.

Justiça Global. (2001). *Massacre at Carandiru*, resource document. http://www.observatoriodeseguranca.org/files/Carandiru%20Prison%20Massacre.PDF. Last accessed 23 July 2020.

Karam, M. L., & Saraiva, H. R. (2017). *Ouvindo as vozes de carcereiros brasileiros*, unpublished. English version: *Hearing the voices of Brazilian correction officers* (trans. Karam, M. L.) *Prison Service Journal, 229*: 48–50.

Macaulay, F. (2014). Whose prisoners are these anyway? Church, state and society partnerships and co-production of offender resocialization. In V. Miller & J. Campbell (Eds.), *Transnational penal cultures: New perspectives on discipline, punishment and desistance* (pp. 202–216). London: Routledge.

Madeira, L. M. (2008). *Trajetórias de homens infames: Políticas públicas penais e programas de apoio a egressos do sistema penitenciário no brasil*. PhD thesis, Federal University of Rio Grande do Sul, http://www.lume.ufrgs.br/handle/10183/15656. Last accessed 23 July 2020.

Madeiro, C. (2017, January 22). *Em Alcaçuz, presos controlam chave de pavilhões e até entrada de comida*. https://noticias.uol.com.br/cotidiano/ultimas-noticias/2017/01/22/em-alcacuz-presos-controlam-chave-de-pavilhoes-e-ate-entrada-de-comida.htm. Last accessed 23 July 2020.

Marques, A. (2010). "Liderança", "proceder" e "igualdade": Uma etnografia das relações políticas no Primeiro Comando da Capital. *Etnográfica, 14*(2), 311–335.

Marques, A. (2014). *Crime e proceder: Um experimento antropológico*. São Paulo: Alameda.

Mendes, L. A. (2005). *Às cegas*. São Paulo: Companhia das Letras.

Mendes, L. A. (2009). *Memórias de um sobrevivente*. São Paulo: Companhia de Bolso.

Mendes, L. A. (2012). *Cela forte*. São Paulo: Global.

Mendes, L. A. (2015). *Confissões de um homen livre*. São Paulo: Companhia das Letras.

Olmo, R. (1981). *America latina y su criminología*. Delegación Coyoacán: Siglo Ventiuno.

Ottoboni, M. (2006). *Vamos matar o criminoso? Método APAC*. São Paulo: Paulinas.

Ramos, H. (2003). *Pavilhão 9: Paixão e morte no Carandiru* (4th ed.). Paris: Gallimard.

Rap, A., & Zeni, B. (2002). *Sobrevivente André du Rap (do Massacre do Carandiru)*. São Paulo: Labortexto.

Said, E. (1978). *Orientalism*. New York: Pantheon.

Salla, F. (2017). Vigiar e punir e os estudos prisionais no Brasil. *DILEMAS*, special edition no.2: 29–43.

Santos, B. S. (Ed.). (2007). *Another knowledge is possible: Beyond northern epistemologies*. London: Verso.

Sozzo, M. (Ed.). (2017). *Pós-neoliberalismo e penalidade na américa do sul*. São Paulo: Fundação Perseu Abramo.

Steinberg, G., & Sacramento, P. (2004). *O prisioneiro da grade de ferro, documentary film*. Brazil: California Filmes.

Varella, D. (1999). *Estação Carandiru*, São Paulo: Companhia das Letras. English version: Varella, D. (2012). *Lockdown: Inside Brazil's most violent prison* (trans: Entrekin, A.). London: Simon and Schuster.

Varella, D. (2012). *Carcereiros*. São Paulo: Companhia das Letras.

Wolfmann, L. C. (2000). *Portal do inferno: Mas há esperança*. São Paulo: WVC.

4

The Extrajudicial Punishment of Rapists Imprisoned in Brazil

Kristen Drybread

Suspected rapists detained in Brazil are judged twice: once by the nation's criminal justice system and once by their fellow inmates. Whereas justice within the formal legal system tends to move slowly for alleged offenders of all sorts, prison-house punishments are summarily meted out on accused sex offenders. As soon as inmates get word that one of their ranks has been charged with sexual assault, they rush to apply *a lei do talião (lex talionis*), a form of punishment in which the offender is made to suffer an injury comparable to that which he perpetrated.[1] Rare is the accused sex offender in Brazil who can survive long behind bars without having his body brutally violated.

The extrajudicial punishments Brazilian inmates impose upon accused sex offenders evince the profound lack of faith that these men have in the nation's criminal justice system—a system that, from its inception in the colonial period, has been dedicated to forcefully preserving the interests of the rich and the powerful at the expense of the security and the safety of the poor (Arias and Rodrigues 2006; Caldeira and Holston 1999; Kant

K. Drybread (✉)
University of Colorado, Boulder, CO, USA

S. Darke et al. (eds.), *Carceral Communities in Latin America*, Palgrave Studies in Prisons and Penology, https://doi.org/10.1007/978-3-030-61499-7_4

de Lima 2004; Larkins 2015). By physically violating the bodies of accused sex offenders, avenging inmates guarantee that these men suffer for crimes that the formal justice system rarely prosecutes effectively.[2] What is more, the traces their imposed punishments leave on the bodies of the accused rapist increase the likelihood that he will be found guilty when he stands trial in a court of law.

When the alleged sex offender turns out to be innocent, the injustice of the prison imposed *lex talionis* is patent. But even when inmates castigate men who are truly guilty of sexually violating their victims, the extrajudicial punishments they impose on accused and convicted sex offenders do not further the cause of justice. In fact, the retributive punishments that inmates impose on sex offenders contribute to shoring up the profound injustices of Brazil's legal system. Not only do the prison-house punishments bestowed on alleged rapists deny the accused his right to a fair and impartial trial, the cringe-worthy nature of the punishments draws attention away from the structural and procedural conditions that encourage inmates to castigate those who have been hailed by the law as rapists. When a sex offender is brutalized in detention, judicial authorities and criminal justice workers who knowingly placed him in harm's way can raise their unsoiled hands, point to the blood shed by avenging inmates, and deny responsibility for the violence. Culpability is reserved for prisoners who, in their efforts to uphold the moral codes they arguably share with their captors, prove their inveterate criminality by requiring the rapist to pay for his crime in kind.

Paradigms of Prison Rape

Despite widespread public knowledge and acceptance of the punitive rape of sex offenders in Brazilian penal institutions, scant scholarship has been directed toward the topic. Most academic studies of incarcerated sex offenders have attended to the experiences of men detained in North America or Europe, where sex offenders are often shielded from the predations of other inmates by being secured in facilities, or wards, with high concentrations of sex offenders. To be sure, across national contexts, sex offenders are perceived to be the most abject of criminals (Lancaster

2011; Moffett 2006).[3] Whether they are detained in Toronto, Toledo, or Tocantins, sex offenders are frequent targets of physical and psychological punishments mandated by the unwritten, yet seemingly universal, con code: "a loosely bound set of behavioral prescriptions and cognitive orientations perpetuated among inmates," which endorses the aggressive punishment of those who do not obey the rules (Schwaebe 2005: 619). But when sex offenders in most North American and European countries are mixed within the general prison population, they have the chance to avoid infamy by denying their sex offender status (Hudson 2005; Ievins and Crewe 2015; Schwaebe 2005; Waldram 2012). Few Brazilian sex offenders have such luck; prison administrators and staff members seldom conspire in keeping rape charges secret. In fact, my research suggests that most at least tacitly support inmate-enforced codes of morality and conduct, which demand that those charged with rape suffer ignominy and, preferably, death (Varella 1999: 144).

The handful of scholars who have studied the punitive rape of Brazilian sex offenders have given little attention to the structural and systemic conditions that support the practice. Instead, they argue that convicts perpetrate sexual violence on inmates who have been charged with sex crimes in order to restore honor to themselves and to the women—real and imagined—who were violated by the rapist's crime (Machado 2015; Marques Junior 2007; Silva 1997; Varella 1999). Their analysis departs from the presumption that incarcerated Brazilian men find imprisonment to be a humiliating loss of honor that throws their masculinity in crisis; the act of sexually violating a more abject prisoner provides a way for an inmate to redeem his own honor and virility, while also restoring to the institution of the family the sanctity that the sex offender had violated (Silva 1997: 125). As such, the rape of an imprisoned sex offender is understood to be an act of "compensatory violence" (Hautzinger 2003: 97; Penglase 2009) perpetrated by one or more relatively powerless inmates seeking to boost their individual status and to shore up their threatened masculinity.

The principal problem I find with this analysis is that most of the Brazilian inmates I have met consider incarceration to have affirmed—rather than to have diminished—their manhood (Drybread 2014). Another problem with this analytical position is that it tends to be based on hypothetical cases imagined by the researcher, rather than on the documented experiences of real-life prisoners (Machado 2015). But what is perhaps most troubling about this analytical approach is its unquestioning reliance upon gender stereotypes that naturalize women as sexual objects and men as active agents of honor and power. In this respect, studies of punitive prison rape in Brazil do little more than repeat the conclusions of academics who have studied prison rape in other contexts.

Scholarly studies of prison rape in the United States and in Europe commonly treat sexual assaults against sex offenders as just one of the many manifestations of "the subculture of sexual violence that permeates prison life" (O'Donnell 2004: 2011). In this view, every act of rape that occurs inside a prison is the aggressor's attempt to shore up his own "hegemonic" masculinity by sexually subordinating, humiliating, and "feminizing" his victim (Giller 2003; Haney 2011; Jewkes 2005; Kupers 2001; Messerschmidt 2001; Michalski 2015).[4] This conclusion suggests that (at least in prison contexts) the maintenance of manhood requires the physical domination of a feminized other.

While the concept of hegemonic masculinity (Connell and Connell 2005; Messerschmidt 1993) has made crucial contributions to complicating the study of gender, the notion arguably reinforces what Bourdieu calls "the doxic experience of masculine domination"(1996: 195). By insisting that subordinated men have necessarily been feminized, studies that reaffirm the explanatory power of hegemonic masculinity keep us trapped in "this infernal circle wherein we unconsciously take as instruments of analysis of masculine domination the unconscious (masculine) categories produced by domination" (Bourdieu 1996: 192). But studying hierarchal and social relationships that shape men's perceptions of gender, and their perceptions of their place in the world, need not entail the feminization of those men who occupy the lowest rungs of the status ladder. The danger of understanding prison rape as an expression of hegemonic masculinity is that this perspective reinforces gender binaries that naturalize the violent domination of women. The argument also shores up notions of the feminine as little more than the exploitable object of male desire. What is more, analyses that consider rape exclusively from the viewpoint of hegemonic masculinity lend credence to the notion that, despite the structural conditions that make violence one of the few forms of agency available to the incarcerated, prisons are violent spaces primarily because inmates are inherently prone to excessive, and self-serving, violence.

Administering Violence in Prison

Recent scholarship on relationships between power, security, and incarceration in contemporary Brazil has begun to challenge some of our taken-for-granted assumptions about prison violence in general, and about prison rape in particular.[5] Specifically, histories of the effective transfer of prison administration and security from state governments to organized criminal networks like the *Primeiro Comando da Capital* (First Command of the Capital, or PCC) and the *Comando Vermelho* (Red Command, or CV) have shown that male prisons need not be sites where individuals violently compete with one another to be recognized as the Alpha male.

In the twilight years of the twentieth century, criminal factions like the PCC and the CV began to consolidate power and to establish a monopoly on violence within state prisons in São Paulo and Rio de Janeiro. The case of the PCC in São Paulo most effectively demonstrates that as inmate organizations bestowing social assistance, demanding solidarity, and enacting their own forms of justice began to organize into an effective administrative body, the constant insecurity and fear associated with the imperative to maintain manhood through violent performances of "hegemonic" masculinity began to abate for most inmates in PCC-controlled penal facilities (Caldeira 2004; Dias 2009; Jozino 2004; Salla 2006). Although the PCC still expresses its authority through purposeful—and spectacular—acts of bloody and brutal violence, the consolidation of power in the hands of a few respected leaders has made such violence predictable; a strapping inmate can no longer violate weaker cell mates at will (e.g. Dias 2009).

Prisons in far-flung corners of the nation, like the small northeastern state where I've been conducting research since 1999, have not (yet) been dominated by criminal organizations from wealthy southern states. Here, crime remains highly unorganized. In local favelas, young men and boys terrorize their neighbors, kill one another, and alternately pledge allegiance to the CV, the PCC, and to other criminal factions from the south, hoping to gain the financial and symbolic capital that seems to magically accrue to those who claim to be affiliated with a small collection of recognizable initials. In prison cells and corridors, and in private interviews with individual inmates, I've frequently heard the powerful and the power hungry invoke the letters representing one or more of the large Rio or São Paulo-based criminal networks when insisting that their fellow prisoners adhere to procedures of administration or codes of conduct that are commonly known to have been sanctioned by the PCC and the CV.[6]

One of the policies I've frequently heard lauded is the PCC's use of tribunals to adjudicate conflicts between prisoners.[7] The procedure allows all parties in a dispute to level accusations, to explain suspect behavior, to present incriminating or exculpatory evidence, and to otherwise bolster their case. The parties are then bound to the verdict decided upon by the collective (Dias 2009: 88). Physical dominance is no longer the ultimate arbitrator of right and wrong, and sexual domination is no longer an acceptable way for one or more prisoners to exercise power over another. In fact, the PCC has explicitly banned sexual assault inside Brazilian prisons.[8] The only exception seems to be in cases when an act of sexual violence is considered punitive, and is imposed upon an inmate who has been identified by the legal system as a rapist (Dias 2013).

Official Ignorance

That members of the PCC and similar criminal factions have cast themselves as protectors of the nation's women does not mean that men in these organizations promote—or even condone—sexual equality or sexual liberation for women (Penglase 2009: 51). Nor does it suggest that any of these men are necessarily innocent of perpetrating sexual violence or coercion. In fact, one could argue that the shared imperative to punish sex offenders does not indicate respect for taboos against sexual violence; it merely indicates the revulsion that members of Brazil's organized criminal factions have for men who've been caught by legal authorities while violating those taboos.

Criminal justice workers seem to share this revulsion, as I learned when I met Henrique, an 18-year-old high school graduate who had been placed in pretrial detention for his participation in a fatal brawl. Henrique had butterscotch skin and light green eyes. His tightly curled hair was the color of wheat. With his unassuming demeanor and his comparatively lettered speech, he was likely to have curried favor with the middle- and working-class men and women who typically served on juries at the court to which his case had been assigned. However, at the police station where his case had been processed, Henrique was somehow identified as a rapist. Sometime between his arrest and his first court appearance several weeks later, the word *tarado* (sex maniac, or pervert) had been etched onto both of his forearms. Each letter was roughly 4 centimeters square and had been slowly burned into Henrique's flesh with the red-hot tip of cigarette after cigarette.

The painful procedure must have taken hours. Yet, not a single officer at the police station where Henrique was first detained admitted to having heard Henrique utter the slightest protest during his stay in their facility; they claim that the branding must have happened either during or after Henrique's transfer to the local jail. The drive from the police station to the jail normally takes about 20 minutes, but transportation logs show that on the day Henrique was moved, the trip took more than an hour—because of traffic. Two officers on the transportation squad vaguely remembered that Henrique was wounded before they picked him up at the police station; the other two recalled that they had delivered him to the jail unscathed. Officers at the police station swear that they turned Henrique over to the transportation squad with nary a scratch on his head. Meanwhile, jail personnel insist that Henrique had been brutalized before they took him into custody. The only thing these officials seemed to agree upon was that no one in uniform had done Henrique any physical harm. "You know how these guys are," an officer on the transportation crew told me, nodding toward the handcuffed inmates who were piling back into his wagon after a day in court. "They don't support rape. There's nothing we can do to impede their [form of] justice. *O papel* (the role) of a police officer is limited."

Promoting "Justice"

Formally speaking, police officers are charged with capturing and investigating suspected criminals, while members of the judiciary are responsible for prosecuting, defending, judging, and sentencing these suspects. The executive branch of government is tasked with "correcting" convicted criminals (Adorno 1994: 108). In practice, however, police officers and prison security guards play an outsized role in deciding who is and who is not judged a rapist within the nation's prisons and jails. Two police officers who spoke to me separately, after I had assured each that I would in no way reveal his identity, admitted that when officers decide to hold someone on a rape charge that seems credible, they make little effort to keep secret the accusation of sexual assault. One of these officers said, "Few are sent up [to prison] for rape. I don't know why. I don't know what happens with the judge. But in my opinion, I don't think it's wrong that when there's enough proof to hold a guy here for sexual assault, he gets a little justice."

Police officers and prison security agents alike admitted to turning a blind eye toward the punishment of accused sex offenders in police holding cells and in jails. A few security guards even hinted that they facilitated the extrajudicial punishment of accused rapists by spreading word of the accusation prior to the suspect's arrival in jail (Marques Junior 2007: 102). Likewise, security agents in local prisons admitted to becoming sidetracked while transporting convicted sex offenders from one seemingly secure location to another inside the prisons where they worked.

All of the punishments imposed on imprisoned sex offenders leave emotional scars on the victims; many leave physical scars as well (Machado 2015; Pimentel and Schritzmeyer 1998; Sliva 1997). In court—if the victims of punitive prison rape survive to see their day in court—these burn marks, lacerations, and bruises serve as evidence of their bearer's guilt. In allowing prisoners to punish accused sex offenders, police officers and security guards help to guarantee their conviction. This is precisely why some of the security professionals I spoke to help to facilitate the extrajudicial punishment of imprisoned sex offenders.

"Doesn't that put you in the position of a judge?" I asked a security officer at the city jail when he boasted to me of his participation in this practice.

"I'm a man, not a judge," he responded. "I have a mother, three sisters, and I might even have a daughter one day. It's my responsibility to protect them. The laws in Brazil are weak. We should have the death penalty like you do in your country [the U.S.]. There, there is justice. Here, it's all broken. It's those guys in there that keep our women safe," he said, nodding to the pair of large, overcrowded holding pens in the center of the jail.

Hostile Judgments

This corrections officer's words give substance to a piece of common knowledge that usually remains unspoken: whether they are suspected rapists held in pretrial detention or convicted sex offenders newly arriving in prison, "rapists are judged again by their fellow prisoners," and they are always found guilty (Machado 2015: 170). Fortunately for select sex offenders in relatively wealthy and politically progressive southern states, some local governments have begun to address the issue of punitive prison rape by constructing facilities dedicated to housing identified rapists. These institutions in no way compare to the therapeutic prisons and residential treatment programs that have been developed to treat convicted sex offenders in places like Canada, the United States, and the United Kingdom. In "first world" programs, prisoners convicted of sexual assault are often physically protected from the dangers they would likely face within the general prison population, while also being provided with rigorous psychological programing intended to reduce their risk of future offending (Ievins and Crewe 2015; Schwaebe 2005; Waldram 2012). The relatively new Brazilian facilities that have been dedicated to housing sex offenders do not provide intensive treatment; they merely isolate "rapists" from inmates who might otherwise try to enforce the con code.

In northeastern states where both the political will and the financial capital necessary to construct facilities earmarked for sex offenders are lacking, prisoners charged with sexual assault either attempt to hide their sex offender status, or they consent to being isolated in "secure" cells where reviled prisoners are allowed to seclude themselves for as long as the good will of prison administrators allows. In one of the prisons I visited regularly in 2014 and 2015, the secure cell that endangered inmates could elect to stay in was an unlit broom closet, roughly two feet wide and three feet deep. Up to eight prisoners at a time called it home. At four-hour intervals, they took turns sleeping in the rear, near the plastic bucket and empty soda bottles that served as a latrine.

As dreadful as the conditions in this secure cell were, some of the judges and public prosecutors I spoke to complained that its existence violated the constitution by providing unequal treatment to the offenders housed within. These legal professionals argued that in a prison system containing roughly two spaces for every three inmates, separating out the 2% or so who have been convicted of sexual assault amounts to privileging them over other prisoners (Marques Junior 2007: 102–104). Other legal professionals I spoke to countered that sex offenders who are placed in the general population inevitably suffer a double penalty: in addition to the sentence of confinement they may receive for sexual assault,[9] they are subject to cruel and unusual punishments, which are also prohibited by the supreme law of the land.

To me, this argument between jurists about the constitutionality of protecting sex offenders from other inmates obscures larger questions about the responsibility of prison administrators and guards to maintain the security of all their wards; it also deflects attention from the culpability that public prosecutors and sentencing judges bear for the violence that befalls inmates who are detained for rape. Brazilian scholars who have studied the attitudes of legal professionals toward accused and convicted rapists repeatedly point out that judges and prosecutors are fully aware of the violence that befalls any prisoner who has been identified as a sex offender. Nevertheless, when making sentencing recommendations and decisions, these legal professionals seldom take into account the extrajudicial punishments that inevitably accompany a rape conviction (Marques Junior 2007: 110, 143). What is more, legal professionals rarely pursue charges against inmates who violate sex offenders while in prison. "It is as if Judicial Authority ignores and/or accepts as 'natural' the fact" that detained sex offenders will suffer rape in prison (Pimentel and Schritzmeyer 1998: 65).

Protective Silence

I observed many instances in which legal professionals expressed tacit acceptance of the prison rape of sex offenders, but only one instance in which a judge attempted to protect a defendant who was eventually charged with sexual assault. The case was being heard in a juvenile court where I had been attending trials for several months. Although I had already signed a binding agreement that required me to maintain the confidentiality of all persons who appeared before the court, the first item on the day's docket demanded from me a deeper commitment to confidentiality. The presiding judge met with me before the trial and demanded that I not breathe a word about the case to anyone—ever. "The adolescent's infraction is very grave," he explained. "If I send him to detention, his life will be at risk. No one other than the [institution's] Technical Team [of psychologists and social workers] can know what he's done. Not even the security staff. If the boy's secret is revealed, it could cost his life." The 14-year-old defendant had been accused of forcing a 10-year-old neighbor boy to suck his dick.

Before the defendant entered the courtroom, it was abuzz with censure. Court personnel had read the charge and the age of the accused on the day's docket and assumed the defendant was an ugly and over-large bully who terrorized neighborhood tots. Instead, a slip of a boy came into the courtroom, teary-eyed and clutching the small cloth he would use to wipe his tears while on the stand. He explained that for months he had been on the giving end of the blowjobs two older teenage neighbors demanded of scrawny local boys. On the day in question, the pair seemed to have decided that it would be fun to watch one of their regular victims be serviced by an even littler kid. In my notebook that night, I noted how uncomfortably revealing the trial was, after all of the judge's pre-trial talk of secrecy: "He made the defendant recount in much, much more detail than usual every last thing that happened before, during, and after the [defendant's] 'crime'." I also noted that no effort seemed to have been expended to bring to justice the two older boys who had abused the defendant.

At the end of the hearing, the judge—and everyone else in the courtroom—seemed to be convinced that the boy on trial was more a victim than a perpetrator. Still, the public prosecutor, in defense of public morals (Foucault 1996: 334–5), successfully argued that the kid should be placed in detention for at least four months, given the "depravity inherent in the infraction he'd committed." Before sending the boy to the local juvenile prison, the judge called a special meeting of the institution's administrators and the court bailiffs who would be transporting official documents related to this case between the juvenile prison and his court. "This boy's life depends on your silence," he warned. "Under no circumstances is any one of you to reveal his infraction. If someone outside of this room asks, let's say he participated in an assault. That way, no one will ask for details."

This case was the only one I had heard about in which an inmate's sexual assault conviction was deliberately shielded from both rank-and-file prison staff and the general prison population. Common knowledge has it that all accused and convicted rapists in Brazil's carceral system (police stations, jails, juvenile detention facilities, and male and female prisons) are eventually exposed as such—either by security staff or by visitors who bring in rumors that had been circulating on the outside. The fact that so many professionals conspired to keep this boy safe by keeping his secret suggests that the real secret in most sexual assault cases is that legal professionals, security professionals, and inmates alike condone the practice of punishing apprehended sex offenders with *lex talionis*.

Conclusion (Screwed)

In its performative aspect (Bourdieu 1986), the Brazilian legal system that names particular prisoners as rapists sets these individuals apart as requiring punishments that have been prohibited by Brazilian laws. In other words, legal authorities knowingly facilitate the extrajudicial punishments that custom demands. At the same time, those who officially judge sex offenders bestow upon poor, and mostly Afro-Brazilian, inmates the blame for the "barbarous" and "archaic" extrajudicial punishments that befall imprisoned sex offenders (Rodrigues do Nascimento and Guimarães 2015: 204–5; Marques Junior 2007: 118, 142).[10] Thus, in allowing—and in many instances facilitating—the prison rape of sex offenders, State authorities transfer the responsibility of corrections to the incarcerated, while also reserving the ability to decry the punishments imposed by the con code as not only "uncivilized," but as also reflective of the "animality" and "irrationality" of criminals (Marques Junior 2007: 118, 142). In this respect, the extrajudicial punishments imposed upon imprisoned sex offenders have little, if anything, to do with avenging the women who may have been violated by the rapist, and have even less to do with protecting the honor of the mothers, sisters, and daughters of the inmates who have taken it upon themselves to avenge the imprisoned sex offender's crimes. In the guise of helping avenge women who have been sexually victimized, those who facilitate or perpetrate the punitive rape of accused and convicted sex offenders reinforce "social divisions and power inequalities" among men (Linger 2003: 113). In the process, both the brutalized sex offender and his attackers end up being—to put it crassly—screwed by the official criminal justice system.

Notes

1. Of course, people of all genders can (and do) commit sexual violence and abuse. Prior to 2015, however, the crime of rape was specifically gendered in the Brazilian national law, which stated that the act of rape could only be committed against a woman. And prior to 2009, the crime was characterized by vaginal penetration. Although legal statutes have been amended, this gendered logic still pervades popular understandings of sexual violence, and thus influences the extrajudicial punishment of those who have been accused or convicted of rape. For these reasons, this chapter is limited to a discussion of male inmates.
2. A mere 15% of rapes reported in Brazil each year are likely to be brought to trial, and fewer than one in ten Brazilian men formally accused of rape is ever convicted (Lima and Bueno 2015; Vargas 2007: 767).
3. This does not, of course, mean that all acts of sexual violence are equally recognized as being criminal. The contexts and discourses that mediate

particular acts of sexual domination and coercion determine whether or not these acts become recognizable as crimes (Morris 2006: 58).

4. Two other arguments appear with frequency in the literature. Some suggest that prison rape is common because men locked in a homosocial setting need to find some outlet for their sexual urges (Hensley and Tewksbury 2002). A less troublesome but still controversial position is taken by scholars who argue that in U.S. prisons, where the perpetrators of prison rapes are disproportionately black and victims are disproportionally white, prison rape is not only an expression of hegemonic masculinity, but also a manifestation of "racial hatred of whites by blacks" (Carroll 1977; Knowles 1999: 278; O'Donnell 2004; Scacco 1975). The racial dimension(s) of prison rape in Brazil is an important area for future research, as race influences the practice of criminal justice in similar, yet analytically distinct ways in Brazil and in the United States (Adorno 1996; Fischer 2004; Schwarcz 2008; Telles 2014).
5. Some authors have begun to suggest that the force prisoners use against prison administrators, and against one another, can be considered tactics for making rights claims, or as a means for serving some notion of the collective good (Caldeira 2004; Dias 2009, 2013; Drybread 2014; Salla 2006). A discussion of the important interventions of this scholarship is beyond the scope of this chapter.
6. In 2001, the PCC formalized in a written statute the 16 principles underlying the organization's goals and actions. The statute has circulated widely in newspapers and online.
   http://www1.folha.uol.com.br/fsp/cotidian/ff250524.htm and in English: www.ft.com/cms/s/0/3381ebb8-e5c6-11da-b309-0000779e2340.html#axzz3zuQE1XdB
7. Similar tribunals are said to adjudicate conflicts in PCC- and CV-controlled favelas (Adorno and Salla 2007; Dias 2009; Goldstein 2013; Larkins 2015).
8. In fact, the heteronormative and patriarchal model of masculine citizenship and self-possession that the PCC and CV promote in their policies of prison administration and security seems to increasingly frown upon consensual sex among prisoners (Dias 2013).
9. The standard punishment for sexual assault is 6–10 years in confinement, but adults found guilty of aggravated rape can be subject to more stringent penalties. Perpetrators under the age of 18 are not sentenced

under the Criminal Code, but under the Children's and Adolescent's Statute (ECA); the maximum sentence they can receive is three years in confinement.

10. The most recent census of Brazilian judges found that roughly two thirds of the nation's magistrates are men, and more than 80% of all judges are white (CNJ 2014).

References

Adorno, S. (1994). Violência, Controlo Social e Cidadania: Dilemas na Administração Da Justiça Criminal No Brasil. *Revista Crítica De Ciências Sociais, 41*, 101–127.

Adorno, S. (1996). Racismo, Criminalidade Violenta e Justiça Penal: Réus Brancos e Negros em Perspectiva Comparativa. *Revista Estudos Históricos, 9*(18), 283–300.

Adorno, S., & Salla, F. (2007). Criminalidade Organizada Nas Prisões e Os Ataques Do PCC. *Estudos Avançados, 21*(61), 7–29.

Arias, E. D., & Rodrigues, C. D. (2006). The myth of personal security: Criminal gangs, dispute resolution, and identity in Rio de Janeiro's Favelas. *Latin American Politics & Society, 48*(4), 53–81.

Bourdieu, P. (1986). The force of law: Toward a sociology of the juridical field. *Hastings Law Journal, 38*, 805–854.

Bourdieu, P. (1996). Masculine domination revisited. *Berkeley Journal of Sociology, 41*, 189–203.

Caldeira, C. (2004). A Política do Cárcere Duro: Bangu 1. *São Paulo em Perspectiva, 18*(1), 87–102.

Caldeira, T., & Holston, J. (1999). Democracy and violence in Brazil. *Comparative Studies in Society and History, 41*(04), 691–729.

Carroll, L. (1977). Humanitarian reform and biracial sexual assault in a maximum security prison. *Urban Life, 5*(4), 417–437.

Connell, R. W., & Connell, R. (2005). *Masculinities*. Berkeley: University of California Press.

Conselho Nacional de Justiça (CNJ). (2014). *Censo do Poder Judiciário: VIDE Vetores Iniciais e Dados Estatísticos*. Brasília: Conselho Nacional de Justiça.

Dias, C. C. N. (2009). Ocupando as Brechas do Direito Formal: O PCC como Instância Alternativa de Resolução de Conflitos. *Dilemas, 2*(4), 83–105.

Dias, C. C. N. (2013). *PCC: Hegemonia nas Prisões e Monopólio da Violência*. São Paulo: Saraiva.

Drybread, K. (2014). Murder and the making of man-subjects in a Brazilian juvenile prison. *American Anthropologist, 116*(4), 752–764.

Fischer, B. M. (2004). Quase Pretos de Tao Pobres? Race and social discrimination in Rio de Janeiro's twentieth-century criminal courts. *Latin American Research Review, 39*(1), 31–59.

Foucault, M. (1996). Truth and juridical forms. *Social Identities, 2*(3), 327–342.

Giller, O. (2003). Patriarchy on lockdown: Deliberate indifference and male prison rape. *Cardozo Women's Law Journal, 10*, 659–690.

Goldstein, D. (2013). *Laughter out of place: Race, class, violence, and sexuality in a Rio shantytown*. Berkeley: University of California Press.

Haney, C. (2011). Perversions of prison: On the origins of hypermasculinity and sexual violence in confinement. *the American Criminal Law Review, 48*, 121–142.

Hautzinger, S. (2003). Researching Men's violence personal reflections on ethnographic data. *Men and Masculinities, 6*(1), 93–106.

Hensley, C., & Tewksbury, R. (2002). Inmate-to-inmate prison sexuality: A review of empirical studies. *Trauma, Violence, & Abuse, 3*(3), 226–243.

Hudson, K. (2005). *Offending identities: Sex offenders' perspectives on their treatment and management*. New York: Routledge.

Ievins, A., & Crewe, B. (2015). 'Nobody's better than you, Nobody's worse than you': Moral community among prisoners convicted of sexual offences. *Punishment & Society, 17*(4), 482–501.

Jewkes, Y. (2005). Men behind bars 'doing' masculinity as an adaptation to imprisonment. *Men and Masculinities, 8*(1), 44–63.

Jozino, J. (2004). *Cobras e Lagartos: A Vida Íntima e Perversa nas Prisões Brasileiras: Quem Manda e Quem Obedece no Partido do Crime*. Rio de Janeiro: Editora Objetiva.

Kant de Lima, Roberto. (2004). Direitos Civis e Direitos Humanos: Uma Tradição Judiciária Pré-republicana? *São Paulo em Perspectiva, 18*(1), 49–59.

Knowles, G. J. (1999). Male prison rape: A search for causation and prevention. *The Howard Journal of Criminal Justice, 38*(3), 267–282.

Kupers, T. A. (2001). Rape and the prison code. *Prison Masculinities*, 111–117.

Lancaster, R. (2011). *Sex panic and the punitive state*. Berkeley: University of California Press.

Larkins, E. M. R. (2015). *The spectacular favela: Violence in modern Brazil*. Berkeley: University of California Press.

Linger, D. T. (2003). Wild power in post-military Brazil. In *Crime's power* (pp. 99–124). New York: Palgrave Macmillan.

Lima, Renato Sérgio de, & Bueno, S. (2015). *Anuário Brasileiro de Segurança Pública*. São Paulo: Fórum Brasileiro de Segurança Pública.

Machado, T. L. (2015). Violência no Cárcere: Análise Sobre os Estupros no IAPEN/AP. *PRACS: Revista Eletrônica de Humanidades do Curso de Ciências Sociais da UNIFAP, 7*(2), 155–173.

Marques Junior, Gessé. (2007). *"Quem Entra com Estupro é Estuprado": Avaliações e Representações de Juízes e Promotores Frente à Violência no Cárcere*. Piracicaba: Universidade Metodista de Piracicaba.

Messerschmidt, J. W. (1993). *Masculinities and crime: Critique and reconceptualization of theory*. Lanham: Rowman & Littlefield Publishers.

Messerschmidt, J. W. (2001). Masculinities, crime, and prison. *Prison Masculinities*, 67–72.

Michalski, J. H. (2015). Status hierarchies and hegemonic masculinity: A general theory of prison violence. *British Journal of Criminology*. https://doi.org/10.1093/bjc/azv098.

Moffett, H. (2006). 'These women, they force us to rape them': Rape as narrative of social control in post-apartheid South Africa. *Journal of Southern African Studies, 32*(1), 129–144.

Morris, R. C. (2006). The mute and the unspeakable. *Law and Disorder in the Postcolony*, 57–101.

Rodrigues do Nascimento, Raul Victor, & Guimarães, R. B. (2015). A Violação dos Violadores: Um Estudo Acerca das Causas e Consequências do Estupro Carcerário de Estupradores no Brasil. *Revista Transgressões, 1*(2), 200–223.

O'Donnell, I. (2004). Prison rape in context. *British Journal of Criminology, 44*(2), 241–255.

Penglase, B. (2009). States of insecurity: Everyday emergencies, public secrets, and drug trafficker power in a Brazilian favela. *PoLAR: Political and Legal Anthropology Review, 32*(1), 47–63.

Pimentel, S., & Schritzmeyer, A. L. P. (1998). Estupro: Direitos Humanos, Gênero e Justiça. *Revista USP, 37*, 58–69.

Salla, F. (2006). As Rebeliões nas Prisões: Novos Significados a Partir da Experiência Brasileira. *Sociologias*, Porto Alegre, *16*, 274–307.

Scacco, A. M. (1975). *Rape in prison*. Springfield: Charles C Thomas.

Schwaebe, C. (2005). Learning to pass: Sex offenders' strategies for establishing a viable identity in the prison general population. *International Journal of Offender Therapy and Comparative Criminology, 49*(6), 614–625.

Schwarcz, L. K. M. (2008). Quando a Desigualdade é Diferença: Reflexões Sobre Antropologia Criminal e Mestiçagem na Obra de Nina Rodrigues. *Gazeta Medica da Bahia, 76*(2).

Silva, Eneleo Alcides da. (1997). Violência Sexual na Cadeia: Honra e Masculinidade. *Revista de Ciências Humanas, 15*(21), 123–138.

Telles, E. E. (2014). *Race in another America: The significance of skin color in Brazil.* Princeton: Princeton University Press.

Varella, D. (1999). *Estação Carandiru.* São Paulo: Companhia das Letras.

Vargas, J. D. (2007). Análise Comparada do Fluxo do Sistema de Justiça para o Crime de Estupro. *Dados, 50*(4), 671–697.

Waldram, J. B. (2012). *Hound pound narrative: Sexual offender habilitation and the anthropology of therapeutic intervention.* Berkeley: University of California Press.

5

Two Regimes of Confinement in Tension: Partial Prison Reform in the Dominican Republic

Jennifer Peirce

The United Nations *Standard Minimum Rules for the Treatment of Prisoners*, known as the "Mandela Rules" and adopted in 2015, set out a vision for prisons based on principles of dignity and humane treatment (UNODC 2015). Implicit in the *Mandela Rules* is the idea that prisons should be neither too strict and isolating nor too chaotic and unregulated. Though more impoverished countries in the Global South often see the *Mandela Rules* as appealing but impossibly unrealistic, some have made a substantial, sustained effort to confront inhumane prison conditions and to implement a human rights approach quite concretely. This typically involves changing infrastructure, laws, policies, personnel training, management tactics, transparency, and oversight. But for these changes to be sustainable and meaningful to incarcerated people, less tangible changes—attitudes and social dynamics—also matter.

Perhaps nowhere is this better exemplified than in the Dominican Republic, where, since 2003, the state has founded a new prison model,

J. Peirce (✉)
John Jay College of Criminal Justice (CUNY), New York, NY, USA

S. Darke et al. (eds.), *Carceral Communities in Latin America*, Palgrave Studies in Prisons and Penology, https://doi.org/10.1007/978-3-030-61499-7_5

oriented explicitly toward human rights, dignity, and rehabilitation.[1] Over the following decade and a half, the government built more than 20 new facilities, spacious and well-equipped, called *Centros de Corrección y Rehabilitación* (correction and rehabilitation centers, CCR), which have professional correctional staff and provide extensive education and vocational programs. In prison slang, they are called *azulitos*, which translates roughly to "the lil' blues," for their identical pastel blue-and-yellow-painted esthetic. By policy, CCR facilities cannot be overcrowded, as they refuse to admit more people once they reach their fixed bed capacity limit. To date, the Dominican government has built 22 CCRs, varying from a hundred to over a thousand people. In 2018, the government launched an ambitious "Humanization Plan,"[2] which aims to build enough CCRs, including a vast 12,000 person "complex," to hold the entire prison population.

This new model exists in parallel with the remaining "traditional" prisons, known as "*cárceles públicas*" (public prisons, i.e. the commoners' prison) or "*rulay*" prisons—a term that refers to life on the street, which is a blend of *barrio* music, parties, and fighting for money and survival. The traditional prisons are located in military or police barracks, most of which date from the Trujillo era. Although the new model sets out a bold and different approach, the *azulitos* hold only a third of the country's incarcerated population, which since 2004 has ballooned from 14,000 to over 26,000 (ICPS 2019). The successes of the new model facilities exist in tension with—and arguably depend on—the capacity of the traditional prisons to absorb the most trenchant of penal state problems—surplus bodies (overcrowding), languishing pretrial detention periods, corruption, abject conditions, and a flourishing illicit economy. While the resources of the CCRs can remedy some of these problems, the interactions between the two models and the influence of the larger judicial system mean that these problems persist, sometimes in new ways.

Although the new system claims to be more humane, prisoners express widely different opinions and preferences about whether they are better off living in an *azulito* versus a *rulay* facility. Some prefer the old system's easy (though costly) access to consumer goods and unstructured time during the days, whereas others prefer the new system's provision of free food and beds and extensive menu of programs. This complexity aligns with ethnographic research from other Latin American countries on informal prison dynamics (Darke and Garcés 2017; Garcés et al. 2013). The mixed views among Dominican prisoners challenge assumptions that implementing internationally established human rights standards automatically improves prison life, particularly in the Global South (Coyle 2003; Martin 2017). Furthermore, the Dominican reform experience raises more abstract questions about how prisoners' subjective perceptions of decency and fairness align (or not) with objective measures of "adequate" conditions (Liebling 2004).

This chapter explores prisoners' experiences and opinions of their physical and social conditions in both new and traditional prisons. Dominican prisoners care about the same things as prisoners anywhere: food, a safe place to sleep, communication with loved ones, opportunities to spend their time productively, and a sense of respect and self-determination. In this chapter, I suggest that variations in prisoners' preferences reveal two competing dynamics: equal access to basic needs versus autonomy to resolve these needs individually. The new model, by aligning with international standards, guarantees some basic needs and protections for all, but to do so, it imposes significant new restrictions and pressures on prisoners' daily routines. This poses a challenge for reformers, as some prisoners—and not just those with power—may resist changes that seem unquestionably positive to outsiders. The question of what parameters of freedom prisoners "should" enjoy—balancing principles of normalization, justice, and public safety—is beyond the scope of this chapter. Rather, my aim is to illustrate the diversity and complexities of prisoners' experiences during the implementation of a more progressive model in a low-resource setting.

Genesis of the Dominican New Model

The remarkable prison reform experiment in the Dominican Republic began through a convergence of initiatives and visionary individuals in the late 1990s and early 2000s. First, two broader reforms converged in the country: a major international aid project to modernize public institutions in the country (facilities, civil service laws, transparency) and the shift from an inquisitorial to an adversarial criminal justice system. Second, a few key players decided to take a chance on "remaking" one single prison, with funds from the modernization project. These included a few directors within the old prison system and several senior professors and deans at the public university. One had himself been incarcerated for political reasons in one of the notorious prisons during the 1970s. The Dominican Attorney General at the time—who has institutional responsibility for prisons—was also involved in generating this bold reform vision, and lent significant political will and institutional leverage to the project. With support from the British Ambassador at the time, as well as guidance from former correctional leaders from the UK, they formed a small team to plan and implement the first conversions of prisons from the old to the new model.

The first reform involved renovating a facility beside a military base, moving prisoners to the new facility, removing the military and police staff from their functions, and directly tackling the internal power of prisoners in key leadership roles, by removing their access to drugs, weapons, and control of money and food flows to the other prisoners. The second major step, over the next few years, was the establishment of a brand-new correctional officer training academy, which accepts only people with no police or military experience. Graduated officers are known as "penitentiary treatment officers" (*agentes de vigilancia y tratamiento penitenciario*) and have higher salaries and a clear career advancement path. With this new staff body, the new model project gradually converted the old prisons into new prisons, through both renovations and new facilities. It also built a coordination institution—located under the Directorate of Prisons (traditional model) but with substantial operational autonomy—and was granted a regular budget from the *Procuraduria* (Attorney-General's Office). After the initial international funding expired, the new model facilities have mostly relied on this budget, except for some specific new initiatives. Meanwhile, the traditional prisons have also made some modest improvements—such as new toilets, health services, and literacy classes—but are severely constrained by their location in cramped quarters.

The Dominican reform experience is widely cited as a reference point and best practice in Latin America, particularly in Central America and the Caribbean, where crime is higher and budgets more meager (Carranza 2012; Justice Trends 2017). Costa Rica has also made significant investments in new buildings and more rehabilitation-oriented programs, but its previous system was never as overcrowded or chaotic as in other countries of the sub-region. The Dominican model attracts international visitors and study tours on a regular basis, and it is now being adapted and implemented in Ecuador (Garcés and Navarrete 2017) and Guatemala (Ministerio de Gobernación 2017). Although there are local studies on changes in specific CCR facilities (Javier Cordero 2015; Paniagua Guerrero 2015), there is surprisingly little research about the system-level change, particularly including a comparison between old and new models. Given the prominence of the Dominican reform project, it is important to explore in more detail its assumptions, limits, and experiences of real-life implementation, with particular regard to prisoners' perspectives.

This chapter describes, in broad terms, the material and social conditions in the two Dominican prison systems, highlighting contrasts between them and with broader international standards for prisons. This depiction is based on research I conducted in old and new Dominican prisons during 2016–2019. This included over 30 visits to about 25 different facilities, during which I spent one to three days in each facility. During these visits, together with a small team of local students, we spent significant unstructured time observing daily activities and conversing with prisoners and staff. We also administered a survey about conditions and perceptions of the social climate[3] and conducted semi-structured interviews and focus groups with prisoners, staff, and key stakeholders in the reform process. This chapter is based primarily on field notes from the prison visits and on the qualitative data from the survey and interviews.

Conceptualizing Human Rights in Practice in Latin American Prisons

Given the dramatic differences in prison realities across regions, scholars have called for new approaches and concepts for comprehending prison dynamics in the Global South (Darke and Garcés 2017; Drake and Earle

2013) and in comparative perspective globally (Skarbek 2020). Some argue that simply detailing severe rights violations—violence, corruption, lack of legal aid—in the vocabulary of international standards is insufficient; in order to facilitate real change, research must seek to understand prison dynamics and logics from the inside of these settings, including the point of view of prisoners and staff (Jefferson 2007). This is relevant to the Dominican case, because we know that institutions do not change in any fundamental way simply because political and institutional leaders suddenly wish to be compliant with international human rights standards (Sabet 2012). A change imposed on a given criminal justice institution with the aim of achieving a particular human rights principle may generate unpredictable synergies and/or tensions with existing practices and interests (Armstrong 2018; Hannah-Moffat 2010).

My aim is not to endorse particular Dominican reforms as positive or justified per se. Rather, this exploration seeks to show the complexities and contradictions of implementing human rights-oriented changes in Dominican prisons "in real time" and in a gradual transition process where previous practices co-exist with new ones. To do so, I draw on Birkbeck's categories of "regimes of confinement" (2011), which provides a useful framework for comparing different types and facets of prison. The categories are: regimentation, surveillance, isolation, social arrangements, formalization, and accountability. Birkbeck suggests identifying the resources, arrangements, policies, and practices that combine to achieve the basic *functions* of confinement, regardless of whether these are official or illicit. These are deliberately descriptive, not normative, categories; this allows comparisons of settings that may be materially very different.

The call for deeper understanding of how prisons work in non-Western settings does not preclude normative assessments, of course. Other analytical approaches explicitly foreground the normative or moral experience of particular reforms or practices. Liebling's (2004) concept of the *moral performance* of prisons hinges on the idea that simply measuring objective square footage and number of meals per day—which is what a UN Rules report might do—tells us very little about whether incarcerated people are experiencing dignity or decency. Research shows too that prison institutions sometimes adopt or coopt human rights language, while pursuing harsh practices (Armstrong 2018; Martin 2017). Furthermore, any international human rights instrument reflects dominant, often Western, notions of what dignity and fairness mean in practice (Joutsen 2015). My research in Dominican prisons reveals some of this tension: prisoners may experience physical violence and not necessarily consider this a rights or fairness violation.

The following section describes several aspects of differences and similarities between the models, following Birkbeck's categories in terms of how a given arrangement functions. This modest window into Dominican prisons "in transition" suggests that, while the new model clearly resolves some of the most serious material problems of the old model, it also creates an emergent set of power relations or restrictions that may or may not generate the sought-after rehabilitation outcomes for different prisoners.

Dimension 1: Regimentation

Regimentation refers to the how a facility organizes prisoners' access to spaces for sleeping and other activities. International standards prescribe separation of inmates by sex, age, remand vs. sentenced, and risk level, among other factors, and advocate for single-cell housing where possible. In the Dominican Republic, though, spatial distribution is shaped mostly be crowding and, in some cases, money.

Entering a traditional prison or *rulay* feels like entering a separate and hidden world: at the gate, I face an imposing concrete barrack wall painted in camouflage pattern, with gleaming military insignia and no sign that hundreds of men live confined behind it. At the gate, family members pass bags of clothing, Styrofoam containers of food, documents, and other packages marked for specific prisoners, to an officer who knows many of them by name. A couple hundred feet behind, a chain-link fence or metal gate separates the prisoners' area from the officers' area, where there is also usually a small medical clinic and administrative offices. There is clanging of padlocks and shouting of prisoners trying to ask who the deliveries are for today. It is hard to tell from this vantage point whether the prison holds a hundred or a thousand men.

After the military or police checkpoint, the prisoners mostly determine their own spatial organization, with a few exceptions. At the gate to this area, certain prisoners are designated *llaveros* and carry the keys for padlocks to enter and leave. Each prison has a *jefe de cárcel,* who usually sits at a table with notebooks and keys, tracking movements. In more than one facility, at the gate, the police or military officer told me quite directly, referring to the *jefe*, that "beyond this point, you need permission from him, not me – and you can trust him."

Each *rulay* has a common area—"patio"—surrounded by tall cement walls, sometimes with an area reserved as a chapel or classroom. Cellblocks are accessible by doors in the cement wall, leading to a narrow transverse passageway along which wooden "rooms" (*goletas*), built from scrap materials and barely high enough to sit up in, are stacked, with makeshift ladders up the wall. These are padlocked and prized by their owners, as they provide privacy. Because spaces are limited, people pay a fee to reside in a *goleta,* which may be individual or shared by up to four people. Typically, this one-time-only purchase takes place upon entrance, paid to an individual who has been released, and/or to the representative of the cellblock; sometimes there is a weekly rental rate. Prices vary by the level of amenities in a cellblock (notably toilets and water). The status of a cellblock is sometimes obvious by its name—some of the tougher ones are called "Vietnam" and "Kosovo," while the "quieter" ones are called "Alaska" or "*buen comportamiento*" (good behavior).

People who cannot pay for their own space are known as *ranas* (frogs), since they sleep in the passageway or bathroom floors, which are often partially wet. These passageways are mostly dark, even in the middle of the day, filled with smoke from cigarettes and hot-plate cooking, and it is hard to see the makeshift electrical wires twisting out of each *goleta*. Prisoners take pride in showing visitors that even in such conditions, the floors (often cement) are clean and each *goleta* resident has tidy shelves and personalized decorations and photos. A typical cellblock holds about 100–150 people, with about a third in *goletas*, and all share one toilet and one water tap.

Some "privileged" cellblocks are much larger, with fewer people, and entirely separate from the common patio area. Residents enjoy extra resources and connections through organized crime or family wealth. Sometimes these cellblocks are designated for religious inmates: a pastor (usually an older inmate) assigns spaces to the most devout, many of whom convert inside prison. Both types of privileged cellblocks prohibit sex between men, drugs, and swearing. A designated police officer liaises with this area and receives a portion of the weekly "taxes" they collect, in exchange for not interfering in the affairs of the cellblock. This results in a spatial regimentation based mainly on ability to pay plus perceived street reputation or risk to the inmate leaders. However, the prison administration retains control—in consultation with the *jefe*—over transferring prisoners to another facility, which most consider a punishment if it takes them far from family members.

In contrast, the new model has invested most of its resources in impressive infrastructure for the CCRs. Prisoners live in "pavilions" that house between fifty to a hundred people, divided into dormitory rooms ("cells") of six to twelve people each. Each person has a bunk bed and a locker—all identical—and a bathroom/shower area inside the module. One man who was a *rana* in the old model told me: "I couldn't believe that I had the same bed as a wealthy man here." In contrast, a young man who used to share a *goleta* said he appreciates having his own bed, but resents that he is not allowed to install shelves for his clothing or have his own fan or TV by the bed.

The main separation in new model facilities is the area designated "maximum security." This refers to a small group of prisoners who are a risk to or vulnerable in the general population—based on their outside-world positions and their crimes, not on any clinical risk assessment. Typically, this group includes people tied to notorious cases, organized crime leaders, and ex-police or ex-government officials. One staff person said: "These people are not themselves dangerous, but they have their reasons for wanting to live separately." Because they have single-occupancy cells, this "security" classification creates a small set of people who enjoy more space and privacy.

So, the new model facilities clearly meet international standards of basic space and amenities better than the old facilities. But prisoners' comments show that a free, clean bed may not outweigh the more intangible spatial considerations, namely privacy.

Dimension 2: Surveillance

Prisons are always sites of surveillance, technological, and human, but in Latin America, formal surveillance by staff is usually limited to the perimeter. Human rights standards emphasize fair, respectful treatment by staff, as well as respect for privacy, lawfulness, and restraint on searches (UNODC 2015; Coyle 2003). In Dominican prisons, the staff–inmate ratios are much higher in the new model than in the old—where there may be a dozen police officers for hundreds of prisoners—but other prisoners can serve a surveillance function in both. But generally, prisoners' perceptions about surveillance refer mostly to staff's attitudes and use of discretion, not ratios or tactics. This reflects Liebling's emphasis on inter-personal dynamics being central to a sense of decency and respect, regardless of the number of officers.

In the barracks prisons, police or military officers patrol from gates and rooftop posts, usually armed, while a few circulate sporadically in the main area with batons, but no weapons. I saw only one metal detector in an old model facility, and it was broken and out of use. According to prisoners, families pay guards to allow the passage of food, phones, clothes, drugs, weapons, and other goods. In order to show power or to enforce payments, guards may search certain cells and confiscate contraband goods, at random. Several prisoners perceive this as an abuse of the "arrangement"—if they already paid for bringing in an item, it is not fair for the police to search a cell for it. The *jefe* and his delegates typically have permission from the prisoner population to search cells, if there is suspicion of a "real" contraband item. For example, in one facility, a prisoner said that the group rule is that people can keep machetes, but not firearms. This generates intra-group accountability, both in setting and in enforcing the rules.

The new model CCRs employ several basic surveillance tools common in other countries: guards at the main entrance gates, entry checkpoints, search procedures, and guards posted at the entry point for each separate area of the facility. Officers usually searched us and other visitors thoroughly and respectfully. There are few cameras or metal detectors. A relatively new method is the use of canine units, to search visitors, cells, and prisoners. The staff move freely in the facility and can enter the sleeping areas at any time. During our visits, when a VTP discovered contraband drugs, in a cell search or a visitor search, they would describe what they found to our research team, as a point of pride.

Prisoners in the new facilities do not complain about the rules on paper, and they generally laud the lesser presence of drugs and weapons inside, but they complain that rules can be enforced without justification. For example, they told me that some searches of their cells and of their visiting relatives seemed arbitrary and unfounded. One foreign prisoner told me he did not understand a nighttime search order, because he does not speak Spanish, but that the staff punished him for not getting out of bed. The new model staff may comply with human rights standards regarding surveillance—their tactics are in no way excessive, from an objective view—but the details of *how* they interact with a prisoner during a search matter most (echoing Tyler's procedural justice findings in policing (Tyler 2006)).

Dimension 3: Isolation

The third category, isolation, refers broadly to how much contact prisoners have with the outside world—family, friends, organizations—through conjugal and regular visits, phone calls, and correspondence, as well as contact with other inmates. It also includes the use of literal isolation—solitary confinement.

In the old prisons, separate cells to punish rule-breaking are known as *la plancha* (the grill, due to extreme heat)—but they are almost never solitary. In my interviews, many people spoke of physical punishment, even deaths, at the hands of other inmates during a stay in *la plancha*. The *jefe* and his delegates can "judge" an inmate's infraction and put him in the punishment cell for a given period, with little or no staff involvement in the decision. The use of the *plancha* is purely retributive, according to descriptions I heard. Prisoners commented that if a *jefe* uses this discretion excessively, other prisoners will protest and challenge his authority.

The new system also has a similar system, with softer language and more oversight. The punishment cell is called the "*Espacio de Reflexión*" ("reflection space"). A "*Junta de Evaluación y Sanción*" composed of staff members assesses infraction allegations. The discourse justifying the use of this "reflection space" echoes nineteenth century prison reformists in the US: repentance through isolation (Rubin and Reiter 2017). But, prisoners report that people are put in "reflection space" for other behavioral objectives, not just punitive—to detox from a drug addiction, to "encourage" school attendance, and for people who have mental breakdowns or suicide attempts.

Prisoners talk about the reflection space in the new model as being essentially identical to the *plancha* in the old model, except that it has more space, fewer weapons, and regular meals. There are varying views on whether using a *plancha* or *reflexión* cell is morally justifiable, but almost all shared the view that the VTP agents use the *reflexión* space arbitrarily, for even minor rule violations. As one man explained: "They put me in *reflexión* for wearing shorts – but I didn't have the money to buy more pants."

Dimension 4: Social Arrangements

Social arrangements encompass formal staff structures, staff–prisoner interactions and communication mechanisms, and informal inmate-led methods of distributing power and resources within the facility. International standards call for alternative dispute resolution methods, eliminating any inmate-led management of disciplinary procedures, and limiting staff discretion in use of force. However, in facilities where there is very little presence of staff or institutional conflict management mechanisms of any kind, some inmate-led solutions fill this function, similar to forms of co-governance documented elsewhere in Latin America (Antillano 2017; Darke 2018; Weegels 2018).

More than ten years ago, powerful individual prisoners, called *provós,* ruled a given facility by force and fear. In the current traditional model prisons, over the past decade, interventions by the administration and police removed these *provós* and replaced them with new "*representantes.*" This "representative" is an influential prisoner nominated by the formal administration and endorsed by prisoners, and he has "delegates" who assist him in managing day-to-day operations. In collaboration with prison staff, the *representante* and *delegados* use a combination of access to authorities, material resources, and threats and sometimes violence to establish order. In one facility, the prisoners uniformly lauded the *jefe* because he had collected funds from inmates and, in collaboration with the prison administration, bought materials to install new toilets and running water. "He can be violent, but he provided a solution to our most urgent needs, so I support him," one respondent told me.

In the new model facilities, the *jefe* structure does not exist. The VTP officers deliberately take prominent roles in all aspects of daily prison operations. Although this reduces abuse by the *jefe* toward other prisoners, prisoners speak with frustration that they have no "direct line" to decision-makers at the facility for conveying their concerns. The *jefe* filled this function, even if inequitably or harshly, and the new model, by not addressing this, leaves a gap.

Dimension 5 and 6: Accountability and Formalization

Birkbeck's final two categories, accountability and formalization, relate to oversight structures and the nature of policies and procedures. In Latin America, oversight mechanisms, where they exist, tend to be through public media coverage and civil society pressure, rather than through courts, except for occasional cases in the Inter-American Court of Human Rights. The UN Mandela Rules call for formal oversight of key services, such as food and sanitation, which are taken for granted in Northern systems—though not always enforced well—and for clear and prompt investigation into disciplinary incidents and complaints. This is in line with Liebling's (2004) emphasis on transparency and fair application of rules, institutional decision-making processes, and disciplinary procedures.

The rules overseeing the Dominican prison system are mainly in Law 224 (the general prison law) and in an online "prison management manual." The principal formal enforcement mechanism is the role of the sentence oversight judge (*juez de la ejecución de la pena*). This is a powerful function, but in practice its effectiveness relies heavily on the discretion and skills of the individual judge. Administrative data is detailed on prisoner population numbers, but there is scarce documentation on other elements of daily life (activities, access to food and lawyers, or program enrolment). A frequent complaint from prisoners is that court documents, which are paper files, are processed very slowly. One example is release orders: these can take weeks or months to move from a judicial decision to a prison director's desk, so prisoners may be stuck inside after their release date has passed.

Prisoners say that the only real way to get attention in the old model is through having a personal connection to a member of the administration or, in extreme cases, contacting a news reporter and hoping for scandal-generated action. The inmate-led governance system (*jefe* and *delegados*), similarly, has clear rules, consequences, and procedures, but, as an unofficial system, there are limited recourse channels. If abuses of rules become too extreme, prisoners may riot or take hostages, but this carries risks of even harsher rules in the subsequent regime (Thompson 2014). In one set of interviews, prisoners described their group's debates about rioting to protest high fees and *cuotas*—but they feared additional reprisals by police and the *jefe*.

The new model system has much more detailed rules about operational procedures, responsibilities, and recourse channels. It also produces more extensive and systematized data on its population, including the basic information described above, as well as documentation of activity participation, behavioral assessments (i.e. rule infraction incidents), and other health, medical, or legal updates. The majority of this information is in an electronic database, managed by the new model headquarters. However, the assessments of a prisoner's "progress" are not consistent across facilities and are not easily accessible to defense lawyers or other people outside the CCR system. Each facility very clearly posts its "daily data"—a count of how many inmates are in which situation and programs.

The prisoners in CCRs acknowledged that there is a formal channel for submitting grievances and requests, through the representatives of each *pabellón* and through the *Junta de Evaluación*. Most noted that the grievance process relies on the discretion of staff, as there is no outside advocate for the prisoner's point of view; this undermines perceptions of fairness (Calavita and Jenness 2014, note the same point in California prisons). The new model also receives extensive media coverage, mostly positive, and is invested in sustaining its reputation as humane and professional. According to staff themselves, when negative coverage occurs, this does put pressure on the administration to make changes, but only for security concerns (the perceived weak flank of the new model). Complaints about poor conditions in the new prisons get little coverage, perhaps because the public already considers them to be generous.

Conclusion

It is perhaps unsurprising that people who held a degree of power and privilege in the internal economy and social order arrangements of the *rulay* prisons would object to being forced to live according to the state's rules and to submit to new forms of state control, surveillance, and restrictions, while those who suffered in the old system would appreciate a respite from the exploitation. The picture of transition is not quite so tidy, though. The themes in this chapter suggest that some of the problems with the traditional system persist in the new system, despite the changes—as scholars of reform elsewhere have also noted (Garcés and Navarrete 2017; Karstedt 2015; Macaulay 2013).

Both formal and informal dynamics are at play in the basic functions of a regime of confinement in the old and new Dominican prisons. Reviewing these through the lens of Birkbeck's categories, we see that in each dimension of prison life, from the perspective of prisoners, there are two inter-dependent realities: on the one hand, a sometimes harsh and unequal system where strong or entrepreneurial individuals can acquire power and resources, and on the other hand, a system of relatively predictable, equally distributed, but inadequate material conditions, with few channels for recourse or finding unofficial solutions.

On space, when payment for more comfortable cells spaces is eliminated, there is equality but prisoners chafe at the lack of privacy and personalization. On surveillance, when staff have the capacity to control contraband and movements inside the facility (not just perimeters), this curtails the illicit drug economy and its related problems, and the majority of prisoners appreciate this. But if staff use these new powers in an arbitrary or punitive way, the benefit of this stability—from the point of view of prisoners—may not be worth it. On isolation, a similar dynamic is at play. Whether it is the inmate *jefe* or the staff security chief who decides to put a person in a punishment cell, or cut off visits and cellphone access, the prisoners are concerned primarily about whether this consequence is imposed in a fair and impartial way. On social arrangements, the shift away from inmate-led governance in the new model seems to have reduced violence and exploitation among prisoners. However, when prisoners lose their ability to organize and solve problems among themselves, but do not have access to other channels for addressing needs (i.e. through a responsive administration), they may resist and resent this new social arrangement. Finally, on formalization and accountability, more capacity and detail on policies, rules, data, and resources seem to create a system in which basic daily movements and requests flow more smoothly. Still, the lack of a neutral, outside advocate for prisoners when they need to take recourse against staff or administrative decisions leads to an ongoing sense of frustration among prisoners—even those who do not yearn for the "good old days" of inmate chiefs.

The "success" of the Dominican new model prisons is undeniable if measured by material indicators: more water, hygiene, literacy, and fewer weapons and diseases. This is the product of gradual institutionalization of new approaches, and is no small feat. Even though this change covers only part of the system, and even though larger success metrics—notably recidivism—remain unclear, the new model has survived political, public, and prisoner skepticism and shows that top-down changes can take hold. However, the new model does not operate in isolation. On many issues, the leaps forward in the new model are outweighed by worsening conditions in the old model—particularly on the issue of overcrowding.

Because the prison institution overall, even with the most visionary leaders, does not have control over how many people are entering the prisons, and for how long, this central tension endures. The Dominican system faces a difficult question: does it invest in building new, healthier facilities for everyone currently incarcerated, even though this is expensive and implies accepting the fact that over half of prisoners are pretrial detainees? Or does it plan for a more appropriate population projection, insist that the courts cut back on prison sentences and pretrial detention, and risk that if this does not happen, people awaiting trial will continue to live in abject, overcrowded barracks?

Policymakers who support improving prisoner rights and well-being must also try to understand how and why certain changes occur, and why actors inside prisons welcome or resist these changes (Mears 2008). In the Dominican context, this requires an honest assessment of how to apply more state control and transparency on the existing self-governance system without inadvertently causing a backlash due to a perception that people are "worse off" without the *jefe* at the helm. The themes emerging from my study suggest that on nearly every dimension of confinement, prisoners value fair and impartial treatment and having a recourse channel for cases of abuse of authority (by a *jefe* or by staff) at least as much as, and sometimes more than, material changes in conditions. But still, the Dominican Republic, with a halfway-implemented new model and a renewed political will for expanding the reforms, may yet be able to generate a hybrid model that combines the decency of equal and stable conditions from the new prisons with the participation channels and autonomy of the traditional prison dynamics.

Notes

1. The new model is officially named the *Modelo de Gestión Penitenciaria*, literally the Prison Management Model, implying that the traditional prisons do not abide by any type of "management model."
2. As of June 2020, some of the new buildings had opened: https://pgr.gob.do/avanza-plan-de-humanizacion-del-sistema-penitenciario-pgr-incorpora-3-nuevos-centros-completamente-remodelados/. The country

held elections in July 2020, and the opposition party won; thus, next phases of the plan are in the hands of the new administration.
3. This survey is adapted from the *Measuring the Quality of Prison Life* survey instrument (Liebling 2004; Liebling et al. 2012) and included closed-answer and open-answer questions. We received 1240 responses from men in 17 different prisons. A detailed analysis of the survey findings appears in other publications and is outside the scope of this chapter.

References

Antillano, A. (2017). When prisoners make the prison: Self-rule in Venezuelan prisons. *Prison Service Journal, 229*, 26–30.

Armstrong, S. (2018). Securing prison through human rights: Unanticipated implications of rights-based penal governance. *The Howard Journal of Crime and Justice, 57*(3), 401–421.

Birkbeck, C. (2011). Imprisonment and internment: Comparing penal institutions north and south. *Punishment & Society, 13*(3), 307–332.

Calavita, K., & Jenness, V. (2014). *Appealing to justice: Prisoner grievances, rights, and Carceral logic*. Oakland: University of California Press.

Carranza, E. (2012). Situación penitenciaria en América Latina y el Caribe ¿Qué hacer? *Anuario de derechos Humanos, 8*, 31–36.

Coyle, A. (2003). A human rights approach to prison management. *Criminal Behaviour and Mental Health, 13*, 77–80.

Darke, S. (2018). *Conviviality and survival—Co-producing Brazilian prison order*. London: Palgrave Macmillan.

Darke, S., & Garcés, C. (2017). Surviving in the new mass Carceral zone. *Prison Service Journal, 229*, 2–9.

Drake, D. H., & Earle, R. (2013). On the inside: Prison ethnography around the globe: Deborah H Drake and rod Earle introduce the articles in the themed section. *Criminal Justice Matters, 91*(1), 12–13.

Garcés, C., & Navarrete, B. (2017). Promise and contradiction in Ecuador's new prison model. *NACLA Report on the Americas, 49*(3), 347–353.

Garcés, C., Martin, T., & Darke, S. (2013). Informal prison dynamics in Africa and Latin America. *Criminal Justice Matters, 91*(1), 26–27.

Hannah-Moffat, K. (2010). Sacrosanct or flawed: Risk, accountability and gender-responsive penal politics. *Current Issues in Criminal Justice, 22*(2), 193–215.

Institute for Criminal Policy Research. (2019). *World prison population list: Dominican Republic.* Retrieved from: https://prisonstudies.org/country/dominican-republic.

Javier Cordero, S. (2015). Efecto de la sobrepoblación de los centro de corrección y rehabilitación del nuevo modelo de gestión penitenciaria en la aplicación del tratamiento penitenciario, Higuey, 2012. [*The effects of overpopulation in correction and rehabilitation centers of the new model of penitentiary in the application of penitentiary treatment*, Higuey, 2012]. (Unpublished Master's Thesis, Economic and Social Sciences, FCES 005). Universidad Autonoma de Santo Domingo, Santo Domingo.

Jefferson, A. M. (2007). Prison officer training and practice in Nigeria: Contention, contradiction and re-imagining reform strategies. *Punishment & Society, 9*(3), 253–269.

Joutsen, M. (2015). International standards and norms as guidance in the criminal justice system. *Idea* 4. Retrieved from: http://www.unafei.or.jp/english/pdf/RS_No98/No98_VE_Joutsen.pdf

Justice Trends. (2017). Dominican Republic: An example of penitentiary reform to follow. *Justice Trends – Innovative Prison Services*. Retrieved from: http://www.justice-trends.press/interviews–entrevistas.html

Karstedt, S. (2015). Cultural peers and penal policies: A configurational approach toward mapping penal landscapes. *Punishment & Society, 17*(3), 374–396.

Liebling, A. (2004). *Prisons and their moral performance: A study of values, quality, and prison life*. Oxford: OUP.

Liebling, A., Hulley, S., & Crewe, B. (2012). Conceptualising and measuring the quality of prison life. In D. Gadd, S. Karstedt, & S. F. Messner (Eds.), *The SAGE handbook of criminological research methods* (pp. 358–372). SAGE Publishing.

Macaulay, F. (2013). Modes of prison administration, control and governmentality in Latin America: Adoption, adaptation and hybridity. *Conflict, Security & Development, 13*(4), 361–392.

Martin, T. M. (2017). Scrutinizing the embrace of human rights in Ugandan prisons: An ethnographic analysis of the equivocal responses to Human Rights Watch reporting. *Journal of Human Rights Practice, 9*, 247.

Mears, D. P. (2008). Accountability, efficiency, and effectiveness in corrections: Shining a light on the black box of prison systems. *Criminology & Public Policy, 7*(1), 143–152.

Ministerio de Gobernacion de Guatemala. (2017, 5 June). *Una nueva guardia para el sistema penitenciario*. Retrieved from: http://mingob.gob.gt/una-nueva-guardia-para-el-sistema-penitenciario/

Paniagua Guerrero, Y. E. (2015). *Variables de Impacto de Gestion de la Reforma Penitenciaria en la Republica Dominicana y su Influencia en America Latina y el Caribe, 2003–2013*. [Variables of Impact in the Management of the Prison Reform in the Dominican Republic and its Influence in Latin America and the Caribbean, 2003–2013.] [Master's Thesis: Penitentiary Administration]. Universidad Autonoma de Santo Domingo.

Rubin, A. T., & Reiter, K. (2017). Continuity in the face of penal innovation: Revisiting the history of American solitary confinement. *Law & Social Inquiry, 43*(4), 1604. https://doi.org/10.1111/lsi.12330.

Sabet, D. (2012). *Police reform in Mexico: Informal politics and the challenge of institutional change*. Stanford: Stanford University Press.

Skarbek, D. (2020). *The puzzle of prison order: Why life behind bars varies around the world*. New York: Oxford University Press.

Thompson, H. A. (2014). Lessons from Attica: From prisoner rebellion to mass incarceration and Back. *Socialism and Democracy, 28*(3), 153–171.

Tyler, T. R. (2006). *Why people obey the law*. Princeton: Princeton University Press.

United Nations Office on Drugs and Crime (UNODC). (2015). *The United Nations standard minimum rules for the treatment of prisoners: An updated blueprint for prison management in the 21st century*. Vienna: UNODC. Retrieved from: https://www.unodc.org/documents/justice-and-prison-reform/Brochure_zon_the_UN_SMRs.pdf

Weegels, J. (2018). *Performing prison power, agency and co-governance in Nicaraguan prisons*. Amsterdam: University of Amsterdam.

6

Fire Next Time: Gangs, Prison, and the Apocalyptic Image in Honduras

Jon Horne Carter

Ashes

"They think they can do this?" my friend Victor exclaimed. "Because everyone hates gangs?" In 2004, the prison fire in San Pedro Sula, Honduras, burned for hours as fire fighters and medical teams stood outside the front gate, locked-out. Those inmates who managed to escape the blaze by beating a hole in the cinderblock walls were executed by a masked firing squad waiting outside. When it was over, state investigators arranged 129 bodies in a grid on the prison lawn. All were suspected gang members. Survivors would claim their ward was firebombed with gasoline, but official investigations ruled it was caused by a refrigerator appliance, illegally hotwired by inmates.

Victor was aghast, because this was the second fire in less than a year. In 2003, a fire had taken the lives of 68 individuals at another prison in La Ceiba. Most people I knew believed that Mano Dura, or "strong

J. H. Carter (✉)
Appalachian State University, Boone, NC, USA

S. Darke et al. (eds.), *Carceral Communities in Latin America*, Palgrave Studies in Prisons and Penology, https://doi.org/10.1007/978-3-030-61499-7_6

hand" policing practices had opened the door to the recent prison fires by putting too much power in the hands of anti-gang security forces. Mano Dura was the formal name for regional emergency measures to control gangs, specifically the maras (gangs MS-13 and Barrio 18), in Guatemala, El Salvador, and Honduras. In Honduras, it granted military and civilian police broad authority to search and detain individuals as suspected gang members on the basis of a tattoo or gathering in small groups (Gutiérrez Rivera 2013; Wolf 2017). Within a year, the national prison system was overcrowded and at the brink of a crisis. Mano Dura had inaugurated mass incarceration in Honduras, before prisons were equipped to handle it. As such, any analysis of prisons in Honduras is also an analysis of particular forms of law enforcement.

Mano Dura had its critics from its inception in 2002, but the fire in San Pedro Sula galvanized the nation in outrage. For the last two years, evidence had been mounting that Mano Dura brigades were responsible for extrajudicial killings of gang suspects and so, for many, the identity of the perpetrators of the SPS massacre was not a mystery—they were uncontrollable elements of Mano Dura authorities, who believed their expanded policing authority actually placed them beyond the law itself. Domestic and international pressure forced the Honduran Bureau of Prisons to respond to the lack of security for incarcerated gang members. State austerity measures prohibited major renovations and so, instead, at the San Pedro Sula prison and Marco Aurelio Soto (MAS) outside Tegucigalpa, the MS-13 and Barrio 18 were each given a multi-level dormitory with a courtyard and perimeter wall, and the keys to lock themselves inside. If the state couldn't protect them, the logic seemed to go, they should at least be able to defend themselves. Locked inside their barracks and reeling from the tragedy of the fires, the maras transformed their interior world. They overhauled the barracks with physical renovations and covered its drab surfaces with vibrant murals of gang life. They limited visitation, fortified the entrances to the barracks, and seemed to turn their incarceration into an occupation—making a fortress of an otherwise abject and abandoned institution.

Flames

I begin with the aftermath of the 2003 and 2004 prison fires because it is there that the state of emergency, carceral experimentation, and criminal community coalesce to shape anti-liberal politics in Honduras. Here I take anti-liberal politics to mean a critical response to the contradictory foundation of sovereign power in Western nation-states, in which the state of emergency is an unmediated expression of the force that is both lawless and yet the condition for law itself (Agamben 2005; Schmitt 2006). As gangs locked themselves inside their independent barracks, shielding themselves from unconstrained emergency power, it was there that gang tattooing intensified. Mara tattoos started to cover the entire upper body, neck, face and head in interlocking images. They were not the popular motifs of gang tattooing seen before, but instead drew from the occult. Eye-sockets were filled with ink to look like a skull. The face of the reaper was drawn at the center of the brow as a third-eye. The numerals 666 crowded the forehead as if branded with an iron. Horns emerged beneath closely cropped hair. Expressionless, zombie vixens stared back at the viewer. A screaming beast tore through the skin, liberating itself into the outside world. Intricate devils, monsters, demons, and living dead circulated over the body as if possessing it. While these tattoos were photographed and circulated through global media during the 2000s, they were never the subject of close analysis and by-passed, I believe, as kitsch. And while gang members' dramatic physical appearances have inspired aesthetic appreciation, photographs of gang barracks during this period more often evoked early twentieth century sociology of crowds, as politically regressive, than the changing face of political agency within the crises of late liberalism (Le Bon 2002; Mazzarella 2010; Povinelli 2011). In the pages ahead, I address this problem by suggesting that the vibrant and hermetic tattoos of incarcerated gang communities in Honduras were both political in nature and, importantly, interdependent. They are not to be interpreted as discrete symbols but as fragments in tension with one another, converting the body into a field of associations that dismembers the self-possessed, liberal subject. Tattooing the devil on one's face, and the apocalypse across one's body, was the foundational praxis of an anti-liberal subjectivity that foisted gang members outside the political sphere and inaugurated a carceral politics of refusal (Carter 2014; Simpson 2014).

Silence

The National Penitentiary Marco Aurelio Soto is 26 kilometers outside of Tegucigalpa and, by the mid-2000s, when I was visiting the prison regularly, home to 2800 inmates. Originally designed for 2000 inmates, everywhere the prison seemed to be crumbling under the stress of overpopulation. The gang barracks were the exception to the rule, though, and sparkled with new paint. Bright murals on the outer wall, a mural announced the transition from one social and political world to another. Inside the barracks of Barrio 18 and that of MS-13, the gangs had painted cemeteries with tombstones personalized to victims of the fires, and to vendettas and innumerable perils of gang life. They renovated the interiors to include billiards tables, cantinas, disco lighting, and a sound system that thumped hip-hop music across the entire complex. The youngest members transported construction materials from delivery trucks in the parking lot, back to the barracks where renovations were constant. Some afternoons I spent time with the prison director who was bemused by the fact that ceding power to the inmates to run the prison's interior had actually improved conditions overall. In retrospect, it was the violence against the maras and their isolation that had initiated co-governance, or shared authority between administrators and inmate leadership, in Honduras. The director laughed. "It's funny," he said. "This way I have fewer responsibilities, so my job is easier. But also, we don't have money and I can't supply the money myself. But these criminal gangs and mafias have so much money they could rebuild this entire prison if they wanted to. So if you go to the MS-13 barracks you'll see that they're changed everything. They've made this place livable. And now that we've given them their own world, we don't hear a word from them. No more trouble. They just want to be left alone now."

When international journalists and photographers arrived to the barracks, the gangs let them inside. The photos had given them global notoriety. Gang members posed in concrete chambers decorated with baroque murals, flat screen televisions, and designer furniture. Outside, they posed in the sunlight, shirtless with their tattoos reaching across their entire upper body, and their faces turned away, as if the tattoos spoke for them. But with domestic reporters, legal advocates, and Christian missionaries, the gangs were painfully aloof. They said little before turning them away. This was especially galling for human rights lawyers who were collecting eye-witness testimony of survivors of the fires, hoping to assemble a criminal case against state actors believed to be involved. But the maras did not come forward to offer testimony.

My friend Angela, a journalist and human rights activist, who had known the maras in Tegucigalpa since the early 1990s, told me she felt betrayed. Angela was one of the original pioneers of gang rehabilitation in the capital during the 1990s, and spent a decade creating job training and therapy resources for gang members who took advantage of her program. More recently, she had worked closely with members of both the MS and Barrio 18 to mount cases against police commanders involved in death squads that targeted gangs during Mano Dura. She was demoralized that the maras, now with their own palatial setting inside the penitentiary, seemed disengaged with that work and were falling out of touch. "Now they have their quadrant of the penitentiary," she said, "and they don't want to talk with us any more? For years we risked our lives trying to help them!" It was true that her work had caused her serious problems with police across the city. "But now I go and some kid who's barely eighteen years old stops me at the door like I'm not welcomed. Now they say they don't accept visitors unless we are family. I'm trying to help them get out of there. What do they plan to do, live in the prison forever?"

Evil

The only person I knew who regularly visited the MS-13 at MAS was Miriam Blanco, a journalist who had been assisting gang members in their court appearances for over a decade. I spent more than a year shadowing her, and as we sat in the courtyard of the MS-13 barracks, I wondered about the tension between the silence shrouding gang life and the prolific image-work across gang members' skin. When thinking about images and politics, few thinkers have been so suggestive as Walter Benjamin, whose "dialectical image" and its relationship to the state emergency tapped into the theatrics of sovereign power (Benjamin 1969). For Benjamin, state violence was not simply a manifestation of sovereign power but equally an opportunity to overturn its mythical foundations. "To articulate the past historically does not mean to recognize it the way it really was. It means to seize hold of a memory as it flashes up in a moment of danger" (Benjamin 1969, 255). From his earliest work, Benjamin was attentive to the image, first in the overwrought symbolism in the Baroque period and in German tragic drama, and later in his work on montage in avant-garde cinema. Benjamin was keen to point out that the disruption of chronological historical time often produced fleeting images, condensations of non-linear affects that challenged the narratives of progress and the phantasmagoria of capitalist production (Benjamin 2019).

Benjamin suggests that images are more than inanimate representations to be decoded or interpreted, but are monads (Leibniz 1991) that house innumerable affects that lie dormant or become animated by historical circumstance. The images on the skin of the maras were especially potent as many were inscribed after the prison fires of 2003 and 2004, intermingling occult motifs with previously inscribed tattoos of Biblical verse and symbolism. This non-synchronous quality implied a historical as well as an ideological tension between them, which turned the body of the gang member into a baroque theatre, in which the struggle between good and evil was allegorized such that their opposition was neither totalizing nor linear. In the wake of the fires, the sacrilegious quality of these tableaux assailed the binary opposition at the founding of the law, in which the mythical authority of sovereign power is juxtaposed with the victim excommunicated from the polis and possessing no rights (Agamben 2005; Benjamin 2007). The maras' iconoclastic embrace of evil is political, before it is moral, insofar as the devil only saturated the image-work of gang life in the moment of their exile from the rights and protections of a legal order. Evil then is at one, not with crisis itself, but with the contradictions on which crisis takes shape as a historical reality. When the MS-13 painted marijuana leaves, Mayan gods, scales of justice, and wild beasts on the exterior of their barracks wall—all of it framed by an outline of the familiar shape of Honduras—such images displaced the customary content of the moral and the legal, uncoupling them from the magic of the state, and visualizing the revaluation of their values (Nietzsche 1989, 34).

Redeemer

But what makes this sacrilegious revaluation of values a political act? In her writing on the origins of messianic nationalism, Jacqueline Rose (2005) describes the first prophet of Zionism, Shabtai Zvi. Zvi is remembered for hacking down the door of a locked synagogue in Smyrna in 1665, and delivering a blasphemous sermon that violated sacred law. Gershom Scholem describes him as "the most hideous and uncanny figure in the whole history of Jewish messianism," who captured the imagination of the Jewish community worldwide by consorting with evil, breaking the law, and becoming a sinning saint. "It is central to Jewish messianism," Rose explains, "to the consternation of official Christianity, that messianic hope is material and carnal as well as spiritual, fully embodied in political time" (Rose 2005, 3). Rose argues that this messianic hope is carnal and part of this world, in contrast to the interiority of Christian metaphysics. "It must be visible," she writes, "not unseen."

Across the mara communities of Central America in 2020, tattooing is now greatly diminished. Gangs benefit more, now, from clandestinity than theatricality. But in the crucible of the prisons of the 2000s, these satanic and apocalyptic images incarnated the gangs' refusal of state sovereignty and its violence, from which the prison was inseparable. The gangs responded to their objectification by the state's asymmetrical violence, with transgressive adornment that remade the body into a ritualized vessel of oppositional values. These aesthetic labors generated an affective immediacy that countered the necropolitical gaze, under which they were already dead. Their embodied revolt appropriated the phantasms of necropolitics (Mbembe 2019) and reconfigured them across the skin—a montage of apocalyptic visions whose destructive force was a clearing. Whereas Christian conversion experiences were individual, internalized, and offered a narrative of the world to come, the maras' visions were external, written across multiple bodies, and offered nothing but empty historical time in which politics might become otherwise.

Naïve readings of this embrace of evil, of course, attracted evangelical missionaries who were a common sight in the penitentiary. Young and old and dressed in formal attire, they came looking for converts. But gang members who experienced religious conversion had to prove its veracity or face a death sentence as defectors, and did so by standing before a Christian congregation and giving their testimony (Brenneman 2011; Wolseth 2011). The structure of the testimony was predictable, going from an ordered life to disorientation in the criminal world, and then a return to order in their redemption. These linear narratives contrasted sharply with the maras' fragmented, tattoo theology, and such redemption narratives restored not only the spiritual life of the convert, but also returned the rational, liberal subject to wholeness after its dismemberment in the criminal world.

Revelations

The texts most commonly used for Christian conversion were that of the New Testament gospels, and one could find no greater contrast with the spiritual work of those chapters than in the coarseness and indifference of the demonic tattoo imagery that resisted a cohesive and humanized subject. Those images did not surrender to the spirit of god but instead generated power in their affective abundance, undoing discourses of humility and passivity, and reversing Christian interiority with thought-puzzles on the exterior of the body. By the mid-2000s, young men shrouded in satanic script stood opposite evangelicals armed with the Bible, transforming the biopolitical architecture of the state prison into a theatrical stage for the allegorical struggle between good and evil. Contrast this fragmented, non-linear art of revolt as it emerges from the interior of the gang world, with scholarly writing on maras that relies on artful testimonies of former gang members (Brenneman 2011; Fontes 2019; O'Neill 2015; Ward 2012).

In the wake of the two prison fires, the intensification of tattoo art served both to exaggerate gang criminality, establishing them as an oppositional community before the law, and to reject their reintegration into the surrounding world, flouting the spirit of the Christian gospels used in rehabilitation clinics recognized by state courts. Holing up in the unreachable and stigmatizing interiors of prisons, the maras rejected a legal-system that favored the powerful, and transformed their outsider ethos into a politics of vengeance. After the fires, the maras rejected not only missionaries themselves but the teachings of the Gospels and the emphasis on brotherly love on which their praxis relied. Instead they adorned themselves in the apocalyptic imagery of the Book of Revelations with its explosive spirit of revenge that lies dormant and repressed within communities of the powerless. If extensive tattooing marked gangs as beyond the reach of rehabilitation, their embrace of the theological imagery of the Book of Revelations declared an irreconcilability with the present in general.

Vengeance

Many historians of religion have undertaken analysis of the Book of Revelations, but it is D. H. Lawrence's 1930 essay titled *Apocalypse* that most compellingly examines the book's pagan and millenarian influences which I find at work in the tattoo art of the maras (Lawrence 1986). Lawrence begins with the admission that in his youth he found the text "utterly unpoetic and arbitrary" (Lawrence 1986, 10). Returning to it later in life (the essay was written just before his death), Lawrence was surprised at its unsettled fullness (Lawrence 1986, 6). The book was a marvel of the New Testament, an abrupt shift in style and register from the Gospels' expansive elaboration of the philosophy of Christian love, and the elegant teachings of Jesus. It is a book of vengeance that appears suddenly, in a different language and tone, with its lumbering, clumsy symbols and with a "pompous unnaturalness" to its gratuitous frenzy (Lawrence 1986, 9).

Lawrence notes that in his hometown the Book of the Apocalypse electrified the worship ceremonies of the churches of the uneducated and the coal mining families nearby. With a nod to Friedrich Nietzsche, Lawrence teases out the different styles of Christian thought that hold the Apocalypse in tension with New Testament theology, as "popular religion…distinct from thoughtful religion" (Lawrence 1986, 9). The Apocalypse is collective rather than inward and individual. It is not of those whose destiny is postponed for another time, as in Nietzsche's construction of *ressentiment* (Nietzsche 1989, 18). Rather, it was an open and impassioned will to power, the triumph of those who find themselves weak but know themselves "chosen," and those who would manifest the annihilation of the powerful in a corrupt and fallen world. Lawrence writes: "The longer one lives, the more one realizes that there are two kinds of Christianity, the one focused on Jesus and the Command: Love one another! – and the other focused…on the Apocalypse. There is the Christianity of tenderness. But as far as I can see, it is utterly pushed aside by the Christianity of self-glorification: the self-glorification of the humble" (Lawrence 1986, 11). If exiting the maras through Christian conversion led one through the effete and refined love espoused in the teachings of Jesus of Nazareth, the political theology of the maras themselves was the text of the Apocalypse: vengeful, collective, and monstrous, without a teleological narrative and dependent on the force of gathering signs and visions.

Prison Theology

Lawrence's analysis is provocative largely for suggesting that the Book of Apocalypse be treated by its reader as an archaeological site, a layered text infused with multiple messianic traditions. Underneath the text, he argues, are the influences of pre-Christian, pagan religions. All but eradicated from other parts of the Bible, here they remained more visible than anywhere else. The authorship of the book has been regularly disputed, but is often attributed to the Apostle John, also author of the fourth Gospel and the Epistles. But, Lawrence writes in rebuttal, "(I)t cannot be that the same man wrote the two works, they are so alien to one another" (Lawrence 1986, 13). For Lawrence, it was not the Apostle John but rather John of Patmos, an obscure figure exiled by the Romans and imprisoned for years on the island of Patmos. In prison, he started the text as a screed against the Romans, finishing the book in AD 96 as he entered his late years. The Book of Apocalypse was, Lawrence tells us, prison theology long before the maras transposed it to images.

In the New Testament, the Book of Apocalypse was unusual for its clunky and unwieldy symbols, which Lawrence attributed to John's influences. John was an apocalyptist composing in the style of his time. Given the details known of his life, it is not likely he would have known anything of the legend of Jesus nor that he would have read the Gospels. But he would have been well versed in the writings of Jewish prophets whose messianic texts had been in circulation for two or three centuries before Christ (Lawrence 1986, 40). These early apocalyptic texts came about after Roman oppression of Jews had dismantled any belief that the Chosen would have their day to rule on earth. Any religious text promising it would have lost authority as it became clear that Judeo-Christian destiny would be postponed. Lawrence writes, "It was no longer a matter of prophecy: it was a matter of vision. God would no longer *tell* his servant what would happen, for what would happen was almost untellable. He would show him a vision…That was what the apocalyptists set out to do: to vision forth the unearthly triumph of the Chosen" (Lawrence 1986, 32).

Pagan Magic

Jewish prophets had lived alongside pagan cults even as they were no longer of them, but those who sought smiting power grand enough to destroy their enemies on earth found such frenzied potential in pagan consciousness of the cosmos (Lawrence 1986, 32). In Lawrence's reading of the Book of the Apocalypse, the early Jewish prophets anthropomorphized and disguised the pagan cosmic forces, inserting them into allegorical frames beneath which were vestiges of pagan religious experience. Lawrence remembers ridiculing the text as a young man, but in his late-reading of the text he sees the symbols anew, and finds in John of Patmos' writing a "brutal paganism" tapping into the vitality and potency of their religious cults. These symbols are not of a second-rate theological parable, but non-representational traces connecting to divine power. Jewish prophets incorporated the power of pagan myth, and later John rewrote their texts. But unlike other authors, John refused to suppress the pagan influences and retained the movement of sensory-consciousness that gives primacy to images (over words). Such "rotary-thought-images" Lawrence describes as opposed to the modern process of progressive thought (Lawrence 1986, 52). "To them a thought was a completed state of feeling-awareness, a cumulative thing, a deepening thing, in which feeling deepened into a feeling in consciousness until there was a sense of fullness. A completed thought was the plumbing of a depth like a whirlpool…As a matter of fact we do very much the same in a crisis. When anything very important is to be decided we withdraw and ponder and ponder until the deep emotions are set working and revolving together, revolving, revolving, until a center is formed and we 'know what to do'" (Lawrence 1986, 51). Can we think similarly of the maras' tattoo images, as working through their historical crisis by carving out new paths of intuition, at once refusing the individualized accounts of the rational, liberal subject, and exploring a visionary politics of collective and worldly transformation?

In his work in rehabilitation clinics across Central America, the sociologist Robert Brenneman describes a threshold in personal transformation in gang recovery. In public testimony of one's descent into sin and subsequent calling to serve God, authenticity of one's account was often measured by the depth of one's emotional and psychological breakdown. This entails uncontrollable weeping and trembling that the subject overcomes in the quest to become whole again (Brenneman 2011, 153–187). This solitary spiritual quest and its allegorical framing of good and evil differs greatly from the collective spirit of transgression of the maras, and the apocalyptic and anti-state vision of mid-2000s gang politics. In the Gospels, Jesus the prophet was also a lone individual who, surrounded by disciples, was never the figure of vengeance they wanted him to be. But much as Judas was essential to Jesus' spiritual realization, the Book of Apocalypse is retained in the New Testament, Lawrence writes, "to give the death kiss to the Gospels" whose bounded Ego is undone by ontological drift and dismemberment (Lawrence 1986, 18).

Zombies

Writing on Lawrence's essay, Gilles Deleuze suggests that "(i)f we are steeped in the Apocalypse, it is rather because it inspires ways of living, surviving, and judging in each of us. It is a book for all those who think of themselves as survivors. It is the book of Zombies" (Deleuze 1997, 36–7). Deleuze finds the rotary-thought of the pagan symbol a "process of action and decision" that opposes the over-determination of meaning in allegory. "It has neither beginning nor end, it does not lead us anywhere, and above all it has no final point, nor even stages. It is always in the middle..." (Deleuze 1997, 48). The rotary-symbol builds what Deleuze calls "connections," which open the flow of life to radical transformations. They are, I think, much like tattoos suspended in a storm of other images which are all mutually constitutive. In Benjamin's political-historical image-theory, he calls these affective connections "constellations"—new configurations of image and concept that, importantly, arise most frequently in moments of danger. In the Honduran prison, the threat of emergency powers at the core of state sovereignty is a constant, and, in that context, there is little that separates Benjamin's dialectical images from Lawrence's apocalyptic visions. Rather than a transcendental escape, they are flashing reminders that we can only transform this immediate world. It is the survivors of state violence, or in Deleuze's terms "zombies," who have been divining such alternative futures on the surface of their bodies. Thinking with Lawrence, we might take a moment to re-evaluate the unsophisticated symbolism of the penitentiary tattoos, where the rotary-thought image summons apotropaic force in the struggle against the mythical foundations of state sovereignty.

Antichrist

Miriam and I were in the central park of Tegucigalpa having coffee before leaving for the penitentiary. We relished the moment. We knew we would be in the barracks of the MS-13 by the afternoon. The sun was warm. Birds on the cathedral squawked. But then in the distance we heard shouting. It was getting closer. Miriam reached for her handbag as if gang members or police might come around the corner and we would need to run. She asked someone what was happening. "There are some people over there," a young boy told her, "that say they worship the antichrist."

Around the corner came a slow-moving group of some 50 people. They held signs with 666, placards with the crucifixion of Christ inside a circle with a slash, and a banner that read, "Creciendo en Gracia, de Miami, Florida" with a photo of their leader Jose Luis de Jesus Miranda. Miranda claimed to be the second coming of Christ and preached against the concept of original sin. In his view, it was a misinterpretation of Christian theology. Miranda argued that Jesus' death absolved humanity of original sin and lifted the Law of Moses (and the Ten Commandments) off the Christian community. What remained was a state of "grace" in which one's salvation was no longer measured in works but in faith. For him, "sin" was an anachronism that religious institutions maintained in order to keep parishioners in submission. Many had tattooed 666 on the inside of their wrists, which they said was not reference to the devil but an expression of their rejection of the teachings of the Catholic Church. That night Miranda would take the stage at the largest arena in the capital, before an audience of nearly five thousand attendees.

When we arrived to the barracks of the MS-13 later that day, the courtyard was alive. People were washing clothes, playing soccer, and minding the communal garden. Jochito stopped to greet us. He was head of the MS-13 in the market district of Tegucigalpa and one of the ranking leaders in the prison. Miriam told him about the parade we had seen.

He smirked. "Yeah they came here. I, personally, told them 'no visitors.'"

"They were here?"

"This was the third or fourth time," he said.

"What did they want?"

"Usually they preach their beliefs – that there is no such thing as sin, right? The Catholic Church lies to us. Their pastor is Jesus Christ, returned to earth. And they want to tattoo everyone with 666."

"Do people here accept what they have to say?"

"No one of us wants to hear that kind of talk," he said. "They come here because they've seen our photos on the internet, with all our tattoos, and they think we are people with no principles. They think we would join their group because they don't believe there are consequences for your actions in this life. They think we are allies in their spiritual war. But actually, like I've told them, what we believe is the opposite."

"So you do believe in consequences?" I asked.

"Of course. I've been Catholic since I was a boy and I'll be Catholic when I die. But in this country, where you have so much corruption and impunity for the rich, there are consequences. We are the consequences."

"You are?" I asked.

Jochito laughed. "Look around," he said, pointing to the busy courtyard, the murals, and the tattoos covering his forearms. "How many times has the state tried to exterminate us? They kill us on the streets and burn us alive in prisons, and yet here we are, stronger than before. We can't hold them accountable because they are too powerful. But we still exist. So when they see us, tattooed and ugly, they know."

"They know what?" I asked.

"We exist because they exist. When your society falls apart because of corruption, and violence, you get people like us. People who have no place in their society but can see it for what it is. The people who run this country think God's judgment happens after death. But for us, they've already broken the world into tiny pieces. Judgment day is now."

"How do you put it back together?" I asked, not expecting an answer.

Jochito removed his shirt. His chest was a field of infernal images. "Each of these (tattoos) is one of those pieces we carry with us." I stared at the interconnected fragments that together were an indecipherable maelstrom.

"And so together the tattoos are a history?" I asked.

"No," he said. "More like emotions. When I look across this courtyard at all the tattoos, I can see our emotions together like a powder keg." For a moment we looked over the courtyard in silence, the tattoos seeming to interlace and circulate from body to body like a blue, electrical current.

"It's amazing what has happened in this corner of the prison," I said.

"Missionaries always promise another world after you die," Jochito said. "But we made one right here."

References

Agamben, G. (2005). *State of exception* (trans: Attell, K.). Chicago: University of Chicago Press.

Benjamin, W. In H. Arendt (Ed.) *Illuminations: Essays and reflections* (trans: Zohn, H.). New York: Schocken Books, 1969. Theses on the Philosophy of History.

Benjamin, W. (2007). Critique of Violence. In P. Demetz (Ed.), *Reflections: Essays, aphorisms, and autobiographical writings* (trans. Jephcott, E.). New York: Verso Press.

Benjamin, W. *Origin of the German Trauerspiel* (trans: Eiland, H.). Cambridge, MA: Harvard University Press, 2019.

Brenneman, R. (2011). *Homies and Hermanos: God and gangs in Central America*. Oxford: Oxford University Press.

Carter, J. H. (2014). Gothic sovereignty: Gangs and criminal community in a Honduran prison. *South Atlantic Quarterly, 113*(3), 475–502.

Deleuze, G. (1997). Nietzsche and Saint Paul, Lawrence and John of Patmos. In *Essays Clinical and Critical*. Minneapolis: University of Minnesota Press.

Gutiérrez Rivera, L. (2013). *Territories of violence: State, marginal youth, and public security in Honduras*. London: Palgrave Macmillan.

Lawrence, D. H. (1986). *Apocalypse*. New York: Penguin Press.

Le Bon, G. (2002). *The crowd: A study of the popular mind*. Mineola: Dover Publications.

Leibniz, G. (1991). *Discourse on metaphysics and other essays* (trans. Garber, D and R. Ariew). Indianapolis: Hackett Publishing Company, Inc.

Mazzarella, W. (2010). The myth of the multitude, or, who's afraid of the crowd? *Critical Inquiry, 36*(4), 697–727.

Nietzsche, F. (1989). *The genealogy of morals*. New York: Vintage Press.

O'Neill, K. L. (2015). *Secure the soul: Christian piety and gang prevention in Guatemala*. Berkeley: University of California Press.

Povinelli, E. (2011). *Economies of abandonment: Social belonging and endurance in late liberalism*. Durham: Duke University Press Books.

Rose, J. (2005). *The question of Zion*. Princeton: Princeton University Press.

Schmitt, C. (2006). *Political theology: Four chapters on the concept of sovereignty*. Chicago: University of Chicago Press.
Simpson, A. (2014). *Mohawk interruptus: Political life across the borders of settler states*. Durham: Duke University Press.
Ward, T. W. (2012). *Gangsters without borders: An ethnography of a Salvadoran street gang*. Oxford: Oxford University Press.
Wolf, S. (2017). *Mano dura: The politics of gang control in El Salvador*. Austin: University of Texas Press.
Wolseth, J. (2011). *Jesus and the gang: Youth violence and Christianity in urban Honduras*. Albuquerque: University of Arizona Press.

7

Carceral Coloniality in Venezuela: Theorizing Beyond the Latin American Penal State

Cory Fischer-Hoffman

Introduction

Recent scholarship on the rise of the Latin American penal state is highly influenced by the central thesis that rising rates of incarceration are not a result of increased crime but a response to heightened "social insecurity" generated through neoliberal restructuring (Wacquant 2009b). Wacquant argues that a loss of industrial jobs and harsh austerity measures have eliminated the social safety net, further criminalizing the poor who no longer have legal means of survival in the neoliberal age (2009a). This framework is utilized to analyze the rise of mass incarceration in the United States and the export of *mano dura* and *zero tolerance* policies to Europe and Latin America (2009b). However, alone this framework is insufficient for examining prisons in Venezuela because the concept of "neoliberal penality" fails to recognize how Latin American countries are geopolitically positioned in the capitalist world-system and how the prison bolsters systems of domination beyond neoliberal capitalism. In

C. Fischer-Hoffman (✉)
Lafayette College, Easton, PA, USA

S. Darke et al. (eds.), *Carceral Communities in Latin America*, Palgrave Studies in Prisons and Penology, https://doi.org/10.1007/978-3-030-61499-7_7

this chapter, I will address these shortcomings by proposing a postulate that I am calling *carceral coloniality*. I assert that Venezuela's penal state is "nested in a matrix of 'the coloniality of power'" (Taylor 2014, p. 126). I am suggesting a different infrastructure—beyond Foucault's *Discipline and Punish* and beyond Wacquant's *Neoliberal Penal State*—for examining prisons in Latin America.

Research on prisons has overwhelmingly focused on the United States and Europe. Attempts to adapt Wacquant's theory to analyze the Latin American Penal State have failed to engage with the particularities of Latin American racial constructs or some explanations fall back on simplistic characterizations, such as "informal" or "corrupt," without sufficiently engaging with the colonial legacy in the region (Müller 2010). Birkbeck (2011) compares incarceration in the Global North and Global South and argues that while control is more restrictive in North America, the less restrictive forms of control in Latin America do not mean that prisoners are not also subjected to forms of external authority, punishment, and discipline.

Latin American de-colonial thinkers have proposed a framework for understanding the expansion of the world system in the sixteenth century through the process of colonization and a "parallel construction of its imaginary both from inside and outside the system" (Mignolo 2000, p. 64). Quijano (2000) refers to this is as "the coloniality of power." Mignolo (2000) argues that the process of colonization "lays the foundation for both modernity and coloniality" (p. 51). Quijano and Wallerstein (1992) argue that "…there could not have been a capitalist world economy without the Americas" (p. 549). This framework insists on thinking about the region outside of the bounds of linear development theories, (including a Euro-centered Marxist analysis); it creates a tool for understanding modernity and coloniality as "two sides of the same coin" and; it offers a lens for analyzing how hierarchies of superiority/inferiority operate (Mignolo 2000, p. 91).

Unlike Wacquant's (2010) construction of the penal state, based largely on the relationship between the growth of prisons and the economic model of Neoliberalism, I argue that global capitalism is not only neoliberal but it is also colonial/modern and Euro-centered and therefore prisons need to be examined on a more complex terrain; what I call *carceral coloniality*. The coloniality of power is constructed on four intersecting and interconnected "controlling ambits of power"; labor, sex, authority, and subjectivity, all of which are shaped by the enduring creation of the concept of race in the sixteenth and seventeenth centuries (Taylor 2014, p. 123). Each of these categories is "structurally linked and mutually reinforcing," and they are also controlled through particular systems and institutions (Quijano 2008, p. 184).

In the control of labor and its resources and products, it is the capitalist enterprise; in the control of sex and its resources and products, the bourgeois family; in the control of authority and its resources and products, the nation-state; in the control of intersubjectivity, Eurocentrism (Quijano 2008, p. 193).

The carceral sits at the intersection of each of these areas, and therefore the prison is an institution in which the control of labor, sex, authority, and intersubjectivity all converge.

Building from the historically framed ethnographic research, participant observation and interviews that I conducted in five prisons in Venezuela from September 2014 to April 2015, I will examine Venezuelan prisons in relation to the coloniality of power by surveying how Quijano's "four ambits of controlling power"—labor, sex, authority, and subjectivity—intersect with punishment, penal institutions, and the carceral world. My approach blends international political economy and cultural studies with empirically and historically grounded ethnographic methods. First, I will focus on the concept of race, which connects with all of the other categories. I utilize Angela Davis' (2003) work on the intersections of punishment, gender, race, capitalism, and colonialism in US prisons; the work of Laura Segato (2007) on the question of color and prisons in Latin America; and I continue to draw on the concept of coloniality from Quijano and Mignolo as well as Mark Lewis Taylor, who examined the "four-controlling ambits of power" in relation to Mass Incarceration in the US. I will conclude this chapter by proposing "border-thinking" as means of creating new way of thinking about prisons in Venezuela (Mignolo 2000).

Race: "The Most Effective and Long Lasting Instrument of Universal Social Domination"[1]

Los pobres negritos. ("Those poor black people") (A Venezuelan government official's response to the El Rodeo Prison riots in June 2013)

The concept of race was created in the sixteenth century, as a mechanism of social classification to distinguish between the conquerors and the conquered and to maintain the system of domination.

From the sixteenth century on, this racial principle has proven to be the most effective and long-lasting instrument of universal social domination…In this way, race became the fundamental criterion for the distribution of the world population into ranks, places, and roles in the new society's structure of power (Quijano 2000, p. 534).

Race replaced the more ancient inter-sexual domination of men as superior to women with a categorization that did not exist prior to colonization. The ongoing domination of conquered peoples was maintained through a classification system based on the idea that conquered populations were *naturally* inferior to those who dominated them (and not simply a result of historical consequences). Prior to colonization, the categories of *Indian*, *black*, *mestizo*, or *white* did not exist and previous categorization based on national origin had not yet taken on a racial meaning in the ways that Spanish, Portuguese, or European came to be associated with whiteness and therefore a 'natural superiority' over racialized 'others.'

Since the present-day racial violence and tensions do not seem to be as extreme as they are in the United State, the concept of "racial democracy" in Venezuela often serves to mask "the true discrimination and colonial domination" of Afro-Venezuelans (Quijano 2000, p. 568). The construction of Venezuelan *mestizaje* projects a concept of racial sameness under the guise of a universally shared mixed heritage, what Wright (1990) refers to as *Café con Leche*. The process of racialization in Venezuela looks different from the rigid "one-drop" rule that shapes racializations in the United States. In Venezuela, some aspects of racial categorizations are more fluid, linked to class (which is a legacy of the racialized division of labor imposed through colonization and slavery), and overlap with concepts of ethnicity—a sense of cultural belonging to a group. Because of these differences, it can be very challenging to have fixed categories of race, like those often utilized in the US. Critical race theories that have focused on racialization as a process shaped by context is much more useful for examining race and identity in Latin America. For example, Denise Ferreira da Silva (2007) examines the concepts of racial democracy and *mestizaje* in Brazil and argues that as opposed to excluding black folks in Brazil, Afro-Brazilians are engulfed in the national (mestizo) subject thus difference is always placed in the past (pp. 248–249).

Race takes on a socio-spatial character in Venezuela; unlike the "inner-cities" of the United States, poor barrios are described interchangeably with the "periphery" (Davis 2006). In El Rodeo I prison, incarcerated young brown and black men largely reassured me that there was no racism in the prison, or in Venezuela. Many compared their own experiences of socially integrated spaces with movies and television shows about prison in the US, where they saw people as organized in gangs based on their race/ethnicity. But through my research, I found that many Venezuelans defined the process of racialization in spatial terms, based on one's association to place. For example, on my third visit to El Rodeo I prison in the Caracas outskirts of Guatire, the crew of guys that I spent the most time with introduced me to three different black men, claiming that these men came from Africa, Haiti, or Barlovento, but when I asked each young man if they were really *foreigners* or from the Afro-Venezuelan rural coast community, all of them confirmed that they were from Caracas. A former prisoner explained the place-based categorizations as *lugareño*, which he described as being "like racism but about a place." Common examples of this place-based discrimination can be found in the association of the countryside with backwardness and the barrio with criminality, both of which, while not explicitly about race, carry racialized signifiers.

While the racial caste system has changed from the colonial period, there is a persistent and enduring process of racialization which "continue[s] to determine access to the most recognizable public spaces" (Harrison-Conwill 2011, p. 169). The young black man who had been incorrectly introduced to me as a "Haitian" challenged the common "color-blind" wisdom of his peers in Venezuela. While pointing to his chocolate brown arm, he argued that he had not been able to get into nightclubs when he was on the outside. The current systems of racial domination relates to skin color but also to other racial signifiers like place of origin, residency, dress, speech, class, or the way one carries oneself or represents one's cultural belonging on a naturalized hierarchy of superiority and inferiority.

The prison is an institution of place-based racialization and social exclusion in Venezuela because criminality and therefore incarceration are still associated with blackness, barrios, and marginalization. The prison is a place of confinement for the racialized poor; "for 'the other' that has the mark of the Indian or African, the marks of historical subordination, who are those that still constitute the vast majority of the dispossessed" (Segato 2007, p. 156) In El Rodeo I prison, a group of young men between the ages of 18 and 28 years all agreed that if you dress like a *malandro*, the police are more likely to stop you; some contended that this was because the *malandro* identity signifies an approximation to blackness.[2] The prison is an institution of race-making in Venezuela because one of its key functions is to reinforce the association between blackness and criminality.

Labor

> *Prison is a business…it is a business. Those who are prisoners and not* luceros *nor* principales *[prans or bosses] but are only just someone who lives in* el mundo *[the carceral world], because in prison there are three ways to be, those who are the chiefs, who have control of the prison, this is within the inmates, not the guards, no. The Christians, who pick up the trash, collect the dead bodies, those who fix problems and cover for people when they are going to kill them; and there are those who are part of the* población, *that live on the outskirts that are not involved in evangelism or nothing and those that are called* malandros, *those who live relatively comfortable, comfortable in the sense that they don't take the trash out or anything like that. The discomfort is that every Sunday, you have to pay la causa, which is something that must be paid every Sunday, and you can't not pay; this is this business. This is the business of the*

prison. (Fernando, a formerly incarcerated person who was present during the 2011 prison riots in El Rodeo, interview, September 14, 2014)

Since the colonial era, the prison has been an instrument for disciplining and controlling the labor force. The racial constructs created to justify colonization and slavery engendered a racialized division of punishment which could been seen through the distinct locales of incarceration based on one's social status (Troconis de Veracoechea 1998, p. 61). The prison itself was an institution that bolstered slavery, one of the most violent forms of control of the labor force, and even after slavery's decline, racially coded labor laws sought to criminalize and control Afro-descendent rural workers as a means of labor discipline (Lombardi 1971, p. 52). The prison population became cheap or free labor on public works projects such as highways. In Venezuela, the long road towards modernity was literally paved by indentured prison laborers (El Universal 2009). Forced labor was construed as educational or job training and was justified as the remedy for the natural inclination towards laziness projected onto criminalized groups. The racialization of people of African descent was built on associations between darker skin color and criminality or laziness; this logic was used to justify a natural inferiority of blacks, which placed them in the lowest ranks of earning within the capitalist system; this logic justified low or no wages for their work (Troconis de Veracoechea 1983).

As the wage system grew under the capitalist production model, labor became associated with time; Davis (2003) explains how "the computability of state punishment in terms of time-days, months, years-resonates with the role of labor-time as the basis for computing the value of capitalist commodities" (p. 44). In order to enforce the incorporation of laborers into the capitalist economy, anti-vagrancy laws served to criminalize the poor, especially those who worked in informal sectors, and those who did not engage in wage labor. Through the 1937 *Ley de Vagos y Maleantes,* those who were not formally incorporated into the wage-economy or perceived to be "vagrants" could be arrested and incarcerated. This crack down accompanied the birth of the penitentiary in Venezuela, which oriented its rehabilitative efforts towards job training so that people in prison could assume their role as laborers in the global capitalist economy.

For women, this training has tended towards laboring in the domestic sphere, which reproduces the concept that women are naturally domestic and nurturing and it strengthens the patriarchal logic that women are subservient to men in a masculinist conception of the nuclear family. Furthermore, since domestic work is perceived as natural to women, women's labor in the prison is less likely to be seen as work and therefore less likely to receive even modest compensation (Davis 2003). For example, in Sargent David Villoria Prison (formerly Uribana), incarcerated men bake bread, do mechanical or agricultural work, and receive modest compensation, while women are expected to do all of the cooking and cleaning to maintain the annex in which they are incarcerated and they are not remunerated for their work.

Within the prisons under carceral self-rule, the *Pran*/prison boss controls the labor of the incarcerated population. *El carro*/the prison organization controls a central bank from which the population is taxed. In order to pay the weekly *causa*, many people in prison must find a way to make an income. The means by which people can pay this weekly tax are by receiving support from family members or by running businesses inside of the prison. The entrance of tools, machines, or supplies needed for their business all need to be negotiated through the *Pran*, so as people gather supplies for their operations, they often start out in debt. In some prisons, incarcerated people pay the *causa* by working directly for the leadership as a type of indentured servitude. Antillano et al. (2016) explain how "economic extraction also operates by appropriating the forced labor of segments of the population," as marginalized groups within the prison population are converted into a "semi-slave work force." Additional aspects related to labor and prison include sex work within the prison both among the incarcerated population and with outsiders who sell sexual services on visiting days. I spoke with three women who sold sexual services at San Felipe prison every weekend and they said that it was their main source of income. Prison labor is also being utilized by the Ministry of Penitentiary Services (MSP) to produce a variety of goods such as furniture, textiles, and plants, but through *Plan Cambote,* new prisons were intended to be constructed by incarcerated people, although economic stagnation appears to have halted these plans. But this case demonstrates how the expansion of the prison complex is predicated on the ability of the state to mobilize the labor of current prisoners.

The premise that the rise of the prison population is a response to loss of industrial jobs combined with a shrinking safety net due to neoliberal restructuring does not fully explain the economic circumstances in Bolivarian Venezuela. And, as Godoi (2016) points out, although this thesis does partially explain the rise of mass incarceration in the United States, it fails to explain the "diverse range of organizational, legal, political and social structures and historical paths that have led to an exacerbated punitivism" in Latin America. Venezuela's reliance on the oil sector meant that the country did not have a significant industrial workforce prior to neoliberalism and as a result of the Bolivarian Revolution, investment in social spending had increased, not decreased. Since the transition from an agricultural exporter to oil producer opened up new possibilities for consolidating the nation-state under a liberal modern democracy in the twentieth century, the prison has been utilized to house the "reserve army of labor." The criminalization of vagrancy, the use of prison labor on infrastructure projects, and the transformation of prisons as institutions of punishment into training schools for marketable skills pushed the rural and urban poor into waged labor in the capitalist modes of production; and therefore, the prison makes the laboring class more exploitable.

Sex and Sexuality

> *"Squat down, push, open your legs, spread your lips, push hard!" Sometimes they make you pee. They make you fart and you are still not pushing hard enough for them. They discriminate against you. They yell at you, they insult you, they tease you and you can't do anything because they will take away your right to visit. But how do the drugs get in? The drugs and alcohol that are inside? So, they humiliate us...and them? For me, there is nothing good here. You arrive here excited because the kids are going to see their father...and you leave demoralized, humiliated, tired, stubborn, and full of hatred. There is nothing good here.* (Anabel, describing being strip-searched to enter prison for visiting day at El Rodeo prison; interview, October 12, 2014)

Much of the punishment of women, especially those who deviate from the norms of the patriarchal nuclear family, continues to be punished in private through physical violence. In the colonial period, "since women were largely denied public status as rights-bearing individuals they could not be easily punished by the deprivation of such rights" (Davis 2003, p. 45). Many of the so-called crimes that women were charged with in the colonial period through the early twentieth century in Venezuela were related to sexual behavior—adultery and prostitution (Troconis de Veracoechea 1983). The criminalization of poor women reinforced a portrayal of *mestiza* and afro-descendent women as collectively *naturally* sexually deviant, whereas elite women accused of similar "crimes" were often portrayed as having mental illness or individual problems. The punishment of women whose "crimes" were conflated with sex demonstrates that the "intersection of criminality and sexuality continues to be racialized" (Davis 2003, p. 68).

The sex segregation of prisoners also marks a difference in the rules and norms of conduct for men and women in prison, which "enables and contributes to the production of masculinity and femininity." (Pemberton 2013, p. 166). In Colonial Venezuela, sex segregation was only practiced with "whites," whereas "non-whites" were not sex segregated, highlighting how sex and gender are inherently racialized in the colonial matrix of power. Women's prisons tend to place emphasis on correcting "womanly behaviors" and the rehabilitative programs that exist aim to train women to do domestic labor, creating "skilled domestic servants among black and poor women" (Davis 2003, p. 64). Demonstrating the intersection between race, class, gender, and labor, the prison in Venezuela produces a domestic labor underclass and "attempts to normalize female prisoners, according to white, middle-class conceptions of acceptable femininity" (Pemberton 2013, p. 166). As I mentioned above, women in Sargent David Villoria prison doing uncompensated domestic work while their male counterparts were compensated for baking bread highlights how women's prisons not only make women more "fit" for domestic work but also maintain the myth that reproductive labor is inherent to femininity, reinforcing domestic work as uncompensated, underpaid, and undervalued (Gilmore 2007; Dalla Costa and James 1975; Fortunati 1975; Federici 2004).

The role of hegemonic masculinities does not only shape the experience of women in prison, men are equally impacted—albeit in different ways—by the gendering of prisons because violence is often equated with masculinity (Davis and Dent 2001, p. 1240). Hegemonic masculinity functions to inferiorize subordinated masculinities through violence and an environment of "toxic masculinity" (Pemberton 2013, p. 168). Subordinated masculinities, those who do not conform to a heterosexist, macho, and violent embodiment of manliness or those who are gay, genderqueer, queer, or transgender, are placed in an inferior position within the context of hegemonic masculinity. The state participates in this ordering through its long history of the criminalization of homosexuality, queer sexual acts, and other forms of sexual 'deviance.' While the Ecclesiastical prisons of the colonial period brutally tortured and punished individuals suspected to be homosexuals, the 1937 *Ley de Vagos y Maleantes* criminalized homosexuality, therefore using state institutions to enforce adherence to hegemonic masculinities and to oppress those who did not conform (Hernández 1977; Heredia 2009). In the face of this oppression, homosexual relationships were often carried out clandestinely and queers who were rejected from their families were often forced into illicit work, including sex work. These circumstances, combined with official state policy that criminalized and policed homosexuality, set the stage for disproportionate rates of homosexuals in prisons because hegemonic masculinity and heteronormative sex is heavily policed. While it is difficult to find statistics on the presence of gay or trans people in prison, through my research I learned that people assumed to be gay faced life-threatening violence, rape, and sexual harassment in prisons.[3]

In the prisons under carceral self-rule in Venezuela, it is common knowledge that rapists and homosexuals are killed by *el carro* upon entrance into the prison. People who are charged with rape, molestation, (homosexual) public sex, and prostitution or are rumored to be gay are often not safe in the general prison population in male prisons. Individuals facing these circumstances might engage in a hunger strike, further dramatized through sewing one's lips together. They may stay on the margins of the physical structure and plead to be transferred to a new regime prison for their own safety, I saw this in action on two separate occasions at El Rodeo I prison. Six out of eight people who I asked at El Rodeo I prison confirmed that they had seen an execution of someone accused of being a homosexual in the years 2009–2015.

There is undoubtedly homosexual/queer/lesbian sex (both consensual and coerced) taking place in male and female prisons, but it is an extremely taboo topic and a dangerous line of inquiry considering that "outing" someone could have devastating implications for them. This example highlights how the prison is not only a depository for the surplus labor pool, it is also an institution that enforces, reinforces, and recreates hegemonic gender norms, homophobia, and transphobia. Social exclusion, alienation, and oppression of subjugated masculinities or femininities outside prison walls is then compounded with state policies and policing of gender norms. Despite significant overlap in prison policies for men and women, the discontinuities demonstrate how prisons are gendered beyond the obvious sex segregation.

For example, despite an increasing number of women in prisons largely as a result of the war on drugs, the fact that women only make up 6% of the prison population in Venezuela means that there are less prison facilities for women (OVP, Informe Semestral 2014). INOF, located in Los Teques, in the northern central capital region, is the only prison specifically for women.[4] INOF is the subject of study for all research on women's prisons in Venezuela and the handful of more remote and less funded women's annexes are under-researched (Suárez 1997). Because there are less prisons specifically for women, female prisoners are more likely to be incarcerated further from their families, creating barriers to receiving financial, material, or emotional support. Since many of the women incarcerated are mothers, their female relatives often take care of their children on the outside and cannot provide additional care for them.

On the other hand, the high rates of incarceration of men creates significant work for the women who support them. Many women cook on a bi-weekly or weekly basis and deliver goods to the prison; which are necessary for the survival and sustenance of incarcerated people. Whether the prison is nearby or a long-distance trip, this work takes time, not to mention resources to cover the costs of transportation and materials that family members bring to their loved ones. This is how Maritza, a woman visiting the father of her child at El Rodeo I explained it:

> It is a little complicated, coming here [to the prison] costs a lot of money. Because to be able to have food, bus fares, and all the things that they need, every Sunday, it's a little bit complicated...one spends a lot of money to be able to come here. I brought him food, if one doesn't bring enough food, they can die of hunger inside. Not everyone would do this. The lines are horrible, this would drive most people crazy.

Additionally, women are often left to care for their children, when their male partners are in prison. I met hundreds of women who spend nearly every weekend at the prison caring for their husbands, sons, brothers, and grandsons. Some women complained about the toll on them and the other parts of their lives that they neglected to make a visit and bring supplies on a regular basis.

The gendered divisions of labor in the family are magnified as family support is converted into an essential resource for the confined in Venezuela; it implies different access to support and resources for male and female prisoners as well as gendered differences in responsibilities for the family members of incarcerated people. When men have to assume reproductive labor within the prison—work done by women on the outside—this contributes to a de-masculinization that is often compensated for through a hyper-masculinity.

Authority

> *At the far end of El Rodeo I prison, propped up along the fence, and tucked away from where most of the action was, stood a make-shift shelter with a bed and there were two guys sitting inside when I approached and asked if I could come in. They welcomed me and offered me a broken plastic chair. Edgar, 24 and Abraham, 26 were both dressed in pristine clean and ironed clothes. Edgar had a cellphone and throughout my stay there, one person after another came by to make a phone call or to use the coveted electrical outlet in the tent. While I still hadn't directly talked to anyone about the Pran or* la causa, *it was hard to ignore the presence of the weapons and the commotion in the tent. The guns were visible and ever-present, few places existed on the ground floor where they were completely out of site, even in this tucked away corner.*

> *Edgar and the others were all calling family members and friends and trying to figure out how they would come up with* la causa *which was 450 Venezuelan Bolívares (VBF) or more accurately, it was 2 payments; 300 and one of 150. On a monthly basis this equated to roughly 35% of the legal minimum wage (November 2014). I saw Edgar making multiple phone calls, pacing a little and looking nervous. He assured me that he would find a way to come up with the money. Abraham; like the others, came from a poor family, was under 30 years old and had been put in prison in the last five years. He had been locked up for three years on charges of kidnapping and murder. In those three years, he had only been brought in front of a judge on one occasion but since his lawyer did not show up, the hearing was postponed. He has never met his lawyer and he is not even sure that he has one. He pointed out to me the irony of his kidnapping charges and the fact that now, he has essentially been kidnapped by the state and is being held for ransom at a price that neither he nor his family would be able to pay. While his family couldn't come up with the amount needed to get him out of prison, he paced back and forth in the tent trying to round up the money he needed just to keep him alive for the week.* (Author's notes, following a prison visit to El Rodeo, November 2014)

Quijano (2008) engages with questions of authority largely in relation to the nation-state. He argues that a modern nation-state is built on the concepts of citizenship and political democracy, but only insofar as citizenship can provide "legal, civil and political equality for socially unequal people" (Quijano 2008, p. 205). Therefore the nation-state, which is largely understood as a centralized power that expresses its domination over a given territory through the use of violence and the creation of an "imagined community" only exists in Latin America through the exclusion of the majorities and through the maintenance of the coloniality of power. Prisons function as concrete manifestations of state authority and control over a territory and its peoples.

Because the Venezuelan nation was constructed on the shared interest in the territory's valuable subsoil, and the state's management of those resources, power, and authority were concentrated in the state apparatus. The state—as negotiator with foreign oil companies, as an institution organized to engage directly with transnational capitalism, and as arbitrator and distributor of oil wealth—has been the significant venue for the exercise of power since the early twentieth century, when oil exports quickly outpaced all other exports (Coronil 1997, p. 76).

The construction, expansion, and "modernization" of prisons are an integral part of the nation-building process in Venezuela. Each phase of consolidation of the nation-state since the late nineteenth century has included reforming, "modernizing," and expanding the prison system. From the formation of the liberal modern state through "Order and Moral Regeneration," through the post-Gomez reorganization of the nation-state that coincided with the 1937 Choissone reforms and the first Penitentiary, to the 1961 reform of penal codes that accompanied the founding of modern rentier liberalism; to the creation of the new regime prisons and MSP in the postneoliberal era; changes in the prison are integral to changes in the organization of the nation-state (Diaz 2001; Choissone 1936; Sánchez 1999; Morais de Guerrero 2011). While reforming the prison system had not initially been prioritized when the Bolivarian Republic of Venezuela was recreated in 1999, the "*revolución penitenciaria*" was taken up in 2011 by the newly created Ministry of Penitentiary Services.

In the huge and diverse territory within Venezuelan borders, the prisons can function as outposts of the nation-state in what is otherwise an indigenous or state-less region. While El Dorado "penal *colony*" in Southeastern Venezuela is perhaps the most dramatic example of this, the prison has also been utilized as a part of the process of consolidation and expansion of the state over territory. But authority is not solely possessed by the nation-state, it can also be understood in how power and knowledge play out in people's daily lives, what Foucault calls "governmentality." This can include the prisonization of broader society, like the increasing reliance on gated communities for the rich and the ways in which the ghetto and the prison "meet and mesh," as well as the proliferation of surveillance in Venezuela (Wacquant 2001; Mallett-Outtrim 2013).

In Venezuela, as is the case for many countries in Latin America, incarcerated people have established their own forms of authority through an organization called *El Carro*. In the prisons, the state lost complete authority over most of the internal management of the prisons and has only recently regained partial control. Through military interventions and careful negotiations, by 2015, the National government had reclaimed the majority of prisons in Venezuela, leaving the government in full control of just under half of the total prison population. The remaining prisons under carceral self-rule have generated their own form of authority, fueled by their ability to utilize deadly force and to mobilize the labor of the hundreds or thousands that they hold power over. Internally, the state has lost the monopoly and internal organizations control the territory through the use of force and through the implementation of a strict code of conduct, *la rutina*, which is predicated on the weekly payment of *la causa*. The state continues to maintain power over the perimeter of the prison, enforcing its role as the creator of a depository of humans who then internally manage life on the inside. There is a growing literature on these forms of self-organization, which some analyze as a model of co-governance and authority sharing (Darke and Garces 2017).

The prison in contemporary Venezuela is a key territory where the state's authority continues to be contested. It is widely assumed that the state *ought* to control the prisons; because prisons are largely understood as necessary institutions of a modern state. The internally self-ruled prison, on the other hand, is described as "an important source of insecurity" that "threaten[s] the country's stability" (Fonseca and Paméla 2015, p. 125).

(Inter) Subjectivities

> *The Penitentiary problem is something that has no solution under capitalism, and we don't yet live in the other society that we have dreamed of.... There were people that dreamed up the society that we are living in today...those Europeans, Locke, Russell, Hobbes, those who envisioned the social contract ...they designed Enlightenment thinking and they constructed Humanism... The capitalist society is based in this concept of humanism; and from there these people designed a lot of things...all of these things were designed, little by little under a logic and all of this created various institutions including the prison that we know today.* (Osmar Romero, Filmmaker with friends and family members in prison; interview, September 13, 2014)

Subjectivities can be defined as "structural practices of Eurocentric white racism," which stem from the process in which, through colonization of the Americas, Europe was not only the economic world power but it imposed dominance through incorporating the world into its way of structuring power relations from a European perspective (Taylor 2014, p. 127; Quijano 2008, p. 188). This Euro-centered perspective was based on two "founding myths": a unilineal development model where humans progressed from a state of nature and from which this development rose to a crescendo in Europe and "a view of the differences between Europe and non-Europe as natural (racial) differences and not a consequence of history of power"(Quijano 2008, p. 190).

In the colonial period, ecclesiastical prisons along with corporal punishment were utilized to enforce Christian beliefs onto those who were "caught" or accused of practicing non-European religions or speaking non-European languages. Today, the police in Venezuela profile people based on the way they walk, talk, and dress. I spoke to a 20-year-old who had been in prison for two years at El Rodeo I prison and he said that the ways that he dressed and talked were "normal" for him, even though the police perceived them as "bad."

The growth of evangelism inside of prisons also marks an intersection of Eurocentric values being perpetuated through the penal institution. In every prison that I visited, there were numerous evangelical churches and incarcerated pastors. In many prisons, evangelical church groups are the only organizations that have regular access to the prisons. The prison is an important nexus of recruitment to evangelical Christianity because the themes of the gospel readily connect with many incarcerated people's own stories of redemption. The penitentiary itself was formulated on the Christian concept of penitence, feeling regret or sorrow for what one has done.

The prison propels Eurocentric subjectivities by functioning as a depository for "the other," from a Euro-centered perspective. The prison maintains "the internal borders" that serve as pillars of coloniality in Latin America.

As much as the occidentalist cooptation as the erection of internal borders in the face of the internal other—autochthonous, afro descendent or both mixed, but never occidental—implies a continuation of the racist modernity that orients and organizes our countries, our knowledge, and the execution of power. It is in this internal border and in this state occidentalist where we find the reason for the color of the prisons (Segato 2007, p. 155).

The prison functions as an institution of domination and dehumanization that is adaptable to the shifting requirements of global capitalism. The prison also functions to produce a Euro-centered system of knowledge that justifies the existence of this institution of domination and even purports the necessity of prisons in modern democracies. This is because the prison is presented as an institution for the punishment of criminals; even though its primary function is the domination of "others" through a Euro-centered perspective. It is that very perspective, constructed through a Euro-centered Christian enlightenment, liberal positivist lens, that distracts us from seeing prisons as multifaceted carceral institutions that reinforce racial regimes of inferiority and superiority, organize and control the labor supply, enforce patriarchal gender norms, and breed subjectivities of the criminalized "other" who remains on the margins of political life occupying a sub-citizenship status.

The structural practices of Eurocentrism is what Quijano (2008) describes as "a mirror that distorts what it reflects" (p. 204). It is this distortion that makes it impossible to truly understand and therefore address the problems facing Latin America (Quijano 2008). Quijano, critical of (Euro-centered) socialist revolutions in Latin America, advocates for decolonizing projects that look to truly uproot the coloniality of power, through challenging Euro-centered perspective and forms of knowledge.

Conclusions: Prison Border Thinking

So, for me, the best is that there are not prisons. That would be the best because the prison is an institution…like the majority of the institutions that we know today that was constructed from war, from hunger, from fear; they were designed from those places. The idea is to construct or dream another society where that doesn't exist and the idea is to think it and so we, for example, we ask people to talk about this: Look, how would you imagine what it would be like if there weren't prisons? And everybody, "No! There would be more deaths, more murders!" "No, there would be chaos!" And then we ask them, "Aja, and what are we living now?" We live in chaos so, "would there be more chaos if there weren't prisons?" But we are going to begin to think about it, to take out the chip in our brains that says that there have to be these institutions of this system because that will only continue feeding it. Yes, for me, the best thing is that there aren't prisons, I can't answer what the alternative would be because it doesn't yet exist, but at least to get to think about it to see if one day it changes. (Osmar Romero, talking about teaching film classes in Yare I Prison in Venezuela; interview, September 13, 2014)

We must fully erase the concept that prisons are simply places where criminals—whether for structural or individual reasons—get punished, the prison "works" in much more expansive and diverse ways than simply as a bureaucratic institution of punishment (Davis 2003). *Carceral coloniality* provides a framework that demonstrates how the prison is an integral institution in the structural practices of global capitalism, masculinist heterosexism, authority, and a Eurocentric white racism that projects Euorocentrism "as epistemological perspective" (Mignolo 2000, p. 87). *Carceral coloniality* expands on the concept of the neoliberal penal state by examining how neoliberalism fits within a broader historical context and how the colonial difference shapes prisons in Latin America. The prison reproduces, protects, and bolsters the coloniality of power by using racialized concepts of criminality to purport white supremacy, by utilizing masculinist concepts of the family and gender roles to reinforce patriarchy and heteronormativity, and by asserting the consolidated power of the nation-state as the arbitrator of justice despite various studies and testimonies that prove discrimination and selectivity in the use of policing and prisons. Carceral coloniality expresses the locus of intersectionality in the forms of marginalization and social exclusion that the prison both *is* and *represents*.

Examining the prison through the lens of *carceral coloniality* also creates an opportunity to "de-link" from the colonial matrix of power because "coloniality carries in it the seeds of decolonial agency" (Mignolo and Tlostanova 2009, p. 145). Mignolo and Tlostanova (2000) proposes "border-thinking"as a starting point for "de-linking...from the sanctified belief that there is only one game in town." (p. 87; Mignolo and

Tlostanova 2009, p. 145). "Border-thinking" is an extremely useful concept because incarcerated people have identified that the "prison is itself a border" (Davis and Dent 2001). This originates from the fact that many people in prison "name the distinction between the "free world" and the space behind the walls of the prison" (Davis and Dent 2001, pp. 1236–1237). In Venezuela, this is the border between "*la cárcel y la calle.*"

It is from this perspective, where people in prison can "think from dichotomous concepts rather than order the world in dichotomies" (Mignolo 2000, p. 85). This way of thinking has to do with a shift in perspectives, not only in content or terms. It is those who occupy the space of the border between "*la cárcel*" and "*la calle*" that have the perspective to think from a place that can de-link with the colonial matrix of power.

Border thinking brings to the foreground the irreducible epistemological difference between perspective from the colonial difference and forms of knowledge that, being critical of modernity, coloniality and capitalism still remain "within" the territory "in custody" of the "abstract Universals" (Mignolo 2000, p. 88).

Building further scholarship on *carceral coloniality* will depend on reconstructing and uncovering past narratives of confinement; examining relationships between slavery, race, and the prison; exploring the criminalization of the poor and racialized others alongside immigration policies; digging deeper into the intersections of colonialism, imperialism, racism, sexism, homophobia, transphobia, classism, and discrimination against addicts—all within the context of the geopolitics of power. This research must rest on ethnographic work in prisons that looks for not only content but perspective, work that explores narratives, testimonies, oral histories, and self-representation and that rejects the Eurocentric focus on individual behavior/choices as a means of understanding crime.

Carceral worlds are already epicenters of cultural production, of a new language, of codes of conduct, of styles, of ways of being. Ultimately, it is incarcerated peoples and their families, those who can contribute epistemologically to prison border-thinking. As the concept of *carceral coloniality* is expanded and critiqued, it will be the perspectives of those who speak from the borderlands, from the varied carceral worlds that will enrich thinking on prisons. *Carceral coloniality* rests on the premise that prisons are institutions of domination, and not solely places of punishment. These findings lead to the logical conclusion that, in Latin America, prisons must be abolished in order to decolonize.

Notes

1. Quijano (2000, pp. 534–535)
2. A Chilean hip-hop artist who had been harassed by the police while touring in Venezuela told me that despite having "light skin" he and his crew drew the attention of authorities because he has "the international style of *pull me over.*" (Personal conversation, June 2015).
3. Most research on LGBT incarceration has been done in the US. Amnesty International released a 2001 study called Crimes of hate, conspiracy of silence: Torture and ill-treatment based on sexual identity" which explores the treatment of LGBT prisons outside of the US, but very little data is available on Latin America. Encarnacíon (2016) argues that despite the expansion of former rights for LGBT people in Latin America, this increase in rights is being accompanied by increasing state violence towards queer and trans people.
4. INOF is the National Institute of Feminine Orientation

References

Antillano, A., Pojomovsky, I., Zubillaga, V., Sepúlveda, C., & Hanson, R. (2016). The Venezuelan prison: From neoliberalism to the Bolivarian revolution. *Crime, Law and Social Change, 65*(3), 195–211.

Birkbeck, C. (2011). Imprisonment and internment: Comparing penal institutions north and south. *Punishment & Society, 13*(3), 307–332.

Choissone Villamizar, Tulio. (1936). *Organización Penitenciara Venezolana.* Caracas: Coop de artes graficas.

Coronil, F. (1997). *The magical state: Nature, money and modernity in Venezuela.* Chicago: University of Chicago.

Dalla, C. M., & James, S. (1975). *The power of women and the subversion of the community*. Bristol: Falling Wall Press Ltd.

Dammert, L., & Zuñiga, L. (2008). *Prisons: Problems and challenges for the Americas*. Santiago: FLASCO.

Darke, S., & Garces, C. (2017). Surviving in the new mass Carceral zone. *Prison Service Journal, 229*, 2–9.

Davis, A. (2003). *Are prisons obsolete?* New York: Seven Stories Press.

Davis, M. (2006). *Planet of slums*. London: Verso.

Davis, A., & Dent, G. (2001). Prison as a border: A conversation on gender, globalization, and punishment. *Signs, 26*(4), 1235–1241.

Morais de Guerrero, María G. (2011). *El sistema penitenciario venezolano durante los 50 años de la democracia petrolera, 1958–2008*. Caracas: Fundación Empresa Polar y Universidad Andrés Bello.

Troconis de Veracoechea, Ermilia. (1983). *Historia de las Carceles en Venezuela (1600–1890)*. Caracas: La Acadamia Nacional de la Historia.

Troconis de Veracoechea, Ermilia (1998). La vida carcelaria en tiempos pasados. *Boletín de la Academia Nacional de la Historia* (Venezuela), 81(324), 61–77.

Diaz, A. J. (2001). Women, Order and Progress in Guzman Blanco's Venezuela, 1870–1888. In R. D. Salvatore, C. Aguirre, & G. M. Joseph (Eds.), *Crime and Punishment in Latin America: Law and Society Since Late Colonial Times* (pp. 56–82). Durham: Duke University Press Books.

El Universal. (2009, April 1). The prohibition is the seed of mafia. *El Universal*. Retrieved from http://www.eluniversal.com/aniversario/100/imp_en_ca3_art_the-prohibition-is-t_01A2217565

Federici, S. (2004). *Caliban and the witch*. New York: Autonomedia.

Fonseca, B., & Paméla, P. (2015). Organized Chaos: Venezuela's prison crisis. In J. D. Rosen & M. W. Brienen (Eds.), *Prisons in the Americas in the twenty first century: A human dumping ground*. Lanham: Lexington Books.

Fortunati, L., & Fleming, J. (1995). *The arcane of reproduction: Housework, prostitution, labor and capital*. Brooklyn: Autonomedia.

Foucault, M. (1975). *Discipline & punish: The birth of the prison*. New York: Random House.

Gilmore, R. W. (2007). *Golden gulag: Prisons, surplus, and opposition in globalizing California*. Berkeley: University of California Press.

Godoi, Rafael. (2016). *Intimacy and power: Body searches and intimate visits in the prison system of São Paulo, Brazil*. Champ Pénal/Penal Field (Vol. XIII).

Gregory, W. (2011). *An assessment of Venezuela's Bolivarian revolution at twelve years. Venezuelanalysis.com*. Retrieved from: http://venezuelanalysis.com/analysis/5971

Harrison-Conwill, G. (2011). The race toward "Caraqueño" citizenship: Negotiating race, class and participatory democracy. *The Annals of the American Academy of Political and Social Science, 637*, 165–183.
Heredia, Iván Urzaíz. (2009). *Control y Exclusión Social: la ley de vagos y maleantes en el primer Franquismo*. Universo de micromundos. VI Congreso de Historia Local de Aragó (pp. 109–122).
Hernández, T. (1977). *La ideologización del delito y de la pena (un caso venezolano: la Ley sobre Vagos y Maleantes)*. Caracas: Instituto de Ciencias Penales y Criminológicas, Facultad de Ciencias Jurídicas y Políticas, Universidad Central de Venezuela.
Human Rights Watch. (1997). *Punishment before trial: Prison conditions in Venezuela*. New York: Human Rights Watch.
Lombardi, J. V. (1971). *The decline and abolition of negro slavery in Venezuela, 1820–1854*. University of Texas: Greenwood Publishing.
Mallett-Outtrim, Ryan. (2013, November 27). 30,000 more security cameras and 17,000 less guns on Venezuelan streets. Venezuelanalysis.com http://venezuelanalysis.com/news/10198
Mignolo, W. & Tlostanova, M. (2000). *Local histories/global designs: Coloniality*. Subaltern Knowledges and Border-Thinking: Princeton University Press.
Mignolo, W., & Tlostanova, M. (2009). Global coloniality and the decolonial option. *Epistemologies of Transformation, 6*, 130–147. Rolskilde University, Copenhaguen.
Müller, M.-M. (2010). The Universal and the particular in Latin American penal state formations. In P. Squires & J. Lea (Eds.), *Criminalisation and advanced marginality: Critically exploring the work of Loïc Wacquant*. Bristol: Policy Press.
Pemberton, S. (2013). "Enforcing gender" the constitution of sex and gender in prison regimes. *Signs, 39*(1), 151–175.
Quijano, A., & Wallerstein, I. (1992, January 01). Americanity as a concept, or the Americas in the modern world-system. *International Social Science Journal, 44*(4), 549.
Quijano, A. (2000). Coloniality of power, euro-centrism and Latin America. *Nepantla: Views from South, 1*(3), 533–580.
Quijano, A. (2008). Occidentalism, globalization and the geopolitics of knowledge. In M. Moraña, E. D. Dussel, & C. A. Jáuregui (Eds.), *Coloniality at large: Latin America and the postcolonial debate*. Durham: Duke University Press.

Salvatore, R. D., & Aguirre, C. (Eds.). (1996). *The birth of the penitentiary in Latin America: Essays on criminology, prison reform, and social control, 1830–1940*. Austin: University of Texas Press.

Sánchez, Rodríguez G. N. (1999). Análisis del discurso de los proyectos de leyes del régimen penitenciario venezolano de 1961 y 1980. *Opción, 15*(28), 59–79.

Segato, R. L. (2007). El color de la cárcel en América Latina: apuntes sobre la colonialidad de la justicia en un continente en desconstrucción. *Nueva Sociedad, 208*, 142–161.

Silva, D. F. (2007). *Toward a global idea of race*. Minneapolis: University of Minnesota Press.

Suárez, Faillace B. E. (1997). *Female criminality : Interviews with inmates in a Venezuelan prison*. Master's thesis, University of Florida.

Taylor, M. L. (2014). Decolonizing mass incarceration: 'Flesh will Wear out Chains'. *Journal for Cultural and Religious Theory, 13*(1), 121–141.

Wacquant, L. (2009a). *Punishing the poor: The neoliberal government of social insecurity*. Durham: Duke University Press.

Wacquant, L. (2009b). *Prisons of poverty* (expanded ed.). Minneapolis: University of Minnesota Press.

Wacquant, L. (2010). Crafting the neoliberal state: Workfare, prisonfare, and social insecurity. *Sociological Forum, 25*(2), 197–220.

Weschler, J., Fellner, J., & Americas Watch Committee (U.S.). (1994). *Venezuela: Prison massacre in maracaibo*. New York: Americas Watch.

Wright, W. R. (1990). *Café con leche: Race, class, and National Image in Venezuela*. Austin: University of Texas.

Part II

Ethnographic Reflexivity

8

The *Mata Escura* Penal Compound: An Analysis of the Prison-Neighbourhood Nexus in Northeast Brazil

Hollis Moore

The Entrance

At the entrance to the penal compound is a guards' base. Its bulletproof windows exhibit the scars of a shootout. In front of the entrance runs a line of dirt-filled barrels serving as crude anti-ram bollards. These artifacts are constitutive components of the compound's boundary, a boundary that embodies and anticipates its own breach. People who spend time in and around this compound know it exceeds this tenuous shell in significant ways. Moreover, beyond the compound's imposing entrance, its edges are strikingly indeterminate. The compound's limits are neither obvious nor absolute. This quality is distilled in the figure of the prison vendor.

Those who arrive at the compound's entrance anytime during the day, are greeted by a dozen or so vendors. Vendors set up shop under bus shelters on either side of the thoroughfare running past the entrance. Some

H. Moore (✉)
Carleton University, Ottawa, ON, Canada

S. Darke et al. (eds.), *Carceral Communities in Latin America*, Palgrave Studies in Prisons and Penology, https://doi.org/10.1007/978-3-030-61499-7_8

vendors have *barracas* (stands), others hawk their wares out of wheelbarrows. Most live in *Mata Escura*, the low-income neighbourhood that abuts the compound. Though these vendors are not officially sanctioned by compound authorities, they nonetheless participate in its day-to-day operations. Consider the experiences and contributions of Dani and Michelle.[1]

Dani, explains how she ended up working here.

> I used to sell my merchandise door-to-door. It was very tiring. Up and down the *ladeiras* (sloping streets). Then, when my husband *caiu preso* [was imprisoned], I started selling to other visitors *lá embaixo* [down below – *in* the compound]. I just stayed in front [of the prison she was supposed to be visiting] and only worked a few days a week [designated visitation days]. This was way easier and I earned more…

When Dani's husband was transferred to a prison located elsewhere, her status as a visitor authorized to enter the compound was revoked. But this temporary setback was ultimately a boon to her business. She relocated her point of sale to the compound entrance where she expanded her customer base and hours of operation. Now she encounters visitors destined for *all* of the compound's seven prisons. Gradually her business grew and, today, she monopolizes an entire bench and sells a would-be catalogue of women's clothing and accessories (e.g., tight jeans, embellished jersey tops, shoes, purses, sexy underwear, hair scrunches, etc.). Dani is the only vendor who sells fashion items, a costlier venture than snacks and drinks. Her array of pretty and pleasing indulgences offers a welcome distraction to bored and belittled female visitors, too drained after the labour of visitation to trek to Salvador's central commercial district.

Like most other vendors, in addition to selling goods, Dani also provides services for a fee. For example, she stores possessions that visitors are not permitted to bring with them into the prisons. The list of prohibited objects is long but the main items that visitors pay to store are purses, cell phones, make-up, and luggage (brought by out-of-town visitors arriving at the compound directly from the long-distance bus terminal). Inside the compound, most of the prisons do not offer visitors access to secure storage.[2] Thus, vendors like Dani step up to meet demand.

Some vendors offer a delivery service. For a fee, they haul visitors' heavy packages of food, hygiene products, and other goods to the prisons. Michelle, for example, uses her wheelbarrow to transport loads partway into the compound. She has worked here for many years and is known to prison staff. Although it is against prison rules for anyone without formal authorization to access the compound, Michelle has negotiated an informal agreement with guards stationed at the entrance. She can travel roughly 300 meters into the compound until she reaches "the tunnel." The tunnel is a dilapidated structure on the side of a dirt road, situated halfway between the main entrance and the compound's largest prison—*Penitenciária Lemos de Brito* (PLB). The tunnel consists of a covered bench and a very run-down bathroom no longer maintained by the state.

The tunnel happens to demarcate an invisible boundary. It is here where Michelle stops and transfers her cargo to a *fardo azul* (blue-uniformed PLB prisoner on work detail). *Fardos azuis* may only venture as far from PLB (and as close to the compound entrance) as the tunnel, though no one is actually monitoring them very closely. On the mornings of visitation days, a small group of these men sit in the shade of the tunnel waiting to be hired to transport visitors' purchases the remaining distance to PLB's four scattered cellblocks.

In this paper, I explore the edges of imprisonment as they manifest in my field site.[3] The figure of the vendor is suggestive of the complexity and richness of these edges. As a visible example of the way locals traverse carceral spaces and engage imprisonment to make ends meet, vendors reveal how imprisonment is woven into the fabric of poor urban neighbourhoods. Dani reminds us that the compound exerts a certain pull, drawing outsiders into this simultaneously stigmatizing and stabilizing social milieu. And, as Michelle's routine illustrates, the boundaries dividing the insides and outsides of carceral spaces—carceral "interfaces" (da Cunha 2014)—are less singular, apparent, and well-defined than we might expect. What does it mean to take the interfaces between the interior world(s) of the prison and the ecology of its social, economic, and urban exterior more seriously?

I attend carefully to such interfaces, approaching them as a window onto the prison-neighbourhood nexus, a "carceral form"[4] of great contemporary importance in this era of "hyperincarceration" (Wacquant 2010). I begin with a brief discussion of "carceral forms" and the heuristic value of this framing, especially in the context of uneven carceral expansion. I then trace the contours of a particular carceral form—namely, the prison-neighbourhood nexus as it manifests within my field site. To grasp this form, I focus on peri-carceral space and examine the material and symbolic flows and stoppages that connect the compound with its proximate sociospatial environment.[5]

Hyperincarceration, Carceral Forms, and the Prison-Neighbourhood Nexus

Between 1997 and 2007, the prison population in Brazil grew faster than that of any other country in the Americas (Walmsley 2010). In a single decade, it more than doubled. By 2011, a total of 515,000 individuals were incarcerated in Brazil. This translates into an incarceration rate of 270 per 100,000 members of the population (Murray et al. 2013). The confined population is overwhelmingly composed of economically dispossessed young men with low educational qualifications (Wacquant 2008: 63; Murray et al. 2013). These young men are usually from low-income, heavily penalized urban neighbourhoods, such as *Mata Escura*.[6] I describe this phenomenon in terms of "*hyper*incarceration" rather than "*mass* incarceration" because the inflation of prison populations that has occurred in most liberal democracies over the past quarter-century has disproportionately affected particular social groups.[7] In fact, triple selectivity—by class, ethno-racial identity, and place—"is a constitutive property of the phenomenon" (Wacquant 2010: 78). Precipitous carceral expansion "is socially tolerable and therefore workable as public policy only *so long as it does not reach the masses*" (ibid.).

My research examines how increasing rates of imprisonment, and the concentration of carceral effects, shape social relations and imaginaries in Northeast Brazil. Uneven rates and patterns of hyperincarceration mean that for some groups the prison is becoming one of the primary institutions that structures experience. Yet, prison studies scholars have traditionally sought to understand the social realities of imprisonment through theoretical and methodological frameworks that construct the prison as a "world apart" (da Cunha 2008). Until recently, the ethnographic study of imprisonment has primarily been dominated by four models: the "prisonization" model (Clemmer 2004 [1940]; Comfort 2008); the "functional-adaptive" or "total institution" model (Sykes 1958; Sykes and Messinger 1960; Goffman 1961); the "importation" model (Irwin and Cressey 1962; Giallombardo 1966; Kruttschnitt et al. 2000); and the "prison in wider society" model (Jacobs 1977). These paradigms have informed numerous studies and set the terms of intellectual debates regarding experiences of imprisonment and carcerality itself. Simon (2000) suggests that contemporary scholars of the prison ought to be mindful, not only of where early studies diverge, but also of what they have in common. Namely, conventional attempts to synthesize or update classic models often leave the category of 'prison culture' largely intact. Accordingly, scholarship on prisons continues to form objects of inquiry and to delineate field sites that correspond to materially 'obvious' bricks-and-mortar parameters of prisons. The prison emerges as a site in which: (a) sociality and quotidian practices appear to be relatively contained and self-referential and (b) incarceration is understood to *sever* prisoners from external relationships and to interrupt 'normal' routines (Reed 1999, 2003; Owen 1998; Crewe 2005; Rhodes 2001, 2004). Such analytic tendencies can obfuscate deep and unapparent linkages between the prison and its social milieu. As Cunha has noted, this may prevent us from identifying and understanding "the ramifying social effects of concentrated incarceration upon both the prison and heavily penalized lower-class neighbourhoods" (2008: 325). While prisons, with their fixed and unmistakable boundaries, remain spatially distinct features of the contemporary landscape, the "edges of imprisonment" are less clear-cut for prisoners, visitors, and other subjects of hyperincarceration.

In recent years, "the 'prison-society' relation and the articulation between intramural and extramural worlds" (da Cunha 2014: 217) has garnered increasing scholarly attention. A growing number of researchers have begun to document and analyse the inter-dependence of the prison and the world in which it remains embedded. Too often, however, this relation is conceived in terms of "collateral damage" (Wacquant 2002: 388; Comfort 2008: 11). In this formulation, the prison appears as an isolated institution external to the social space that it harmfully intrudes (Wacquant 2002: 388). By positioning the prison as the catalyst of social suffering, scholars risk obfuscating the extent to which: carceral institutions are imbricated with other organizations; harms and hardships endured by those most affected by hyperincarceration stem from sources other than the prison; and practices of imprisonment may not have wholly disintegrative and damaging results. In this chapter, I demonstrate the insufficiency of studying the prison as a world unto itself and the inadequacy of a damage assessment approach by documenting: the historical co-development of the compound and *Mata Escura*; the accomplishments of creative social actors who have managed to shape prison regimes and derive some benefit from their engagements with the compound; as well as material and symbolic continuities underlying the emergence and unity of this assemblage.

In this chapter, I gain analytic purchase over prison-society relations through assemblage theory (Deleuze and Guattari 1988) and a focus on what I call "carceral forms." In short, carceral forms are emergent unities joining together heterogeneous components—namely, elements that have *come* to be distinguished as carceral and other sociocultural phenomena. Carceral forms result from a process of mutual constitution and embody the impossibility of distinguishing absolutely between properly carceral and non-carceral constituent parts. Carceral forms are interrelated and overlapping; they exist at different scales of production and levels of abstraction. Some correspond quite directly with meaningful emic, "socially recognizable" categories, while others are better understood as heuristic theoretical "conceits" that bring otherwise hidden and highly abstract connections into view. This conceptualization of my object of inquiry helps to suspend assumptions about the location and nature of carceral boundaries, rendering "carceral closure" as a processual possibility to be investigated rather than a *fait accompli.*

My analysis of the prison-society relation in terms of carceral forms contributes to a relatively disparate and emergent body of scholarship recently identified as "interface studies" (da Cunha 2014). Ethnographers working in this vein have taken up the challenge to focus on the interfaces shared by prison and 'non-penal spaces' (da Cunha 2004, 2008; Gilmore 2007; Combessie 2002; Comfort 2008; Gowan 2002), interrogating the extent to which life inside and outside the prison is inextricably intertwined and emphasising the curiously *symbiotic* relation between practices of imprisonment and other social institutions. Although this trend is highly significant because it suggests a break from conventional prison studies debates and approaches, the notion of "interface" and its emphasis on and assumption of the "sensitive perimeter of the prison" (Combessie 2002) may conceal: the coextensiveness of the prison and its milieu; contestation of closure or efforts to reimagine "once-carceral space" (Schept 2015: 252); and processes of disconnection and differentiation which prefigure the 'separateness' of prison and society. My analysis of the penal compound and the neighbourhood's common qualities and 'effects,' historical co-production, and constitutive capillary flows (and stoppages) brings processes of becoming, undoing, fusion, and rupture into focus. In what follows, I argue that interfaces *as well as indeterminacy* condition the carceral.

The penal compound introduced at the outset of this chapter, in combination with the adjacent neighbourhood of *Mata Escura*, is helpfully understood as an emblematic instantiation of an increasingly common carceral form: the prison-neighbourhood nexus. The Penitentiary Complex of the State of Bahia (*O Complexo Penitenciário do Estado da Bahia*) is a sprawling penal compound housing the state's largest concentration of prisons and prisoners. In lieu of its proper name, the media and various publics refer to the compound as "*O Complexo da Mata Escura*" (The *Mata Escura* Complex). On one level, this label simply denotes the compound's location. But, talk of the compound that elides "the State" and inserts "*Mata Escura*" is also productive. *Mata Escura* is discursively sutured to the prison as "the State" is backgrounded or rendered not-fully present. Indeed, Brazilian prisons—a fundamental institution of the state apparatus—often appear in popular consciousness as frontier zones just beyond the control of government officials (see French 2013). The naming of the compound alerts us to a way in which it resembles *Mata Escura*: the state conspicuously fails to enforce the law in both of these conjoined spaces. Rather than operate as an aspirational "blue zone" showcasing a high degree of state presence, effective bureaucracy, and a properly functioning legal system (O'Donnell 1993: 1359), the penal compound has become a monument to failure of good governance that seems to index the *limits* of state capacity. These limits are thrown into relief as the integrity of the compound and its workers is unveiled to be thoroughly compromised.

Insecure Boundaries

A relatively low concrete wall extends from the compound entrance to The Center.[8] The compound's strikingly low (and incomplete) perimeter barrier is bemoaned by guards as a shameful symbol of problematic permeability.

On one side of the wall runs the thoroughfare. On the other side, there is thickly forested state-owned land, the compound's verdant margin. Children of the Center fear this forest; three boys once told me they had heard screams emanating from it—the last cries of a murder victim. Generally speaking, residents of Salvador da Bahia (*Soterpolitanos*) are wary of this terrain—the kind that gives *Mata Escura* (Dark Forest) its very name—because it is widely assumed to harbour "bandits." Note, the threatening figures presumed to inhabit this forest are not escaped convicts but local opportunists taking advantage of the coverage and isolation this margin offers. The penal compound's low wall demarcates, without effectively securing, its territory. The wall *is* successful in one important respect though. As an announcement of the state's usage of (or intent to use) this land, it has largely prevented further encroachment by people looking to build homes in the region. In fact, the wall was built, primarily, to protect state property from its appropriation by "insurgent citizens" (Holston 2008). The problem of carceral permeability, in this case, derives more from the desire to protect state property from common appropriation—keeping the public out and the possibility of future prison construction here alive—than from concern over "public security" and keeping prisoners in.

Across the road from the compound entrance is a significantly higher wall which surrounds the compound's "open regime"[9] prison. Guards bitterly point out the irony that an open-regime prison—which requires all prisoners to leave for work on a daily basis (Monday to Friday)—is "effectively secured." Years ago, funds were allegedly allocated to construct a similarly high and complete wall around the main part of the compound. However, guards tell me this secure perimeter never materialized because "someone ate the funds."[10] The sorry status of the penal compound's enclosure presents a symbolically-charged, counter-intuitive image of the prison to *Soteropolitano* observers. Guards, for instance, claim that it is actually *illegal* to wall-in an open-regime prison.

On the far side of the penal compound, another major thoroughfare—*Avenida Gal Costa*—hems in the carceral form. Travellers along this road have a good view of the compound's prisons perched up on a forested hill. One of these—the Special Disciplinary Unit (UED)—is a maximum-security prison reserved for men identified as the state's most dangerous prisoners, namely, members of state and national-level prison-based drug trafficking organizations (Lourenço and de Almeida 2013; Penglase 2008; Leeds 1996).

In April 2013, in the early hours of the morning, men incarcerated in UED broke locks, exited their cells, and detonated an explosive to fell the door of their cellblock. Meanwhile, a small band of armed accomplices, some disguised as police officers, crept through the forest and managed to subdue military police stationed in a guard tower. Ultimately, the escape attempt was stymied because the cellblock door withstood the explosion. The armed band of invaders, having already neutralized the exterior patrol, retreated back through to the forest. But they did not leave the penal compound empty-handed. They left with weapons commandeered from their temporary captives.

In media coverage of this escape attempt, a city councillor is quoted remonstrating that UED, like the compound more generally, is not surrounded by a wall: "There are fences. Any person knows that beyond UED there is a forest that ends at the edge of [the road], and this is exactly the route the bandits took to arrive and escape" (Bocão News 2013). After the incident, police found two stolen cars abandoned on *Avenida Gal Costa.* One of the cars contained a discarded police uniform.

This was not an isolated incident; escapes and attempted escapes from the compound are relatively regular occurrences. However, this particular case draws attention to a common concern that is expressed about prisons, police/prison guards, and low-income peripheral neighbourhoods like *Mata Escura*: their vulnerability vis-à-vis crime. Understaffed and infrastructurally-inadequate prisons do not reliably *contain* prisoners or redress the fear of crime. Rather, Brazilian prisons are widely perceived to exacerbate insecurity by, for example, incubating and enabling notorious organizations of criminals (see Biondi 2016). Likewise, police/guards are incapable of preventing incursions by well-armed bandits. And, just as funds allocated for a secure perimeter wall were "eaten," so to may police be consumed by corruption. In Brazil, the boundary dividing police and bandits is in fact so problematic that an intermediary figure has emerged—the *policial-bandido* (police-bandit) (Goldstein 2003: 188; Caldeira 2002: 249). The police uniform found inside one of the abandoned vehicles invites suspicion about its origins. The status of the guards taken captive by the invaders also raises questions of complicity and corruption; while they claim to have been beaten, it seems they did not in fact sustain serious injuries (Bocão News 2013).

Agentes Penitenciários (guards) assigned to particular prison units regularly accuse the military police charged with patrolling the compound's perimeter of incompetence and corruption. At a public meeting organized by the *agentes'* union, there was much talk of how exactly contraband flows so readily into the prisons. Shifting attention from their own possible roles in such violations, *agentes* drew attention to visitors' vaginas and a dearth of modern security technology (e.g., x-ray machines and working metal detectors). When the spectre of large machetes was raised as proof that visitors are not solely responsible for the entry of contraband, *agentes* shifted the blame again, explaining how cellblocks' open-air structure permits large items to be thrown inside by prisoners' allies hidden in the forest. This possibility hinges on inadequate securitization of the compound. Guards allege that some military police tasked with this duty are paid or extorted to look the other way as bandits approach and breach the units.[11]

The problematic nature of public authorities and institutions within the prison-neighbourhood nexus gives rise to multiple insecurities, including the insecure boundaries of the penal compound. But insecurity, unequally distributed throughout the population, is also a condition of this carceral form's emergence. In the following section, I consider this emergence, charting the historical co-development of the penal compound and *Mata Escura*.

The Emergence of a Prison-Neighbourhood Nexus in Salvador

In 1549, Portuguese settler colonists founded Salvador da Bahia and the north-eastern coastal city became the commercial and administrative hub of an Atlantic-orientated economy based on the enslavement of Africans and the export of sugar and other plantation products (Gledhill and Hita 2009: 6). Slavery, as well as colonial land distribution patterns, have shaped social relations (Brown 2000) and the emergence of a prison-neighbourhood nexus in contemporary Brazil.

In the nineteenth century, Imperial Brazil resembled a patchwork of small villages, parishes, and large plantations (the legacy of colonial land grants and the diversity of local territorial claims). During this period, the forested area where *Mata Escura* is currently located supplied water to the surrounding region. It was also the site of *quilombos*—settlements of run-away enslaved peoples (Amado 2007)—as well as *terreiros*—"sacred place[s] of worship for Candomblé practitioners" (Perry 2013: 30). In 1880, a private company purchased part of this land from plantation owners and constructed two dams which supplied water to the growing city of Salvador until 1987.

In 1950, construction began on PLB. This prison, the first public institution in the area, was erected amid a vast expanse of uncultivated land. A shantytown emerged in its shadow which, over time, developed into *Mata Escura*. Until the early 1960s, there was no road access to *Mata Escura* from the city center. At least part of the 10-km journey had to be made on foot. The distance and isolation of this area from the city center were principle factors motivating officials to acquire the land for prison construction (see, e.g., Combessie 2002). Major infrastructure improvements, including the extension of power lines and roads to the area, did not occur until the early 1970s. These improvements were not, of course, primarily intended to benefit residents of *Mata Escura* (Oliveira 2012: 73). New roads, for example, did not bring public transportation with them; PLB staff relied on an employee shuttle service to/from the city.

In the late 1970s and 1980s, Bahia's prison system began to expand; PLB was enlarged and new prisons were constructed in its vicinity. During this period, there was a total absence of prisons in the interior of the state; Bahia's entire penal population was concentrated in the capital (primarily in "the *Mata Escura* Complex"). People migrated to *Mata Escura* to be in proximity of imprisoned relations, contributing to the neighbourhood's creation, consolidation, and development (Conceição Silva 2014). Of course, the pull of the prison was not the only factor that brought people to *Mata Escura*. In particular, urban revitalization of central and coastal areas of the city has etailed "the violent demolition of homes and the mass explusion and displacement" of people from prime inner-city land to the city's distant and underserviced periphery (Perry 2013: 9). In the 1990s, even as Bahia's prison system entered a phase of systematic "interiorization" (which has entailed the construction of 14 prisons in the interior of the state), *Mata Escura* and 'its' penal compound continued to grow. Today, in addition to PLB, the compound contains six separately administered prisons confining a total of approximately 3200 men and 200 women.

As is the case with other neighbourhoods of the *periferia* (periphery), marginalized zones typically situated on the outskirts of Brazilian cities, a significant portion of *Mata Escura*'s growth was informal and 'unplanned.' People appropriated and occupied unused land (a process known as "invasion" in Brazil), gradually auto-constructing their own houses and infrastructure (see Holston 1991). At the beginning of the twentieth century, 70 percent of the Brazilian population inhabited the countryside; by the turn of the century, over 70 percent were urban dwellers. Brazilian cities subsequently developed in an unjust, disorderly, and illegal manner. As elites modernized city centers, "they expelled the working poor and forced them to reside in undeveloped hinterlands… [usually] in precarious and typically illegal conditions" (Holston 2008: 8).

Yet, rapidly expanding periphery regions (or "*favela*" zones) also frightened urban elites (Skidmore 2009: 138). The association of these communities—"where the majority of [B]lack working-class people live in

Brazil's major cities" (Smith 2016: 2)—with the illicit extended beyond the issue of usurped land. Historically, *favelas* have been represented as enclaves of lawlessness and major *sources* of social problems. The media, experts, and politicians tend to depict them "...as a perversion of the city's social, moral, and economic order" (Hayes 2011: 81). The space of the *favela* itself is associated with crowded, unsanitary conditions that breed disease and crime; it is often represented as a safe harbour for illegal activities "populated by vagrants, drunks, criminals, prostitutes, and other social undesirables" (ibid.). In short, it has been common for the periphery to be problematized as criminogenic.

In the case of *Mata Escura*, the taint of the illicit far surpasses this general "territorial stigmatization" (Wacquant 2007): the neighbourhood has suffered from image problems over harbouring a prison in its very center (Caldas et al. 2007: 16). Amado observes that "[t]he prison serves as a reference, saddling the community with a marginal identity, which diminishes local self-esteem" (2007—my translation). *Mata Escura* is inextricably linked to the penal compound in the popular imagination. Many understand the neighbourhood as fundamentally *of* the prison more than as a distinct and relatively independent *neighbouring* entity.

By approaching *Mata Escura* as part of a carceral form, I have been able to grasp the shared history and meaning of the neighbourhood and penal compound. Before there was an "interface," there was an imminent carceral form, pre-conditioned by transnational anti-Black violence (Smith 2016), patterns of socio-economic inequality and responses to it by officials, elites, and the poor. In the final section of this chapter, I present an ethnographic account of subterranean and symbolic flows of people and things constitutive of this prison-neighbourhood nexus. This account highlights features of carceral forms—namely, their co-authorship by targets of the criminal justice system and the extent to which their closure is contested—that are important to those of us struggling to destabilize dominant carceral logics.

Flows and Stoppages Constitutive of the Carceral

Today, formerly incarcerated people and prison visitors continue to establish residences in *Mata Escura*. Posters around the compound entrance advertise rooms available for rent. I knew of a few relatively mobile young women (wives of prisoners in the early phases of marriage) who, at least temporarily, took up residence in the vicinity of the compound. One such woman, Taise (28), explained how renting a room nearby was not a purely pragmatic decision: "At night I can see the lights of [the cellblock] when we talk,[12] when I cook him a meal [that she will bring on her next visit]. I can see his light and I can sleep because he is close."

Taise, ultimately, relinquished her rented room. Following a very rocky period in her marriage, she happily told me that she and her incarcerated husband were expecting their first child (together). Pregnant, Taise became more enmeshed with her affines and began living with them in another area of the city.

Rymunda (52), another wife of an incarcerated man, has also taken up residence in *Mata Escura*. Unlike Taise, Rymunda had been married to her husband for years before his imprisonment. They have three children together and hail from a rural area in the interior of the state. Due to the prohibitive distance separating their home from the capital, Rymunda and her sons are only able to visit when time and money permit them to stay in Salvador for month-long stretches. During such stints (which generally overlap with school holidays), Rymunda and her youngest son, Enrique (7), stay within walking distance of the compound. They rent a small one-room brick outbuilding in the back garden of "Sr. Antonio's" family home. The room contains a bed, an old stove, an empty fuel tank covered with a sheet, and a single shelf.

On the agreed-upon day of my visit, the garden is lush and cool, shaded by mature fruit trees. The trees' branches droop under the weight of almost-ripe mangos and five different species of banana. The area is pleasantly smoky. *O Senhor* is tending a campfire because, at the moment, he is out of fuel. Enrique and three other boys are in the midst of a water fight in the outdoor bathing area. They emerge, dripping and naked, asking for change to buy a Popsicle. Rymunda scolds them for splashing (dirty) water back into the well before she allows me to give them money to buy us all popsicles from a neighbour's household shop. Accustomed to water shortages typical of Bahia's semi-arid interior, Rymunda is appreciative of Sr. Antonio's two-meter-deep well: "here we never lack water." This is one of a few reasons Rymunda is contemplating a more permanent move to *Mata Escura.*

Generally speaking, residents of *Mata Escura rarely* lack water. When the public water company (*EMBASA*) first extended infrastructure to the area, the pipes only ran as far as the prison. Enterprising residents bought their own materials and were permitted, by profiteering police and prison administrators, to "pirate" (Telles and Hirata 2007) the prison's water supply and extend pipes to their households. This, as one research participant recalled, involved excavation of pipes "at the prison's front door." Then, state actors, acting unofficially, proceeded to extract fixed monthly fees from residents of the growing neighbourhood. Now, years later, water redirected from the prison is free to those who are connected to this covert infrastructure.

Eventually, EMBASA extended a legal water supply to the neighbourhood itself. The presence of an alternative licit resource stream undermined the system of monthly pay-offs. Residents now had a choice and were in a position to denounce state agents' corruption and alert the media.

Today, the majority of *Mata Escura do* pay monthly water bills. However, there still exists a covert network of underground pipes enabling many residents to pay a "*taxa minima*" (minimum rate). Some households have two water taps: one that is connected to a billing meter and one that spouts prison water, compliments of the state. Those who can afford to be official consumers strategically use *both* taps, for example, drawing cooking water from the official tank and using a clandestine tap in the garden for everything else. This allows them to avoid the scrutiny of water company investigators. Additionally, receiving monthly water bills can be helpful when one is required to demonstrate proof of address, a common demand of many bureaucratic rituals. The case of the pirated prison water reveals the deep interconnection of the compound and the neighbourhood. Moreover, the presence of an illicit subterranean infrastructure produced by local residents reminds us how difficult it is to determine where the carceral begins and ends.

Salvador's topography helps to condition the carceral form. The city expanded out from its center over a series of hills and ridges (Gledhill and Hita 2009: 10). Senhor Antonio's house—where Rymunda and Enrique stay—is located at the base of a valley in the part of *Mata Escura* residents call "*Inferninho*" (or "little hell"). This area, abutting the tall grey wall of the compound's open-regime prison, is the zone of *Mata Escura* most strongly associated with imprisonment. Around 5000 people live on *Inferninho's* twenty *travessas* (lanes). Sandoval, a resident of *Mata Escura*, shared an account of the origins of the area's name:

> Many years ago in *inferninho* there lived prisoners who had left [the prison]. They had control over the location and police couldn't enter. Even people from other areas couldn't enter. Now the situation has improved. Prisoners died, the power of the state arrived, and there has been an influx of *moradores de boa indole* [residents with strength of character] with good conduct who do the right thing on the side of the law and *justice.*

To walk to/from the main entrance of the penal compound (an exhausting 15-minute journey, more like a hike than a walk), Rymunda and Enrique must ascend and descend a series of steep and narrow footpaths which, in many places, have been roughly paved by the residents themselves. The rippling effect of hand-poured concrete provides traction for those who negotiate these slippery slopes. Rymunda and Enrique navigate flooded patches by jumping or picking their way across makeshift balance beams. Towards the bottom of the hill a felled door bridges a filthy stream of sewage running between two concrete houses. Marilene, a resident of one of these houses, complains that she is still suffering from a sinus infection caused by rank fumes. She continues to decry the situation, explaining that a neighbour's child recently died after a rat bite. With an expansive gesture, she attributes the death to "these conditions." Indeed, regular flooding encourages zoonotic diseases, such as Dengue and Dengue Haemorrhagic Fever, to flourish in the area. Marilene recalls that during the rainy season it was impossible to sleep at night because of the mosquitoes: "The lids popped off the sewers and it was like a river down here. The sewage flows down from the prison. It's impossible to walk at night." *Mata Escura is literally saturated by excessive and mismanaged prison waste to the point that some residents are nocturnally confined within their homes.*

The presence of the penal compound may amplify *Mats Escurans*' vulnerability to life-threatening health risks in yet another manner. The municipal government considers *Mata Escura* an area at risk of a Dengue epidemic. This diagnosis intersects consequentially with the neighbourhood's reputation as a violent, crime-ridden incubator of risk—problematically analogous to the prisons it adjoins. Violence, or its perception, impedes the efforts of health workers to combat the spread of infectious diseases within certain areas. Workers are advised to suspend their projects and leave the location immediately should they feel endangered (*O Correio* 28/06/2012). The director of Epidemeological Security at the State Health Ministry has identified "*tráfico e a criminalidade*" (drug trafficking and criminality) as the greatest obstacle to effective dengue prevention (ibid.).

Even among some local residents, *Mata Escura*, specifically *Inferninho,* is considered to be a relatively violent space. The following headline and excerpt from *Massa!,* Salvador's most pulpy tabloid (primarily marketed to and read by the city's poorest), touts the imprisonment of an *Inferninho* resident in an illustrative manner. Note the paper's play on the word "hell".

> [Headline:] Upon arrest, Chris, a resident of *Inferninho*, simply moves from one hell to another.
>
> Chris goes to prison hell: The guy is the official killer of the gang of traffickers of *Inferninho*, Mata Escura.
>
> General Panic – Local residents of *Inferninho* report, on the condition of anonymity, fear of living in an area with disputes between dealers. "They do not mess with us, but there is a fear of being on the street when there is a shootout...," says a street vendor. "They go around armed right over there..." says a retired man. (*Massa*! 05/12/2012 – underlining my own.)

I had lived in *Mata Escura* for months before I began to go "*lá embaixo*" (down there—to/through *Inferninho*), always accompanied, always during the day. Teens at the Center assured me: "it's only dangerous for *caguetes, X-9* [snitches, police informants]. It's fine if you go, see, and leave it [what you see] there." One afternoon, I paid a visit to Vania (47) in *Inferninho*; the father of her 4-year-old is incarcerated in the penal compound. Our interview was cut short when she received a call from him. She apologized for the interruption and instructed her daughter Estephanie (9) to escort me back up the hill. As we walked through the narrow, winding streets we passed a group of young men lounging against a low wall. The smell of marijuana was strong. I averted my eyes, hoping they would recognize me as part of The Center. Many residents of *Inferninho* have had positive experiences with the Center which, in addition to sheltering children with incarcerated parents, operates a daycare that serves its wards as well as members of the wider community. The nun who runs the Center, aims to integrate rather than isolate sheltered children and, in the process, offers assistance to poor residents in need of support.

Rymunda (Sr. Antonio's tenent) tells me that she is thinking of relocating more permanently to *Mata Escura*, at least until her husband is released. Times are tough in the interior and travel back-and-forth is tiring, costly, and disruptive to Enrique's schooling. School absences are particularly problematic because they can trigger an interruption and/or suspension of monthly *Bolsa Família* (federal cash transfer) payments. Rymunda has heard of the Center and the kinds of support the nun is 'rumoured' to extend to families of (ex-)prisoners living in the area. For example, Sister Adele has helped formerly incarcerated people find employment and housing; she has invited neighbourhood children and youth to participate in *reforço* (after-school study sessions) and other programs at the center; and she has provided *cestas básicas* (staple food baskets meant to last a month) to people in need. Rymunda muses: "I could find work if the Sister would watch Enrique when he's not in school."[13]

While *Mata Escura*'s close association with the prison may deter some service providers and outreach workers, the long-standing problematization of this neighbourhood has also attracted various charitable agencies and given rise to certain targeted interventions. Similarly, both virulent waste and valued resources flow from the penal compound. Ultimately, the concentration of state agents and institutions within the prison-neighbourhood nexus give rise to insecurity as well as opportunity for guards, inmates, visitors, vendors, and others to creatively negotiate the edges of imprisonment.

In our ethnographic investigations of imprisonment, by moving from 'prison culture' to prison interfaces to carceral forms, I suggest we are best able to understand the dynamics and diffuse reverberations of hyperincarceration throughout the social landscape. Carceral forms permit a dual, but non-binary, way of viewing prison interiors and exteriors, or prisons and their contexts, without re-inscribing the prison as a primarily pathological "world apart" in which captives construct society. Conceptualizing a plurality of carceral forms helps us to make sense of the experiences of growing numbers of people whose lives are intensely entangled with prisons. These subjects of hyperincarceration work with and against carceral logics, living their lives in a manner that extends but also exceeds, and possibly transforms, the carceral.

Notes

1. Names of research participants have been modified to preserve anonymity. All conversations took place in Portuguese. Translations are my own.
2. Elsewhere, I describe a project mounted by the men incarcerated in a specific cellblock. Following a prison-wide ban on purses, they accumulated funds, coordinated with prison administrators, and had a visitor waiting area—complete with a bank of lockers—constructed at the cellblock entrance.
3. This analysis is based on 17 months of ethnographic fieldwork conducted in and around the aforementioned penal compound from 2010 to 2012. I use the ethnographic present when I am able to draw directly from field notes written during this period.
4. Carceral from the Latin *Carcer* ("a prison") + *-al* ("of, pertaining to"). Foucault (1977) concludes the fourth and final part of *Discipline and Punish*, on "Prison", with a chapter on "The Carceral". Here he writes of a "carceral archipelago" that transports "the penitentiary technique" from the penal institution throughout the social body.
5. This chapter was written in 2015 and reflects my thinking at the time. It takes inspiration from Wacquant's provocative account of how the U.S. "Ghetto and Prison Meet and Mesh" (2001, 2002).

6. *Mata Escura* is a poor Black neighbourhood located on the outskirts of Salvador da Bahia (pop. 2.675 million), capital of the north-eastern state of Bahia.
7. Alves (2014) contextualizes Brazil's uneven carceral expansion within the country's enduring system of anti-Black racism.
8. While carrying out the ethnographic research upon which this analysis is based, I lived next door to the compound at *Centro Nova Semente* (henceforth: "the Center"), a shelter for children with incarcerated parents that was founded by an Italian nun.
9. In Brazil, convicted prisoners are sentenced to serve time in closed, open, or semi-open regimes. Officially, prisoners are meant to progress through these regimes in preparation for release.
10. "*Alguem comeu as verbas*"—a popular expression to indicate corruption or misspending.
11. Garces has written about similar dynamics in Ecuador's prisons (2014:3).
12. Taise's husband*, like many incarcerated men, has access to a contraband cell phone.
13. In Brazil, public schools have two daily sessions. Students attend either before or after lunch. This makes it very difficult for parents of young children (viz., mothers) to work. Someone must be available to accompany children to/from school, provide them with lunch, and supervise them for the portion of the day when they are not in school. The crisis of child supervision is even more acute in neighbourhoods with an active gang culture; parents fear their children will be caught in the crossfire or recruited into a marginal lifestyle (see Millar 2014).

References

Alves, J. A. (2014). On mules and bodies: Black captivities in the Brazil racial democracy. *Critical Sociology, 42*(2), 229–248.

Amado, D. (2007). Desenvolvimento Social na Mata Escura: uma abordagem a partir do LTECS. *IV Simpósio de Excelência em Gestão e Tecnologia Associação Educacional Dom Bosco*. Web. 29 Nov 2012.

Biondi, K. (2016). *Sharing this walk: An ethnography of prison life and the PCC in Brazil.* J. F. Collins, Ed. and Trans. Chapel Hill: University of North Carolina Press.

Bocão News. (2013, April 1). *Unidade invadida por bandidos abriga os presos mais perigosos da Bahia*. Web. 14 Aug 2020.
Brown, A. K. (2000). 'A black mark on our legislation': Slavery, punishment, and the politics of death in nineteenth-century Brazil. Special Issue, State, Society, and Political Culture in Nineteenth-Century Brazil, *Luso-Brazilian Review*, *37*(2), 95–121.
Caldas, A., et al. (2007). Tecnologia Social: Cooperação Universidade/Comunidade Para o Desenvolvimento Urbano Regional e Local Sustentável. *Revista de Desenvolvimento Econômico, 16*, 16–25.
Caldeira, T. (2002). The paradox of police violence in democratic Brazil. *Ethnography, 3*(3), 235–263.
Clemmer, D. (2004 [1940]). Prisonization. In *Classics of criminology*. 3rd ed. J. Jacoby, Ed. Long Grove: Waveland Press.
Combessie, P. (2002). Marking the carceral boundary. *Ethnography, 3*(4), 535–555.
Comfort, M. (2008). *Doing time together: Love and family in the shadow of the prison*. Chicago: University of Chicago Press.
Crewe, B. (2005). Prisoner society in the era of hard drugs. *Punishment and Society, 7*(4), 457–481.
da Cunha, M. I. P. (2004). From neighbourhood to prison: Women and the war on drugs in Portugal. In J. Sudbury (Ed.), *Global lockdown: Race, gender and the prison industrial complex*. New York: Routledge.
da Cunha, M. I. P. (2008). Closed circuits: Kinship, neighbourhood and incarceration in urban Portugal. *Ethnography, 9*(3), 325–350.
da Cunha, M. I. P. (2014). The ethnography of prisons and penal confinement. *Annual Review of Anthropology, 43*, 217–233.
da Telles, V. S., & Hirata, D. V. (2007). Cidade e práticas urbanas: nas fronteiras incertas entre o ilegal, o informal e o ilícito. *Estudos Avançados, 21*(61), 173–191.
Deleuze, G., & Guattari, F. (1988). *A thousand plateaus: Capitalism and schizophrenia*. London: Athlone Press.
Foucault, M. (1977 [1975]). *Discipline and punish: The birth of the prison*. A. Sheridan, Trans. New York: Pantheon.
French, J. H. (2013). Rethinking police violence in Brazil: Unmasking the public secret of race. *Latin American Politics and Society, 55*(4), 161–181.
Garces, C. (2014). Denuding surveillance at the carceral boundary. *South Atlantic Quarterly, 113*(3), 447–473.

Giallombardo, R. (1966). *Society of women: A study of a women's prison*. New York: Wiley.
Gilmore, R. W. (2007). *Golden gulag: Prisons, crisis, and opposition in globalizing California*. Berkeley: University of California Press.
Gledhill, J., & Hita, M. (2009). *Anthropologies of the urban periphery: Salvador, Bahia* (BWPI working paper 97). University of Manchester, Brooks World Poverty Institute.
Goffman, E. (1961). *Asylums; essays on the social situation of mental patients and other inmates*. New York: Anchor Books.
Goldstein, D. M. (2003). *Laughter out of place: Race, class, violence, and sexuality in a Rio shantytown*. Berkeley: University of California Press.
Gowan, T. (2002). The nexus: Homelessness and incarceration in two American cities. Theme issue, The Ethnography of the Prison, *Ethnography* 3(4): 500–534.
Hayes, K. E. (2011). *Holy harlots: Femininity, sexuality, and black magic in Brazil*. Berkeley: University of California Press.
Holston, J. (1991). Autoconstruction in working-class Brazil. *Cultural Anthropology, 6*(4), 447–465.
Holston, J. (2008). *Insurgent citizenship: Disjunctions of democracy and modernity in Brazil*. Princeton: Princeton University Press.
Irwin, J., & Cressey, D. (1962). Thieves, convicts and the inmate culture. *Social Problems, 10*(2), 142–155.
Jacobs, J. (1977). *Stateville: The penitentiary in mass society*. Chicago: University of Chicago Press.
Kruttschnitt, C., Gartner, R., & Miller, A. (2000). Doing her own time? Women's responses to prison in the context of the old and the new penology. *Criminology, 38*, 681–718.
Leeds, E. (1996). Cocaine and parallel polities in the Brazilian urban periphery: Constraints on local-level democratization. *Latin American Research Review, 31*(3), 47–83.
Lourenço, L. C., & de Almeida, O. L. (2013). 'Quem quer manter a ordem, quem quer criar desordem' – dinâmicas das gangues prisionais no estado da Bahia. In *35º Encontro Anual da ANPOCS GT 38 – Violência, Criminalidade e Punição no Brasil*.
Millar, K. M. (2014). The precarious present: Wageless labor and disrupted life in Rio De Janeiro, Brazil. *Cultural Anthropology, 29*(1), 32–53.

Murray, J., de Castro Cerqueira, D. R., & Kahn, T. (2013). Crime and violence in Brazil: Systemic review of time trends, prevalence rates and ricks factors. *Aggressive Violent Behaviour, 18*(5), 471–483.

O'Donnell, G. (1993). On the state, democratization and some conceptual problems: A Latin American view with glances at some postcommunist countries. *World Development, 21*(8), 1355–1369.

Oliveira, B. A. (2012). *Presos na Fé: Ethos de um trabalho evangélico dentro da Penitenciária Lemos Brito, de Salvador*. Dissertação de Mestrado. Universidade Federal da Bahia.

Owen, B. (1998). *In the mix: Struggle and survival in a women's prison*. Albany: Suny Press.

Penglase, B. (2008). The bastard child of the dictatorship: The Comando Vermelho and the birth of "Narco culture" in Rio de Janeiro. *Luso-Brazilian Review, 45*(1), 118–145.

Perry, K.-K. Y. (2013). *Black women against the land grab: The fight for racial justice in Brazil*. Minneapolis: University of Minnesota Press.

Reed, A. (1999). Anticipating individuals: Modes of vision and their social consequence in a Papua New Guinean prison. *The Journal of the Royal Anthropological Institute, 5*(1), 43–56.

Reed, A. (2003). *Papua New Guinea's last place: Experiences of constraint in a post colonial prison*. Oxford: Berghahn Books.

Rhodes, L. (2001). Toward and anthropology of prisons. *Annual Review of Anthropology, 30*, 65–83.

Rhodes, L. (2004). *Total confinement: Madness and reason in the maximum security prison*. Berkeley: University of California Press.

Schept, J. (2015). *Progressive punishment: Job loss, jail growth, and the neoliberal logic of carceral expansion*. New York: New York University Press.

Silva, J. M. C. (2014, November 30). Encarcerados. Bairro que cresceu ao lado do presidio da Mata Escura convive com violência. *O Correio*.

Skidmore, T. E. (2009). *Brazil: Five centuries of change*. New York: Oxford University Press.

Smith, C. A. (2016). *Afro-paradise: Blackness, violence and performance in Brazil*. Urbana: University of Illinois Press.

Sykes, G. (1958). *The society of captives: A study in a maximum security prison*. New York: Rinehart.

Sykes, G., & Messinger S. (1960). The Inmate Social System. In R. Cloward et al., (Eds.), *Theoretical studies in social organization of the prison* (pp. 5–19). New York: Social Science Research Council.

Wacquant, L. (2001, April/May). Deadly symbiosis: Rethinking race and imprisonment in twenty-first-century America. *Boston Review, 3*(1), 95–133.
Wacquant, L. (2002). The curious eclipse of prison ethnography in the age of mass incarceration. *Ethnography, 3*(4), 371–397.
Wacquant, L. (2007). Territorial stigmatization in the age of advanced marginality. *Thesis Eleven, 91*(November), 66–77.
Wacquant, L. (2008). The militarization of urban marginality: Lessons from the Brazilian metropolis. *International Political Sociology, 2*, 56–74.
Wacquant, L. (2010). Class, race & hyperincarceration in revanchist America. *Daedalus, 139*, 74–90.
Walmsley, R. (2010). *World prison population list*. London: King's College International Center for Prison Studies.

9

The Community of Believers: Law, Rituals and Magic in a Self-Governed Bolivian Prison

Francesca Cerbini

It was April 2006 when I received the authorization to visit daily the prison of San Pedro, set in the centre of La Paz, in order to carry out my ethnographic research.[1] I was granted access to all the prison sections to converse with my interlocutors without any surveillance nor any time limits, which are factors that frequently hold up fieldwork activities in similar contexts (Cunha 2014).

According to a well-established practice, the penitentiary police merely guarded the entrance of the prison, checking the licit as well as illicit traffic of people and goods crossing the gate, while inside, the inmates could circulate freely, organize their time and manage their space. Dispensing with "the fetishism of law and the enchanted faith in constitution" (Comaroff and Comaroff 2006: 25), they practically live with no rights an independent and self-regulated[2] life, disconnected from any international treaties currently in force on the protection of prisoners.

F. Cerbini (✉)
Centre for Research in Anthropology (CRIA), University of Minho, Braga, Portugal

S. Darke et al. (eds.), *Carceral Communities in Latin America*, Palgrave Studies in Prisons and Penology, https://doi.org/10.1007/978-3-030-61499-7_9

While the penitentiary, as an institution, regulated the relationship between the inmates and the outside world by means of a complicated bureaucracy and a muddled judicial system; inside the confinement, customary laws were enforced, mostly relying on exceptions, informality, privileges and inequalities. These in turn were often the cause of vexations, deprivations, distressing conditions of subjugation and unusual expenditures. For instance, once imprisoned, the inmates had to pay for their "admission" to the prison. These incomes would be passed on to a council of eight inmates elected by the convicts' community, who were in charge of the eight sections in which the jailhouse was divided. Each section had a main gate, some common areas, and cells where people lived and went on with their daily activities. Even though the majority could not afford the minimum living conditions, they still had to care for their basic needs one way or another, since the state did not provide them with either a cell or a bed, and not even enough food to be fed. Moreover, cells were part of some kind of real estate business, so that inmates could rent, build or redevelop the units according to everyone's financial means.

As a rule, the best cells, the most spacious and top furnished, were mainly bought by politicians or drug dealers who sought all the comfort. By the same token, most of the prisoners had to rent a place to live or be hosted by someone who could employ the deprived guests for daily chores, treating them as a sort of servant in exchange for the opportunity to live in their "home". Hence, a few luxury cells and a multitude of hovels lodged according to the two relevant inmate varieties. They both constituted a dichotomous human environment and a rather odd architectural landscape.

Arguably, looking at a panoramic picture of La Paz city centre, it was hard to tell the facility apart from the rest of the city. The former looked like a neighbourhood set in one of the most vibrant urban areas sprawling across business outlets and tourist attractions. San Pedro prison itself resembled a small village where some of the inmates had been tacitly allowed to do time with their wives and children. This kind of mimetic link between the city and the prison thus suggests a review of many concepts: inside and outside, legal and illegal, order and disorder, inclusion and exclusion. It prompts redefining the notion of margins, and its variables, ambiguities and instabilities (Harris 1996; Das and Poole 2004; Greenhouse et al. 2002).

By all means, San Pedro was a real "rattrap" mostly for indigenous people—peasants, labourers, miners, small traders and minor drug dealers—"the disinherited of the colonial policies" described by Segato (2007: 145). Aymara or Quechua were the mother tongues of most inmates, who would hardly ever get used to speaking Spanish. They were socially and economically disadvantaged and could only use their scarce resources to deal with their legal issues and the so called "*abogangsters*"[3] described by the anthropologist Alison Spedding during her imprisonment in a Bolivian jail.

For many inmates coming from rural areas as well as from the city, the language and the internal logic of the law were something utterly unfamiliar until they entered the prison. They were acquainted with the unwritten rules of the indigenous justice system experienced in their communities of origin.[4] Their ideas were rooted in doing justice through the "agreement" and the balance between the parts or *taypi*, that is a typical feature of the traditional justice system, where the concept of punishment is not paramount, nor are the ethical and moral issues concerning the notions of good and evil.

In the Andean world, justice means the removal of discordance, so that harmony can be restored to the community (Fernández Osco 2000; de Sousa Santos and Exeni Rodríguez 2012). As Bazurco Osorio and Exeni Rodríguez (2012: 55–56) emphasize, even though indigenous justice is based on "traditions", "ancient norms" and "ancestral customs",—and thus might seem to be encased in the past—it is in fact rather contemporary and dynamic, resulting from changes, ruptures and transformations in the rural, urban as well as peri-urban environment. Even so, the symbolic value of indigenous justice relies on "uses and customs" as a mighty reference to the communities and social groups' identity. By this perspective, indigenous justice can constitute an antagonistic discourse strategically used to gain a higher degree of self-governance, or else to oppose the state inefficiency. As a matter of fact, people with Aymara and Quechua background are constantly looking for alternatives to the state legal system (see Goldstein 2003), which is considered ineffective to solve legal problems. Most of them consider imprisonment as an unnecessary overload of suffering and a dangerous entanglement in the state apparatus. Accordingly, for many inmates living in San Pedro, to be in jail might be reckoned a consequence of a curse from envious neighbours or relatives. This aetiology of misfortune shapes the entire vision of legal issues, the jailhouse space, and the relationships between inmates and the authorities.

In this scenario, religion, spirituality, beliefs and rituals are securely tied to the world of traditional justice and, in a broader perspective, justice is to be considered a kind of healing practice used to reinstate a dimension of wellness as a whole (Taussig 2004: 126). This bond indeed exemplifies a significant means to resist and survive in such a disordered and violent environment.

The following pages attempt to shed light on how spirituality and rituals are employed to create a community, produce new subjectivities and a certain knowledge of the prison space. I will argue how Andean rituals, magic and witchcraft may offer a system and a practice of order within ambiguous circumstances, where legitimization processes are to be constantly redefined and negotiated and where different powers are set against each other to create or destroy likewise.

Andean Rituals in Prison

The spiritual and religious domain in the prison of San Pedro mirrored faithfully the external society. The facility, which occupied one block of the city of La Paz, was one of the places in the country with the greatest concentration and variety of cults. At the heart of the vestiges of the panoptical[5] structure, an imposing Catholic church dominated the architectural landscape, while the Pentecostals temples[6] were located in strategic areas. They were ideally devised as shelters of decorum, morality and order in stark contrast to the environment of the more ill-famed sections of the prison, where these places of worship generally found space and followers. The strategies of colonization of the prison space by Protestant congregations were similar in the city neighbourhoods and rural communities. Once settled in San Pedro prison, their principal contrast emerged with the indigenous ritualistic tradition—indissolubly tied with the Catholic saints—and especially with the Andean ritual specialist, called, in Aymara language, *yatiri*[7] or *master* (*maestro*).

The *yatiris* played an important role in this self-governed prison, solving a wide range of problems concerning imprisonment. For this reason, they became amongst the most relevant subjects of my ethnography.[8]

I could not participate myself in the rituals held in prison, basically because they were officiated during the night, surreptitiously, away from the notice of the Pentecostals. I knew about their occurrence and I recorded some accurate descriptions of them in the long hours I spent in jail talking with Mariano Vilca, Julio Durán and Nacho Chura, who were inmates, Andean ritual specialists, traditional healers and witchcraft practitioners. They would stealthily perform rituals to help their clients face prison and to facilitate their release.

Within the microcosm of the penitentiary, the *yatiri* would create around himself a community of believers united by the desire to seek a solution to their daily jail problems, to cope with the highest rates of despair, their loneliness and family abandonment. The *yatiri* Julio Durán explained to me: “In here, when for example [men] are left by their wives, they no longer come [to visit them] [...] So you call their *ajayu*[9] and the women come back”.

It was primarily by chewing coca leaves (*pijchar*) on Tuesdays and Fridays, as required by the traditional calendar, that *yatiris* and inmates strengthened their ritualistic relationship. Only then, they set on elaborating in their social circle, ideas and opinions related both to the prison experience and the life conditions everyone left outside. As a client expressed clearly his urgencies, so similar to many other inmates’ concerns: “Will my family abandon me? Is my wife faithful? Are my children all right? The yatiri helps you understand the truth”. Therefore, the *master* would naturally be summoned to help in emergency situations, to cope with the distress typically experienced during the first months in prison, and in any other dire straits afterwards. The ensuing support, the relevant exchange of information, together with the ritual coca leaves chewing, would produce a feeling of belonging amongst the *yatiri’s* followers, besides a network of useful experiences to be applied as a tool to interpret daily life in prison.

The Ritualistic Legal Domain and the Performance of Ritual Offerings for Release

In the Andean cosmology, justice and the extra-human sphere have never been separated. It clearly follows that inmates convinced of the value of certain ritualistic practices considered the *yatiri* as the vehicle of a correct osmosis of principles and norms between the supernatural world and humans, since the *master* is the interpreter and guarantor of the law (Fernández Osco 2000: 90).

Within the community of origin (and beyond), the *yatiri* is usually employed to solve disputes, or to find thieves and murderers through ritualistic tools. As already mentioned, justice rests basically on the principle of harmony. That is why for many *yatiris*, working for the police, or else for an alleged criminal,[10] by and large does not make much difference. In accordance with their professional mandate, they refrain from any ethical judgement on their clients, assisting whoever is in need. Without any prejudice, regardless of their clients' guilt or innocence, they consult the *Pachamama* and the *Achachilas,*[11] which are the most important supernatural entities in this ritualistic legal domain.

In general, the inmate-customers would have already experienced the reading of coca leaves and related remedies even outside the prison and they would be satisfied with the outcome. In this regard, they typically recounted episodes when the *yatiri's* work had been paramount in clarifying difficult situations or in achieving what was required. They then hoped the *yatiri's* help would work again, even in prison, to assess legal matters and to organize spiritual defence strategies. Their hope stretched to such an extent that a client stated: "*The master is the lawyer... to be safe (in prison), right? [...] They do some ch'alladas*[12] *at the Tío,*[13] *at the Pachamama.*[14] *That works, and nothing else*".

The first move in the defence strategy devised by the *yatiri*-lawyer of the inmates consisted of reading the coca leaves. This was essentially when the convict explained to the *master* how the facts had actually occurred, as telling the truth may lead to the best conclusion. The consultation at this stage looked like a proper penitential sacrament by which the client confessed their own hardship, suffering and, quite likely, their crime too, so that the ritualistic session could be the most specific and effective.

Based on the coca leaves' response, the *master* would then craft a ceremonial "pro-freedom offering" (*ofrenda de libertad*), namely to get his client out of prison. The objectives of this kind of ritual offerings are "tailored" on the penal code and could be summed up as follows: to regain freedom either by acquittal or by suspension of the prison term; to achieve release due to the expiry of the custody time limit; to obtain a less severe conviction so as to reduce the jail time originally sentenced to; to get a bail term less severe than expected to pay at the end of jail time.

During the ritual performance, the *yatiri*'s invocations and supplications were filled with technical juridical jargon, evoking the legal proceeding. The very terms "pardon" or *retardación* de *justicia* (release due to expiry of custody time limit) would be invoked with all the power and might of a magic spell.

As a matter of fact, it is worth stressing that the complex language of the penal code would be hardly accessible to the *yatiri* and his clients, who would usually be from poorly educated backgrounds. Essentially, what the prisoners learnt in the attempt to understand their own and other inmates' cases, stemmed from the many rumours circulating in the prison about the functioning mechanisms of official justice. The *yatiri's* group in turn produced a wide record of experiences as a basis to provide interpretative tools of the penal process and of the state representatives' actions, which, otherwise, would come across as totally incomprehensible to this audience. That was particularly true for those in pre-trial detention, when the indications for decoding laws and analysing verdicts often proved vital to cope with anxieties and misunderstandings.

Hence, the *master* acts as a sheer interpreter of the criminal code for the benefit of all those who are not familiar with the Western legal system, the State institutions and the Spanish language. He is available for all who think that ritual negligence is dangerous to the successful unfolding of the legal course, as well as to the ones who do not feel properly represented by their official lawyer.

Clearly, in a congested justice system, bribery and widespread cross-cultural discrimination often transform the judges and public prosecutors into negative and unjust characters to be fought against, by all means, including curses and witchcraft:

> We are completely cursed [...] here people come completely cursed [...] We are as if in a sheep ground, all together, there is no selection, good people, bad people, we are all in a pit [...] you smoke, you chew coca leaves to get rid of all this curse [...] Even judges and prosecutors are cursed [...] because they take money, and it's no use. A person like that is really cursed. With what sacrifice, with what effort is money found? It's just a matter of getting paid, taking money away. They say [the lawyers] "Let's do this, now you get out, let's do this and that" and they do nothing! We give them money for nothing! [...] they get paid for a reason and they don't do anything. For example, now I curse my lawyer [...] because he couldn't get me out of here [...].
>
> Doesn't the curse come back on you?
> No. If it had been witchcraft for other reasons it would have returned to me, but in this case it doesn't (Julio Durán, San Martín section, *yatiri* inmate, June 29, 2006).

People are usually wary of revealing their ability to cause harm through witchcraft. In jail, however, the black magic employed against the representatives of law and order—usually regarded as outright criminals—is not even surreptitious anymore, and can be stated openly without fearing the hex to return to the original sender. On that account, quite the opposite stands: cursing the key law representatives becomes a due act of justice accomplished pursuant to a fair and acceptable rationale which implies sending back the evil to the sender.

The Supernatural Trial

During the research, Nacho Chura, the most powerful *master* of the prison, told me about a time-consuming and rather complex black magic ritual he had performed to obtain the release due to expiry of the custody time limit for a client in pre-trial detention, accused of murder:

I helped him [the client]. He had his first hearing and I got it cancelled. Then I got the second one annulled, and the third [...]. They have to tell me exactly how things stand. And depending on that, I can figure out how to defend them. He was supposed to serve 30 years and now he's about to be released.

Is it thanks to your work?

Yes, thanks to my work. I worked with black candles, black offerings, black incense, and I also blew skull bone dust, and they didn't convict him. They tried to convict him recently, but they cancelled the hearing again and now he's leaving. That's good, right? I've caused several postponements. I called the soul of the accusers who came here to discuss how this could be settled. (Nacho Chura, yatiri inmate, June 20, 2006)

The *yatiri* immediately claimed that through this kind of ritual he had succeeded in releasing from prison innocent people as well as thieves and killers: it makes no difference to him. He is above judgement, simply after the agreement of the parties.

In another instance, Nacho Chura was called to supervise the ritualistic part of the penal proceedings in a very special way. The description of the ceremonial session was rather impressive as the *yatiri*, possessed by the spirits of all participants (human as well as extra-human ones), impersonated all their voices setting up a sort of a mock trial.[15] The coca leaves epitomized all the relevant characters which would come into play in the legal proceeding: the defendant, the lawyer, the victim and their family, the defendant's family, the public prosecutor, the judge and distinctly the supernatural entities recipient of the ritualistic offering: *Pachamama* and *Kunturmamani,*[16] the latter being the symbolic representative of the inmate's home. After intense pleadings, the *master* summoned all the spirits, evil and kind ones alike, who came accompanied by St. Expedito, and together would find a solution to please and appease all the stakeholders.

Using the whole panoply of suitable tools, the *yatiri*, through the coca leaves, tries to negotiate the terms of the release in order to reach an agreement to the benefits of his client. Summoning the adverse party is basically done in an attempt to strike a "deal" before the actual hearing takes place in court.

Once the spirits have been dismissed, he prepared the offering. In doing so, he considered the symbols to be employed: on the one hand, the ones metaphorically embodying the objects and circumstances of the daily life the client wants to recover with the sought freedom; on the other hand, the symbol representing the court, venue of the final verdict. As a formal act, in order to pledge the arrangement achieved during the ceremony, the *yatiri* burnt the pro-freedom offering on his cell rooftop.

The Prison as a Sacred Space

In normal circumstances, the mighty places of the Bolivian high plateau are the proper setting to successfully stage ritualistic sessions. The highlands have always been sacred venues where humans, ancestors, the souls of the deceased and the Andean supernatural beings engage with one another. The rivers and the mountains possessed by the spirits called *Achachilas* have always stood out as the chosen places to leave ceremonial offerings. The most important *Achachilas* are the snow-capped peaks of the Andean Cordillera, always in sight from great distances. In La Paz, the Mounts Illampu and the Illimani, the Mount Sajama or the majestic Huayna Potosí are customarily mentioned during ritualistic ceremonies and are duly worshipped. In the city as well as in the highlands, they are always evoked with great care; even if not all of these mountains are in sight, libations (*ch'allas*) are usually directed towards their sites. These spiritual entities are especially important at times of crisis for the individual or the community, and accordingly they were necessarily invoked during the rituals. There are *Achachilas* more important and powerful than others, but during the prayers, efforts are made not to overlook any of them, since every supernatural entity could turn whimsical and dangerous towards disrespectful humans. To invoke their names implies urging their presence and asking for their protection; likewise pouring on the soil some of the drink one is having (*ch'allar*) is a sign of respect and invitation to *Pachamama*.

Suffice it to say, albeit in jail this scenario was inaccessible, the *yatiri* would not despair: the cell roof—always shielded from the Pentecostals' judgement—would turn into a mountain from where the smoke of the burnt offerings would rise to reach the sky:

> There isn't a mountain here [in prison], so I climb the roof. Outside I go to the Illimani, Huayna Potosí, Laguna, Cumbre de Caranavi mountains, these are powerful [...] and I go there and do what I have to do. I told you, if one has faith, then everything becomes possible. I make the soul of the prosecutor or the judge in this mountain speak (Nacho Chura, Álamos section, yatiri inmate, August 2, 2006).

From the top of a wobbling cell roof, the visual contact could be extended to the mighty Illimani Mountain, and the sites of all the other mountains could be worked out so as to rightly direct the invocations pleading for protection. Likewise, the sewages of the prison would turn into rivers suitable to receive their offerings. Lastly, even the prison itself would come into play as a powerful clue that had to be included in the ritualistic invocations:

I always sprinkle alcohol *(ch'allo)* in all the sections, and when I don't go there, I call them out (the section names) and I drink a little with their permission. There are seven sections: Pinos, Álamos, Prefectura, Palmar, Cancha, San Martín, Guanay, Posta [...] and then I sprinkle alcohol (*ch'allo*) when I do my rituals, always remembering them, and even when I'm working upstairs (on the cell roof), I gotta get all these names out.

> Do you name all the sections when you do an offering here?
> Yes, I also mention the saint. I nominate Los Pinos, Álamos, Prefectura...
> Which saint?
> St. Pedro.
> Why do you name each section?
> Because each section has its own misfortunes, with all the various people that are there, so it's always powerful (Nacho Chura, *yatiri*-inmate, section Álamos, 2 August 2006).

Conjuring all sectors of the penitentiary shows and tells the essence of this close-fitting, concentrated cosmos. The sections share with the wild areas of the highlands an ambiguous character. They are both a space for life in common and for subsistence activities during the day, which rather easily turns into a peculiar, dangerous and fearful place by night. Through the sprinkled alcohol (*ch'allas*), all the powerful places in the prison are greeted one by one, just like it would be done in the highland ritual environment, so that each of the evoked places feels summoned to perform their protective function (Bouysse Cassagne 1987: 43–44) and no one is consigned to the dangerous oblivion of unspoken words.

Whether inside or outside the penitentiary, the places appointed behave as "guardians" of the norms set by the prison community of believers in the desire to bring order to the world and the circumstances experienced, so that things would take on meaning in space and through time.

San Pedro, representing both the saint and the prison, is mentioned along with the sections and their names in the prayers to appease the destructive forces possessing them, pleading for help and shelter in the same way as is done with every *Achachila.* This is because in the Andes not only people but also places require special care.

To the *yatiri,* naming all the sectors of the penitentiary was a way to tame that "wild" unwelcoming and violent space, exactly as it is with the wild untamed highlands that are continuously recalled in the ceremonies so as to prevent them from causing harm to the humans.

During the burning of the ceremonial offering on the cell roof, the most dangerous and "powerful" places of the prison were unceasingly invoked: the little squares and burrows, the hovels, the dark corridors where aggressions and killings would take place, were mentioned with scrupulous insistence in order to gain protection, courage and strength. In this way, through the lens of the ritual, the space of the penitentiary was being reinterpreted and neutralized in its most violent and threatening expressions.

Conclusion

In Local Knowledge, Geertz (1983: 184) conceives law as a system of symbols and meanings which are "part of a distinctive manner of imagining the real". Paraphrasing Geertz's understanding, Merry (1988: 886) describes the law "as a species of social imagination" that shapes identities (Merry 1995) and outlines relationships within the power of the state.[17] Like the law, ritual is a powerful ordering force that creates and changes the social experience.

With regard to the *yatiris'* work in prison, rituals frame and give meaning to everyday life, expectations and sorrows, marking an important arena of hope and contention.

As Waldram (1997) underlines in the Canadian context, the indigenous spiritual chiefs in prison act as a normative model needed to make sense of such a context. Ultimately, *yatiri*s provide an alternative interpretation of the prison experience and its world, recreating a community of believers that struggle against a dispossession of their sense of "familiar". They act as "cultural intermediaries" between some domains of life that, though intertwined, would normally appear as incompatible in their many facets: the safe and the dangerous, the bizarre and the conventional, law and justice, prison and free world. Consequently, this case study highlights a space of ambiguity concerning the different social actors and categories involved, which turns the distinction between who is harming whom into a complex affair.

Matters like magic and black magic are simultaneously accessible and inaccessible, knowable and unknowable. Thereby, magic is a force that can be bent for criminal purposes as well as for reinstating a sense of justice, which is gone completely lost in a place like San Pedro prison. Accordingly, these rituals can also be regarded as a form of political statement for people with no access to the formal legal scene (Goldstein 2003), who, through the rituals, attempt to communicate "grievances against the inadequacies of the State's official legal order" (Goldstein 2003: 23).

The community of believers is in the throes of the structural injustice of the post-colonial state and the "little injustice" (Nader 1981, in

Goodale 2008: 224) of everyday life in the prison of San Pedro like "in thousands of rural hamlets, urban favelas, and neighbourhood associations and *sindicatos*, as well as in the offices of provincial police officers [...] in which indigenous peoples, *campesinos*, miners, and the urban poor are able to employ a wider range of legal strategies than their elite counterparts" (Goodale 2008: 224).

Can "the excessive disorderliness of post colonies on the one hand and their fetishism of law on the other describe a concrete reality? (Comaroff and Comaroff 2006: viii)". Arguably, in this scenario, ritualistic practices are acknowledged to signify a *Weltanschauung* and an established form of concreteness. They do not represent an exotic belief, but rather a valuable insight into daily life in prison. In this perspective, rituals arrange things in the right place: the space and its dwellers, and the whole legal experience. It serves as a way to transform "unruly subjects" into "lawful subjects" of the state (Das and Poole 2004: 9) within a specific local knowledge.

As the lynching described by Goldstein (2003), the pro-freedom offerings are not to be deemed as necessary antagonistic to the power of the state. Nonetheless, these rituals claim a reaction, and set a challenge to the inefficiency of the judicial system; by condensing "micro-acts of resistance" (Merry 1995: 15), they also feature an aspect of the "ritual activism" described by Burman (2011). They hold like a sort of "tactical" attitude, or a low-level guerrilla warfare in which Andean tradition reinvents itself and adapts to a new scenario in order to display unexpected assemblages and social imaginaries.

The ethnography of ritualistic practices in the prison of San Pedro sheds light on the inmates as subjects acting through cultural categories stemming from a specific tradition, then elaborated and adapted to the prison microcosm. The whole detention experience, including all the subjects and objects belonging to such unfamiliar space, needs a cultural mediation, so that the inmates can develop a creative and instructive strength which, bypassing laws, can at once make sense and put all in order, within and beyond the prison.

In this unusual context, the Andean ritualistic tradition calls to mind rather powerfully the "dilemmas of modernity" which Goodale (2009) described in his essay on the fluid nature of justice in Bolivia. This "flow" is indeed rather well depicted by the internal functioning of the self-governed prison of San Pedro. No wonder then, if ambiguity and secrets, magic and witchcraft are quintessential to the self-regulation and control of this place.

Notes

1. The topic analysed in this work, the objectives and methodology of the ethnography have been deeply and widely addressed in Cerbini (2012).
2. See: Cerbini (2017), Darke and Garces (2017), Darke and Karam (2016).
3. This rather suggestive term coined by Spedding (2008: 29) does not need further explanation than its etymology, composed by the word *abogado* (lawyer) and gangster.
4. See: de Sousa Santos and Exeni Rodríguez (2012).
5. At the end of the nineteenth century, the prison of San Pedro was built on the architectonic model of the panopticon. The facility recalled the famous North American penitentiaries of Philadelphia, Boston, Baltimore and Albany.
6. These churches generally belonged to the current of the third Protestant reform. See Cerbini (2012: 125–161).
7. I use the term *yatiri* as it was used by the inmates of San Pedro, who came mostly from the Aymara linguistic area. See: Fernández Juárez (2004, 2004a).
8. See: Cerbini (2012: 93–124).
9. According to the indigenous conception of the human being, the person is composed of different "souls" called *ajayu*, *animu*, *curaji* or *qamasa*. See: Fernández Juárez (2004a).
10. See: Risør (2013).
11. The term *Achachila* designates the spiritual notion of "mountain".
12. The *ch'allada* is a ritual action that consists of sprinkling alcohol or wine on the ground or on objects that make up a ritual offering.
13. *Tío* is a supernatural figure dispensing fortune, prosperity and wealth, often identified with the "devil".
14. *Pachamama* is the Mother Earth.

15. This ritual practice is carried out by a powerful *master*, called *ch'amakani* (see: Fernández Juárez 1995: 212–213).
16. The word aymara *Kunturmamani* is the ritual term to designate the house.
17. See also: Goldstein (2003).

References

Bazurco Osorio, M., & Exeni Rodríguez, J. L. (2012). Bolivia: Justicia indígena en tiempos de plurinacionalidad. In B. de Sousa Santos & J. L. Exeni Rodríguez (Eds.), *Justicia indígena, plurinacionalidad e interculturalidad en Bolivia* (pp. 49–144). Ediciones Abya-Yala.

Bouysse Cassagne, T., & Harris, O. (1987). Pacha: en torno al pensamiento aymara. In T. B. Cassagne et al. (Eds.), *Tres reflexiones sobre el pensamiento andino* (pp. 11–59). La Paz: Hisbol.

Burman A. (2011). Yatiris en el siglo XXI. El conocimiento, la política y la nueva generación, Nuevo Mundo, Mundos Nuevos [On line], Debates, EHESS. http://nuevomundo.revues.org/61331; https://doi.org/10.4000/nuevomundo.61331.

Cerbini, F. (2012). *La casa de jabón. Etnografía de una cárcel boliviana*. Barcelona: Ediciones Bellaterra.

Cerbini, F. (2017). From the panopticon to the anti-panopticon: The 'art of government' in the prison of San Pedro (La Paz, Bolivia). *Prison Service Journal, 229*, 31–34.

Comaroff, J., & Comaroff, J. L. (2006). *Law and disorder in the post-colony*. Chicago: University of Chicago Press.

Cunha, M. (2014). The ethnography of prisons and penal confinement. *Annual Review of Anthropology, 43*, 217–233.

Darke, S., & Garces, C. (Eds.). (2017). Informal dynamics of survival in Latin American prisons. *Prison Service Journal, 229*.

Darke, S., & Karam, M. L. (2016). Latin American prisons. In Y. Jewkes et al. (Eds.), *Handbook on prisons* (pp. 460–474). Abingdon: Routledge.

Das, V., & Poole, D. (2004). *Anthropology in the margins of the state*. Oxford: Oxford University Press.

de Sousa Santos, B., & Exeni Rodríguez, J. L. (2012). *Justicia indígena, plurinacionalidad e interculturalidad en Bolivia*. Quito: Ediciones Abya-Yala.

Fernández Juárez, G. (1995). *El Banquete Aymara. Mesas y Yatiris*. La Paz: Hisbol.

Fernández Juárez, G. (2004). *Yatiris y ch'amakanis del altiplano aymara: sueños, testimonios y prácticas ceremoniales*. Editorial Abya Yala.
Fernández Juárez, G. A. (2004a). animu, kuraji: el "susto" y el concepto de persona en el Altiplano aymara. In A. Spedding (Ed.), *Gracias a Dios y a los Achachilas: ensayos de sociología de la religión en los Andes* (pp. 185–218). La Paz: ISEAT/Plural.
Fernández Osco, M. (2000). *La Ley del Ayllu. Práctica de jach'a justicia y jisk'a justicia (Justicia Mayor y Justicia Menor) en las comunidades aymaras*. La Paz: PIEB.
Geertz, C. (1983). *Local knowledge. Further essays in interpretive anthropology*. New York: Basic Books.
Goldstein, D. M. (2003). "In our own hands": Lynching, justice, and the law in Bolivia. *American Ethnologist, 1*, 22–43.
Goodale, M. (2008). Legalities and illegalities. In D. Poole (Ed.), *A companion to Latin American anthropology* (pp. 214–229). Blackwell Publishing.
Goodale, M. (2009). *Dilemmas of modernity. Bolivian encounters with law and liberalism*. Stanford: Stanford University Press.
Greenhouse, C. J., Mertz, E., & Warren, K. B. (2002). *Ethnography in unstable places*. Durham: Duke University Press.
Harris, O. (1996). *Inside and outside the law. Anthropological studies of authority and ambiguity*. London: Routledge.
Merry, S. E. (1988). Legal pluralism. *Law and Society Review, 22*(5), 869–896.
Merry, S. E. (1995). Resistance and the cultural power of law. *Law and Society Review, 29*(1), 11–26.
Risør, H. (2013). "Captured with their hands in the dough": Insecurity, safety-seeking, and securitization in El Alto, Bolivia. In M. Holbraad & M. A. Pedersen (Eds.), *Times of security ethnographies of fear, protest and the future* (pp. 57–79). London: Routledge.
Segato, R. (2007). El color de la cárcel en América Latina. Apuntes sobre la colonialidad de la justicia en un continente en desconstrucción. *Nueva Sociedad, 208*, 142–161.
Spedding, A. (2008). *La segunda vez como farsa. Etnografía de una cárcel de mujeres en Bolivia*. La Paz: Editorial Mama Huaco.
Taussig, M. (2004). *My cocaine museum*. Chicago: University of Chicago Press.
Waldram, J. B. (1997). *The way of the pipe. Aboriginal spirituality and symbolic healing in Canadian prisons*. Orchard Park: Broadview Press.

10

Carceral Alliance: Vernacular Professionalization and Containment in Puerto Rican Drug Rehabilitation

Caroline Mary Parker

The Graduation Ceremony

On a hot, cloudless Sunday, the parking lot is filling fast. Cars and limousines line up and snake around the corner. Puerto Rico's elected officials—the chief justice, the town mayor, and scores of representatives of the legislative assembly—have come together with over eighty families to pay tribute to this year's graduating class of rehabilitees. On the stage, a reformed ex-addict turned therapeutic community director breaks out with the opening speech:

Honorable ladies and gentlemen. Today is a special afternoon. We are here to award certificates to this year's *re-educados*, the graduating class of 2017 who have demonstrated, yet again, *sí, se puede*. Like all of you graduating *re-educados* here today, I am here too as a product of the justice system. And I would like to thank our friends here in the Department of Justice who have got us to where we are today; I can tell you all that it's a

C. M. Parker (✉)
University of Manchester, Manchester, UK

S. Darke et al. (eds.), *Carceral Communities in Latin America*, Palgrave Studies in Prisons and Penology, https://doi.org/10.1007/978-3-030-61499-7_10

beautiful privilege to be here. To our honorable directors, today is a proud day for you too. You have all spent years as *internados*, you have all made enormous sacrifices as mentors and guides, and you all know how much effort it takes to make the journey to re-educate oneself. *Graduados*, now that you have all put in the effort, after all that work and sacrifice you can now start to enjoy the success. You can return to your community as *hombres certificados*, as leaders in your communities. *Para que nunca vuelvas, su honrado certificado re-educado* (in English, "So that you may never return, certified re-educated honoree").

Watching the graduation, I felt that a certain drama was unfolding before my eyes. On the stage, criminalized and addicted men were applauded by the powerful in recognition of their hard-earned sobriety, and in celebration of the opportunity that surely lay ahead. Shirts starched and shoes shined, these drug offenders stood tall and proud as they shook the hand of the town mayor and received their certificates under gaze of family and town. Center-stage for all to see was the embodied, best-case scenario that court-mandated drug treatment can offer: ex-offenders and ex-addicts now reformed and remade as "honored and certified re-educated ex-addicts" and catapulted to equivalence, for today, with the governing class, the professions, and the whole of working Puerto Rico that stands apart from the street. Aspiration filled the air.

Ostensibly, the graduation ceremony is a civic ritual celebrating the re-integration to civil society of drug offenders upon their completion of court-mandated residential drug treatment. Less ostensibly, graduation ceremonies dramatize what I have come to recognize as an increasingly important strategy in the contemporary carceral era: the improvisation of work by way of "vernacular professionalization." This is a dual strategy of two components: first, an entrepreneurial life project through which criminalized subjects create and demarcate a labor market niche and domain of expertise that simulates the professions—in this case, the para-professional category of the "certified and re-educated ex-addict." Second, it is also a governing strategy through which the state pursues containment. Across the Americas, vernacular professionalization has flourished in self-help therapeutic communities in particular, where drug offenders will often be diverted as a cheaper alternative to prison. Here, my focus is on Puerto Rico, a "commonwealth" and colonial territory of the United States,[1] though analogous trends towards a professionalization of rehabilitation have been documented elsewhere in Latin America and the Caribbean (Hansen 2018; Garcia 2015; O'Neill 2014; Darke and Garces 2017).

In this chapter, I explore vernacular professionalization ethnographically, considering its history, performance, and tactics and examining the ways these improvised channels of certification and qualification mimic existing educational structures. While many consider these credentials to be 'informal' or 'just ceremonial' or even 'phony,' I show that the 'certified re-educated ex-addict' now constitutes a state-recognized class of workers whose members perform vital under-waged work as therapists and social workers on behalf of the carceral state. The tendency of *re-educados certificados* to short-circuit the ordinary credentialing requirements that typically restrict and qualify entrance to these professional categories is tolerated, I argue, because of the utility these subjects present to various state actors. But even as this alliance gives rise to job opportunities for drug offenders, it also encloses its subjects with a regime of unwaged and underwaged labor and ultimately it fails to open a viable route to social standing and professional mobility outside of this circumscribed carceral circuit. Before examining vernacular professionalization in more detail, let me begin by articulating this construct's theoretical underpinnings.

The notion of the vernacular has often figured in studies of the global movement of languages and discourses. Levitt and Merry (2009), for example, use the term "the vernacularization of human rights" to refer to how global ideas about human rights are appropriated and customized in diverse local communities. Similarly, Anjum (2017) writes of the "vernacularization of Islam" to refer to the adjustment and adaptation of Islam outside Arabia. In line with this work, I use term "vernacular professionalization" to refer to how ideas and discourses about professionalism—including pedagogies, certification systems, hierarchies, and symbols—are appropriated, customized, and adapted in communities ordinarily considered to be located outside of the professions. I use the term "vernacular" rather than "informal" for two reasons: first, I wish to do away with the notion of a clear-cut distinction between formal and informal work, a binary already subject to thoughtful critique elsewhere (Millar 2018). Second, I want to highlight the transfer and blending elements of this process: like the vernacular languages that derived from Latin in Europe, the local systems of professionalization that are improvised and created here are influenced by a template, in this case, global ideas of "the professions," which are then adapted and modified according to local conditions.

The emergence of vernacular professionalization in Puerto Rico makes sense for several reasons. First, a precipitous increase in drug convictions has further compounded employment barriers for men. Second, the entrance of the non-profit sector and specifically of self-help therapeutic communities into the work of rehabilitating drug offenders has opened an institutional space that drug offenders have capitalized upon by creating alternative job opportunities for themselves as paraprofessional drug rehabilitation experts. Third, the enormous public expenditure on drug-related law enforcement and incarceration since the 1970s—now estimated to exceed $5 billion in the commonwealth (Ferrería 2012)—means that the commonwealth state has historically been very favorably disposed to lend its support to innovations that have the potential to lower containment costs. In Puerto Rico, criminalized men's efforts to improve their life circumstances have found an unlikely affinity in efforts to lower containment costs, linking the punitive politics of the war on drugs to the dreams and ambitions of Puerto Rico's poor.

To better understand the nature and dynamics of vernacular professionalization, this first examines *re-educados'* labor histories before historically situating the formation of this paraprofessional labor niche in relation to the carceral turn. Then, it argues that vernacular professionalization promises *re-educados* job opportunities and recognition, but it does so through confining them to work as unwaged and underwaged paraprofessionals on behalf of the carceral state. Ultimately, it argues that this unequal alliance has proven exceptionally effective in delivering cheap containment.

Drug Convictions and Becoming a "Certified and Re-educated Ex-addict"

Like many *re-educados,* Salvador describes himself as *producto del sistema judicial,* a reference to the fact that his entrance into therapeutic community treatment was precipitated by a drug charge, and his first four years of internment were spent under court order. Previously, Salvador had worked as a janitor in an *urbanización*, while also dealing cocaine on the side to supplement his meager salary. Drug dealing ultimately led him to acquire five drug-related charges between 1975 and 1985, during which time he spent a total of six years in prison. In 1985, he was diverted from prison to a therapeutic community where he spent four years as an *internado.* After he completed his mandatory treatment period he graduated as a "certified re-educated ex-addict" and chose to stay and live at the same program for an additional three years. During this time, his official title was "therapist." He did not receive a salary, but he did enjoy free room-and-board along with a sub-minimum wage stipend ($6000 per year). Eventually, Salvador went on to establish his own therapeutic community, *Mesón de Dios.* By the time I interviewed Salvador in 2016, *Mesón de Dios* was home to twenty male residents. Reflecting on his life trajectory, Salvador attributes his professional successes directly to his court order.

> Before this, I hadn't done a thing with my life. All I knew was drugs and the street. But the program, it helped me to discover talents in me that I never knew I possessed. So, after I graduated, I decided to stay, me certifique y me profesionalice, and after a few years I followed my dreams and started my own program. And thanks to God I'm still here today, as the founder and director of a program, sixteen years and counting. Me, a director... even though I don't have sixth grade.

Like Salvador, the work histories of *re-educados* often spanned illicit economies and low-waged sectors of licit economies, sometimes traversing Puerto Rico and the mainland. Prior to enrolling in therapeutic community care, for example, Miguel had been a security guard in a mall; while Carlos, the director of a therapeutic community in Cataño, had formerly worked as a cleaner in *Pollo Tropical,* an American fast-food chain restaurant. Each had initially wound up in therapeutic community care via a drug charge.

In therapeutic community settings, professional titles, such as caseworker, social worker, therapist, and leader, are highly coveted designations that carry significant social capital, but only rarely conform to wage labor arrangements. Most *re-educados* who have chosen to stay and work after graduation will receive free accommodation, sometimes supplemented by a sub-minimum wage stipend. Most organizations can only support a small number of waged positions, usually through corrections grants, and these will typically be reserved for directors. Thus, the majority of *re-educados* who choose to work after completing a court order do so for less than minimum wage.

The drug conviction to *certificado re-educado* pipeline, common in the labor histories of many *re-educados,* is a trend that stems directly from Puerto Rico's dovetailing of mainland US drug policies. Since the 1970s, carceral expansion in Puerto Rico has closely mirrored that on the mainland, with the number of people incarcerated rising from 4221 to 14,691 between 1981 and 2000 (World Prison Brief 2016), and the incarceration rate rising from 130/100,000 to 582/100,000 between 1981 and 2003 (World Prison Brief 2016; Santiago-Negrón and Albizu-García 2003).

Carceral expansion in Puerto Rico was driven both by legislative change and by stricter enforcement of existing laws. Particularly important was the introduction of the Commonwealth Law of Controlled Substances in 1971, which soon became the most common conviction among Puerto Rico's prison inmates, applying to 33.94% of the total prison population in 2003 (Santiago-Negrón and Albizu-García 2003:1422). Federal laws and courts also played a role. Key was the Federal Anti-Drug Abuse Act of 1986, which increased penalties and instituted mandatory minimum sentences for most drug offenses, and the Federal District Court of Puerto Rico, which convicted thousands of Puerto Ricans of drug-related offenses (O'Neill and Gumbrewicz 2005).

By the early 2000s, Puerto Rico could claim the third highest incarceration rate in the world, surpassed only by mainland United States and Russia (Santiago-Negrón and Albizu-García 2003).

Mass incarceration was facilitated by large increases in spending, with the budget for the Department for Justice rising from $25 million in 1984 to $62 million in 1992, and that of the Department for Corrections rising by 262%, from $147 million in 1992 to $532 million in 1998 (Departamento de Justicia 1992; Departamento de Justicia 1986). By 2011, the pooled annual budget for Puerto Rico's Police Department, the Correctional Administration, and the Judicial Branch was $1.5 billion (Ferrería 2012). To put that into perspective, that same year, the annual budget for the Mental Health and Anti Addiction Services Administration (ASSMCA), the department responsible for overseeing all addiction prevention and treatment on the island, was just $96 million (Ferrería 2012).

In the face of soaring containment costs, the commonwealth state has experimented with a variety of prison-diversion schemes, starting with the Treatment Alternatives to Street Crime program (TASC), a federal initiative introduced in the 1970s, but also various other legislative mechanisms.[2] For their part, therapeutic community leaders have played a proactive role historically in establishing various ex-addict-led organizations to oversee treatment among court-ordered residents. These have included the Social Association for Rehabilitated Ex-Addicts (Spanish acronym, ASEAR), and the Association for the Services of Rehabilitated Ex-addicts and Ex-convicts' (Spanish acronym, ASEER).

With the help of these paraprofessional organizations, the Department of Correction and Rehabilitation has diverted hundreds of inmates each year to self-help therapeutic communities, who typically receive a per diem for each court-ordered resident. The numbers diverted rose steadily during the 1970s and 1970s, but, by the early 1990s, it was diverting roughly 1800 people (overwhelmingly men) annually from prison to therapeutic communities of the non-profit sector (Department of Correction and Rehabilitation 1994:30).

Anthropologists have observed similar trends towards prison-diversion in North America (Kerwin Kaye 2010; Tiger 2013), and through them, have begun to elaborate changing philosophies, rationales, and governing strategies of the juridical system. Many have noted a late twentieth-century shift towards "therapeutic jurisprudence" (Wexler 1990), an approach to the law that seeks to maximize the therapeutic benefits of the legal system, through reconfiguring judicial processes to channel people into institutions of treatment. But what stands out about Puerto Rico's carceral turn and its particular conviction-to-paraprofessional pipeline is the extent to which the targets of these carceral interventions have seized upon (and creatively melded) the opportunities that these corrections projects have presented. This opportunity-seizing element challenges us to ask what more, besides any therapeutic endeavor, underwrites this labor regime.

Certification by Way of Simulation

"I certified myself," ex-trafficker Héctor Vayaz announced early in an interview. We were seated in a dilapidated office where water dripped loudly into a trashcan from a peeling ceiling, and the shelves of an ageing bookcase drooped tiredly, struggling under a weight attributable not to books but to an extensive collection of trophies. The assortment of goblets and shields came in various shapes and sizes: plastic figurines of painted gold, small embossed silver cups, and large black-diamond plaques. Following Héctor's gesture, my eyes floated upwards to a black and white framed photograph that was hanging on the wall. At the center of the photograph was Héctor, flanked on both sides by a dozen residents. "In Recognition for Services to the Free State of Puerto Rico," read the inscription. They stood smiling in rows with medals around their necks like a high school soccer team. We settled into an interview.

> "I passed through a program. I saw the hurt. I knew what was happening with the youth in Puerto Rico, [and] I'm not gonna be hanging around on the corner, watching. So I did something. I graduated, I got certified in addiction."
>
> "Oh cool," I said. "Where did you get certified?"
>
> "I got certified at my old program," he said. "That's how it is here."

Vernacular professionalization is a highly entrepreneurial strategy. It proceeds through both simulation and improvisation and ultimately entails the cultivation of a domain of expertise that mimics the professions in symbol, insignia, and representation, but that is "extra-professional" in the sense of originating from without. Contrary to popular conceptions of *re-educados* as revering 'lived experience' over and above all other forms of professional preparation (people in public health repeatedly told me this, "they think only addicts can treat addicts"), professional accreditation is upheld by *re-educados* as a dominant cultural value. This helps to explain, in part, why therapeutic communities go to great lengths to devise a parallel world of titles, trophies, rewards, and ceremonies that mimic the professions. It also adds some context to some of therapeutic communities' more curious rituals: the elaborate reward ceremonies, the sometimes-grandiose titles—*exadicto honrado* and *re-educado certificado*—and the appropriated professional designations: *terapista, trabajador de caso, trabajador social.*

Some therapeutic communities—particularly the larger ones—actually operate internal training schemes known as *aprendizaje* and *la práctica* for graduated *re-educados*, which confer internal forms of accreditation. These programs vary in form and content from place to place, and tend not to follow any specified curriculum, at least not one that I could find written down.

In 2017, I attended six training sessions for *re-educados* at two different addiction shelters. I found myself watching Manuel, a long-standing and evidently much beloved director of a therapeutic community in Guayama. His official title was "district training official," and he was responsible for coordinating and delivering training across several different shelters. In a previous life, Manuel had been a shop assistant, then a drug trafficker, but, in 1991, he'd been court-mandated to a therapeutic community—where we were now all gathered—and he'd stayed there ever since.

I watched Manuel teach four classes. He was charismatic and often paced up and down the room as he talked. He always wore a suit and tie and would start each session by inviting the group to give a round of applause and a welcoming cheer to each attendee. Following lively introductions, he'd invite the group to hold hands in prayer: "Being here together, *profesionales entre profesionales,* this is what we strive for. We are happy, we are motivated, we are grateful. *Gracias a Dios.*"

In format, practicums had a hybrid structure and atmosphere that lay somewhere between seminar and office party. Between ten and fifteen of us would sit around a table stacked with worksheets and refreshments. The facilitator would introduce the topic and, for the next few hours, we'd listen to a lecture, complete various exercises, and watch online videos. In terms of content, it was a hodgepodge of lessons determined by the presenter's choice. The six trainings I attended covered a mixture of topics, some based on scientific research (e.g., "substance use and DSM-V" and "domestic violence") others on pop-science ("managing stress" and "achieving your potential"), and others on bible-based thoughts for the day ("the power of prayer") or on recent news items.

For example, in a session dedicated to "leadership and authority," Manuel talked us through the ideas of John Maxwell, an Evangelical American author whose pop-psychology books on leadership have sold millions of copies across the United States. After the presentation, we watched several online videos and performed role-play exercises. In another session, we watched a TED talk delivered by an academic researcher about the long-term health consequences of childhood trauma. In another, we discussed how the Christian notion of sacrifice applied to *re-educados'* work, with attendees asked to enumerate specific sacrifices they had made ("sleeping on the floor when there aren't enough beds" and "working hard for little pay").

The hodge-podge content of these training sessions—pop-science, Christianity, and public health doctrine—highlights the mimetic manner in which vernacular professionalization operates in Puerto Rico. Lacking any stable curriculum and unrestricted by theoretical allegiance, this improvised education system mimics and borrows its structure, content, and discourses from its surroundings, mixing and melding Christianity, medicine, and popular culture into an improvised project of self-betterment.

Consider a session I attended on "substance use and DSM-V," led not by Manuel but by a visiting graduate student with a BSc in psychology from the University of Puerto Rico. The student began the session by reminding attendees that "addiction" was just a lay term, and that "as professionals talking among professionals, we should all be trying to use the correct DSM-V term, 'substance use disorder'." Before giving his presentation, he asked the class to enumerate some of the characteristics that someone with a substance use disorder might display. "Being manipulative!" shouted one attendee. "A loss of social values!" suggested Manuel. Consistent with the characterological approaches that had defined their own therapeutic careers, "aggressiveness," "irritability," and "conflict with authority" were among the other suggested responses.

After noting the responses, the lecturer then turned to his next slide, which listed "eleven reportable or observable symptoms of substance use disorders according to DSM-V." Unlike the characterological explanations offered up by the *re-educados* in attendance, these symptoms were mostly behavioral and included such things as consuming more substances than originally intended, continued use in spite of harm to personal relationships, and spending large amounts of time in consuming or obtaining substances. After the presentation, we completed a quiz in groups about observable symptoms of substance use disorders. Once Manuel had thanked the speaker, he delivered an off-the-cuff recap: "Today's addicts are complicated. It's not like before, when addicts were just addicts. Now, they have trauma, mental health, dual-diagnosis, domestic violence. Addicts have changed," he said, "and we have to change too."

To me, this session stood out as a striking dramatization of how vernacular professionalization operates as a kind of *bricolage* (Lévi-Strauss 1966) for the cultivation of social capital—in this case, a highly coveted and valorized professional kind of cladding. At play in this session was an encounter between two seemingly distinct therapeutic epistemologies: a clinical epistemology grounded in the norms of biomedicine and the diagnostic criteria of DSM, and then a therapeutic community system, grounded in Eriksonian psycho-analytical theory and character-building therapies. Yet, the extremely accommodating orientation of *re-educados* to what (to outsiders) might seem like high-stakes framing tensions reflects the fact that 'theory' here (whether of the scientific, popular, or spiritual variety) functions not primarily as a guide for therapeutic practice, or as a tribal allegiance within a contested landscape of addiction treatment. Instead, vernacular professionalization draws on whatever is around, blending diffuse kinds of theory and knowledge that self-improving subjects can appropriate and meld, via self-certification, into a kind of honor based on modern notions of middle-class success, skilled work, and education.

For the day's trainees, attendance was rewarded with the bestowal of small prizes: an embossed certificate for each attendant, a plastic medal for newcomers, and for the person deemed "most promising leader," a plastic shield. The ceremonial conferral of these prizes was marked by a round of applause, one for each member, with absent members calling in to deliver their congratulations on loudspeaker. These were joyous occasions. At the end of each session, we'd pray, and Manuel's energy never dropped. "We are so grateful for these opportunities we have been given. Remember to have your certificates in a safe place," he called out to the exiting throng. "That way, if anyone says you aren't qualified, you can show that you are."

Outside, after the workshop, a *re-educado* delivered to me an enthusiastic lecture about the harms of drug use. Seeming satisfied, he finished: "Me, a therapist! When I came here, I didn't know at that moment there were many things I didn't believe I could do… That I could get certified, that I get professionalized." He seemed content as we watched the others play basketball.

For some, the trainings on offer here might read like a glorified imitation of a higher education, a fanciful counterfeit and a flashy kind of group theater whose artificiality is apparent, and, for those to whom the status value of educational qualifications matter, problematic. Certainly, this was the view of many Puerto Rican public health officials, who often dismissed these credentials as fraudulent, opportunistic, and even immoral. But dismissing this vernacular job training system as phony relies upon a host of obfuscations, the most pressing of which is that the commonwealth state has not only relied upon *re-educados* as a workforce, but it has also variously endorsed and recognized *re-educados* claims to professional expertise. The legislative archive proves instructive here.

For several decades now, the commonwealth state has taken steps to elevate and legally recognize *re-educados* as a legitimate para-professional category. This was done most recently in the Mental Health Act of 2000, when legislators passed a law that granted *re-educados* recognition as "specialist guides in community treatment" (Legislative Assembly of Puerto Rico 2000). This legal promotion was accompanied not by any stipulation of required training, but, instead, by a statement commending the "monumental labor of rehabilitated and re-educated ex-addicts" in handling Puerto Rico's drug problem. To this day, the Mental Health Act positions *re-educados* outside of key government regulations through its stipulation that therapeutic communities are exempt from minimum standards of care set out in the Mental Health Act and instead may "continue providing their community services according to their historic, traditional and customary practices" (Legislative Assembly of Puerto Rico 2000).

Legal endorsement of *re-educados* as a paraprofessional category can also be found in earlier legislation, such as in Law 60 of 1973 (Estado Libre Asociado de Puerto Rico 1973:8–9). This amendment exempted *re-educados* from the usual minimum credential requirements at the Department for Services Against Addiction (DSCA, 1973–1993), facilitating their mass hiring at government-run addiction programs during the 1970s (Parker 2020). While this amendment could be read as the state acknowledging *re-educados* lack of qualifications, when considered from the perspective of its intended outcome (hiring low-cost workers in government programs), the amendment seems instead to index a tacit endorsement of their expertise.

Such acts of strategic deregulation and direct and indirect legal recognition are significant in that they bring into sharp relief the problem with characterizing this work as straightforwardly informal. In the case of *re-educados*, their unorthodox professional training can hardly be characterized as 'off the books' or 'unofficial.' Evidently, it does have some legal basis and evidently it is conferred kinds of state endorsement. But the more important idiosyncrasy of this work is not its confounding of distinctions between work that is 'formal' or 'informal,' a binary already subject to thoughtful critique in prison research elsewhere (Weegels 2018, 2020). Most significant to this analysis are the mimetic practices of simulation that underlie this labor regime. The thing about simulation, Baudrillard (1983) tells us, is not that something pretends to be real, or even that something masks or distorts what is real, but rather that it "threatens the difference" between what is real and imaginary (1983:

454). This point seems apposite here, where vernacular professionalization is not just tolerated, but is widely treated by state actors as perfectly equivalent to other forms of professional preparation. Via simulation of the professions, *re-educados* have successfully curated not a secondary copy, but, as Baudrillard describes it, "a programmatic, metastable, perfectly descriptive machine," one "that offers all the signs of the real" but "short-circuits all its vicissitudes" (1983, 454). Thus, it is because of this mimetic simulation that I call this work vernacular rather than 'lay' or 'informal.' I wish to emphasize the copying, blending, and adaptation elements of this process.

The question remains, of course, how well can vernacular professionalization be said to serve *re-educados*? In the final section, I explore the limits of this alliance and the differential distribution of both its proceeds and unacknowledged harms.

Carceral Coalition and Its Discontents

Through vernacular professionalization, *re-educados* work to improve their life circumstances by demarcating a domain of professional expertise. But what these improvised education systems conceal is the fact that vernacular professionalization is rarely a one-way ticket. My own notes and life histories of dozens of *re-educados* show that they routinely oscillate, over the course of many years, between an *internado* and a *certificado re-educado* position, with the interim period often being one of extreme vulnerability. It was not uncommon in fact for directors and other senior staff members to find themselves back out—*pa' la calle* (i.e., on the streets)—even after several years of dutiful service. Outside the compound, many *re-educados* find themselves in very similar conditions of vulnerability to those that preceded their enrollment.

Consider Jorge, a *re-educado* and attendee of the graduation ceremony that opened this chapter. By the time I attended his graduation in 2017, Jorge had actually already graduated three times before, racking up nearly five years of unwaged and under-waged experience as both an *internado* and therapist in several different communities, nearly all while under court order. The incident that precipitated his most recent re-enrollment came in 2013. After two consecutive years of sobriety, Jorge had used cocaine and had been promptly expelled from the program, thereby forfeiting his therapist position, his only means of income, and his home. Soon after he returned to his hometown and resumed a life he really hoped he had left behind. He squatted in abandoned buildings, he begged for money at traffic lights. "I thought I was ready. I wasn't expecting it at all." After several months of homeless injection drug use, he was eventually brought back to his old therapeutic community by way of outreach initiative. He re-entered at the bottom of the pyramid, with no privileges and none of his previously earned responsibilities, his "honored and certified" status and years of experience counting for nothing.

Luis' story was not dissimilar. By the time we met in 2017, where he was the director of an Evangelical center (at that time for eight years and standing), he had already graduated three times before. Upon his first graduation he had worked for twenty months as a live-in social worker at a small program, for which he'd received a modest stipend ($8000). Figuring it was time to try something else, he had taken a job as a janitor in a mall, a position he lost soon after he started using crack again.

> "I guess I wasn't ready," he said. "I ended up on the street. I used to sleep on cardboard boxes and it was really hard to understand what was happening".

Not that there were no lasting success stories. I did encounter *re-educados* who had retained a position for many years and who had acquired stable salaries via corrections contracts that permitted them to live off-site. By all accounts, Manuel (the onetime-trafficker-turned-trainer) was an example of this. By the time I met him, he had had the same job for twenty years and his salary was relatively high ($24,000) compared to the sub-minimum wage income of many of his colleagues. That said, oscillations, ascensions, and devastating precarity seem to be part and parcel of the *re-educado* career. So when public officials exclaim "after all your work and sacrifice you can start to enjoy the success and return to your communities as qualified and certified people of means," these statements seem cruel tributes given the catastrophes awaiting so many of these men.

In this respect, there is an obvious and fundamental lie here, that simply passing through a therapeutic community can open doors and even catapult you into the middle-class professions. This improvised education system prepares its students for one thing and one thing only: the thing they just came from. Whatever recognition may have been gained on the inside is legal tender only within a highly circumscribed economy. Outside this therapeutic market, these alternative credentials count for very little, often to the great peril of the individual whose viability was dependent on it. And unlike other forms of educational credentials, which, barring exceptional professional foul play, are retained by the bearer whatever life's eventualities, the "certified honored and accredited *re-educado*" is a title constantly at risk of forfeiture. It can be revoked at any moment, and it is substance use, relapse, or drug charge—precisely the trigger events that kick-start this labor cycle—that are most likely to exact such a penalty.

For the sake of cheap containment, the Puerto Rican state has facilitated and constructed a legal environment where criminalized men can be repackaged as paraprofessional social workers, therapists, and caregivers. Pursuing job opportunities and recognition, it is precisely those most likely to be victims of the carceral turn who rush to seize these openings: men from low-waged and insecure ends of the licit economy, handlers and distributers in illicit markets, and men whose drug use or addiction has seen them stripped of their liberty.

> I know what it is to suffer in prison, I know what it is to be addicted to drugs, to be hungry, to sleep without a roof. And I feel proud of what I have achieved here. I'm proud that I got certified and I'm proud that I can work here in the same place I came to seek help.

So this man stays and works at the therapeutic community from which he has just graduated. He works not just hard, and gratefully, because at last, after years in prison, he has finally landed on a viable and even rewarding career trajectory....

Personally, for me it's a pleasure, a joy. I love it and I'm proud that I can be helpful to other men like me. I don't do this job for money, I do it from the heart.

Notes

1. Puerto Rico's status as an "unincorporated territory" of the United States (since 1901) and "commonwealth" (since 1952) place it within an ambiguous field of sovereignty that has been a hallmark of American imperialism since at least the nineteenth century (Stoler et al. 2007). As a commonwealth (or in Spanish text, *Estado Libre Asociado*), Puerto Rico has some autonomy in some domestic areas, including elections, taxation, education, and health. But it remains subject to federal legislation at the discretion of Congress, it does not have representation in US federal government, and Puerto Ricans do not have the right to vote in US elections. Federal government remains in control of most state affairs, including citizenship, immigration, customs, defense, currency, foreign trade, and diplomacy.
2. Such as rule 247.1 of the Puerto Rico Rules of Criminal Prosecution, and various amendments to the 1971 Law of Controlled Substances.

References

Anjum, T. (2017). Vernacularization of Islam and Sufism in South Asia: A study of the production of sufi literature in local languages. *Journal of the Research Society of Pakistan, 54*(1), 190–207. AsiaNet Pakistan (Pvt) Ltd.

Baudrillard, J. (1983). *The precession of simulacra.* New York: Semiotext(e).

Darke, S., & Garces, C. (2017). Surviving in the new mass carceral zone. *Prison Service Journal, 229*, 2–9.

Departamento de Justicia. (1986). *Departamento de Justicia Explicación Del Prepuesto Funcional Año Fiscal 1985–1986.* Departamento de Justicia. Biblioteca Legislativa de Puerto Rico.

Departamento de Justicia. (1992). *Departamento de Justicia Memorial Explicativo Año Fiscal 1991–1992.* Departamento de Justicia. Biblioteca Legislativa de Puerto Rico.

Department of Correction and Rehabilitation. (1994). *Intermediate sanctions plan*. Departamento de Corrección y Rehabilitación. Biblioteca Legislativa de Puerto Rico.

Estado Libre Asociado de Puerto Rico. (1973, April 6). *Senate session 495 of 1973*. Biblioteca Legislativa de Puerto Rico.

Ferrería, J. N. (2012). Colossal cost of subsidizing failure: How the drug war impacts Puerto Rico's budget. *Revista Jurídica UPR, 81*, 1139.

Garcia, A. (2015). Serenity: Violence, inequality, and recovery on the edge of Mexico City. *Medical Anthropology Quarterly, 29*(4), 455-472.

Hansen, H. (2018). *Addicted to Christ: Remaking Men in Puerto Rican Pentecostal Drug Ministries*. University of California Press.

Kerwin Kaye, B. (2010). *Drug courts and the treatment of addiction: Therapeutic jurisprudence and neoliberal governance*. New York: New York University.

Legislative Assembly of Puerto Rico. (2000). *Ley No. 408 – Ley de Salud Mental de Puerto Rico* (Act No. 408 – Puerto Rico Mental Health Act). https://www.mindbank.info/item/3074

Lévi-Strauss, C. (1966). *The savage mind*. Chicago: University of Chicago Press.

Levitt, P., & Merry, S. (2009). Vernacularization on the ground: Local uses of global Women's rights in Peru, China, India and the United States. *Global Networks, 9*(4), 441–461.

Millar, K. M. (2018). *Reclaiming the discarded: Life and labor on Rio's garbage dump*. Duke University Press.

O'Neill, K. L. (2014). On Liberation: Crack, Christianity, and Captivity in Postwar Guatemala City. *Social Text, 32*(3), 11–28.

O'Neill, L. A., & Gumbrewicz, J. (2005). Our forgotten colony: Puerto Rico and the war on drugs. *The Modern American, 1*, 8–11.

Parker, C. M. (2020). From treatment to containment to enterprise: An Ethnohistory of THERAPEUTIC COMMUNITIES in Puerto Rico, 1961–1993. *Culture, Medicine, and Psychiatry, 44*(1, Springer), 135–157.

Santiago-Negrón, S., & Albizu-García, C. E. (2003). Guerra contra las Drogas o Guerra contra La Salud? Los Retos Para La Salud Pública de La Política de Drogas de Puerto Rico [war on drugs or war against health? The pitfalls for public health of Puerto Rican drug policy]. *Puerto Rico Health Sciences Journal, 22*(1). http://prhsj.rcm.upr.edu/index.php/prhsj/article/download/740/531

Stoler, A. L., McGranahan, C., & Perdue, P. C. (2007). *Imperial formations*. Santa Fe: SAR Press.

Tiger, R. (2013). *Judging addicts: Drug courts and coercion in the justice system*. New York: New York University Press.

Weegels, J. H. J. (2018). *Performing prison: Power, agency and co-governance in Nicaraguan prisons*. Amsterdam: University of Amsterdam.

Weegels, J. (2020). Prison riots in Nicaragua: Negotiating co-governance amid creative violence and public secrecy. *International Criminal Justice Review, 30*(1), 61–82. Los Angeles: Sage Publications.

Wexler, D. B. (1990). Including therapuetic compliance through the criminal law. *Law and Psychology Review, 14*, 43.

World Prison Brief. (2016). *Puerto Rico (USA) | World prison brief*. http://www.prisonstudies.org/country/puerto-rico-usa

11

The Futility and Necessity of Human Rights in an Era of Carceral Hyperinflation

Loïc Wacquant

Over the past dozen years, I have had the opportunity and privilege to share my research on the nexus of incarceration and urban marginality with a broad range of non-academics. I have spoken to and debated with the leadership and staff of the prison services of France, the Netherlands, Brazil, and Argentina; I have engaged officials and professionals concerned with criminal justice trends and policies at the United Nations, the OECD, the Italian parliament, and a smattering of regional and city governments (ranging from the district of Seine-Saint-Denis, northeast of Paris, and the Generalitat de Catalunya to cities as far flung as Rotterdam, Rome, and Rio de Janeiro). I welcome this opportunity for dialogue and mutual learning with the Gendarmeria de Chile on this day in Santiago.[1]

L. Wacquant (✉)
University of California, Oakland, CA, USA

Centre européen de sociologie et de science politique, Paris, France

S. Darke et al. (eds.), *Carceral Communities in Latin America*, Palgrave Studies in Prisons and Penology, https://doi.org/10.1007/978-3-030-61499-7_11

The Prison in Professional Practice and Social Theory

First, let me make clear that I am not here to inculpate or disculpate the Gendameria by my words or deeds, not because I am timid or squeamish, but simply because *sociologists are not moralists*. We are not in the business of passing judgement on institutions, deciding who is "guilty" and who is "innocent," and assigning blame for undesirable social conditions and unwanted human outcomes. We are in the business of analyzing the ordinary operations, built-in contradictions and ramifying effects of institutions, the social functions they fulfill, and the collective fictions they sustain.[2] I want to stress this at the outset to dissipate a mistaken view of what sociologists are about, prevalent among the educated citizenry as well as among many of my colleagues (who think that putting the adjective "critical" before sociology does more than waste a bit of ink and paper).

Second, I am not here to give lessons to the Gendarmeria de Chile: academics should always be careful when addressing professionals, because they reside for the most part in an abstract world of texts, suspended above and sheltered from the urgency of practical tasks. By contrast, professionals have their hands dirty from getting things done in whatever domain they operate. I have no experience running a prison, but I have enough of a sense of the complexities it entails to know that I am badly placed to instruct anyone who does on how to administer their establishment. I would not count my morning-long visit of La Penitenciaria, however instructive it has been, as a basis for leveraging advice. Prison tours are interesting to get a feel for what the warden wishes to showcase to outsiders; they tell us more about the view that officials want to project than about the daily realities of life in under lock.

But here is the advantage of being retired from a given institution: you can study it, dissect it, break it down into its constituent elements, and learn from comparison across units, epochs, and geographical boundaries. The contribution the sociologist can make to the discussion about human rights behind bars is to provide a broader outside view; bring the lessons of historical and international experience to bear on contemporary debates in a given country; supply an *analytic frame that makes it possible to step back* from the urgency of practice and the fire of political debate, reformulate questions, and point to some of the unforeseen consequences and hidden contradictions of penal confinement, as well as link the prison to other pertinent institutions beyond its walls.

Different theoretical traditions in the social sciences articulate different connections of punishment to non-judicial institutions. Roughly put, we can distinguish five theoretical strands and organizational linkages:

1. *Class and the economy*: the neo-Marxist tradition portrays criminal justice as a material instrument of control whose primary target is the poor and whose trends mirror those of the sphere of production, particularly the state of labor. Its typical topic is the macro-level correlation between incarceration and unemployment. Rusche and Kirschheimer's ([1939] 1995) *Punishment and Social Structure* is generally cited as the canonical text of this tradition—mistakenly, in my view, since it puts forth a multifactorial model, taking into account extra-economic variables, such as fiscal capacity, religion, and sexuality, that puts it closer to Weber than to Marx.
2. *Community and morality*: the tradition descended from Émile Durkheim and the French school of sociology construes punishment as a language, a means of symbolic communication that captures collective emotions to spotlight and elevate shared norms. The target here is not the criminal but the law-abiding citizen, and a favorite topic is crime scares and judicial ceremonials that embody the passionate tenor of punishment and serve to draw boundaries between insiders and outsiders. A paradigmatic study is Kai Erikson's (1966) dissection of the Salem witch trials in the seventeenth century Puritan colony of Massachusetts in *Wayward Puritans*.
3. *Professionals of rationality, elite mentalities and cultural sensibilities*: a third line of works takes after the classic analysis of law, bureaucracy, and rationalization by Max Weber and his epigone, Norbert Elias. It stresses the emergence of official specialists in the management of crime, the changing attitudes of elites toward the body, pain, and deviance, and how these shape the gradual "civilizing" of punishment. The Dutch historian Pieter Spierenburg (1984) offers a classic

statement of this position in his book *The Spectacle of Suffering*, which charts the disappearance of the public infliction of physical punishment from the sixteenth to the nineteenth centuries in Europe. I put Foucault within this broad neo-Weberian tradition, given his concern for the uniqueness of the West and the de facto rationalization of domination through the societal diffusion of "disciplines" designed to make bodies "docile and useful" in *Discipline and Punish* ([1975] 1977).
4. *Forging criminal deviance, penal identity, and the self*: Foucault also offers a link to a distinctively microsociological tradition rooted in the North American school of symbolic interactionism, concerned with the social mechanisms that produce deviance, shape identity, and mold the self of the criminal and the inmate. Erving Goffman's (1961) *Asylums* and John Irwin's (1970) *The Felon* are exemplary statements of this approach, which gives us an understanding of punishment from the standpoint of the punished and their coping strategies.
5. *The state as symbolic power and bureaucratic field*: the last and most recent theoretical strand draws on the work of my mentor and friend, the late French sociologist Pierre Bourdieu. Bourdieu ([1993] 1990) gives us two concepts to rethink punishment: the notion of "symbolic power" points to the monopolization of the capacity to impose classifications on society and to inflict dishonor on its members in the form of penal sanction; the notion of "bureaucratic field" suggests that there is a *struggle going on inside the state* between rival agencies that purport to resolve social problems by applying supportive social treatment (the feminine Left hand) or disciplinary sanctions (the masculine Right hand). In my book *Punishing the Poor* (Wacquant 2009), I adapt these two notions to show that the resurgence of the prison over the past thirty years partakes of the building of the neoliberal state and its policy of penalization of poverty.

This brief overview is intended to point out that, far from being an isolated institution, the prison is simultaneously linked to a multiplicity of social institutions and forces, themselves interlinked: the economy, civic emotions, elite sensibilities and bureaucratic forms, the identities elaborated by the punisher and the punished, and patterned struggles inside the state on how to define and distribute public goods, including the negative good of criminal punishment.

Here I want to spotlight this last variable: the notion of human rights is typically invoked by educated elites with a stake in expanding the role of the Left hand of the state in opposition to their counterparts of the Right hand who invoke economic rationality and budget necessities to undermine the extension and enforcement of costly rights. The ministry of justice, where it oversees the prison system, is itself traversed by the same tension between a Left pole wedded to rights and rehabilitation and a Right pole infatuated with retribution and the rigid implementation of law and order as a matter of state authority. I suspect that in this very room there are members of the Gendarmeria de Chile who are committed to upholding and expanding human rights behind bars and others who see the same human rights as a useless luxury and a feckless distraction from their mission, if not a Trojan horse for leftist sedition. The fact that I am invited to give this address today and the look of stern military attentiveness of my audience indicate that the struggle between these two poles is uncertain if asymmetric.[3]

The Bourdieusian approach invites us to make three moves that are useful to situate the debate over human rights in prison (see Wacquant 2011 for an elaboration). The first is to *decouple crime from punishment* and to acknowledge that, from the time of its historical invention in the late sixteenth century, the penal prison has always served as an implement to manage urban marginality and to assert the prerogatives of the ruler through the theater of penal sanction. The second move is to treat social welfare policy and penal policy as *two sides of the same coin of poverty policy* and to acknowledge that these two policy streams must be understood together, insofar as they treat the same population and deploy the same discursive tropes and administrative techniques. The third move is to *hold together the material and the symbolic moments of punishment* and to realize that its functions of control and communication, associated with the Marxist and the Durkheimian schools, respectively, are not antinomic but complementary and even mutually sustaining. When you arrest a suspect and incarcerate a convict, you are simultaneously exerting physical force and symbolic force: you are curtailing the material entitlements of that person as well as broadcasting a moral message by amputating his membership in the civic compact and soiling his dignity.

Connecting Human Rights Inside and Social Rights Outside

The question of human rights is primarily a juridical and moral question, not a sociological one, so I feel ill-positioned to tackle it. I am aware that there is a broad and dynamic domain of research at the intersection of law, political sociology, and peace studies that deploys this notion (Somers and Roberts 2008; Clapham 2016). But my summary view is that, in the current context of carceral hyperinflation and bolstering of the penal state across Latin America (Müller 2012; Hathazy and Müller 2016), human rights form what Kenneth Burke (1957) calls a *terministic screen*, a discourse that veils the reality of the utterly catastrophic conditions of mass detention, reminiscent of captives in medieval dungeons (Geltner 2008), in a set of formal categories obfuscating the interests of those who invoke them.[4]

So I would turn the question around and ask: when are *human rights* invoked behind bars? Answer: when fundamental *social and economic rights* are routinely violated beyond bars, as is the case throughout Latin America due to the combination of extreme social inequality, rampant poverty, and the political reality of the (un)rule of law (Hoffman and Centeno 2003; Mendez et al. 1999). At the risk of seeming to court paradox for its own sake, I will argue that talk of human rights in the prisons of societies that ongoingly violate basic standards of human dignity at the bottom of their class structure is at once futile and indispensable.

To speak of human rights behind bars is an *exercise in futility* for two basic reasons. The first is that the prison itself is fundamentally an *outlaw institution:* it functions *exlex*, outside of the law. Under the press of necessity, correctional authorities everywhere violate the legal rules they are supposed to uphold. Proof is the suffusive brutality and shocking material penury that afflicts inmates throughout Latin America. Even in advanced countries, penitentiary legal codes are underdeveloped, weak, and solipsistic, incapable of effectively allocating inmates a core set of rights. This is because the confined are by design *zombie citizens,* existing in the shadow of the law but not in its light. The second reason is that the prison is a deeply *damaging institution*: it is a place of concentrated violence and vice; it assaults the personality, distorts the sociality, and erodes the physical and mental well-being of those placed in it. Moreover, it seems absurd to grant and enforce human rights behind bars when these same rights are denied beyond them due to the weakness of the social and economic rights of citizenship that are their minimal condition of actualization.

And yet there is definitely a *utility to human rights*: legal discourse can serve as guide and goad to improve correctional funding and functioning, as a weapon to curb penal illegality and to minimize human damage within carceral facilities. For this reason, we must invoke them, insert them among correctional standards, and seek to enforce them so long as we do not know how to do better and until such time as we engage in a more fundamental political reflection on the purposes of incarceration, or lack thereof.[5] But we must do with no illusions about their limits and by constantly connecting human rights inside and social rights outside.

So how are we to deploy human rights to minimize the interlinked illegality and social destructiveness of the prison? I propose that we follow three principles. First, *minimize the footprint of the carceral institution* by maximizing alternative ways of managing marginality and crime, including social, medical, and economic treatments of problematic conditions and conducts, all of which focus on preclusion and prophylaxis rather than punitive reaction.[6] Second, *relink inside and outside*, for the prison is not a closed and hermetic space. Contrary to the official vision, its walls are doubly porous, by which I mean that external forces seep in and affect its operations and output (concretely, think of the flow of service providers and visitors who come into its perimeter daily and of the streaming contraband of drugs, cell phones, and indispensable goods like food, medicine, and toiletries) and that, going the other way, the prison deeply affects the neighborhoods of relegation that are its primary feeders. This is true everywhere, but nowhere truer than in Latin America, where, due to lack of sufficient funding, prisons rely on this constant tide *trans muros* for their basic operations and routine order maintenance. Third, take into account the deleterious long term impact of incarceration both *within and across generations*: confinement warps the life trajectories not just of the inmates but of entire lineages, from their wives and parents to their children and grandchildren and many of their kin and friends in between.[7] The prison is a poverty-perpetuating and crime inducing-institution, both within and beyond its walls.

Some of you may complain that these principles are overly broad and generic and that they fail to provide a guide for concrete and immediate action, beyond the indispensable goals of reducing staff mistreatment, inmate violence, and improving access to programs (Sanhueza et al. 2017). So let me end by making a few practical, if politically unlikely, recommendations to the Gendarmeria de Chile and, beyond it, to the prison services of the various Latin American countries that can find inspiration in Chilean reforms that would make this country a *continental trend-setter for decarceration* after being leader in incarceration for so long.

1. ***Reduce grotesque overcrowding***: human rights are a joke so long as inmates are packed like dead sardines. According to official data, the national occupancy level of Chile's custodial establishments is 118% and reaches 130% in La Penitenciaría. But this is a total charade: these figures are meaningless because they are obtained by cramming six men in tiny cells that should house at most two people. So the actual overcrowding rate is closer to 330%. Reducing overcrowding can be obtained by reducing sentence length across the board for good behavior (day for day), increasing early releases and expanding diversion programs (to minimize entries on short-term sentences).
2. ***Set a low prison population target and institute a cap***: launch an active policy of decarceration with an ambitious goal. Chile should aim to return to a rate of about 100 inmates per 100,000, similar to the rate it sported in 1981 and close to the average for Western Europe. Starting from today's rate of 300, this can be achieved by shaving about 12 points every year for 15 years, which represents a subtraction of about 1700 inmates annually. This rate of 100 can then be treated as an absolute cap, motivating the courts to find creative and effective alternatives to incarceration whenever it comes within reach.

3. ***Move the prison from the justice ministry to the Ministry of Social Development*** (where it belongs) and provide effective programs in health (including mental health), marital and family counseling, job training and employment under what I will call the *two for one rule*: two units of any service will be provided in the dispossessed districts symbiotically linked to the prison for every one unit delivered within the prison. For instance, offer construction jobs both inside and outside according to this ratio. Boosting social and economic rights on both sides of the prison walls simultaneously will deflect the politics of resentment (which falsely portrays the provision of correctional services as a zero-sum game that takes resources away from law-abiding citizens) and help create popular support for those programs.
4. ***Reduce the shocking squalor of the physical plant*** of penitentiaries as part of a large scale public housing program. Close down older facilities unfit for human housing and replace them with new ones built as part of a dual construction policy: for every peso invested in building a new prison, invest two pesos in improving the housing stock, and infrastructure in the neighborhoods of relegation that are the primary feeders of houses of confinement. Effectively, treat prisons for what they are everywhere: a central component of low-income or social housing.
5. ***Integrate public services behind bars*** such as education, health care, and social work with regular public services outside: create a mandatory "national service" for teachers, nurses, doctors and psychiatrists, and family counselors to serve two years inside prisons on government payroll; one year right after they obtain their degree and one year a decade later. Such service will both dramatically improve conditions for inmates and lift the concern of professionals outside for what happens to convicts. Provide tuition credit for university students who come to teach high school courses inside prisons. Make universal literacy mandatory for all inmates: no one should come out of prison without knowing how to read and write.
6. ***Elevate the status and quality of prison staff***: increase the baseline qualifications, periodic training, and pay of the staff to make the position of correctional officer a valorized and attractive one. Teach them applied rudiments in sociology, psychology, and social work instead of

tutoring them only in order-maintenance techniques. This will valorize their work as well as make them attuned to rights behind bars. In particular, drill into them that the full respect of the law and fair treatment of each inmate in every circumstance is the foundation of their job (we know that procedural justice, not fear, is why people obey the law, as shown by Tyler 2006).
7. ***Triple the correctional budget*** in fifteen years and make prison gradually more expensive so that budget-minded politicians actively seek alternative solutions to incarceration. Proposition 3 to 6 above will require significant increases in public funding. Together with propositions 1 and 2, they will raise the per capita cost of incarcerating offenders, which will create a built-in incentive for not overtaking the carceral cap.
8. ***Run a public information campaign on the failure of current penal policies***, making it clear to the citizenry that the prison is a *bankrupt institution*, a blunt and brutal implement that does not resolve the crime problem but merely hides and displaces it; that incarceration does not reduce recidivism and expand the ability of convicts to lead a lawful and productive life once they return to society (which nearly all of them do); and that confinement is enormously more costly than alternative responses and is becoming more expensive as human rights standards are implemented in custodial facilities.

This platform for action will not by itself deliver human rights in custody, but it will facilitate their insertion and defense. More importantly, it will directly curtail the built-in illegality and reduce the human corrosiveness of the prison. Ultimately, we must question the dichotomous offering of human rights behind bars and citizenship rights beyond bars. For inmates are citizens and, as such, they should be entitled to a modicum of social capacities and dignity both inside and outside the gates of the penitentiary.

Notes

1. This is a revised version of notes prepared for a keynote address to the Gendarmeria de Chile, Division of Human Rights, 16 October 2013, at the Gran Palace Hotel, Santiago de Chile. I thank the Gendarmeria de Chile for this invitation. I am grateful to Alejandro Arevalo, head of the Unit for Protection and Promotion of Human Rights, for involving me in this debate; to Guillermo Sanhueza for his tireless work behind the scenes; and to Megan Comfort for her astute observations during and after our visit of the prison of La Penitenciaría.
2. Max Weber (1948) put it best in his essays on *The Methodology of the Social Sciences*: our task is to "analytically order empirical reality," which is different from assessing its aesthetic value, moral worth, or political tenor.
3. I would hypothesize further that supporters of human rights within the polarized social space of the Gendarmeria are likely to be younger, more feminine, endowed with university credentials and with career paths starting outside of law enforcement, whereas their detractors sport the opposite properties. For backdrop, see the astute and thorough study of the recent transformation of penal institutions and policies in Chile by Paul Carlos Hathazy (2013), *Democratizing Leviathan*.
4. On this point, I recommend reading Nicolas Guilhot's (2005) *The Democracy Makers*, which shows how the transnational movement for democracy and human rights has been hijacked by experts and turned into an instrument of neoliberal reform. For dissenting views documenting a more positive role for human rights, see van Zyl and Snacken (2009) for Europe, and Sikkink (2007) and Cardenas (2011) for Latin America.
5. David Garland (2003) shows that we do not really know why we incarcerate any more due to "the crisis of penal modernism."
6. I discuss these alternatives in Wacquant (2009: 281–286), "How to Escape the Law-and-Order Snare."
7. See the work of Comfort (2008) on the girlfriends and wives of convicts, Black (2010) on brothers, and Wakefield and Wideman (2013) on the multisided impact on their children.

References

Black, T. (2010). *When a heart turns rock solid: The lives of three Puerto Rican brothers on and off the streets*. New York: Vintage.

Bourdieu, P. ([1993] 1994). Rethinking the state: Genesis and structure of the bureaucratic field. *Sociological Theory, 12*(1), 1–18.

Burke, K. (1957). *The philosophy of literary form*. Berkeley: University of California Press.

Cardenas, S. (2011). *Human rights in Latin America: A politics of terror and hope*. Philadelphia: University of Pennsylvania Press.

Clapham, A. (2016). *Human rights: A very short introduction*. Oxford: Oxford University Press.

Comfort, M. (2008). *Doing time together: Love and family in the shadow of the prison*. Chicago: University of Chicago Press.

Erikson, K. (1966). *Wayward puritans: A study in the sociology of deviance*. New York: Wiley.

Foucault, M. ([1975] 1977). *Discipline and punish: The birth of the prison*. New York: Vintage, New Ed. 2012.

Garland, D. (2003). Penal modernism and postmodernism. In T. G. Blomberg & S. Cohen (Eds.), *Punishment and social control*. New York: Aldine de Gruyter, 2nd expanded edition.

Geltner, G. (2008). *The medieval prison: A social history*. Princeton: Princeton University Press.

Goffman, E. (1961). *Asylums: Essays on the social situation of mental patients and other inmates*. New York: Anchor.

Guilhot, N. (2005). *The democracy makers: Human rights and international order*. New York: Columbia University Press.

Hathazy, P. C. (2013). *Democratizing leviathan: Bureaucrats, experts and politics in the transformation of the penal state in Argentina and Chile*. Berkeley, Unpublished PhD dissertation, 332p.

Hathazy, P., & Müller, M.-M. (2016). The rebirth of the prison in Latin America: Determinants, regimes and social effects. *Crime, Law and Social Change, 65*(3), 113–135.

Hoffman, K., & Centeno, M. A. (2003). The lopsided continent: Inequality in Latin America. *Annual Review of Sociology, 29*, 363–390.

Irwin, J. (1970). *The felon*. Berkeley: University of California Press, 1987.

Méndez, J. E., O'Donnell, G. A., & Pinheiro, P. S. (Eds.). (1999). *The (un) rule of law and the underprivileged in Latin America*. South Bend: University of Notre Dame Press.
Müller, M.-M. (2012). The rise of the penal state in Latin America. *Contemporary Justice Review, 15*(1), 57–76.
Rusche, G., & Kirscheimer, O. (1939). *Punishment and social structure* (Vol. 2003). New Brunswick: Transaction Books.
Sanhueza, G., Brander, F., & Fuenzalida, F. (2017). First survey on prison life in Chile: A social work call for prison reform. *International Social Work*. in press.
Sikkink, K. (2007). *Mixed signals: US Human Rights Policy and Latin America*. Ithaca: Cornell University Press.
Somers, M. R., & Roberts, C. N. J. (2008). Toward a new sociology of rights: A genealogy of 'buried bodies' of citizenship and human rights. *Annual Review of Law and Social Science, 4*, 385–425.
Spierenburg, P. (1984). *The spectacle of suffering: Executions and the evolution of repression*. Cambridge: Cambridge University Press.
Tyler, T. R. (2006). *Why people obey the law*. Princeton: Princeton University Press.
van Zyl Smit, D., & Snacken, S. (2009). *Principles of European prison law and policy: Penology and human rights*. Oxford: Oxford University Press.
Wacquant, L. (2009). *Punishing the poor: The neoliberal government of social insecurity*. Durham/London: Duke University Press.
Wacquant, L. (2011). The wedding of workfare and prisonfare revisited. *Social Justice, 38*(1–2, Spring), 203–221.
Wakefield, S., & Wildeman, C. (2013). *Children of the prison boom: Mass incarceration and the future of American inequality*. New York: Oxford University Press.
Weber, M. (1948). *The methodology of the social sciences*. Glencoe: Free Press.

12

Competition and Collusion Among Criminal Justice and Non-State Actors in Brazil's Prison System

Fiona Macaulay

Introduction

Most of the chapters in this book focus on the internal logics of prison life in Latin America, where state abandonment encourages prisoner self-governance, in its many modalities, and relegates the most immediate representatives of the penal state (prison guards) to collaborators. However, prison populations are produced in the first instance by criminal justice actors and institutions. The latter shape the penal experience, for they act not just outside the prison system, as the funnel that directs particular social groups into existing carceral communities, but also within. Their discretionary practices and institutional power determine much of the context of prison insecurity and survival dynamics that is closely analysed by other authors in this volume. Unlike Anglo-Saxon prison systems, which are managed largely by the executive branch, Latin American judicial institutions are integral to prisoner and prison system

F. Macaulay (✉)
University of Bradford, Bradford, UK

S. Darke et al. (eds.), *Carceral Communities in Latin America*, Palgrave Studies in Prisons and Penology, https://doi.org/10.1007/978-3-030-61499-7_12

management. This creates territorial competition on several levels (philosophical, legal and material), but also collusion, when there should be a separation of functions and oversight. In addition, a number of non-state actors and prisoner organisations are also now competing for control over parts of the carceral archipelago in Brazil and offering alternative formal and informal governance and penal experiences.

This chapter examines how both the formal and informal dispositions and practices employed by criminal justice-related institutions in Brazil have created the conditions for the prisoner self-governance and survival strategies analysed by other authors in this volume. It looks at how extra-mural criminal justice institutions have created and sustain such an enormous prison population, how these exercise an intra-mural role in shaping the carceral experience for inmates and how they interact with the non-state actors active in the carceral space. These dynamics are complex, sometimes contradictory, and can shift between competition and co-operation. The process of mapping these relationships is also incipient, with ethnographic work on the prisoner experience (Dias 2013; Biondi 2016; Darke 2018) but little ethnographic data on the justice system, its operators and its institutional micro-cultures. I first embarked on researching the Brazilian prison system in 1997, on behalf of Amnesty International, and since then have visited dozens of penal institutions, of different types, and spoken to many criminal justice operators in diverse levels of administrative responsibility, and to civil society groups involved with prisons, all around the country. This chapter draws on those observations, conversations and poking-and-soaking in the Brazilian penal field.

Informal institutions are here understood as shared sets of practices, values and unspoken rules of behaviour that may be at odds with the formal rules and purposes governing the organisation in question (Helmke & Levitsky 2006). Often, they emerge in organisations as a form of resistance to being governed and directed by other actors, either those in a hierarchically superior position, or in a separate branch of government or sphere. In Brazil, this is accentuated by horizontal relations between the three major institutions of the criminal justice system (police, prosecutorial service and courts) that are characterised by fragmentation, compartmentalisation, territorialism and hyper-autonomy. As a result of institutional design, individual judges and prosecutors are accorded excessive personal discretion—it was not until late 2004 that the principle of binding precedent was introduced, weakly, into Brazilian law. Therefore, the formal criminal justice institutions have relatively weak vertical controls, which in turn encourages informal corporate values and practices that influence individual actors in the aggregate. Territorial competition for governance of the incarcerated is also visible as a number of state and non-state actors jostle for influence over the prisoners and the resources that they represent, and over the way in which prisoners' rights are framed.

Roberto Kant de Lima, the pioneer in legal system ethnography in Brazil, has argued that these institutions do not form a criminal justice *system* as such, as in Anglo-Saxon countries, given the bifurcation between public security professionals (police, prison authorities) and criminal justice professionals (judges, prosecutors and public defenders), and the hyper-autonomy of each of the agencies, driven by distinctive institutional goals and philosophies (Lima 2010: 28). Others have argued that the two domains—of law-and-order, or 'public security' as Brazilians call it, and justice—often find themselves counterposed in political discourse and public policy as a choice between *defesa social*, that is, defending the society of 'decent people' from the 'bad people', and *garantismo*, that is, upholding constitutional and legal rights of criminal suspects and convicts. All the actors and institutions of the criminal justice system have to position themselves in relation to this apparent binary. And, at times of moral panics about crime and violence, fuelled by punitivist talk by politicians, judicial actors tend to identify as part of the state's crime-fighting apparatus more than as rights protectors. A survey of judges in the criminal courts in Rio de Janeiro in 2011 found that, when sentencing, they were putting a general concern about social order over the specifics of the individual case and the rights of the accused in front of them (Casara 2015). This preoccupation was even evident in a key Supreme Court ruling on a legal challenge alleging the unconstitutionality of mass incarceration and consequent poor prison conditions in Brazil.[1] This slippage of identities and institutional overlap means that whilst criminal justice institutions often engage in inter-institutional competition for resources, they also collude when their moral philosophies around crime coincide. This results in agencies that should exercise distinctive functions and mutual oversight collaborating in sending too many criminal suspects to prison and keeping them there.

Formal and Informal Practices of Incarceration

By the end of 2019, Brazil's prison population had topped the 750,000 mark, putting it third in the world in absolute numbers after the USA and China. Its prison population rose more than six-fold from 1992, and its imprisonment rate nearly quintupled, from 74 to 357 per 100,000 population. This seemingly inexorable rise in mass incarceration, which shows no signs of abating, has been produced not just by the changing patterns of crime (particularly the violence and insecurity created by trafficking in narcotics and associated goods) but also by the operational and philosophical preferences of criminal justice agencies for arrest, detention and the carceral disposition (Melo 2020). Brazil's prisons are the product of a central tension in governance: the system is understood to be highly dysfunctional and unsustainable, yet it continues to grow. The political branches of government have often been pulling in different directions. The national legislature tended to lead in introducing hyper-penalising legislation, adding new crimes to the statute books and ramping up penalties, often in response to periodic moral panics around crime.[2] The executive branch, up until 2016 at least, sponsored diversionary legislation, intended to take the pressure off a system that it part-finances, understanding that the building of new prisons can never catch up with the inflow of new detainees. But its decarcerating laws have only slowed the rate of increase, not reversed it, because the judicial branch (judges and prosecutors), at a subnational and individual level, has tended to resist such moves, and maintained an informal institutional bias in favour of incarceration as a form of *defesa social* (Carvalho 2010: 60). These judicial actors have a double, conflicting, interest in prisoners, simultaneously responsible for placing them in custody, and for upholding all the legalities of their detention, and this conflict of interest plays out in the rituals and decision-making in courts every day. The fate of three such initiatives—the 2006 drug law, the 2011 precautionary measures law and the 2015 custody hearing policy—is illustrative of how judicial and prosecutorial cultures have undermined the intention of both the federal government and the governing body of the judiciary to tackle Brazil's prison crisis.

In 2006, the law was changed to divert those convicted of possession of drugs for personal consumption into education, community service and treatment, and away from prison. Yet, after the change in the law the proportion of individuals incarcerated for minor drug offences actually *doubled*, accounting at one point for one quarter of all custodial sentences. The law had left enough loopholes for discretion on the part of law enforcement officials and justice operators, who simply reimposed their own preference for imprisoning the young black men at the *boca de fumo* (street-corner retail sales point) rather than the consumers and intermediaries in the drug chain. As these young men were moved through the hands of the various agencies of the justice system, their fate was sealed by an escalating punitive process. Police routinely recorded the amounts of drugs found on suspects as 'excessive for personal use', and this assessment was almost never revised by further post-hoc investigation.[3] Analysis of the cases of prisoners in two large prisons in São Paulo revealed that prosecutors then had a marked tendency to super-penalise, upgrading a third of all the offences listed in the police crime reports to a more serious one once they formally brought charges. Offenders arrested for an 'attempted' crime would find themselves charged as if they had actually committed the crime in question (ITTC & Pastoral Carcerária Nacional 2012: 61). Then, once the cases reached court, the judges frequently decided that anyone selling drugs must automatically be a member of a criminal organisation, which carries an even higher prison sentence.[4] Yet, a study of 800 sentences handed down in eight Brazilian states from 2013–2015 for 'drug trafficking' showed that two thirds of the accused were low income, 80 per cent were first-time offenders, firearms were present in under 10 per cent of arrests, there was no accomplice in 70 per cent of cases, and the average value of cash confiscated was just £45 per person (Semer 2019), confirming findings in other studies based on police, prosecution and court records (Boiteux 2010; Valois 2016; Machado et al. 2019).

This judicial drive to incarcerate has made it difficult to reduce the number of pre-trial prisoners, who continue to make up nearly one third of the prison population. They are often held in the worst conditions in terms of overcrowding and legal neglect and, as such, are particularly in need of the protections offered by the prisoners' organisations, or *comandos*, that substitute for the state in so many facilities. 'Preventive detention' is a legal tool available to judges to stop suspects from absconding,[5] or committing more crimes, but tends to be used as a form of pre-emptive extra-legal punishment. The country's legal culture—its *sensibilidades jurídicas*—is underpinned by an a priori presumption of guilt, an inquisitorial logic that seeks to arrive at a presumed 'truth' about the offender and offence, and the judge's prerogative of 'interpreting' subjectively the facts put before them (Lima 2010). In over 90 per cent of cases examined in São Paulo, the judges handling cases of *in flagrante* arrest did not even bother putting down a reason for upholding the pre-trial detention, tending to view the detainees as a broad category, rather than as individuals with specific circumstances to be considered. Pre-trial detention was also applied where the individual had been accused of a crime that would not even result in a custodial sentence (ITTC & Pastoral Carcerária Nacional 2012). Such detentions violate the provisions of the 1998 Alternative Penalties law, the first serious diversion and decarceration initiative by the executive branch, which allows first-time offenders who have committed offences carrying a tariff of under four years in jail to receive an alternative sentence, such as community service. Such illegal detentions would be equivalent to state kidnapping, an argument I make more widely for pre-trial detention without legal counsel, justifiable charge or for excessive periods, which is still very common in Latin America (Macaulay 2019).

The Precautionary Measures (*medidas cautelares*) law passed in 2011 was the first executive-led attempt to offer judges a range of options to ensure that criminal suspects were still available to stand trial without holding them in detention. However, case data and interviews with justice system operators in Rio de Janeiro revealed that the latter initially boycotted the new philosophy: 98 per cent of those accused of drug offences continued to be held in pre-trial detention for the duration of their case (Lemgruber et al. 2013). The same was true of 90 per cent of cases involving illegal ownership of a firearm, for which bail conditions are explicitly set out in the law, and for well over 50 per cent of non-violent offences against property such as theft and receiving stolen goods (ibid: 10).

Given that local judges were ignoring the spirit and intent of national legislation, the governing body of the judiciary, the National Justice Council (*Conselho Nacional de Justiça* – CNJ), was convinced by NGOs active in promoting criminal justice reforms and prisoners' legal rights to introduce new procedures that would oblige judges to justify the necessity of preventive detention in each case (Macaulay 2018). In 2015, backed by the Ministry of Justice, the CNJ introduced compulsory custody hearings (*audiências de custódia*), requiring law enforcement authorities to bring suspects arrested in flagrante before a judge within 24 hours. The hearings are intended to uncover abuse or torture by police, and a decision is made immediately about bail conditions, whereas previously suspects would have waited an average of six months in pre-trial detention for a first hearing. Reducing the pre-trial prison population was also seen as means of regaining governance over parts of the carceral space: it was a notorious outbreak of gang violence, gruesome murders and escapes in Maranhão that led that state to pilot these hearings in October 2014. However, as with the previous initiatives, the system absorbed and adapted in order to maintain the *status quo ex ante*. CNJ data shows that 60 per cent of prisoners are still remanded in custody, and only one per cent are released without any conditions at all. The hearings and outcome are public and so have been the subject of both observational studies and quantitative analysis, which revealed that they are conducted in a formulaic manner that still does not pay attention to the individual cases, and routinely ignores illegalities in the arrest (abuse, lack of evidence) that they were intended to flag up (Instituto Pro Bono 2018). Judges are, in effect, practising *Täterstrafrecht*, a German legal term for offender-based criminal law that criminalises the actor, rather than the act.

And, of course, there is considerable variation across the country. Unusually for a large federal country, Brazil has a single, national criminal code. However, its criminal justice agencies are governed by the relevant political and judicial authorities in the 26 states and the Federal District. This decentralisation produces a high degree of autonomy and discretion, and quite localised judicial cultures, institutional mechanisms and informal practices. For example, the legal culture in São Paulo state has long been known as one of the most punitivist in the country (Koerner 2005). This *paulista* judicial culture is maintained by a process of professional socialisation among prosecutors and judges, through attending the same prestigious law school, personal networks and patronage. This culture can be seen reflected in the higher sentences handed down for drug offences, even though the seriousness of these offences is lower than elsewhere (Semer 2019). Their preference for incarceration is also institutionally maintained by two filter mechanisms unique to the state. Since 2013, the São Paulo appellate court has exercised direct control over the entrance and exit portals to the prison system through the police investigation department (*Departamento de Inquéritos Policiais* – Dipo) and the sentence serving department (*Departamento Estadual de Execução Criminal* – Deecrim). In the first, judges oversee cases of police in flagrante arrests, including the resultant custody hearings, and police crime investigations (except of murder or misdemeanours), which are then distributed to the courts to try. In the second, judges make decisions on petitions for regime progression, benefits, parole and release. The appointment of these judges is at the discretion of the appellate court, and therefore judges are selected, or removed, at will on the basis of their alignment with the state judiciary's maximalist position on incarceration (Zapater 2015). For example, the appointment of a 'tough' judge at the end of 2017 saw the proportion of pre-trial prisoners remanded in custody rise markedly under her tenure. Judge Patrícia Álvarez Cruz had a clear position that the common judicial practice of dismissing 'trivial' offences (known as the *princípio de insignificância*) had no basis in law: she herself was notorious for having jailed a woman for the theft of a bottle of shampoo and conditioner.[6] My personal observations of custody hearings in São Paulo in this period confirmed this pattern of excessive control even of those accused of the most minor crime. One case I witnessed involved the theft of a salami from a supermarket, but as it was a repeat offence the judge, prosecutor and public defender engaged in debate about the need for preventive detention. In the end, the homeless person accused of the theft was required to report to a police station once a month until trial.

This philosophical orthodoxy in the judiciary is applied when policing its own ranks. In at least one instance, a judge was removed from the DIPO at the request of prosecutors for being too concerned with upholding prisoners' rights.[7] A justice in the appellate court initiated disciplinary proceedings against fellow justice Kenarik Boujikian after she signed off on the release of 11 prisoners whose pre-trial detention period had exceeded any sentence they could have received for the charges they faced. Her colleagues resented her failure to consult with them and thus allow them to veto the decision. The case was struck down by the CNJ, which will correct poor judicial decisions retroactively, but is very wary of disciplining poor judges due to the principles of federalism and judicial autonomy.[8]

Contests Over Prisoners and Prison Regimes

In 1997, I visited the Roger prison, the main men's facility in João Pessoa, the capital of the north-eastern state of Paraíba, following reports of prisoner-on-prisoner violence. On 29 July 1997, eight prisoners were brutally killed after they had taken hostages in a failed escape attempt. The military police stormed the prison before negotiations had been completed; the hostages escaped and police shot and wounded the hostage takers. Prison officers and a number of 'trustee' inmates from the kitchens then took over and used crowbars and knives to murder the eight injured prisoners.[9] This incident was typical of the intra-inmate violence in Brazilian prisons where the authorities had lost effective control of the carceral space. What was more unusual was the allegation that *defensores públicos*—legal aid lawyers employed by the state to represent these prisoners and defend their legal rights—had stood on a balcony overlooking the yard and egged on the violence. Two researchers from Human Rights Watch went to investigate. As they were talking to inmates in the prison yard, a *defensor* suddenly appeared, brandishing a habeas corpus decision issued by the local *juiz da vara de execução penal* (the judge and court locally designated to oversee the serving of prison sentences in that jurisdiction). This habeas corpus writ purported to 'protect' the inmates from 'interrogation by foreign individuals'. Despite its spuriousness, the researchers were ejected from the prison.

About a month later, I went, on behalf of Amnesty International, to test whether this attempt to prevent scrutiny of the prison still stood. It did, and I sat through a tense meeting in the prison administration block in which the *defensores públicos* used the habeas corpus decision to prevent me entering the prison, to the very evident discomfort of the prison governor, who was being over-ruled in his own establishment. I then paid a visit to the local *juiz de execução penal* who had issued the decision, one Dr. Hitler Cantalice.[10] White linen-suited, he was every inch the old-style *coronel*, and very aware of the discretionary patronage power that he held over the prisoners, who had to petition him, via the *defensores*, for all their entitlements, such as parole, sentence remission for work, eventual transfer to a lighter regime, and even final release. My first attempt to meet with him had failed. Although his secretary had informed us that he was 'just coming up in the lift', an hour later he had still not appeared. But sitting waiting on a sofa in his office, I overheard one side of a phone call taken by one of his staffers, which went as follows, 'Yes, yes, keep the prisoner in solitary for a few days – until the marks disappear.'

Although this incident was extreme, in one sense, and occurred over two decades ago, it is illustrative of continuing dynamics in many parts of Brazil's carceral archipelago. Rather than exercising their formally mandated roles as advocates and guarantors of the prisoners' fundamental human rights, both the *defensores* and the *juiz* were informally using their positions to act as powerful gatekeepers, standing in the way of inmates' legitimate rights claims. Prisoners indicated to me that the former had been extorting them in exchange for legal representation.[11] These judicial actors had de facto replaced the prison bureaucracy as the arbiters of prisoners' physical safety, and were acting in a way that contradicted their formal responsibilities as laid out in the Constitution and the law governing the serving of sentences (*Lei de Execução Penal* – LEP). Moreover, civil society actors were actively excluded from exercising their legal independent oversight role in the prison, and this has been the pattern across Brazil. The most significant institutional shift has occurred in the *defensoria pública* which, in the intervening years, has become a key judicial agency advocating and protecting prisoners' individual and collective rights.

The other actors in this scenario were, of course, the prisoners themselves who were dictating the life and death of other inmates. A key feature of the last two decades in the Brazilian prison system has been the shift from the apparently random chaos of prisoner-on-prisoner and state agent-on-prisoner violence to a more structured and hierarchical system of order imposed by inmate organisations in many prisons (Biondi 2015; Darke 2018; Manso & Dias 2018). Many structural factors continuing to drive ordinary inmates into the fold of these groups can be laid at the door of judicial institutions that are directly responsible for hyper-incarceration and a failure to provide legal representation, judicial oversight and physical protection. This creates a situation of two-fold 'prisoner capture'. First, punitivist legal cultures and institutions have produced mass, and very often illegal, detention of hundreds of thousands of individuals who are then left unprotected, in a situation of 'bare life'. Then, once trapped in the carceral space, they become a source of rent and manpower for the gangs and criminal groups operating inside and outside the prisons (Macaulay 2019), as many of the chapters in this book explore. They also represent a captive audience for religious organisations, particularly the neo-Pentecostal ones that appreciate the financial benefits of converted souls.

Determining Prison Regimes

Once prisoners have been funnelled into the penitentiary system by judges and prosecutors, those same actors have considerable power to determine the quality of the prison regime and the quality of life for inmates. Although the executive branch is responsible for maintaining security and providing infrastructure and basic services, the judiciary, as a primary 'owner' of imprisonment as a punishment and therefore of prisoners, retains a central role in the oversight regime. In Brazil, several different governmental (executive and judicial) institutions are empowered to inspect penal establishments. At the state level, the key bodies are the internal affairs department of the prison administration, the prosecutor's office, *juizes de execução penal*, and, since 2010, the *defensoria pública*. The last three have a potential conflict of interest, as they are involved in prisoners' parole and transfer hearings, which may impinge on the impartiality with which they treat prisoners' complaints, whilst the internal affairs department cannot be considered independent and is structurally prone to collusion with the state prison authorities.

The *juizes de execução penal* are legally required to inspect local prisons once a month and tend to the collective concerns of prisoners, but they also have discretionary power over individual prisoners, conceding or denying specific benefits, as the Roger incident above illustrates. In the two dozen or so interviews I have conducted with such judges around the country, they fall into two camps. Some—a minority—embrace their responsibility and become supporters of greater civil society involvement (Valois & Macaulay 2017). Such *garantista* judges often find themselves at odds with the judicial and law enforcement establishment locally, and suffer petty persecutions and legal harassment, for 'siding with the prisoners'.[12] For example, when a judge inspects a prison and orders it shut down immediately, the prison bureaucracy resists compliance because the constant overcrowding of facilities leave it few options. But most judges remain completely uninterested, take on the function of the *execução penal* as part of their career trajectory and set foot in the prisons in their jurisdiction only when forced to (for example, after an outbreak of violence). They are reactive, not proactive, bureaucratic, and apparently uninterested in the actual penal regime that they are meant to be supervising, whose normative parameters are laid out in Brazil's 1984 *Lei de Execução Penal.* During my research into small prisons in São Paulo state co-governed in a state-civil society partnership, I sat through the inspection visit of the two *juizes corregedores* from the state appellate court. They neither toured the prison nor spoke to prisoners but focused solely on minor flaws in the prison's paperwork. Some local judges never visited at all and declined to use the purpose-built rooms designed for court hearings or business related to sentencing, insisting that prisoners be escorted to the courthouse by the police, thus creating a barrier to prisoners' claiming their rights. Whilst decentralisation of *execução penal* creates a very dispersed and heterogeneous field that is hard to evaluate, the centralisation of this function, as in the Deecrim in São Paulo, brings its own dangers of orthodoxy. The relatively little ethnographical research conducted into the attitudes and practices of these judges indicates that they view the prison law as impossibly utopian, as 'an idea out of place' (Schwarz 1992). Given judges' scepticism about rules governing the formal institution, they default to an informal and collective common sense (Marques 2009). A 2002 study of 339 petitions brought to the *vara de execução penal* in São Paulo city demonstrated that, even after prisoners had been sentenced, judges used their discretion to hyper-penalise, extending the original prison tariff (Teixeira & Bordini 2004).

Since the CNJ (*Conselho Nacional de Justiça*) was set up as a watchdog body for the nation's judiciary as part of the judicial reform process in 2004, it has tried to compensate for the inaction of the local level judges by carrying out periodic inspections of selected prisons as well as conducting joint custodial efforts (*mutirões carcerários*), sending in teams of lawyers to clear the backlog of pending legal problems facing detainees. Between 2008 and 2014, they examined 400,000 case files, conceded 80,000 benefits to prisoners, and released 45,000 who had exceeded the end of their sentences. These *mutirões*, which were meant to be one-off events, became routinised informal institutions that also failed to dent the level of pre-trial detention. Since 2019, the CNJ has set up a centralised database, making the tracking of prisoners' legal situation more transparent, although this does not solve the problem of highly variable and negligent action by local judges.[13]

In São Paulo, the prison bureaucracy responded to the blockages created by the judiciary by 'de-judicialising' some of the processes prescribed by the prison law. Nagashi Furukawa, state secretary for prison administration from 1999–2006 and himself a retired *juiz de execução penal,* introduced a computerised system that allowed prisoners to be released on time by the prison authorities, without having to wait for a judge to sign off on the paperwork. The sheer size of the carceral machine in the state of São Paulo has resulted in more extensive de facto dejudicalisation, as the prison bureaucracy has acquired a level of autonomy from both the political executive and the judiciary in relation to operational decisions, such as transfer and movement of prisoners, and the regulation of the supply of goods to prisoners through the state, family members and, of course, the prisoner organisations (Melo 2020). Other *juizes de execução penal* also support the transfer of certain administrative functions away from judicial actors (Valois & Macaulay 2017). The removal of such gatekeeping power elicited inevitable resistance from the state judiciary. On the other hand, it has shown little interest in exercising its legal powers of oversight, not least as this would bring it onto a collision course with the state political authority, with which it has a demonstrable relationship of accommodation and collusion (Cardoso 2018).

As noted above, the *defensoria pública* has become a counterpoint to the institutional cultures of the prosecution service and judiciary, using new legal powers to advocate for prisoners individually and collectively where other official and social oversight bodies had made little discernible difference. Despite the *defensoria pública* being listed in the 1988 Constitution as a key judicial function, not all states had one until 2012, and it was only in 2004 that a constitutional amendment guaranteed its 'administrative and functional autonomy' putting it, in principle, on a par with the courts and prosecution service. Even now, there are far fewer *defensores* than prosecutors, with whom they do not enjoy parity of salaries, benefits or status. In the state of São Paulo, legal aid had been provided by the *Procuradoria de Assistência Judiciária*, a branch of the state prosecution service, creating a clear institutional conflict of interest. It was civil society demand that in 2006 created an independent *defensoria pública* which increasingly adopted an activist stance, aiming to see all incoming remand prisoners within two weeks in order to get them released on bail.[14] In 2007, the law changed nationally to allow the *defensorias públicas* to engage in class actions (civil legal action), an area previously the preserve of the prosecution service, which naturally opposed the change as encroaching on its legal prerogatives. This boost to their powers has seen the *defensorias públicas* in São Paulo and Rio de Janeiro, for example, Rio de Janeiro file many successful lawsuits, for example, in relation to health care provision to prisoners. This is a means both of jousting with a largely unresponsive executive branch (the prison administration) and getting around judicial vetoing of other instruments, such as writs of mandamus (which order public bodies to do their job properly), and the inaction and collusion of the *juiz corregedor de presídios* with the prison bureaucracy and judiciary.

Non-State Actors and Incarceration

A number of non-state actors have also become involved in the prison system. Some play no role in sentencing and imprisonment but exercise oversight functions, whilst others get involved in the delivery of prison regimes. In recent years, the Brazilian Bar Association (*Ordem dos Advogados Brasileiros* – OAB) has become a lot more proactive in monitoring prisons, with dedicated committees in every state branch. These undertake legal actions, get involved with state penitentiary councils and even run rehabilitation projects. This contrasts with the weakening of the activity of other civil society actors, such as the Catholic Church's ministry to prisoners (*Pastoral Carcerária*) and the civil society community councils (*conselhos da comunidade*), which, according to the prison law, can be set up in any jurisdiction with a prison at the discretion of the local *juizes de execução penal*. The councils' lack of legal autonomy and resources, subordination to the local judge and territorial fragmentation mean that they have not 'laid claim' to prisoners in the manner of other civil society actors. There are very few studies on how they function and their effectiveness and a national initiative to support and empower them fizzled out as they were increasingly encouraged to focus on service provision to prisoners exiting the system, rather than on oversight (Ministério da Justiça 2010).

The OAB, on the other hand, has a formal national, state-level and municipal structure and membership giving it a presence in every locality with a prison and a reach and clout like no other civil society organisation. Undeniably, its members have a professional vested interest in the prison system, often being paid by the state to provide private legal aid, and thus form part of the 'crime industry' (Christie 2000). However, state-level *defensorias públicas* have fought legal battles to release themselves from contractual obligations to recruit auxiliary lawyers only from the OAB's ranks. This separation and the OAB's increasing activism in the prison field has encouraged the two bodies to collaborate on class actions and structural issues. For example, during the Covid-19 pandemic, the OAB used the latter's inspection reports of health conditions in prison facilities to serve compliance notices on the state prison authorities in São Paulo.[15]

When it comes to the *direct* management of prisons, penal regimes and prisoners, a variety of non-state actors are now competing with the state and prisoner organisations. The sheer size of the prison population and estate in Brazil offers commercial opportunities, chiefly for the supply of services to the sector. Bid-rigging in procurement auctions to provide meals to prisons has been perennial, right across the country, and results generally in extremely poor-quality food and significant overcharging. For instance, in February 2020, police investigated the food contract awarded by Rio Grande do Norte, a state with one of the most chaotic prison systems, where gang-related massacres broke out in January 2017, discovering that the winning bid should have been disqualified and would have cost an excess £2 million a year.[16] Yet, despite the honeypot potential of the prison sector and some flagship projects, privatisation of prisons in Brazil has not progressed far. The first prison governed under public-private prison co-administration opened in 1999 in the state of Paraná. By 2020, there were still only 32 such units. Most operate in a hybrid arrangement (termed *co-gestão*) that sits somewhere between the US and the European models of privatisation, with the state financing construction of the prison, providing the warden, deputy warden, and head of discipline inside the facility and state military police for external security, and retaining ownership of the infrastructure. The private firm provides the in-prison services and the guards. Public sector cash flow problems then led to Brazil's first public-private-partnership (PPP) prison opening in January 2013 in Belo Horizonte, the capital of Minas Gerais state, operated by a consortium of five companies. Two factors could drive greater private sector interest in Brazil's mass incarceration. The first is the ongoing fiscal crisis, which would favour a PPP model. The second is the lobby power of the private security providers in a congress that saw the highest ever number of legislators linked to law enforcement (many former police officers) enter in 2018, on the coattails of President Jair Bolsonaro. There is sympathy for privatisation in a right-leaning congress, but little coherent direction in government driving this agenda. Perhaps the most significant blockage to private sector prison expansion, however, is the presence of the prisoner *comandos*, which the state tolerates as informally institutionalised co-administrators of the prison environment (Dias 2013).

One of the novelties in the Brazilian penal landscape is the partnership between the state and not-for-profit civil society groups in the running of some smaller local prisons. In 1972, in São Paulo state, a group of Catholic laymen formed an NGO, the Association for the Protection and Assistance of Prisoners (APAC), to provide services to detainees in the local lock-up. From 1984, they formally ran the jail without guards, with security provided by the inmates. The model was replicated and institutionalised in São Paulo state by Dr. Furukawa, who established 22 similar small prisons, known as Resocialisation Centres (*Centros de Ressocialização* – CRs). In these, the state provided the infrastructure, guards and external security whilst the partner NGO handled the day-to-day running of the prison and rehabilitation of prisoners. Unlike the APACs, the CR model did not stress religious conversion as the keystone of rehabilitation, and it sought to work with, not as an alternative to, the state (Macaulay 2015).[17] Meanwhile the original APAC group moved to Minas Gerais state, found support among justices in the state appellate court, and is being replicated in various states in Brazil (Darke 2015). There is interest in the Bolsonaro administration in the model, very likely because of its emphasis on religiosity. The model will only ever cater to a very tiny minority of prisoners in Brazil and will not affect the dispositions governing the prison experience of the mass of inmates. Much more significant within the mainstream prison system is the growing presence of neo-Pentecostal groups. These evangelical ministries are double-edged—on the one hand, conversion offers community and spaces that constitute a socially acceptable exit escape from the endemic violence of prison and gang life. On the other hand, as others in the volume point out, they also function as partners to both the *comandos* and the state prison bureaucracy for the purposes of social control. The neo-Pentecostal groups are increasingly enjoying privileged access to prisons and prisoners. The most organised and hegemonic churches, such as the Universal Church of the Kingdom of God, have the resources to pursue this as a clear national strategy of recruitment, in much the same way as the *comandos* do, tying together their expansion inside and outside the prisons. Both levy dues on these members so, for both, the lost souls in the prison system and their families are a source of rent and influence.

In summary, the carceral field, both inside and outside the prisons, is complex, with a multitude of state-sector and non-state actors interacting, sometimes competing, sometimes colluding, in the maintenance of many illegal and dehumanising forms of incarceration. There is a dynamic process whereby the creation of new laws, procedures and mechanisms, as a formal response to over-incarceration and its consequences, is met by informal practices of neutralisation and even subversion. As Darke (2018: 69) notes, there are still very few ethnographic studies of the 'institutional culture of penal policy makers'. As this chapter has demonstrated, these cultures are plural, overlapping and contradictory, and intersect in ever mutating ways with intra-mural prisoner survival strategies in Brazil's vast and troubling carceral spaces.

Notes

1. The court's ruling in favour of ADPF 347 is available at http://redir.stf.jus.br/paginadorpub/paginador.jsp?docTP=TP&docID=10300665
2. This legislation is tracked and analysed annually by NGO Instituto Sou da Paz.
3. Most *in flagrante* arrests are made by the uniformed military police, who patrol the streets. Further evidence would be sought by the civil (investigative) police.
4. Under the heinous crime law, those convicted of criminal conspiracy are not eligible for parole, early release or regime progression, thus filling up the maximum security prisons with small-time drug users/dealers.
5. It was often applied in cases of 'no fixed abode' or the lack of a recognised address, as would be the case of those living in informal settlements.
6. https://www.conjur.com.br/2018-fev-18/entrevista-juiza-patricia-alvarez-cruz-chefe-dipo-sp
7. The case was of Judge Roberto Luiz Corciolli Filho, who was rotated *away* from the criminal courts against his will.
8. https://www.conjur.com.br/2017-ago-29/10-votos-cnj-anula-condenacao-juiza-kenarik-boujikian
9. This incident was followed by more violence in the prison, leaving 11 dead and scores injured over a three-month period. During a riot on 8

September 1997, 89 prisoners were stabbed and beaten by other inmates (Amnesty International 1999: 8).

10. This was his real given name. Apparently his mother had named his two other brothers Gandhi and Luiz Gonzaga (after a very well-known north-eastern country singer).
11. I managed to speak in English to one Caribbean inmate, and afterwards was handed a sheaf of handwritten letters from the prisoners, passed on by a local politician.
12. Examples are Luis Carlos Valois in Amazonas and João Carlos Buch in Santa Catarina.
13. https://www.cnj.jus.br/sistema-carcerario/mutirao-carcerario/
14. Interview with *defensoria pública* staff in São Paulo, September 2014.
15. https://www.oabsp.org.br/noticias/2020/05/oab-sp-e-sua-comissao-tematica-agem-para-resguardar-o-direito-a-saude-tambem-no-sistema-penitenciario.13524
16. https://g1.globo.com/rn/rio-grande-do-norte/noticia/2020/02/07/policia-investiga-se-houve-improbidade-em-licitacao-que-geraria-prejuizo-de-r-12-mi-ao-ano-aos-cofres-publicos-do-rn.ghtml
17. Over the years, the APAC acronym has stood for a number of very slightly different names, now most commonly *Associação de Proteção e Assistência ao Condenado.* Some confusion is caused by some of the NGOs working in the CRs in São Paulo state having adopted the APAC acronym.

References

Amnesty International. (1999). *No one sleeps here safely*. London: Amnesty International.

Biondi, K. (2016). *Sharing this walk: An ethnography of prison life and the PCC in Brazil.* Chapel Hill: University of North Carolina Press.

Boiteux, L. (2010). Drugs and prisons: The repression of drugs and the increase of the Brazilian penitentiary population. In WOLA (Ed.), *Systems overload: Drug laws and prisons in Latin America*. Washington, DC: Washington Office on Latin America.

Cardoso, L. Z. L. (2018). *A politíca da justiça: Blindar as elites, criminalizar os pobres*. São Paulo: Hucitec.

Carvalho, S. (2010). *O papel dos atores do sistema penal na era de punitivismo (O exemplo privilegiado da aplicação da pena)*. Rio de Janeiro: Editora Lumen Juris.

Casara, R. R. R. (2015). *Mitologia processual penal*. Rio de Janeiro: Saraiva.
Christie, N. (2000). *Crime control as industry: Towards gulags, western style*. London: Routledge.
Darke, S. (2015). Recoverers helping recoverers: Discipline and peer-facilitated reform in Brazilian faith-based prisons. In V. Miller & J. Campbell (Eds.), *Translating penal cultures: New perspectives on discipline, punishment and desistance*. London: Routledge.
Darke, S. (2018). *Conviviality and survival: Co-producing Brazilian prison order*. London: Palgrave Macmillan.
Dias, C. C. N. (2013). *PCC: Hegemonia nas prisões e monopólio da violência*. São Paulo: Editora Saraiva.
Helmke, G., & Levitsky, S. (Eds.). (2006). *Informal institutions and democracy: Lessons from Latin America*. Baltimore: Johns Hopkins University Press.
Instituto Pro Bono. (2018). *Audiências de custódia: Pensando estratégias de combate ao encarceramento provisório: Dossiê*. São Paulo: Instituto Pro Bono.
ITTC & Pastoral Carcerária Nacional. (2012). *Tecer justiça: Presas e presos provisórios da cidade de São Paulo*. São Paulo: Instituto Terra, Trabalho e Cidadania.
Koerner, A. (2005). Judiciário, juizes e prisões em São Paulo nos anos noventa. In A.-J. Arnaud (Ed.), *Globalização e direito I: Impactos nacionais, regionais e transnacionais*. Rio de Janeiro: Editora Lumen Juris.
Lemgruber, J., Fernandes, M., Cano, I., & Musumeci, L. (2013). *Usos e abusos da prisão provisória no Rio de Janeiro: Avaliacão do impacto da lei 12.403 2011*. Rio de Janeiro: ARP/CESeC.
Lima, R. K. (2010). Sensibilidades jurídicas, saber e poder: Bases culturais de alguns aspectos do direito brasileiro em uma perspectiva comparada. *Anuário Antropológico*, II: 25–51.
Macaulay, F. (2015). "Whose prisoners are these anyway?" church, state and society partnerships and co-production of offender "resocialization" in Brazil. In V. Miller & J. Campbell (Eds.), *Translating penal cultures: New perspectives on discipline, punishment and desistance*. London: Routledge.
Macaulay, F. (2018). Non-governmental organisations and the rule of law: The experience of Latin America. In C. May & A. Winchester (Eds.), *The Edward Elgar research handbook on the rule of law*. New York: Edward Elgar.
Macaulay, F. (2019). Prisoner capture: Welfare, lawfare and warfare in Latin America's overcrowded prisons. In R. Sieder & K. Ansolabehere (Eds.), *Routledge handbook of law and society in Latin America*. New York: Routledge.

Machado, M.R., de Souza Amaral, M.C., de Barros, M. & de Melo, A.C.K. (2019). Incarcerating at any cost: drug trafficking and imprisonment in Brazilian court reasoning. *Journal of Illicit Economies and Development, 1*(2), 226–237.

Manso, B. P., & Dias, C. C. N. (2018). *A guerra: A ascensão do PCC e o mundo do crime no Brasil.* São Paulo: todavia.

Marques, G. (2009). A lei de execuções penais e os limites da interpretação jurídica. *Revista de Sociologia Política, 17*(33), 145–155.

Melo, F. A. L. (2020). *A burocracia penitenciarista: Estudo sobre a configuração da gestão prisional no Brasil.* Curitiba: Brazil Publishing.

Ministério da Justiça (Ed.). (2010). *Fundamentos e análises sobre os conselhos da comunidade.* Brasília: DEPEN/OSPEN.

Schwarz, R. (1992). *Misplaced ideas: Essays on Brazilian culture.* London: Verso.

Semer, M. (2019). *Sentenciando tráfico: O papel dos juízes no grande encarceramento.* São Paulo: Tirant Lo Blanch.

Teixeira, A., & Bordini, E. B. T. (2004). Decisões judiciais nas Varas de Execuções: punindo sempre mais. *São Paulo em Perspectiva, 18*(1), 66–71.

Valois, L. C. (2016). *Direito penal da guerra às drogas.* Belo Horizonte: Livraria D'Plácido.

Valois, L. C., & Macaulay, F. (2017). O judiciário e a crise do sistema penitenciário (entrevista). *Revista Brasileira de Segurança Pública, 11*(2), 78–87.

Zapater, M. (2015). Gargalos tampados. *Boletim IBCCrim, 23*(270), 9–11.

13

The Ghost of the Massacre Still Tells His Tale. Death and Social Order in Colombian Prisons

Libardo José Ariza and Manuel Iturralde

> Prison, where guerrilla fighters and paramilitary soldiers, like colossal infantry battalions, are locked in mortal combat in their war to conquer one more cell block. (Canderipo 2003)

> Until one night the bomb went off. (Molano 2004: 85)

> The court hereby orders an inquiry into allegations made herein regarding alleged acts of torture and homicides carried out by members of illegal armed groups imprisoned in *La Modelo* penitentiary where victims' bodies may be buried in unmarked graves. (Criminal Court 56, Circuit Court of Bogotá 2013)

A similar version of this chapter was published in the *International Criminal Justice Review. See* Ariza, Libardo and Manuel Iturralde (2020). "The Bullet in the glass: War, Death, and the meaning of penitentiary experience in Colombia". *International Criminal Justice Review*, 30(1): 83–98. Copyright © 2019 Georgia State University. DOI: https://doi.org/10.1177/1057567719836475

L. J. Ariza • M. Iturralde (✉)
School of Law, Universidad de los Andes, Bogotá, Colombia

S. Darke et al. (eds.), *Carceral Communities in Latin America*, Palgrave Studies in Prisons and Penology, https://doi.org/10.1007/978-3-030-61499-7_13

The Ghost of the Massacre Still Tells His Tale

Almost twenty years passed since the last massacre in *La Modelo*, one of the most representative Colombian prisons, located in Bogotá. On the night of March 21, 2020, death once again walked through the corridors and yards of the penitentiary, leaving behind twenty-four dead inmates, most of them shot by the prison's guards (Semana 2020). Hundreds of prisoners were protesting against a different kind of death: that caused by the COVID-19 pandemic. Without access to essential health services, crammed in pavilions where water is a scarce and precious good, under deplorable hygienic conditions, inmates at *La Modelo* knew that it was only a matter of time for the pandemic to arrive. They were not prepared for it, and the authorities were doing nothing about it. Their only response was a complete lock-down. And not having visitors or contact with the outside world is another kind of death for many prisoners. Tension increased, and a riot broke out.

After a few hours, the riot became a massacre. Inmates recorded ghastly images in their smuggled smartphones and sent them to their contacts and to the social media to denounce what was happening. Soon, these images were in the screens of thousands of mobiles and later on the web and TV newscasts. A massacre was being broadcasted, live. Twenty years ago, under different circumstances, another massacre marked the grim history of *La Modelo*. Between the 26 and the 27 of April 2000, hundreds of prisoners died, charred and gunned down, caught in the cross-fire between guerrillas and paramilitaries, in one of their several confrontations to rule the prison. For twenty years, the tale of the ghost of the massacre (known and transmitted by inmates and guards) told the story of the horrifying events that took place in *La Modelo*. Such a tale has now a new chapter that reminds us that horror and death are still molding penitentiary experience at *La Modelo*.

In this text, we attempt to assume a contextual perspective to comprehend the meaning of horror and violence for depicting imprisonment in the local context. The memory of past massacres, and the threat of their irruption in prison daily routines, mark carceral experience in Colombia and Latin America. The extreme violence that destroys the bodies of the condemned, dismembered, burnt by the flames of prisons' arsons, or shot dead by the bullets that seek to suppress a riot, are common features of penitentiary punishment in the region. From *Carandiru* and its 111 dead inmates in Brazil (Ferreira et al. 2012), through *Retén de Catia* and its sixty-five dead and thirty-five disappeared prisoners in Venezuela (Inter-American Court of Human Rights 2006), to the massacre of 133 convicts of *El Frontón* penitentiary in Peru (Inter-American Court of Human Rights 1995), massive killings have spread through Latin American prison corridors like a disease, plunging them into a state of terror, and conforming a penitentiary social order of violence (Ariza and Tamayo 2020).

To develop our argument, we employ the findings of our own fieldwork, carried out over the past six years at *La Modelo* penitentiary in Bogotá. This research sheds light on how institutional memory is transmitted and flows from the prison milieu to the open space of free society primarily through the discourses of penitentiary subjects, as well in the narratives of long-serving prison guards and convicts. We seek to trace the above-mentioned discourse by drawing upon texts written by several ex-convicts which make up part of non-academic, nonscientific sanctioned literature (Foucault 1980), and have proven to be valuable sources in revealing *La Modelo*'s recent history. We believe that these penitentiary memoirs, told from the point-of-view of subjects who have passed through the Colombian penitentiary system and suffered its violence, whether as inmates or guards, are indispensable in understanding that shuttered world. Because we have been assiduous visitors to *La Modelo*, and, as such, are recognized as being stable members of a group attentive to the issues that the local prison population confronts, we write about the stories we have been told to introduce us to the world of confinement. In doing so, we write about our own sensitive experience on the Colombian penitentiary field (Jewkes 2012; Drake and Harvey 2014). Indeed, we are trapped in "the old theological question of how to be *in* but not *of* the world" (Liebling 2001: 475) of *La Modelo* Prison.

We attempt to rescue oral history, as passed on by long-serving guards and prisoners who accompany visitors on their walks through the penitentiary's corridors. During these walks, the prison inhabitants repeatedly recall the tales of horror that are inscribed on the prison's walls and in its yards and cell blocks. On every prison wall, they point out the signs of a past that refuses to go away. This daily prison walks, like a museum tour, conducted by guards and yard leaders, takes the visitor to zones where emotions are disrupted when it cannot be concealed that the institution is also a graveyard full of terrifying memories (Morrison 2012; Crewe et al. 2014). We hope to contribute to an understanding of the stability of a concrete and contextual penal social order characterized by violence, and which have been described as a massive and systematic violation of prisoners' fundamental human rights (Ariza 2013; Iturralde 2011; Garces et al. 2013). This discourse on past events at *La Modelo*—the deaths, mass graves, kidnappings and dismembered bodies—plays a fundamental role in the acceptance of today's penitentiary experience, despite its indignity, notwithstanding its violence and asphyxiating overcrowding which reinforces class segregation and stigma inside the walls (Ariza 2011a). These events, which happened not so long ago, seem to have become lodged in institutional memory, shaping how imprisonment is told and experienced.

The Horror of Prison Life

Looking up from the path, muddy in winter and dusty in the dry season, worn smooth by the passing of guards and inmates, it is possible to make out, to one side of the prison's soccer pitch, the dark-colored cell block where, inside, prisoners are hanging out their clothes to dry on its damp, sun-starved walls. A few convicts are playing soccer on the green field, at the other end of which sits The Mental Health Ward fronted by a cemetery-like garden where a few red roses and white calla lilies manage to survive. The peaceful atmosphere, filled with the smell of bread being baked in the prison's ovens, and broken only by a few happy yells coming from the improvised soccer game, is in sharp contrast with the legend of horror that hangs over the site and shocks the visitor who hears it for the first time.

The guard, a veteran of many prisons and witness to countless battles, who accompanies the visitor, smiles, and points to a grate on the second floor of the cell block. On closer look, one sees a small window covered with rusty bars, and then suddenly, the green soccer field is engulfed by the darkness that seeps out from inside the prison. The gloom of the penitentiary overwhelms the atmosphere and brings with it a feeling of suffocation and the unbearable urge to run away. This prison block, classified as not fit to live in, has been closed off several times during the last years—it is a restricted area. Not even the asphyxiating pressure of overcrowding can open its barred doors, except on those days when inmates use it to hang out their clothes to dry and as a place to make the corn mash brew which is passed around on days of mourning or holidays.

The guard assumes an air of severe decorum and begins his tale; meanwhile, a group of rookie guards gathers round to listen closely once more to a story they have heard many times before. He recalls how both the young and old guards pass through this zone as fast as they can on their nightly rounds. The new guards—the ones who have just graduated from Penitentiary School and who still do not know what horrors prison holds, especially this one, are always in the biggest hurry. Their rite of initiation commences with the tale and then the assignment to make the night rounds outside the Mental Health Ward. On different shifts, old and young guards alike have seen—and they have not made this up—a shadowy figure standing at the entrance to the cell block.

Multiple conjectures exist on who the person standing behind the bars could be. Each one recalls a quintessential experience that exposes the suffering of penitentiary existence. Some say he is a convict who hanged himself when told of his sentence; others, that he is one who did the same when his family stopped visiting him; one rookie guard swears that the condemned man died alone, sad, old and forgotten; this version is corrected by another guard who is sure that the man is one of the many dead begging to be dug up from their mass grave and given a Christian burial. That mass grave, he explains, next to the soccer field, hides the victims of the paramilitary soldiers' war to take control of the prison. The man on the other side of the barred window, in the words of the guard who makes a gesture to express his horror, is the ghost of a massacre, a vanquished soul who stands pointing to the mass grave where his body lies.

The sensation that overwhelms the visitor upon discovering he is treading upon a mass grave sharpens his knowledge that imprisonment, in itself something terrible, can turn into horror, into evil. Struck by the visitor's expression of consternation and disbelief, as he stares at the earth he is standing upon, the rookie guards smile nervously, trying to conceal their fear. A veteran guard comes forward to confirm the truth of the terrible event: a few years ago, when the soccer field turf was being torn up and the rotting goal posts torn down to be replaced with new ones, workers inexplicably began to unearth bones and, without meaning to, profaned the penitentiary's mass grave. Those bones, according to what one hears from prison old wardens, most likely belong to inmates who lost their lives during the war inside Colombia's penitentiaries between guerrilla fighters and paramilitary soldiers who battled to control the nation's prisons. They are the remains of one of a multitude of unknown convicts, who now lie in a mass grave, and who, like night-time fog, spread their endless sorrow through the corridors of *La Modelo* penitentiary.

What is not known, however, is in which battle the ghostly prisoner—cloaked in the horror of prison and the tormenter of guards and inmates alike—met his death. Newspapers of the time may be another piece of the jigsaw of penitentiary horror, tracing back the flow of the discourse of punishment. The first massacre to be reported on, albeit not too clearly, took place on April 26 and 27 in the year 2000. Under the headline, "Hell in *La Modelo*", the Colombian newsweekly *Semana* published the testimony of a prisoner, who had spent four years behind bars and was still awaiting sentence: "I had never seen as much blood as what I saw on Thursday, April 27, when – in act of settling accounts – 25 prisoners at *La Modelo* National Penitentiary were machine-gunned to death in yard four" (Semana 2000). This event, referred to as "the massacre in yard four", is one of the first to be described by the local media in the penitentiary war.

This press account deals with the event as "a settling of accounts"—apparently just another display of the routine violence that rules life behind prison walls. But other versions place the massacre in yard 4 within the context of the wider war in which every inmate must take sides against everyone else. It is all a part of the ongoing combat that rages inside the penitentiary, not only of that between the traditional boss—*Cacique*—and the big-time drug baron, but also of the lethal confrontation in the all-out war between imprisoned rebel fighters and paramilitary soldiers. Shortly after the massacre, "the government ordered the immediate transfer of four FARC members out of *La Modelo* for having been indirectly implicated in the slaughter of 27 people over the weekend, as a result of retaliations between paramilitary forces and subversives" (Caracol 2001). The long list of battles, retaliatory homicides, murders, massacres and ephemeral alliances occurred during the relatively short term of two years. Faced by officialdom's total silence, it is difficult to estimate the number of dead and wounded; nevertheless, there are fragments of this infamous story that illustrate the horror of the penitentiary war.

The second scene, wherein destruction rose to an unparalleled level, took place one Monday of July 2001. According to a press release on that day, the battle began at 5:30 pm, "after visiting hours had ended at *La Modelo* National Penitentiary, a murder was committed by a member of the FARC, imprisoned in block 1, who had complained about non-payment of an extortion debt to a common criminal who was known to be in the service of the paramilitary forces" (*El Tiempo* 2001). This murder, the text goes on to say, "lit the fuse of what could be considered the biggest, all-out battle in recent years, in the country's largest penal institution, among convicted rebels, common criminals, drug-traffickers and paramilitary soldiers" (Ibid.). This scene of penitentiary warfare lasted 17 hours and resulted in ten deaths and fifteen wounded. Below, we transcribe the chronicle of this unfortunate event, as it appeared that day in the media:

Once the common criminal had been killed, his fellow prisoners, held in cellblock 3, sought the help of the paramilitary convicts, residing in cellblocks 4 and 5. When the news reached one of the paramilitary leaders, held in maximum security at *La Modelo*, he gave the order to 150 of his men to attack the subversives. Several drug-traffickers then joined forces with the paramilitary soldiers. The call to battle was to take cellblocks 1 and 2 to bring an end to the extortion racket which, according to both prisoners and the authorities, had been set up by the guerrilla forces years before. However, nearly 400 members of the FARC (Revolutionary Armed Forces of Colombia) and the ELN (National Liberation Army), imprisoned in these cellblocks, caught wind of the paramilitary soldiers' plans and were waiting for them. The *guerrilleros* had taken their weapons from caches hidden under floors, in bathrooms and behind walls and barricaded themselves behind prison walls and in corridors. In this case, the confrontation took place because the *guerrilleros* had been charging fees from six hundred thousand to three million pesos to anyone who came to live in the cellblocks which they controlled. Similar sums were also being charged by the paramilitary groups. Speaking from his cell in *La Modelo* yesterday, John Jairo Veláquez Vásquez, alias "Popeye", former head of military operations for the Medellin drug cartel, declared that the inmates were tired of what the guerrilla fighters had been doing and that was why the clash had taken place (Ibid.).

Almost a decade later, during their testimonies at the Justice and Peace hearings,[1] Daniel Rendón Herrera, a.k.a. "Don Mario", and Manuel de Jesús Pirabán, a.k.a. "The Pirate", recalled a number of times, "that paramilitary soldiers imprisoned in *La Modelo* in Bogotá had killed people and hidden their bodies inside the penitentiary itself".[2] This was the time when visitors would enter the prison and were never seen or heard from again, when dismembered corpses were stuffed down tunnels and sewer pipes, when horror and violence turned the prison into a cemetery.

When asked about their role during those times, some of the most experienced guards, who survived the war, recall how their part was mainly to remain behind the old iron doors of the cellblocks of the prison, opening and closing them stoically. As one guard explains:

> The paramilitaries wanted to control the whole prison, but the guerrillas opposed them. They had built trenches and an electric system, wired to all the doors with dynamite so they controlled the perimeter where they ruled. Guerrilla inmates controlled the access to their wing; they opened the pavilions' gates for you and when they knew that the war was coming, they told you, "Commander, go away, we all are going to die here".[3]

The guards were relegated to routine and smaller tasks of the government of the prison: searching the visitors, writing down names in old books, opening and closing doors. The guards could not impose a daily routine, neither they could involve themselves in the resolution of the conflicts between prisoners; they were forced, or paid, to turn a blind eye. During those years it was not exceptional that a guard who would not comply with the whishes, or orders, of *La Modelo* power groups, ended up being shut down in the street by *sicarios* (contract killers). This is the case of prison guards Salazar and Argüello, as one of their colleagues recalls:

> Salazar was shot down because he confiscated two AK-47 rifles from the paramilitaries. He also tried to enforce the prison's rule of counting inmates at four in the afternoon, which displeased the paramilitaries' leaders. They threatened him, but he disregarded them. They killed him outside the prison, one weekend when he was leaving Bogotá on a trip to the *Llanos Orientales*. He was shot in the head. A law-abiding guard who tried to enforce the prison's regulations, was of no use to them. Such was the case of Argüello. He was also very strict in enforcing those rules; they didn't like him, so they killed him.[4]

Guards were even kidnapped by guerrilla and paramilitary groups inside *La Modelo*. Such groups made demands in exchange of their release:

> It was pretty common. Once, they kidnapped, from Sunday to Friday, all the guards that were inside the pavilion that the paramilitaries controlled, including me. Among those who were kidnapped with me I remember Arévalo, Cañón, all those bastards, Manfla as well. I remember that Manfla went crazy, he lost it. The paramilitaries realized that he was indeed out of control; he vomited, did not sleep and said crazy stuff, so they let him go.[5]

When asked if guards tended to align with a specific group (guerrillas or paramilitaries), a guard answered:

> We had no control at all inside the prison. The north side of the prison belonged to the guerrillas, and the south side to the paramilitaries. They even had armed patrols that checked the perimeter of the areas they controlled. We did not interfere with them. Why would we?

This sort of "hands off" strategy of the guards regarding internal control issues, was only interrupted when occasionally the media condemned a prisoner's escape, a video of FARC members training, in uniform, inside the jail, which was leaked to the public; or when the armed confrontation within prison walls was so brutal, that it was impossible to ignore. In such rare occasions the prison special forces, as well as the police and the army, made symbolic demonstrations of state power by violently recovering, for just a few days, the long-gone state control of the prison. There were some dead or wounded prisoners, a few transfers of troublemakers to other prisons, and a first page photo in the newspapers of hundreds of kneeling naked men in the football playground. Messed-up inmates' belongings, as well as the destroyed cells, were displayed as a symbol of the reconstruction of state order. However, after a few days the prison came back to its daily routine.

The tale of the prison war and the hundreds of disappeared men in *La Modelo* recently reemerged after other members of the paramilitary groups provided testimonies to the Justice and Peace Jurisdiction, which confirmed the information about the mass murders and disappearances between 1998 and 2001. Such testimonies finally gave rise to a criminal investigation by the Attorney General's Office, which caught the attention of national and international media. During their testimonies at the Justice and Peace hearings, paramilitaries leaders Daniel Rendón Herrera, a.k.a. "Don Mario", and Manuel de Jesús Pirabán, a.k.a. "The Pirate", recalled a number of times, "that paramilitary soldiers imprisoned in *La Modelo* in Bogotá had killed people and hidden their bodies inside the penitentiary itself".[6] This was the time when visitors would enter the prison and were never seen or heard from again, when dismembered corpses were stuffed down tunnels and sewer pipes, when horror and violence turned the prison into a cemetery (*El Espectador* 2016).

The Bullet in the Glass

> This main corridor, the everyday walk-way, main street in prison city, was without a doubt thought up by a devout disciple of a certain kind of punitive architecture: long, very long, bordered by high grey walls stingily lit by needle-sized skylights, the monotony broken only by iron bars blocking the passage from one cellblock to the other, the floor dirty, shadows of prisoners shuffling about like ghosts stuck to the walls. (Tulio Bayer, Blind Hook. 365 days and one night in *La Modelo* prison 1978).

At the end of a long corridor that leads to the heart of *La Modelo*, one comes to the Main Guard Post. At this checkpoint, the visitor is registered first by having his fingerprint stamped onto a page in a worn accounting book and then by handing over his state identity card; in exchange, he receives a numbered, blue token and is allowed to walk down the corridor that leads to the prison cellblocks. A statue of the Virgin of Mercy, patron saint of Colombian prisoners, appears to be watching over the conversations between lawyers and their clients that are taking place below her. As he pockets the token and pulls up his sleeve to have his armed stamped with invisible markings by a seated guard, the visitor catches sight of the seven bullet holes that pock the glass shield of the Main Guard Post (Image 13.1).

And on every visit, that shield will still be there. The guards have decided that the glass shield can never be removed; it stands as a reminder to the penitentiary war, to the days when it protected them from endless rounds of bullets fired from the north and south sides of the prison, by

Image 13.1 Bullet holes in the glass shield of the Main Guard Post at *La Modelo* Prison in Bogotá. (Juan Antonio Monsalve®)

guerrilleros and *paramilitares*, alike. The bullet in the glass conjures up memories of the prison's past; it casts a shadow over the daily life of prisoners who, day after day, fear the return of penitentiary violence and terror. Nowadays, it is common to hear both guards and inmates say with relief that the prison is not what it once was. They tell the visitor not to worry, that the prison is safe now, that there are no longer kidnappings, murders, dismembered or missing bodies, that there is no danger in visiting the cellblocks, while at the same time ironically remarking that it is best to keep that visitor's token put well away; otherwise, the guards explain to the visitor, "you could be staying while someone else takes your place, just like in the old days." And this joke, about the risk of staying in and not being able to get out, that produces nothing else but fear, is told every time the visitor receives the blue token.

The meaning of the bullet in the window contained into the stock of social knowledge (Berger and Luckman 1966) shapes the objective meaning of penitentiary life, as does the tale of the unknown prisoner who points out the gravesite where he was massacred. These emotionally charged prison zones (Crewe et al. 2014) are crucial to the meaning of penitentiary existence. They mark the spots where prison initiation rites take place and evoke the horror that amounts into prisoner's suffering. Those spaces and rites generate acceptance of daily life behind bars amid a painful, but bearable, present that seems nothing compared with an even more brutal past. And these stories, which flow from the long-term warden, encrypted on prison space, stop for a moment on the prison notebook of ex-convicts which lay forgotten in some library shop of downtown Bogotá.

The available narrative sources produced by convicts who lived through the era of terror corroborate the history of what took place inside the penitentiary. In his autobiography, *Modeling in Hell*, which covers his years spent imprisoned in *La Modelo*, Agudelo (2010) provides a detailed description of the events he witnessed in the all-out war between guerrilla fighters and paramilitary soldiers for control of the prison. Under the title, "Block Four, Sixteenth Corridor", Agudelo commences his chronicle on "the biggest massacre that ever took place" in *La Modelo* National Prison in Bogotá. He goes on to say that "this happened in the month of

July, 2003" when paramilitary soldiers "in one day, slaughtered 130 men in the most savage manner imaginable. This was never denounced in public" (Agudelo 2010: 31–35). His account continues with a "footnote" in which he mentions that "on that same day, 95 prisoners were massacred in cellblock 5, which brought the total number of convicts who were viciously murdered to 225. The fourth cellblock was declared a mass grave". On the pages that follow, he provides a description of how in the yard of cellblock 4, in the laundry and garbage areas, "the bodies were dismembered, stuffed into garbage bags and loaded onto the garbage trucks that come in and out of the prison (...) Other body parts were crammed into sewer drains, which, in effect, were turned into common graves" (Agudelo 2010: 35–40). As in Foucault's narrative on the dismembering of Damiens, with which he begins *Discipline and Punish* (1989), the object of penalization is the body of the condemned; however, in this case, the exercise of punitive power falls not to the sovereign but rises up from the condemned themselves, who take on the task of destroying one another.

These emotionally terrifying prison zones—from the empty prison cells overlooking the soccer field, which is now a clandestine mass grave, to the glass shield with seven bullet holes in it, and on into cell blocks 4 and 5 where massacres and corporal dismembering have taken place—remind newcomers to the penitentiary world that the past was not always better. Prisoners, guards, lawyers, members of the penitentiary's clergy, student interns and judicial functionaries will inevitably see the bullet holes in the glass shield and hear the story of how they got there. This discovery of the institution's past—through the memories passed on in the oral tradition by the veteran guard or by the long-serving prisoner, or in the historical clues found on prison walls, as well as by the memories laid out in books by ex-convicts that have yet to reach the reading public—will help forge a better understanding of prison existence and contribute to greater recognition of its current state.

Prison and Context

Canderipo, who served prison time during the years of the penitentiary terror is the author of *The Cemetery of Living Men*, one of the few books that breathes life into the discourse on what a Colombian convict must live through.[7] In this biographic account, he declares that deciphering the penitentiary spirit is essential to comprehending what it means to be a prisoner: "it is a difficult phenomenon to understand because it obliterates all other differences" (2003: 34). In order to understand precise and contextual prison experiences, Agudelo also suggests to take into account the concrete disparities among correctional institutions: "*La Modelo* can only be *La Modelo*, *La Picota* can only be *La Picota*, Valledupar, which is maximum security has its unique environment, and so on, and each one has a lifestyle of its own" (2003: 34). In order to capture this spirit—concrete and contextual—of the penitentiary experience, the discourse on the institution's past provided by long-serving prisoners and guards is indispensable in improving comprehension on current prison conditions. Over the long term, this comprehension, afforded by the diversity of institutional history transmission, leads to the understanding of how the social order in a specific penal facility is transformed.

Yet, these important contextual differences, that original life style at each penitentiary, seem to get lost in the abstract language in discussions about penal reclusion in its overall institutional context. Although it is true that seminal research on internal prison organization dealt specifically with the penitentiary environment, the respective analytical perspectives have tended to concentrate on understanding the social order from the perspective of the penitentiary administration's dominion as opposed to the individual and collective agency of the imprisoned, thus distancing themselves from the specific context in which the prison is placed.[8] The institution itself seems to be given more importance than its particular context allows. As summed up by Sykes, several years after the publication of his ground-breaking work on prison society, penitentiary studies were trapped by the disarray of the "(…) the fact that they didn't degenerate into perpetual chaos on the one hand, or, on the other into the frozen order of masses of men locked in solitary confinement." (Sykes

1995: 83). This is further exemplified in Goffman's (1961a, b) metaphor of the total institution, which is a plea for governance and administration in all aspects of life. In this sense, the emphasis is placed on understanding, however not exclusively, daily prison life from the perspective of the social order, which, in turn, is understood to be the penitentiary government. This perspective is evident in practices such as the penitentiary administration's reliance on gangs and organized crime to keep the peace inside the institution,[9] as well as the tolerance of certain infractions committed by inmates and the acceptance of contraband as a means to alleviate the hardship of confinement—all of which exemplify penal administrative power.[10]

The importance of understanding the penitentiary's symbolic universe, which has its own prison argot to describe daily life—"the shop", "the car", "the piranha"—is indisputable; but, we believe that interpreting penitentiary culture through its argot vocabulary should be complemented by an analysis of discourse transmission mechanisms in narrations on the institution's past and the effects they have on the person who now identifies him/herself as a prisoner. As Crewe (2013) pointed out, it is not a matter of limiting penitentiary cultural analysis to biographical events, but also of understanding the importance of individuals who, deprived of their liberty, construct historical narratives that reflect on the meaning of their captivity. In this regard, we believe that discourse analysis centered on penitentiary subjects—inmates, guards and habitual visitors—whose narratives transmit and reproduce institutional memory, is fundamental in understanding the conformation of the penitentiary social order. The foregoing could be considered an attempt to decipher local penitentiary culture (Clemmer 1958; Finkelstein 1993) —expressed and constituted through discourse displayed by penitentiary subjects on the meaning of living though punishment and the privation of liberty—in a concrete context.

The emphasis on the "peculiar" aspect of the penitentiary world—that interest in discovering strange features that differentiate it from the world of the free—can result in limited comprehension on how social relations develop within prisons. If, indeed, it would be unwise to maintain that no differences exist between free society and captive society, neither would it be advisable to assume that the opposite were true, that the two worlds tend to be same. Excessive emphasis on the privations associated with punishment can obscure the contextual molding process that evolves within the penal institution. We do not argue that individual actions cannot be interpreted as attempts made by inmates to import fragments of the outside world. Our point is that reconstructing the flux of penitentiaries discourses may help to bridge the symbolic gap between the world of imprisonment and free society.

The denominated importation model—as opposed to the privation model—has been indicated as being important in understanding the influence of prior exterior factors in the conformation of the penitentiary social order.[11] As Thomas and Foster pointed out, the importation model "is related to the assertion that factors external to the prison situation affect patterns of adjustment within the prison" (1973: 228). We believe that the influence of the exterior—as an instrument used for adapting to confinement—should not be interpreted exclusively as an imprisoned individual's importation of his/her prior context. This would presuppose conceptualizing prison-society relations in terms of separation and autonomy and that coincidence between the two settings is generated by individual agency seeking to adjust to prison life. That is to say, that coincidence could only be established between the space of confinement and the space of free society if individual actions were oriented by adjusting strategies. Furthermore, the incidence of the exterior world would be primarily a matter of individual agency performed by imprisoned individuals in an effort to adjust to the new structure to which they have been forced to submit. Alternatively, a contextually oriented interpretation of the penitentiary world would reveal that the institution is being molded by a wider range of characteristics and transformations experienced by a concrete society and, therefore, the institution should be conceived as contextually defined, porous and permeable (Cunha 2014).

The molding of the internal penitentiary order, drawn from the incidence of proper contextual phenomena, is fundamental to understanding the significance of penitentiary confinement in the local context. The bullet in the glass shield presupposes having committed oneself to the task of thick description (Geertz 1992) of prisons and their rituals, to understanding the penitentiary experience in a contextual and deep-rooted way and to rescuing the peculiarities of confinement in a given place and time. Taken from this perspective, the individual mechanisms and strategies employed in adapting to confinement may be better understood as significant social actions oriented by concrete, symbolic penitentiary universes characterized by their intense level of permeability[12]; by the private appropriation and stratification of prison space; their plurality of power sources, their religious sublimation and their judicialization. All of these features should orient the mechanisms for confinement adaptation, and, through these, the reproduction of the penitentiary social order (Ariza 2011a).

And one of these contextual characteristics, which is derived from the widespread porosity of prison, is the incidence of juridical language in the constitution of internal relations (Ariza and Angel 2015). In a socially stratified prison, characterized by a legal punishment that adopts the infrahuman conditions of confinement, where daily life is spent under the shadows of a terrifying war—reflected in the bullet-pocked glass shield—the language of the law allows for prison injustice to be simultaneously denounced and accepted. Members of the legal profession visit the prison to learn about the horrors of confinement; this knowledge is then taken into account in sentencing, thereby cementing the penitentiary's unmarked graves into the foundations of Colombia's judicial history on life behind prison walls. The legal text is the last stop for the prison discourse on war and horror travel from inside the walls.

The Flow of Penitentiary Discourse

In spite of the fact that this is not the place to describe the intense judicialization process that has taken place in local Colombian penitentiaries during recent years, particularly through the growing appropriation by penitentiary inmates and administrators of the human rights discourse (Ariza 2013; Ariza and Angel 2015), we do wish to interpret a part of the process by briefly describing the narratives incorporated into judicial procedures that deal with the terrifying war between paramilitary and rebel military forces, and which have left their indelible stamp upon the ethos of the local penitentiary. Toward this end, we consider the interpretation of "the flow of social discourse" to be fundamental in the analytical process which seeks to signify cultural artifacts—in this case, prison.

In this text, we endeavor to interpret the flow of penitentiary discourse on war, horror and the past. At the same time, we intend to conclude our participation in this discourse flow—one which, on this passage, we have fulfilled in the roles of rapporteurs—by reiterating the importance—in order to reach a contextual comprehension of penitentiary existence—of delineating how discourses created by penitentiary subjects find their way out of prison and into the outside world. These discourses, whose primary function is to serve as introductory rites to confinement by concretely transmitting the meaning of penitentiary existence, also reach the outside world by means of grey literature written by ex-convicts, in haphazard news reports on the horrors of what goes on in penitentiaries, through academic writings—such as this one—and in judicial sentences wherein these rites and myths get drawn into political representations.

These discourses strongly effect the meanings we, individually and collectively, confer on prison and punishment. In this sense, far from embarking on a process of ascertaining the truth of these penitentiary narratives, we have taken the first steps in analyzing their true effects (Foucault 1980), their incidence, in shaping our notions on prison and punishment. We would, therefore, like to conclude our analysis by showing what we intuitively grasp to be the final perceptible stop on this passage that tells the tale of penitentiary war and massacres, of the discourse flow on the possibility of death and disappearance in prison, when justice pays prison a visit.

Justice visits prison to learn about the horror of confinement, to write it into its sentences, thereby turning its unmarked graves into a fundamental part of Colombia's judicial-penitentiary history. Judicial sentences related to the world of confinement become narrative sources, pieces of the puzzle that has yet to be solved on how the local penitentiary landscape is supposed to be put together. Judicial discourse incorporates the narrative of horror into its enunciations, thereby granting it veracity, and making it possible to govern it, and organize it within proper judicial language (Bourdieu 2000). The penitentiary massacre will now become a matter of judicial inquiry, and its narrative will be performed by a court clerk.

The final stage in this passage was made patent in the sentence handed down by the Bogotá Circuit Penal Court 56, which ordered the partial closure and suspension of prisoner remittance to the penitentiary for the first time in its history. This ruling was precipitated by the court's visit to *La Modelo* in response to a suit brought by an inmate who sought "to have a mattress upon which to properly sleep, a sheet and toiletries". (Criminal Court 56, Circuit Court of Bogotá 2013). During this visit, the court encountered firsthand the horror of confinement; and thenceforth, what had only been part of the initiation rite and legend of war, massacres and disappearances was converted into a judicial issue. The sentence begins by reporting on the prison visit which took place on "the 22nd day of the current month, at which time judicial inspection was carried out in the facilities of the *La Modelo* National Prison, with the collaboration of the National Institute of Legal Medicine and the Department of Technical Investigation of the Office of the Prosecutor General of Colombia" (Ibid.). In the words of the judge, it is "a prison which would best be described as a concentration camp", an impression that was further clarified in the following description:

> (...) upon inspecting the run-down facilities, holes in the ceilings and floors, bathrooms overflowing with feces, no toilets, garbage and filth, convicts who must eat with their hands, standing up or lying down on the floor, who must wash their "chow scoops" (dishes) in urinals and drains, handmade electric hook-ups exposed to the elements, thus putting prisoners lives at risk, in sum, gross negligence.

And as the court clerk continues to wander through the prison, through its corridors that lead her deeper into the shadows of confinement, she must face the intangible fear that seeps from the mass grave, and, as in the case with any other visitor, she is inducted into the legend of horror, of the remembrance of the massacre, of the unmarked graves where the bones of the unknown prison lie: the one who, in his unending doom, roams the prison that will not let him rest in peace. In the judge's log of her visit, she records "As we were carrying out our judicial inspection, several prisoners drew near to denounce deeds for which they could provide no proof under penalty of murder; one of which, the gravest, was the existence of mass graves where powerful groups within the prison bury their victims after having tortured them to death (Ibid.).

The judge is unable to find out whether these crimes are taking place or have taken place. In prison, the past merges with the present, and both are turned into an undifferentiated mass. Time stands still inside prison and every day seems like the one before and the one to come. Prison doesn't change even though the tales it tells may vary: the legend of the penitentiary's mass grave and its phantom, the seven bullet holes in the glass shield, the ex-convicts' memoirs, the articles in the press, the judicial sentence and finally, this academic paper. The war that was and the current stable social order inside the penitentiary are intertwined in the recent history of the Colombian penal system.

Notes

1. In the year 2005, the United Self-Defense Forces of Colombia (AUC in Spanish), right-wing paramilitary groups– negotiated their demobilization with the Colombian government, led by president Álvaro Uribe. As a result, Law 975/2005, better known as the Justice and Peace Law, established the legal and institutional framework that allowed for reduced prisons sentences to be accorded with those subjects who, upon handing over their weapons and undergoing demobilization, should choose to collaborate with judicial investigations and contribute to truth and reparations efforts for victims. As part of this process, the denominated open testimonies have proven to be an important source of factual accounts on the atrocities committed during the conflict, thus reinforcing the on-going research carried out by the Commission on Historical Memory.
2. "Judicial statements of paramilitaries block known as *Bloque Centauros*". Available at: https://www.verdadabierta.com/justicia-y-paz/versions/526-bloque-entauros/2638-los-desaparecidos-de-la-modelo
3. Interview with JA, Long-term prison officer at *La Modelo*. Bogotá, November 2019.
4. Interview with JA and AR, Long-term prison officers at *La Modelo*. Bogotá, November 2019.

5. Interview with JA, AR, HC, Long-term prison officers at *La Modelo*. Bogotá, November 2019.
6. "Judicial statements of paramilitaries block known as *Bloque Centauros*". Available at: https://www.verdadabierta.com/justicia-y-paz/versions/526-bloque-entauros/2638-los-desaparecidos-de-la-modelo
7. Other qualitative and biographic accounts of prison experience in Colombia may be found in Carrillo (2001); Molano (2004); and Arteta (2007).
8. Every prison context has "its own sets of normative expectations and criteria of legitimacy, and its durability as a form of "order" in large measure depends on these being fulfilled". (Sparks and Bottoms 1996: 301).
9. This perspective is grounded on a governmental perspective, which emphasizes the informal arrangements for power sharing.
10. As Kalinich and Stojkovic pointed out, "the contraband market place is a factor that is instrumental to the development of a legitimate form of inmate governance. Contraband is defined as materials that are unauthorized by the formal prison administration (...)" (1994: 214).
11. Sykes argues that "much of the behavior of inmates could be interpreted or understood as attempts, conscious or unconscious, to meet and counter the problems posed by the deprivations of prison life, including the potent threats to the ego" (Sykes 1995: 82).
12. As Goffman pointed out, "Another dimension of variation among total institutions is found in what might be called their *permeability*, that is, the degree to which the social standards maintained within the institution and the social standards maintained in the environment society have influenced each other sufficiently to minimize differences." (Goffman 1961b: 28).

References

Agudelo, F. (2010). *Modelando en el Infierno*. Cali: Digicali.

Ariza, L. (2011a). Reformando el Infierno. Los tribunales y la transformación del campo penitenciario en América Latina. In L. J. Ariza & M. Iturralde (Eds.), *Los Muros de la Infamia. Prisiones en Colombia y América Latina* (pp. 18–108). Bogotá: Universidad de los Andes, Colección Estudios CIJUS.

Ariza, L. (2011b). Dados sin números: un acercamiento al orden social en la cárcel La Modelo. *Revista de Derecho Público, 26*, 1–21.

Ariza, L. (2013). Economic and social rights, prisons, and the Colombian constitutional court. In D. Bonilla (Ed.), *Constitutionalism of the global south*. Cambridge: Cambridge University Press.
Ariza, L., & Angel, C. (2015). En el Corazón del Buen Pastor. La apropiación del discurso de los derechos humanos en el contexto carcelario. *Antípoda, Revista de Antropología y Arqueología, 23* (septiembre–sdiciembre).
Ariza, L., & Tamayo, F. (2020). El cuerpo de los condenados. Cárcel y violencia en América Latina. *Revista de Estudios Sociales, 73*, 83–95.
Arteta, Y. (2007). *Relatos de un Convicto Rebelde*. Bogotá: Debate.
Bayer, T. (1978). *Gancho Ciego: 365 Noches y una Misa en la Cárcel Modelo*. Medellín: Ediciones Hombre Nuevo.
Berger, P. L., & Luckmann, T. (1966). *The social construction of reality*. London: Penguin.
Bourdieu, P. (2000). Elementos para una sociología del campo jurídico. In *La Fuerza del derecho* (pp. 155–220). Bogotá: Siglo del Hombre Editores.
Canderipo, J. (2003). *El Cementerio de los hombres Vivos*. Bogotá: Printed by the author.
Caracol. (2001, May 1). *Ordenan traslado de presos tras masacre carcelaria*. Retrieved August 14, 2020, from http://www.caracol.com.co/noticias/actualidad/ordenan-trasaldo-de-presos-tras-masacre-carcedlaria/20000501/nota/92736.aspx
Carrillo Leal, W. (2001). From my prison cell. Time and space in prison in Colombia, an ethnographic approach. *Latin American Perspectives, 116*(1), 149–164.
Clemmer, D. (1958). *The prison community*. Boston: Rinehart.
Crewe, B. (2013). Writing and reading a prison: Making use of prisoner life stories. *Criminal Justice Matters, 91*(1), 20–20.
Crewe, B., Warr, J., Bennett, P., & Smith, A. (2014). The emotional geography of prison life. *Theoretical Criminology, 18*(1), 56–74.
Criminal Court 56, Circuit Court of Bogotá. (2013, January 30). Acciónn de Tutela, radicación 11001310405620l3–00016. Oscar Orlando Pérez vs Cárcel La Modelo de Bogotá.
Cunha, M. (2014). The ethnography of prisons and penal confinement. *Annual Review of Anthropology, 43*, 217–233.
Drake, D., & Harvey, J. (2014). Performing the role of ethnographer: Processing and managing the emotional dimensions of prison research. *International Journal of Social Research Methodology, 17*(5), 489–501.

El Espectador. (2016, February 18). *¿Qué pasó en La Modelo?*. Retrieved August 14, 2020, from https://www.elespectador.com/noticias/judicial/que-paso-en-la-modelo/

El Tiempo. (2001, July 4). *La extorsión prende la cárcel Modelo*. Retrieved August 14, 2020, from https://www.eltiempo.com/archivo/documento/MAM-431150

Ferreira, L. M. A., de Assis Machado, M. R., & Machado, M. R. (2012). Massacre do Carandiru: Vinte anos sem responsabilização. *Novos Estudos CEBRAP, 94*, 5–29.

Finkelstein, E. (1993). *Prison culture: An inside view*. Aldershot: Averbury.

Foucault, M. (1980). Two lectures. In C. Gordon (Ed.), *Power and knowledge. Selected interviews and other writings 1972–1977* (pp. 78–108). New York: Pantheon Books.

Foucault, M. (1989). *Vigilar y Castigar*. México: FCE.

Garces, C., Martin, T., & Darke, S. (2013). Informal prison dynamics in Africa and Latin America. *Criminal Justice Matters, 91*(1), 26–27.

Geertz, C. (1992). *La Interpretación de las Culturas*. Barcelona: Gedisa.

Goffman, I. (1961a). *Asylums: Essays on the social situation of mental patients and other inmates*. London: Penguin Books.

Goffman, I. (1961b). The characteristics of total institutions. In G. Matthews (Ed.), *Imprisonment*. Darmouth: Ashgate.

Inter-American Court of Human Rights. (1995, January 19). Case of Neira Alegría et al. v. Perú.

Inter-American Court of Human Rights. (2006, July 5). Case of Montero Aranguren et al. v. Bolivarian Republic of Venezuela.

Iturralde, M. (2011). Prisiones y Castigo en Colombia. La construcción de un orden social excluyente. In L. Ariza & M. Iturralde (Eds.), *Los Muros de la Infamia* (pp. 110–194). Bogotá: Universidad de los Andes.

Jewkes, Y. (2012). Autoethnography and emotion as intellectual resources: Doing prison research differently. *Qualitative Inquiry, 18*(1), 63–75.

Kalinich, D., & Stojkovic, S. (1994). Contraband: The basis for legitimate power in a prison social system. In S. Henry (Ed.), *Social control* (pp. 209–240). Aldershot: Dartmouth.

Liebling, A. (2001). Whose side are we on? Theory, practice and allegiances in prison research. *British Journal of Criminology, 41*(3), 472–484.

Molano, A. (2004). *Penas y cadenas*. Bogotá: Planeta.

Morrison, W. (2012). *Criminología, Civilización y Nuevo Orden Mundial*. Barcelona: Anthropos.

Semana. (2000, June 5). *Infierno Modelo*. Retrieved May 8, 2018, from https://www.semana.com/nacion/articulo/infierno-modelo/42189-3

Semana. (2020, June 7). *10 horas de terror*. Retrieved August 14, 2020, from https://www.semana.com/nacion/articulo/en-exclusiva-masacre-carcel-la-modelo-pruebas-del-amotinamiento-carcelario/677853

Sparks, R., & Bottoms, A. (1996). *Prisons and the problem of order*. Oxford: Clarendon Press.

Sykes, G. (1995). The structural-functional perspective on imprisonment. In S. Cohen & T. Blomberg (Eds.), *Punishment and social control* (pp. 77–84). New York: Aldine de Gruyter.

Thomas, C. W., & Foster, S. C. (1973). Importation model perspective on inmate social roles: An empirical test. *The Sociological Quarterly, 14*(2), 226–234.

Part III

"Dangerous Subjects" and Biopolitical Inversion

14

Beyond the Cemetery of the Living: An Exploration of Disposal and the Politics of Visibility in the Nicaraguan Prison System

Julienne Weegels

While Nicaraguan prison authorities enforce the penitentiary both as a dumpster for "animals" and as a reformatory for "doubly failed men"—not only failing to abide the law, but also to become uncatchable career criminals—prisoners' lives and livelihoods become doubly precarious. Disposed of into the prison system through a politics of mediated naming and shaming, Nicaraguan prisoners' commonplace refrain of being stuck in the "cemetery of the living" grounds my chapter's focus on the ways in which prisoners both reckon with and attempt to undo their socio-legal disposal by engaging in a politics of visibility. Institutionally, revival from social death is prescribed through penal reeducation, geared at what prison authorities call prisoner "change of attitude" (*cambio de actitud*). Central to such a subjective shift appears to be the requirement of transcendence; thinking, moving, and acting within yet beyond the gravesites of everyday institutional life. Performing changes of attitude may offer prisoners opportunities to imagine and to see themselves in a

J. Weegels (✉)
CEDLA, University of Amsterdam, Amsterdam, Netherlands

S. Darke et al. (eds.), *Carceral Communities in Latin America*, Palgrave Studies in Prisons and Penology, https://doi.org/10.1007/978-3-030-61499-7_14

different light—as if they were already outside. But to what extent are these cruelly optimistic imaginations? And how do these performances articulate with(in) the violent realities of prison life? Drawing from my field research in the Nicaraguan prison system—specifically from a prison theater training program hosted at two different facilities[1]—I problematize the institutionalization of disposal by analyzing (former) prisoners' parallel engagement in performances of violence and change.

First, I sketch the legal and ideological underpinnings of the contemporary Nicaraguan prison system for a better understanding of the local continuities in ideologies of crime control. I then briefly describe how these effectuate the disposal of (specific) young men into the prison system through a politics of mediated naming and shaming. I move on to unpack prisoner survival strategies at the hand of the "cemetery of the living" metaphor, explaining that, to undo the cemetery, maintaining or achieving visibility toward the outside world and/or the authorities is paramount. In doing so, I draw on both the prisoners' informal practices to undo their imposed exclusion, and the formal channel of social revival through participation in penal reeducation and the performance of a change of attitude. I highlight the management of (former) prisoners' visibility as protagonists of change in the face of their civil evanescence by discussing the exceptional case of a day-release, prison theater tour *outside* the facility itself. In all, it appears that the existence of the "cemetery" produces the very desire to "revive," which establishes the parameters for prison to be co-governed by prisoners and authorities, who together provide both the licit *and* illicit means to maintaining or regaining social visibility and eventual moral reincorporation.

Prisons and Crime Control in Nicaragua

To understand the prison system's focus on change of attitude and its institutional discourse of penal reeducation, a brief exploration of Nicaragua's recent institutional history is necessary. The foundation of the contemporary penitentiary system was laid in the wake of the 1979 Sandinista Popular Revolution (1979–1990), when the revolutionary government sought to replace the torturous jails of ousted dictator

Somoza and his *Guardia Nacional* (National Guard), who had run the prison system since 1927. With the exception of La Modelo, the capital city's penitentiary constructed in 1953, and a handful of police jails, all of Somoza's prisons were decommissioned and scrapped, with new, barrack-style penitentiaries built to supplant them during the '80s (Berendse 1998: 12; Centeno Mayorga 2012). These are the facilities currently in use throughout the country.[2] In the same period, the Sandinistas transferred the custody of prisoners from the National Guard—which was dissolved creating separate army and police institutions—to a novel government commission supervised by the Ministry of the Interior. The FSLN's (Sandinista National Liberation Front) revolutionary government also ratified a variety of human rights agreements,[3] established a maximum sentence of 30 years imprisonment, and designed a new political constitution, which was ratified in 1986, thereby completing the process of state transformation. Just as all other legislation, the Sandinista government replaced the old penal legislation by new formal procedures regulating prison security, prisoner reeducation, and work between 1986 and 1987 (Centeno Mayorga 2012: 49).

Today the penitentiary system still operates with the four types of regimes established in the '80s: closed, restricted, semi-open and open (Berendse 1998; Grijalva 1997). An additional regime was added in 2003 with the passing of the Penitentiary Law (Law No. 473,) called "*convivencia familiar*" (family life). In practice both the open and the family life regimes function under conditional freedom. These regimes mark levels of security and are phases that nearly all prisoners will pass through in preparation for (early) release—because, in effect, that is what the system claims to be geared toward: not the mere, long-term lock-up of prisoners but the "progressive assignment of privileges" based on good behavior and participation in reeducational programs. Such reeducational programs can be institutional (such as formal schooling, basic literacy, primary and secondary education), spiritual (evangelical, Pentecostal or Catholic worship activities), cultural (sports and arts programs) or work-related (vocational training or employment, available irregularly across different penitentiaries). A prisoner will always enter first into the closed regime, but "his"[4] behavior (*conducta*) and participation in reeducational programs, in short the perceived effort he puts toward his *cambio de actitud*, will determine how fast he progresses from one regime to the next. Depending on the willingness of the judge and the convincingness of the prisoner's change of attitude, which should be substantiated by penal reports on his behavior and participation recorded on his *Tarjeta de Control de Interno* (TCI, Inmate Control Card), sentence reduction can become as substantial as "*hacer el 2 por 1*"—having one physical day in prison count for two days of the sentence.

To a large certain extent the original reeducational premise of the new prison system had to do with the ideological reeducation of counter-revolutionary (*Contra*) prisoners during the bloody civil war that followed the Revolution in the '80s. Yet even as the Revolution suffered its electoral defeat in 1990, at the hands of the UNO-coalition of opposition parties, the reeducational premise of the penitentiary system remained in place at least in part due to the interest of the FSLN to retain some level of control over the institutions of governance. The civil war, including a US embargo, had nonetheless left the country in economic ruin and thus the first institutions to be downsized were precisely those related to the Ministry of the Interior. Entering the first period of structural adjustment almost 80 per cent of the army was discharged and the obligatory draft was annulled. The neoliberal turn that pushed several structural adjustment programs also led to the privatization of many former government-run services and companies. In this period all of the government institutions that had been erected during the revolutionary period (including the police, military and penitentiary system) were moreover "de-sandinistized." As such, the Sandinista Police, for instance, became the National Police and the Sandinista Popular Army became the National Army. Importantly, the Ministry of the Interior was replaced by the newfound Ministry of Governance, which would now oversee the prison system. Yet, even after these reforms, much of the institutions' internal power structure, loyalties and ideological orientation remained Sandinista (Rocha Gómez 2007). This becomes important in relation to the institutional continuity alluded to by the Sandinistas since their return to power in 2007.

As the FSLN disarmed and stepped down from government in 1990, they promised to continue to "govern from below." Throughout the 16 years of neoliberal government that followed the electoral defeat, the country was often paralyzed by national strikes, student marches and protests. Effectively, very little legislation could pass without the (tacit) approval of the Sandinista bench. This "control of the streets" may have provoked, at least in part, the softer implementation of zero-tolerance policing strategies in spite of a regional Central American turn to much more punitive criminal and penal policies directly following US models of crime control (e.g. see Gutiérrez 2013; Hume 2007; Levenson 2013; Rodgers et al. 2009). But this does not mean that Nicaragua has not witnessed a trend of increasing incarceration in relation to the War on Drugs: the prison population has close to quadrupled over the past two decades[5] with the implementation of policies designed to curb both "youth violence" (1990's and early 2000's) and small-scale drug dealing and trafficking (2010's).[6] Even if these policies are not overtly of the zero-tolerance stamp, they do indicate a turn to punitive control. Interestingly, the most recent and sharpest increase in the penal population, tripling in the past ten years, has been under the current Sandinista government (2007-present). This most notably holds relation with the expansion of the reach of the police force, its "proactive communitarian policing model," the implementation of anti-drug policy *Plan Coraza Popular* (Plan Popular Armor), and as of the massive anti-government protests in 2018 also with the criminalization of political dissent. Arguably, then, even the context of a vaunted "progressive regime" does not escape the global turn to increased incarceration to remedy structural social issues such as inequality and unemployment.[7]

Finally, much as Rocha (2007: 546) predicted, the return to government of the FSLN has meant that most state institutions operate in a much more homogenous manner due to the strong command of their (originally) Sandinista structure. Since their return to power, the FSLN has steadily reinforced its influential power over the state institutions, most notably those of crime control (such as police, military, prison and the judiciary—their original strongholds). In practice, this has brought about an implosion of the executive, legislative, and controlling powers into a single "government." Over the past decade, the political landscape surrounding the institutions of governance and justice has thus arguably "re-sandinistized" (see also Collombon and Rodgers 2018). Cementing their power with the 2011 reelection of President Daniel Ortega, the politicization of the institutions of crime control accelerated—by 2014 reforms to the Police Law for instance made Ortega "supreme chief of police." This political control has reached into the prison system, too: to work in penal reeducation involves overt political alignment with the government's "Christian, solidary and socialist" agenda. Adherence to government discourse poses contradictions in itself, however, as the National Police for example promote a "soft" community policing model while implementing "hard" anti-drug policies. Similarly, the penitentiary system balances the (legal and political) discourse of reeducation with a reality of institutional poverty and structural violence. In all this time, since the early '90s, hardly any structural renovations have been made to the penitentiary system's infrastructure, which was heavily deteriorating due to underfunding and overcrowding. Even as the government has begun to invest in repainting buildings and opening new cellblocks, conditions remain dire with the persistence of overcrowding and the inadequate provision of basic needs such as food, running water, and bedding. Moreover, human rights organizations have been barred from inspecting the prison system since 2008. The saturation of the penitentiary system has furthermore spilled over to adversely affect the conditions of police jails, which are in many cases worse. The city police jail included in this research, for example, ran at more than triple its designed holding capacity, also warehousing more convicted prisoners than pretrial detainees.[8] These extra-legal situations complicate the adequate execution of the Penitentiary Law's reeducational promises and make of most prison experiences more schools for coping with direct and structural violence than projects for self-improvement.

Disposal into the System

In line with the promotion of the "humane character" of the prison system,[9] politicians, scholars, and police alike have promoted the country as "the safest in the region" drawing on the "revolutionary mystique" of the communitarian policing model (Granera 2010; Rocha Gómez 2007; Schrader 2017). Nicaragua's so-called "wall of containment" against the gangs of the Northern triangle, the police claim, is "our youth." With such an ideal presentation of the perseverance of community policing, the mediated presentation of a certain sector of the young, urban population as "corrupted, delinquent elements" becomes all the more telling. They are often pictured cuffed in the back of police pick-ups, cussing, fighting, stabbed, or dead on national television news shows—visually connected whenever possible to holding spaces and prisons (Weegels 2018). The apparent natural state for these youth, then, becomes violent and excluded from "community." These "dramatic portrayals of police work, and of the nature of crime and criminal justice, perform an important symbolic function" and help to keep in place what Jewkes has called a "mythology of policing" (2004: 147).[10]

By examining routine and special report news items, especially those featuring youthful detainees complying to a specific, drug-related stereotype, I was able to pinpoint a politics of disposal and exclusion toward a particular segment of youth from the barrio community.[11] The imagery of this *pinta* detainee largely conflates with the collective imaginary of the "standard prisoner." The *pinta* is he who literally "looks like" a common felon or hoodlum (*vago*). This imaginary especially surrounds particular groups of urban adolescents and young men, who are portrayed as poor, uneducated, substance-abusing, small-arms-reeling, menacing, and *dañino*-looking assailants sprawling from the popular neighborhoods. Their intimidating walk, slang-talk, and (mostly) drugged state of mind apparently warrants a harsher treatment at the hands of the police. As the *pinta*-detainee is cuffed in the police pick-up or presented in front of the police jail, he is visually prepared for disposal into the prison system before the television audience. His routine presentation at the site of social disposal contaminates the imaginary of the prison population in general (see also Weegels 2020). What is more, the supposed "antisocial" or anti-communitarian behavior and values of the *pinta*-detainee appear to justify his exclusion. This moral presentation underlines the need for reeducation, and the moral role police and penitentiary personnel play in this correction.

Upon disposal into the prison system the detainee-turned-convict is confronted with a harsh reality of prison norms and regulations. If he was not already beat upon arrest, he is mostly likely to be beat into subordination by the police upon arrival at the *preventiva* (police jail) or by his cellmates.[12] Though authority abuse of prisoners is slightly less common in the penitentiaries than the police jails,[13] prisoners quickly learn they need to grace both their custodians and their cellmates by complying with a series of internal norms, both formal and informal. These norms are in part established through the assignment of privileges according to compliant behavior. Arguably, the formal privilege system poses a double advantage for prison governance: it not only makes individual non-compliance unattractive, but also works against collective non-compliance (Goffman 1961). If we see this in the light of the Nicaraguan system, where sentences are generally not very long and natural life sentences do not exist, combined with the realistic (though arbitrary) prospects for early release, almost every prisoner will have something to lose in the face of disruption. Yet subtle *and* overt non-compliance is ubiquitous (e.g. see Weegels 2019 on prison riots). The rational-choice underpinning of the progressive privilege system may then explain the general compliance of prisoners with the authorities, but it does not begin to explain widespread engagement in the system's illicit undercurrents. In order to understand this dynamic between compliance and subversion, we must understand that the prison is *not only* governed by the authorities, but also by a prisoner-led, norm-based social order enforced through a clear set of practices of violence and solidarity, which the overcrowding of the prison system has only strengthened. These internal practices of order, are engrained in prisoners' performances of their change of attitude, their affective relations, and their management of prison's illicit economies, and provide opportunity to undo their social disposal by engaging in a politics of visibility.

Survival in the Cemetery of the Living

A long-sentenced prisoner of the regional penitentiary once explained to me that for him "prison"—the metaphorical dumpster of social waste—is a "cemetery of the living,"

> I mean, you aren't quite dead, but you become worthless (*ya no vales nada*). For those on the outside, you simply don't exist. (Manuel, regional penitentiary, 2010)

Even as there is a way out of prison, as there is an end to the sentence, the time spent in prison is time that cannot be recovered—it is dead time. There appears to be a continuous tension between being *alive* yet not being able to *see* or *be seen* by the outside world. Invisible behind the prison's walls, prisoners are subjected to governance from both the authorities and their fellow prisoners. Each enforces its own normative order; there seems to be no way around either. In practice, these norms determine the speed and ceiling of ascent in the cell's hierarchy, are reflected in codes of prisoner solidarity (e.g. toward "*donados*"—prisoners abandoned by their families), and dictate when physical violence may be legitimately used.

Aside from their adaptation to the authorities' governance system, new prisoners often pass through a process of trial and error in their own cells: the under-surveilled spaces where they will spend most of their time in prison.[14] Learning how to survive in these economically precarious, overcrowded, and potentially violent carceral spaces becomes paramount. In order to avoid disappearing into the cemetery, most prisoners go out of their way to stretch the boundaries of their confinement and to reconnect with their homes and communities via the use of illegal cellphones. The lengths to which prisoners will go in order to remain in touch with the world outside is something that perhaps only other prisoners and former prisoners would understand. In the face of seemingly all-enveloping social death, prisoners are willing to sacrifice important aspects of what would otherwise be indispensable parts of their masculine gender identities (e.g. Weegels 2014). When stashing their treasured cellphones, or other illegal objects, the rectum may be used. Using this highly sexualized orifice, however, comes at the risk of emasculating its bearer—in Nicaragua, the homosexual stigma sticks only to the passive partner participating in a sexual relation. Men can thus "get away" with most homosexual activities, so long as they remain the active partner and their rectum remains "virgin" (ibid., Lancaster 1992). But during *requisas* (search and confiscations), there may be no place else for prohibited objects to be hidden away. Bobby, a 23-year-old former La Modelo prisoner, who spent the past 6 years in and out of prison, felt the need to explicitly point out to me that this stashing is "*sin cochonadas*"—without "gayness":

> You have to keep your cellphone on you and be very careful who you lend it to *para que no se lo canten muerto* (so they [fellow prisoners] don't rob it). [...] During a *requisa* everyone will stash theirs. [...] Not under the bed of course! *Sin cochonadas,* I would keep it there [up my rectum]. It was small though. (Bobby, Managua 2015)

Beside the risks it poses to a prisoners' manhood (note how Bobby also feels the need to express that "it was small though"), the smuggling and stashing of cellphones or SIM cards is illegal and prisoners caught with cellphones run the risk of sanctions and the revoking of privileges. It is however a thriving business and access to a cellphone in prison is pivotal, as the device constitutes a direct lifeline with the outside world. It is a prisoner's most valuable possession. Keeping in touch with family, partner or friends on the outside is a direct form of countering the effects of social disposal into the cemetery of the living: it constitutes the permanence of one's existence on the outside.

The prisoner's body is not only conditioned in the use of its orifices; however, it is also conditioned in its movement and rhythm. In the face of the scarcity of resources that overcrowding produces, much of the self-ordering violence that occurs in most prison cells has a clear political economic backdrop resulting from the distribution of scarce goods along lines of hierarchy and fairness: space to sleep, food to eat, and water to drink, wash, and shower with. The resources are controlled through a tight, hierarchical system based on reputation, the amount of time one has served, and one's economic position—be this derived from receiving money and goods from the outside or by involvement in illegal prison economies. Quickly learning to live with such spatial restrictions on one's bodily movement is part and parcel with good cell relations. Clear rules are set by cell-leaders regarding the behavior, presentation, and personal hygiene of their cellmates. If these informal protocols are not met, they are imposed—not necessarily by the leader, but by the cell-collective. "If you don't shower we'll make you!" Bobby told me. "We'll throw water at you – you're not going to be stinking in nobody's space."

Particular to the capital's penitentiary is the ominous threat of being stabbed; a reality that makes the cemetery metaphor particularly crude. Learning how to deal with the threat of the "*puñal*" has to be done fast. When I asked Bobby, "but when they stab you they don't mean to kill you, just to hurt or scare you, right?" He shook his head and answered,

> Their idea is to kill you. There are guards who have been stabbed in these fights [...] [so] when there's a confrontation they [the guards] get nervous: they see that you're being stabbed and they can't even open the door. *That's* when you're killed. When there are maybe ten or five [prisoners] on you, and all of them have a *puñal*, how are you supposed to live? (Bobby, Managua 2015)

Though most prisoners manage to escape the blade and transfer cells on time—as Bobby did because, he added, "you are always warned"—the stories and experiences of occurred stabbings keep the threat alive. It is most steadily mobilized to subordinate fellow prisoners, and to sanction or scare prisoners out of stealing from their cellmates. Both stealing and "*bombear*" (snitching) is punished, mostly severely, by fellow prisoners.

Contrary to what the reinforcement of the "peace" inside the cell through these practices of violence might suggest, many prisoners recall their cells as being spaces of sharing. Bobby talked of his cell as being a "small community in which we would rotate cleaning and cooking duties and share food brought in by visiting family members." Prisoners from the city police jail mentioned a similar dynamic of sharing food and cleaning duties—only cell leaders would be exempt from complying with the latter, but much of the respect they garnered would derive from their generosity in "taking care" of their cellmates. Such practices of solidarity, however, always hinged on the simultaneous disposition to deploy violence against rule-breakers.

From their invisible positions in the cemetery of the living, prisoners also engage in what Goldstein and Williams Castro have called "creative violence" (2006: 381). They will often engage in episodes of such creative violence against prison authorities to make *visible* situations they experience behind the prison walls (suffered physical violence, arbitrary denial of visits, the absence or inadequate provision of basic human needs such as running water and food). With prison riots and other, smaller, yet unambiguously personal expressions of institutional discontent, prisoners find their way into the public eye (e.g. Weegels 2019, see also Symkovych 2018). There are inmates who will cut themselves, sew their eyes or mouths shut to demand a family or conjugal visit, better food, or the alleviation of overcrowded spaces. With the help of cellphones, prisoners' expressions of creative violence against the authorities can make their way to the public. On 26 March 2014, for example, a group of cellmates in La Modelo smuggled out a protest video in which the whole cell had sewed their mouths shut, denouncing abuses of power allegedly committed by prison officers.[15] Prisoners are well aware that the media remains biased against them (as they are unequivocally named, shamed, and forgotten), but the media also serve as a powerful tool for their visibility as human beings, or even victims, when they can pass as "victims of the system."[16]

Changing Attitudes and a Prison Theater Tour

Switching from the prisoners' to the prison's norms and governing mechanisms, I turn to discuss the *cambio de actitud* that the prisoner is urged to achieve in order to be (re)included into society's moral order upon release. As the co-founder and assistant to a prison theater training program that ran with long-sentenced prisoners in a regional penitentiary for four years (2009–2013), and at a community center with convicted prisoners sitting out shorter sentences in a city police jail for one year (2015–2016), I witnessed many performances of changed attitudes.[17] I call these *performances* due to the frontstage character of such attitudes when interactions with the outside world occur (not only prison guards and personnel, police officers and state psychologists, but especially people facilitating reeducational, religious, sports, or cultural activities—including myself and my husband, who was the theater facilitator, and the occasional volunteer or government-aligned journalist). Prisoners generally readily manage their stories of personal change when confronted with an audience. This is not to say that such personal change is not *real* but rather that the occurrences and feelings of the backstage *can* diverge from what is expressed on the frontstage. At the latter location, multi-leveled and daily interaction with the prisoners and former prisoners who participated in the theater training program provided pivotal insight into this shifting between the front- and the backstage.[18] This shifting occurred in almost every interaction between the presentation of changed attitudes and the tacit enforcement of cell-based hierarchies, between practices of compliance and those of resistance.

"We want to show that we can be different, that we can change," Brayan, one of the prisoner-actors, tells the audience after the performance of their play at a small-town high school. The students are eager to ask the group members question; girls pose with the youngest ones, taking selfies alongside them with their smartphones. All but two of the prison theater group actors are still in prison—the other two are former prisoners who enrolled in the theater training program while serving their sentences at the city police jail, and stayed with the group after their release. One of them says,

> This is our chance to show who we *really* are [...] I'm an ex-prisoner and am still with this group even though I'm free to do whatever I want, that's how much this experience changed me. (Wiz, after a theater performance, 2015)

In an attempt to undo the negative imagery that stuck to them upon their arrests—more often than not being portrayed on the local televised news as thugs, dealers, or delinquents—the prison theater tour provided an important opportunity to convince the public of the participating (former) prisoners' change of attitude, literally. Not only were the prisoner-actors actively involved in "achieving" their change-of-attitude by participating in the program, they were also able to demonstrate and perform this change not only before the police but perhaps most importantly, the public eye.

In 2015 the local chief of police granted permission for the realization of a tour with the play that the prison theater group had created after we managed to forge an alliance with the Sandinista Cultural Movement, the party's youth organization, and the local police direction for Juvenile Affairs operating the community center where the theater training program was hosted with 13 convicted prisoners sitting out their sentences at the city police jail. On six individual days over the course of two months, twelve performances of the play were realized at local high schools and on public squares throughout the province, including a special performance at the National Theater in Managua. Due to the novelty of the initiative, the party and institutional backing, and its warm reception among youthful audiences, both the prison-theater initiative and the tour received considerable media attention. Yet we soon noticed that the visibility did not only benefit the prisoners. The police also seized the opportunity to emphasize how this tour was an example of "the government's preoccupation to restitute prisoner rights" (which the participants—ever aware of the ways they could be manipulated—in turn saw as "the police using us to 'block the sun with one finger'," as noted by Marlon). Still, participating prisoners and former prisoners also took advantage of the media attention, jumping at every opportunity to voice their stories, which powerfully centered around their *choice* to step away from crime. The most vociferous group members readily made themselves visible as changed men. Rather than being portrayed as disposable antagonists of the barrio community, prisoner-actors were now heralded by the press as examples of positive change.[19] The prisoner-actors in turn creatively managed their visibility, and voiced with us their hopes that this would generate spin-off effects for them, especially in the form of early or temporary release permits.

Posed as a correctional ideal, the *cambio de actitud* is to be visibly performed by the changing prisoner if it is to be observed by reeducational officers. As such, participation and visibility are rewarded, and such rewards are tangible and highly valued among prisoner community as they come—*if* they come—in the form of early release or permissions for 24-hour or weekend furloughs from the cemetery of the living. Being respected as a "changed man" on a long-term prison sentence can ease relations with prison authorities and expedite family and conjugal visits, making life on the inside significantly less lonely. These coveted rewards, especially any type of (temporal) release, however, are not guaranteed nor distributed equally, but they are given frequently enough to continue forming one of the driving forces behind prisoner compliance and participation in penal reeducation.[20]

Transcendence Required

In order to focus on their change of attitude, prisoners are urged to transcend the prison walls—both metaphorically and literally—for their eventual "social reinsertion." Though the prisoners in the initiative described above had the opportunity to actually move beyond bars, the great majority of prisoners cannot literally leave the prison, and the group of prisoners I worked with during the first prison theater program in the regional penitentiary in fact never did. Still, and this includes the prisoners who spend their weekdays at the community center, prisoners are constantly urged through the reeducational and progressive privilege system to work toward their futures away from confinement while still confined. Fludernik explains that this "topos of transcendence [...] functionalizes the notion of escape (getting out of the confinement behind walls) within the non-physical, spiritual, or merely mental realm" (1999: 62). In their minds, the prisoners are able to leave the prison or transcend their daily realities, for example through dedicated participation in reeducational programs or worship. Yet, in this way, "[a]ctual physical imprisonment is replaced by mental liberation, real corporal restraint by an abnegation of the body, and the suffering of actual physical pain is consequently disavowed as a reality" (ibid.: 62–63).

This ideal of transcendence confronts us with the paradox inherent in the requirement of changing attitudes. While the disciplining power of prison and prisoner governance pushes the prisoner to engage in a series of conditioning activities, both in and outside their cells, the topos of transcendence (in other words, the correctional ideal of reeducation) simultaneously denies the importance of the constraints that the material environment imposes on them because "the mind is free" and "change comes from within." If we take into account the context of structural and direct violence governing much of prison life in Nicaragua, then the prescribed change of attitude and its promise of early release can easily become a form of "cruel optimism" imposed on the prisoner (Berlant 2011; O'Neill and Fogarty-Valenzuela 2015); for how can we stress a prisoner to think *not only beyond* the prison's direct walls but also of an outside world and a future that is significantly more welcoming of him than the reality he lived *before* going to prison? On the other hand, if the prisoner does not transcend the walls from time to time, albeit through illicit phone calls with their loved ones or a hit from a prison spliff, does he not run the risk of sliding deeper and deeper into the cemetery, bringing with it its own risks to the precarious prison order, an order that is balanced exactly through the prisoners willingness to keep their heads in the face of the promise of early release? In Nicaragua, prisoners have a name for this very thing—"*quemar cable*", indicating a state of (over-) worrying and anxiousness about one's sentence, loved ones, or life down the drain—trying to burn away the bars while ever more confined to the walls of one's own towering thoughts.

Trapped in this balancing act and focused on the promise of early release, many prison theater group members arduously kept up their performances of change at the community center, venting their discontent with the arbitrariness and slow pace of the system only occasionally and "*en confianza*" (in trust). Eager to be released, Araña would willingly and repeatedly step into the spotlight to display his change, not only to make it visible but to convince others of his worthiness. The police gladly made use of his eagerness to talk about his lessons learned. After two other group members were released on a collective pardon, partially brought about by a prison riot one month earlier, Araña got his hopes up. A year into his two-year sentence, he spent six weeks on end, right up to Christmas, buying into the promise that he would be released "next week." When his mom came around the week before Christmas after visiting the courts, she told him (visibly shaking and upset) that the judge was not even *aware* that he was participating in the rehabilitation program. By then he had protagonized much of the tour of the prison theater play as well. I sat across from him and his mother at the table we had just shared lunch at, as he laid down on the bench, coping with the reality of spending another Christmas behind bars. It dawned on him that all the time he had spent making himself visible to the police was doing nothing in the way of helping him toward an early release. A short hour later, he regrouped:

> I've done everything possible. I've participated as one of the best students in almost all of the courses here. [...] I really thought they [the police] would at least acknowledge what I've done, but what can I say? That's the way it is, *ni modo*. I'm not going to let it get me down. (Araña, community center, 2015)

The police captain in charge of reporting prisoner behavior at the jail should have sent over his report of good behavior for the judge to read, mentioning Araña's participation in the Juvenile Affairs-run community center. In turn, the police captain in charge of Juvenile Affairs should have sent over such a report as well. Neither did, and even though we, as facilitators, vouched for his excellent participation in the theater training program and tour, such a letter of recommendation is of little effect when essential police documentation is missing. In his mind, Araña was doing "*el 2 por 1*," but so long as the judge in charge of the application of sentence reduction was kept in the dark, his performances of change may well have gone by invisibly.

But why would Araña trust the authorities to do their administrative duties in the first place? He was surely aware how the system worked and cognizant of its backdoor negotiations. One explanation is that Araña was "short-timing." United States prison researcher Josh Seim (2016: 444) has argued that more often than not, short-timers' future-oriented perceptions and practices of reentry are "prison-centric," making them much more a part of prison life than of the reentry process. Arguably, short-timing makes participation in reeducation both so seemingly transcendental and instrumental (the future being both at work and at stake through it), and disappointing, because it holds out a reward that is simultaneously engrained in the structures of penal domination. It can also be seen as a coping strategy in relation to the prison sentence and the resources (family, penal privileges—i.e. "points" on the TCI—money, and faith) a prisoner is able to mobilize to shorten it. With these resources in place, it becomes less necessary to "accept" the sentence and "face" prison time. While Araña's frustration came from the sudden and painful confrontation with his prison time, which was a hard blow indeed, it was one from which he rapidly recovered, focusing again on the resources he could deploy in a second, or twentieth, round against hard time. In effect, currently serving a second and much lengthier prison term, it is a strategy he continues to deploy.

A Politics of Visibility

Though participation in reeducational activities is optional, the presentation of a *cambio de actitud* remains pivotal for obtaining early release. The arbitrariness of the system's allocation of privileges, however, stands in contrast to the direct benefits that can be reaped from participation in the cell-based prisoner social order. It should then come as no surprise that most prisoners will first attempt to establish a position within the prisoner social order before participating in reeducation, if they participate at all. Daily confrontation with the ubiquitous and myriad forms of violence prevalent throughout the prison system ties into the strongly performative nature of "change" in the face of everyday adjustments to life inside the cemetery. Some of the most convincing performers of a *cambio de actitud* may simultaneously be some of the best enforcers of the direct physical violence it takes to keep the hierarchical prisoner order in place. Even when "changing" prisoners may simultaneously excel in navigating the cell-based economy, with its informal rules, modes of violent discrimination, and illicit undercurrents—as was the case with Araña. Whether or not participating in reeducational activities (including those of religious, sports, or cultural nature) *actually* changes the participant is not the point here. Instead, we must understand that change is mapped onto prison's space and scheduled into its time in particular ways. Is it transcendental? Is it transformative? Or might we better understand it as made up of temporary, performative transpositions—balancing acts that allow for a consideration of the parallel nature of imprisonment, the parallel nature of change itself?

In his ethnography of Christian piety and "soft" security in the context of the Guatemalan gang crisis, anthropologist Kevin O'Neill (2015) briefly mentions the notion of parallel-ness when he describes the involvement of an imprisoned gang leader ("Gustavo") in the murder of four police officers during a prison riot. Gustavo was, however, also converting to Christianity. And after Gustavo was murdered himself, O'Neill finds himself standing in the prison with the pastor who had been working with Gustavo on his conversion. Describing his interaction with the pastor, he notes how "Pastor Morales tried to reason through Gustavo's compartmentalizing his emerging Christianity from these killings. It was a different (meaning parallel, rather than past) part of his life. The distinction proved too tedious to explain" (ibid: 42). But is this distinction really too tedious to explain, or is it key? Change and violence, reeducation and co-governance, co-exist inside prison and in the lives of prisoners. For them, violence exists in a parallel rather than past sense in relation to their process of changing, while the performance of change itself is both prison-centric and future-oriented.

By drawing on these parallels, I have tried to shed light on both prisoner-based norms that mold the prisoner's movement in his most intimate space (his overcrowded cell), as well as the movement that the reeducational ideal of a *cambio de actitud* is productive of. By touching on these aspects of the prisoner's navigation of the carceral-correctional field, I have drawn attention to the contradictory politics of prisoner and former prisoner (in)visibility in this chapter. I touched on the media's hypervisible disposal of criminal subjects; on the invisibility of passing time in the gravesite of the "cemetery of the living;" and on prisoners' strategies to resist this predicament, including the (illicit) forms they seek to make themselves visible to the outside world and their formal institutional performances of changing attitudes—performances that are simultaneously charged with the expectations of early release and successful social reinsertion. The contradictory discourses that the government emits through its institutions and in the media—on the one hand "restituting" prisoner rights, on the other hand engaging quite clearly in a mediated disposal of "delinquent subjects"—do little if nothing in the way of actually ameliorating the conditions of life inside prison or the prospects for former prisoners upon release. Rather, it may be more pertinent to conclude that the existence of the "cemetery"—its dire conditions, overcrowding, and the ontological threat to disappear behind its walls—produces the very desire to "revive." This in turn establishes the parameters for prison as a co-governed space, governed by both prisoners and authorities, which together provide both the licit and illicit means to regain visibility and social worthiness from behind bars.

Notes

1. I was co-organizer and co-facilitator of this prison theater training program together with my husband, a Nicaraguan theater director and actor. The program formed my access to two prison facilities: a regional penitentiary and a city police jail. In all, I conducted 31 months of graduate and doctoral field research between 2009 and 2016, 25 months of which were spent with prisoners participating in these theater training program. I also followed up with them post-release, and conducted a series of interviews with former prisoners from capital city penitentiary La Modelo. As the majority of my research collaborators were also theater program participants, I do not specify the name of the program or the location of the prison facilities and use pseudonyms throughout the chapter to safeguard their anonymity.
2. Nicaragua counts eight regional penitentiaries, including La Modelo, and one women's prison. It is important to note that the penitentiary law does *not* apply to police jails which, therefore, are under no obligation to organize reeducational programs.
3. The Sandinista revolutionary junta signed and ratified the American Human Rights Convention in September 1979, followed by the ratification of civil and political rights and economic, social, and cultural rights in 1980. The human rights as declared by the United Nations were taken up in the new political constitution ratified in November 1986 (La Gaceta 1979, 1980, 1987). The second coming of the Sandinista government, however, has barred human rights organizations from inspecting the country's prison system since 2008, despite increasing citizen reports of human rights violations. As of the 2018 anti-government protests, the situation has further deteriorated and both armed state violence and political imprisonment have returned.
4. I refer to prisoners with the masculine prefix as the great majority of Nicaraguan prisoners are men, and my research has been focused on male prisoners.

5. The total amount of prisoners in the penitentiary system was 5064 in 2000 and rose to 21,351 by 2020—an incarceration rate of 322 per 100,000, much on par with the rest of the region (PDDH 2000; Ministerio de Hacienda 2020). Implementation of anti-youth crime policies led to a significant increase in incarceration in the late '90s, doubling in only three years from 3692 in 1996 to 7198 in 1999 (Walmsley 1999, 2000). The number of prisoners dropped back down to 5064 in 2000 (PDDH 2000: 12) remaining relatively stable for the next five years at 5610 in 2006 (Walmsley 2007). Since the return to power of the FSLN and with the expansion of the police force and the implementation of anti-drug policies, it had shot up to 10,569 by 2015 and further doubled to 21,351 over the past five years (Walmsley 2015; Ministerio de Hacienda 2020). It is important to note that the official capacity of the Nicaraguan penitentiary system was only 5125 in the mid-'10s (CENIDH 2014).
6. I have argued elsewhere (Weegels 2018) that the sector targeted by both anti-youth violence and anti-drug policies remained much the same over the past two decades.
7. Similar trends took place in Venezuela, Brazil, and Ecuador.
8. In the month of December 2015, the city police jail that the prisoners I worked with were held at held an average of 175 pretrial detainees and 275 convicted prisoners, functioning at more than 300% its capacity. Only 35 prisoners participate in the rehabilitation program at the local community center. By comparison, the regional penitentiary I conducted research at was also steadily overcrowded, though much less so, holding between 700 and 1000 convicted prisoners between 2009 and 2013, thus running at 130–190% its official capacity. Throughout, according to the Penal Reeducation Direction's internal reports, 70% of the prison population participated in a variety of reeducational programs and sports and cultural activities organized on the prison's premises. It must be noted that by law, once convicted, a prisoner should be transferred from the *preventiva* (pretrial police jail) to the *sistema penitenciario* (penitentiary system), but many irregularities occur—both by sending detainees directly to the prison system (as has been done with many political prisoners since 2018), and by keeping convicted prisoners in police jails, as is still the case at present for the city police jail where I conducted my research.

9. The official slogan of the National Penitentiary System is "Serving the People with Vocation, Dignity and Humanism" (www.migob.gob.ni/spn/ last visit 30 March 2016).
10. See Fassin (2013) and Denyer Willis (2015) for similar dynamics regarding the exclusion of criminalized youth by way of the police in France and Brazil.
11. See Weegels (2018) for an in-depth exploration of the mediated representation of policing and youth crime on the Nicaraguan televised news.
12. Though the latter depends on a variety of factors relating to the prisoners' outside position (see Weegels 2017).
13. Yet many protests at La Modelo center around penitentiary personnel abuse of authority—one such instance was caught on film by a prisoner with a smartphone on 21 December 2015, and can be found here https://www.youtube.com/watch?v=jdQL2Kl_tIQ, visited 13 August 2020.
14. Nicaraguan prisons are not built as panopticons and they do not have electronic surveillance systems. Though the outer perimeters are secured by guards armed with automatic-weapons, rounds in the corridors of the cellblocks are walked by unarmed guards bearing truncheons. During rounds, the open iron-bar fronts of cells are peered into, however, visibility into the cell is usually impaired by series of hammocks and bags with personal belongings which are hung from the bars. Prisoners hence spend much time un- or under-surveilled by authorities.
15. "Denuncian maltrato", article published in the popular newspaper *Hoy* and on their website, with a link to the video report that the inmates shot (http://www.youtube.com/watch?v=gyWRakohAec, visited 30 March 2016).
16. This is especially clear in the extensive reporting, especially by print media, on the predicament of political prisoners since the 2018 anti-government protests.
17. Participants in both prison theater groups formed my key pool of research collaborators. Each group consisted of a fluctuating amount of regular participants, generally between eight and fifteen. A large share of my research participants, including interviewed former prisoners that did *not* participate in the prison theater training program, were released before the end of their sentences.
18. Between September 2015 and January 2016, I was generally at the community center from Monday through Friday, for three to seven hours a day, during the intense physical theater trainings, hanging out over

lunch, listening to music, rapping, dancing, sharing food, meeting family, and waiting for tortillas around the corner; but also on the tour of the prison theater play with the whole group throughout the province packed into the minivan, talking, joking around, and vouching for the group's good behavior. I also spent ten Sundays on end traveling with former prisoners (two of whom just-released members of the community center prison theater group) to a radio station in another city, talking about prison, discrimination and post-release life on air between slots of reggaeton, but mostly during the long bus and car rides there.

19. In most media, the National Police and government received significant credit for creating the opportunity for these youth to have participated in a cultural program with such an outcome. Effectively, the discourse of Nicaraguan exceptionalism played an important part in uniting both Sandinista and oppositional news outlets in their positive appreciation of the prison theater tour.
20. See Cheliotis (2014) for a comparable analysis of the use of temporary release in a Greek prison.

References

Berendse, W. (1998). *Justitie en Detentie in Nicaragua*. Working paper with master thesis mensenrechten in Nicaragua, 1979–1998, University of Amsterdam.

Berlant, L. (2011). *Cruel Optimism*. Durham: Duke University Press.

CENIDH. (2014). *Derechos Humanos en Nicaragua: Informe 2013*. Available online: http://www.cenidh.org/media/documents/docfile/Informe_CENIDH_2013_FinalWEB.pdf. visited 28 Dec 2015.

Centeno Mayorga, D. (2012). *Manual de Derecho Penitenciario Nicaragüense*. Managua: SENICSA.

Cheliotis, L. K. (2014). Order through honor: Masculinity and the use of temporary release in a Greek prison. *The South Atlantic Quarterly, 113*(3), 529–545.

Collombon, M., & Rodgers, D. (2018). Introduction. Sandinismo 2.0: reconfigurations autoritaires du politique, nouvel ordre économique et conflit social. *Cahiers des amériques latines, 87*, 13–36.

Denyer Willis, G. (2015). *The killing consensus: Police, organized crime, and the regulation of life and death in urban Brazil*. Oakland: University of California Press.

Fassin, D. (2013). *Enforcing order: An ethnography of urban policing*. Cambridge: Polity Press.

Fludernik, M. (1999). Carceral topography: Spatiality, liminality and corporality in the literary prison. *Textual Practice, 13*(1), 43–77.
Goffman, E. (1961). *Asylums: Essays on the social situation of mental patients and other inmates*. New York: Anchor Books.
Goldstein, D. M., & Williams Castro, F. (2006). Creative violence: How marginal people make news in Bolivia. *Journal of Latin American Anthropology, 11*(2), 380–407.
Granera, A. (2010). *Modelo Policial de Nicaragua 2010*, Panama, October 2010. The presentation can be retrieved online: http://www.policia.gob.ni/cedoc/ModeloPolicialfc.pdf (visited 26 August 2014).
Grijalva, S. A. (1997). *Nicaragua: Situación del Sistema Penitenciario.*
Gutiérrez, L. (2013). *Territories of violence: State, marginal youth, and public security in Honduras*. New York: Palgrave Macmillan.
Hume, M. (2007). '(Young) men with big guns': Reflexive encounters with violence and youth in El Salvador. *Bulletin of Latin American Research, 26*(4), 480–496.
Jewkes, Y. (2004). *Media and crime*. London: Sage Publications.
La Gaceta. (1979). Ley que aprueba y ratifica la Convención Americana sobre Derechos Humanos celebrada en San José, Costa Rica, 1969. Decreto No. 174, aprobado el 25 de septiembre 1979 por la Junta de Gobierno de Reconstrucción Nacional de la República de Nicaragua. *La Gaceta* No. 67(1979).
La Gaceta. (1980). Aprobación y adhesión del gobierno de Nicaragua al pacto internacional de derechos civiles y políticos, su protocolo facultativo y al pacto internacional de derechos económicos, sociales y culturales. *La Gaceta*, No. 25(1980).
La Gaceta. (1987). Constitución Política. Aprobada el 19 de noviembre de 1986. *La Gaceta*, No. 5(1987).
Lancaster, R. N. (1992). *Life is hard: Machismo, danger, and the intimacy of power in Nicaragua*. Berkeley: University of California Press.
Levenson, D. (2013). *Adiós Nino: The gangs of Guatemala City and the politics of death*. Durham: Duke University Press.
Ministerio de Hacienda. (2020). *Presupuesto General de la República*. Managua: República de Nicaragua.
O'Neill, K. L., & Fogarty-Valenzuela, B. (2015). On the importance of having a positive attitude. In J. Auyero, P. Bourgois, & N. Scheper-Hughes (Eds.), *Violence at the urban margins*. Oxford: Oxford University Press.
O'Neill, K. L. (2015). *Secure the soul: Christian piety and gang prevention in Guatemala*. Berkeley: University of California Press.

PDDH (Procuraduría para la Defensa de los Derechos Humanos). (2000). *Situación de las Personas Privadas de Libertad en el Sistema Penitenciario Nacional*. Available online: http://www.iidh.ed.cr/comunidades/ombudsnet/docs/docsomb_pac/Nicaragua-Publicaciones/PHD-NIC%20Personas%20privadas%20de%20libertad.pdf. Visited 30 Mar 2016.

Rocha Gómez, J. L. (2007). Mapping the labyrinth from within: The political economy of Nicaraguan youth policy concerning violence. *Bulletin of Latin American Research, 26*(4), 542.

Rodgers, D., Muggah, R., & Stevenson, C.. (2009). Gangs of Central America: Causes, costs, and interventions. In *Small Arms Survey* (Occasional paper 23). Geneva: Small Arms Survey.

Schrader, S. (2017). Nicaragua: Central America's security exception. *NACLA Report on the Americas, 49*, 360–365.

Seim, J. (2016). Short-timing: The carceral experience of soon-to-be-released prisoners. *Punishment and Society, 18*(4), 442–458.

Symkovych, A. (2018). Negative visibility and 'the defences of the weak': The interplay of a managerial culture and prisoner resistance. *Theoretical Criminology, 24*(2), 202–221.

Walmsley, R. (1999). World prison population list, no. 88, first edition.

Walmsley, R. (2000). World prison population list, no. 116, second edition.

Walmsley, R. (2007). World prison population list, 8th edition.

Walmsley, R. (2015). World prison population list, 11th edition.

Weegels, J. (2014). The Prisoner's body: Violence, desire and masculinities in a Nicaraguan prison theatre group. In G. Frerks, A. Ypeij, & R. König (Eds.), *Gender and conflict: Embodiments, discourses and symbolic practices*. Farham: Ashgate.

Weegels, J. (2017). Prisoner self-governance and survival in a Nicaraguan City police jail. *Prison Service Journal, 229*, 15–18.

Weegels, J. (2018). 'The terror and scourge of the barrio': Representations of youth crime and policing on Nicaraguan television news. *Journal of Latin American Studies, 50*(4), 861–887.

Weegels, J. (2019). Prison riots in Nicaragua: Negotiating co-governance amid creative violence and public secrecy. *International Criminal Justice Review*. https://doi.org/10.1177/1057567719849485.

Weegels, J. (2020). From *pinta* to changed man: Performing reinsertion and escaping *color* at the Nicaraguan margins. *Latin American and Caribbean Ethnic Studies*. https://doi.org/10.1080/17442222.2020.1798075.

15

Spiritual Life and the Rationalization of Violence: The State Within the State and Evangelical Order in a Venezuelan Prison

Luis Duno-Gottberg

Introduction: A World Upside-Down

On August 19th 2012, a clash between two prison gangs left 26 people dead and 43 wounded inside the Parahuachón[1] prison complex, one of the most notorious penitentiaries of Venezuela. Among the dead were several evangelical pastors, known as *Men of Fire*, who tried to mediate in this confrontation. As I explain in this chapter, *mediation is a function within a complex structure of regulation or rationalization of violence* inside the prison, when the Venezuelan State seemingly delegates the internal control of the facility to the inmates, and, in turn, the gang leaders delegate certain regulatory or disciplinary functions to the evangelical community.

I would like to thank the Boniuk Institute for Religious Tolerance for their generous support during the Summer of 2015. Thanks to David Smilde, Andrés Antillano, and Chris Garces for their illuminating comments.

L. Duno-Gottberg (✉)
Rice University, Houston, TX, USA

S. Darke et al. (eds.), *Carceral Communities in Latin America*, Palgrave Studies in Prisons and Penology, https://doi.org/10.1007/978-3-030-61499-7_15

The tragic event started with an accidental shot fired during a meeting between *Prans*,[2] the rival leaders of "The Administrative" (a former office space now controlled by inmates) and "The Workshop" (an area formerly devoted to the teaching technical skills). At the root of this violence are the well-known issues of overcrowding, lack of due process, corruption, and the wide availability of weapons for those inmates controlling the prison. Statistics are compelling: Parahuachón had the capacity to house 750 inmates but as of 2012, the prison population amounted to 2372. At that moment, this represented an overcrowding of 316%.[3] To make things worse, weapons smuggling had been rampant and included pistols, grenades, shotguns, and automatic rifles.[4]

The 2012 massacre might be also rooted in an event that took place two years earlier, when a group of inmates housed in the administrative wing of the prison took over a section known as "The Tower." Among those subdued in the 2010 confrontation were the members of several evangelical churches housed in *La Torre*. These congregations ultimately would come back, but only under the supervision of the "secular power" that had taken over Parahuachón after the confrontation. A new *Pran* was to organize the church by, as one informant explained to me, "purifying the congregation with fire", and "bringing restitution to a world upside-down". This was "God's design". Those who would not or could not accept this new order and whose lives were spared, escaped to another section of the prison, known at *Los Talleres*, or "The Workshops." The *Admisitrativo-Tower* section and the *Talleres* were, from that moment on, two completely separated communities, not only at odds with each other, but also with distinctive codes and modes of organization. By subjugating or expelling their rivals, a new order ensued. One in which a secular inmate power group would supervise and benefit from the religious inmate community. In this manner, the structural issues of Venezuelan penitentiaries intertwine with a very particular context in which, as I argue, a "state-within-the-state" (or an inmate parody of the state) instrumentalized religious structures and practices to consolidate its power and to regulate violence.

I am interested in this dynamic established between the evangelical religious community inside the prison, and the secular power that actually rules over one large section of Parahuachón. The existence of a well-defined social order, known as *la rutina* ("the routine"[5]), entails a political rationality, conversing with different groups inside and outside the facility. The evangelical church happens to be one of them.

The first two sections of this chapter, "A Foundational Myth for a Modern Inmate Order" and "The Cleansing of the Temple," describe the way in which the evangelicals understand/represent the current power structures in the prison, and the relationship between the religious and the secular. The last three sections, "Rituals of Confinement," "Rituals of Containment," and "Capturing Labor," describe the economic and social functions fulfilled by the of the religious sphere in Parahuachón.

This research began towards 2010, when I was invited to teach several workshops organized by the School of Penitentiary Communication (*Escuela Popular de Comunicación Penitenciaria*), a non-governmental organization providing audiovisual instruction to inmates. In that context, and over the last five years, I visited Parahuachón to provide support to different film projects, as well as to teach film appreciation and Latin American political history. Throughout that time, I came to learn about the role of the evangelical church inside the prison. Here I draw from interviews with members of the evangelical congregation and pastors. I also draw from my observations of ceremonies and daily life inside the prison. Like other ethnographies, this one could be framed as "Witnessing" (Behar 1996; Scheper-Hughes 1992; Malkki 1995), although, in the context of prisons, such concept becomes loaded with difficult implications. The juridical connotation is perhaps the most unsettling aspect, when the fieldwork adjoins, even unwillingly, the police field. Other epistemological, methodological, and ethical challenges of witnessing in prison ethnography have been rightly called to our attention by Angel-Ajani. As she explains in her study of European prisons, anthropological "witnessing" has frequently functioned as an attempt to reassert the authority of the ethnographer. With these concerns in mind, the collaborative nature of my visits to Parahuachón, but also the *rutina* itself, imposed the framework in which conversations and meaning emerged.

The kind of witnessing that ensued can be defined as "engaged witnessing," in that it presupposed a sense of ethical responsibility (Sanford and Angel-Ajani 2006) throughout a lengthy engagement with the interior life of the prison. The project is also characterized by the weight of a double framework in which power and authority shift: on one side, the exchanges between confined men rendering their testimony to an engaged academic (who bears witness); on the other hand, the normative pressure of *la rutina*—which applies to both sides of the conversation, and presupposes strict hierarchies and rules. This tension determined the development and the limitations of my work.

A Foundational Myth for a Modern Inmate Order

The origin of this "inmate order" has been recast by members of the evangelical church as a genealogical myth: a narrative of fall and redemption. Their stories make sense of the bureaucratization of an inmate power structure that successfully rationalized and contained many forms of violence inside the prison through, certainly, their own monopoly of force, but also through the supervision and administration of the existing evangelical community.

This transformation of the religious and secular spheres in Parahuachón evokes, perhaps in a parodic or carnivalesque mode, the process of secularization that accompanied the emergence of the Modern State. In fact, the subordination of the religious order to the secular power inside this prison reminds us of the rise of Absolutism. If the analogy seems extreme, allow me to recall that during Feudalism, the Church and the social elite (the aristocracy) restrained monarchical power; but with the end of feudal partitioning and the consolidation of power in the Monarch, we see the rise of the State and the emergence of professional bureaucracies and armies. This is precisely what I see in Parahuachón: the consolidation of a social order governed by a vertical and highly efficient State-of-sorts, with a sophisticated administration to implement policing and punitive actions, as well as with a diverse number of strategies and practices for extracting labor and generating revenue.

It is my theory that in Parahuachón, a new social order emerged from the utter lack of administration of justice on behalf of the State. In turn, this led to the creation of an autonomous rule where evangelicals function as a branch of a secular (*inmate*) power that delegates certain forms of punishment and other services to the Church. These transformations are not isolated. They are tied to larger shifts taking place in Latin American prisons in the last few decades, as national states appear unable or unwilling to exert control over these spaces of confinement and punishment.

There is a carnivalesque dimension to this reshaping and reconstitution of power inside the prison (see Antillano and Duno-Gottberg, this volume). An all-around subversion of the *status quo* is at the heart of all Carnival traditions, since ancient times. The carnival perspective is, in this sense, the temporary overthrow of the world order and the instauration of a provision order "from below"; a moment of freedom of sorts. Bakhtin has famously portrayed carnival as an expression of a "second life" of the people, against their submission to the dominant powers. Such rupture, even if momentary, points to the fragile unity of dominant systems of power. That being said, the transgressive and regenerative vitality of Bakhtinian carnival has its limits, as it does the subversion of State power and inmate power in Paraguachón. The carnivalesque reproduction of state dynamics from below would not hide, as we will see in this chapter, its oppressive and exploitative dimension.

My research converses with work from others in this book, particularly Chris Garces, Sacha Darke, Fischer-Hoffman, Sepúlveda, Pojomovsky, and Andrés Antillano. I am interested in Garces' assertion that "para-state networks" migrate from and into the state prison system.[6] As my own ethnographic work shows, this flow of social and economic relations turns out to be multidirectional. The existence of a highly sophisticated, some might even say "fluid," structure of carceral governance connects the inside and outside of the prison: barriers are rendered porous by family links, business interest, but also by religious practices. Also important for my argument are Darke and Antillano's reflections on inmate governance (this volume). The latter, working on Venezuela, sees a continuation of a neoliberal carceral order in the context of the Bolivarian Revolution. In spite of the expansion of the state apparatus and the social programs helping the poor, the internal functioning of the prison seems paradoxically to reproduce the logic of neoliberalism: the void left by the receding State is filled by the inmates who, in turn, develop their own administrative/bureaucratic structures in order to extract rent, to regulate daily life, and to monopolize violence. Finally, I draw on the extensive work by David Smilde on the practical functions of evangelical conversion amidst situations of extreme violence (2013). As he explains, this practice provides people from the popular sectors, a way to escape the logic of *la culebra* ("the vendetta"), thus protecting themselves from situations of vulnerability. Inside the prison, evangelical conversion equally provides a safe haven against violence; but Parahuachón reveals an important additional element: the church itself can function as part of a punitive system controlled by the reduced group of inmates that run "el carro", the inmate government (see Antillano, this volume). Freston's and Steigenga's work on Pentecostalism in Latin America is also important for my argument, as it clearly identifies the participation of evangelical groups in the political arena and the potential for authoritarian turns.

The Cleansing of the Temple

Parahuachón's evangelicals rendering of the events leading to the current carceral order draw on a Biblical narrative. Several accounts focus on the reasons why the "cleansing" of "The Tower" annex took place, and the reason why the inmates from the *Adminstrativo* annex (many of them formerly connected to the police or military apparatus), successfully took over.

When listening to these testimonies, one cannot avoid thinking about the story of Jesus chasing the merchants out of the Temple, as it appears in the four canonical gospels of the New Testament.[7] Jesus and his disciples travel to Jerusalem for Passover, to find that moneychangers and merchants have taken over the "'house of God". In Parahuachón, the taking over of the Tower and the reorganization of the evangelical churches has been described in rather similar terms by a few of the pastors: "the church had lost its way and God sent his punishment," "Some Pastors were living in sin, doing illegal businesses, and behaving in an immoral manner." Then, when it was too much, "a man, strong and smart, was sent to bring order," and so the new churches emerged. This new man, nevertheless, was not a religious one, but representing the forces of an inmate power structure—a man with enough weapons to control and expel those who opposed him; a man clever enough to organize the prison from within. The "cleansing of the temple" thus took place under a secular force that would then create the conditions for the emergence of three churches: The *Iglesia Madre* ("Mother Church"), *La Iglesia Luz de Los Hombres* ("The Light of Men Church"), and *El Centro de Rehabilitación* ("The Rehabilitation Center").

Rituals of Confinement

Not paying one's debts or breaking the codes of conduct of the prison can all-too-easily cost an inmate his life. In Parahuachón, nevertheless, this type of event rarely occurs. Infractors are sent by the gang leaders to one particular church, named *El Centro de Rehabilitación*, where they perform a sort of penitence under the supervision of a pastor. The name of the church is telling of the bureaucratic rationality organizing this space—a name that seems closer to that of a medical institution than to a religious congregation.

El Centro, the smallest and poorest of the three churches in Parahuachón, is located at the entrance of The Tower, and was built by the inmates to house those who break the codes of the prison (*la rutina*). While living at *Rehabilitation Center*, inmates are held as prisoners (inside the prison), and are required to follow a rigorous schedule that includes hard work, on top of attending religious services. These inmates can rejoin the general population after serving "their time," or may choose to become *trillos*—those who are being groomed to be permanent members of the congregation. This space, a prison-church-inside-the-prison, functions under a pastor, but also under the watchful eye of a secular power: *el pran*. While the ultimate authority rests on the "secular power" of the latter, conferencing and mutual agreements reached with the pastor is the norm.

The Rehabilitation Center thus fulfills a punitive function that avoids death, as much as possible. This standard institutional recourse is no less violent, needless to say, as scars from blows to the face and the head usually mark those who are sent to the Center. The fact that those housed within Rehabilitation Center are required to shave their heads (showing more clearly their scars), and being required to wear a tie and button-down shirts to move around certain parts of the prison, entail an intricate code that interconnects the secular and the religious. The cost of not following these rules is high (Image 15.1).

Rituals of Containment: *Varones de Fuego*

When shootouts take place, the *Men of Fire* (*los varones de fuego*) respond in ways that combine fierce courage and magical power. They walk into the cloud of bullets, branding their Bibles in the air while shouting: "Jesus is alive. The blood of Jesus heals." If in peace with the Lord, bullets won't harm them. In turn, those branding their weapons would know better than killing these holy men who mediate during outbursts of violence. Their presence inspires admiration, but also restores order: they gather the wounded or the dead; they invite a cease of fire, or arrange conversations between enemies. In Parahuachón's local parlance, these are the *Men of Fire*, mythical pastors who earn the respect of the *Pran* and his army. They are the ultimate mediators between the divine and the profane; but more immediately, between *malandros*[8]—"criminals"—in dispute. These, priding themselves of being brave and unyielding, would only drop their weapons if a worthy "varón" intercedes. Their status would not be tarnished then, if responding to the demands of a divine mediator. Prestige and reputation are not at risk when a truce is reached by these holy, magical means.

Image 15.1 Inmates are assembled by the pastor to watch a movie produced inside the prison. These men are serving time in Parahuachón and, at the same time, they are confined to *El Centro de Rehabilitation* for breaking *la rutina;* this is, committing different kinds of infractions, such as not paying debts, disrespecting members of "*el carro,*" breaking the moral codes of the prison. A double form of imprisonment, these inmates cannot leave Parahuachón, obviously, nor leave the *Centro de Rehabilitation* without the proper authorization from el *Pran* and secondly, from the pastor. The rigidity of daily life in this space clashes with the "freedom" in other buildings in the prison. (Photo LDG 2014)

The *Men of Fire* prove themselves through their "testimony," as one of the pastors explained to me. These are men who have shown to be virtuous in their behavior, and deeply knowledgeable of the Holy Book: "You gain your *testimony* through a life of rectitude and bravery. Only in that way you gain respect from *Malandros*," another of them explained to me, after being released from Parahuachón. "You cannot lie", he said. "*Los mundanos* [those who are not part of the church] would stop you and ask you to recite a verse of the Bible. And then, a little bit further, someone else would ask you for a different verse. If you don't know, they would hit you and even crack your head open. So you have to prove yourself." After listening to many similar accounts, it becomes clear that the secular force remains the ultimate authority but also, that this authority recognizes the value of the Church in terms of administering and reorganizing the community. As one of the "*principales*"[9] expressed to me, "they [the evangelicals] do their thing, and we do our thing; but while at it, they keep the [inmate] population in peace so we don't have to intervene" (June 2014).

Capturing Labor

As I have explained, in Parahuachón non-lethal punishment is delegated to the evangelicals. Other functions that make survival of the community possible also rest on them. They cook and provide food for those without relatives or money to pay the *causa* (a "tax" of sorts). They clean the facility, and take care of those who are ill. When confrontation occurs, they tend to the wounded; and often gather the dead, bringing them to the National Guard who police outside the facility. In short, evangelicals provide a labor pool in a context in which manual work is considered degrading for *malandros*.

"On one side of the Tower, the pile of shit was as high as a person standing," explained a Man of Fire, while raising his hand over his head. "The stench was horrendous and inmates kept on throwing excrement through the windows. No one would do anything. *Malandros* don't clean. They see it as degrading. It's a *mancha* (a stain). So living there, in those conditions was impossible. One day I told the *pran*: give me a pair of rubber boots and a shovel and I'll clean it. The *pran* liked the idea but he didn't think I could do it. And I went in; and I did it. I had to shovel the crap and take it away in a wheelbarrow. The following day, there was more excrement, but I kept on cleaning and cleaning until things began to change. The *pran* was impressed and I gained my *testimonio*".

In this account, a Man of Fire may gain his legitimacy (or "*testimonio*"), not only through acts of bravery, but specially through his work in the most disgusting (and therefore degrading) task within the facility. His efforts in improving sanitation, granted him access to the *pran,* and eventually, mobility throughout the prison. But this is not the case among other evangelicals and much less among those sent to the *Centro de Rehabilitación* for punishment. Their labor doesn't grant them any other privilege than being exempt from acts of violence.

To be sure, the *carro* (the *malandro* government) and the general population benefit in many other ways from this pool of free labor: unloading trucks, preparing food, and organizing events during family visit days are activities carried out primarily by members of the church.

This pool of workers corresponds to a mechanism for capturing labor through institutional salvation from the constant threat of violence. The relationship between the secular and the religious spheres have a clear transactional nature; but not all parts benefit equally. In the negotiations between the *Pran* and the members of the church, there is a significant difference between the coercion experienced by *mundanos*[10] ("worldly men") undergoing punishment, the *trillos* preparing to be permanent members of the congregation, and the Men of Fire.

Conclusion: A Carceral State, Within

In five years, I saw different pastors running the congregations of Parahuachón. Some remained in their post, but others had been released and joined other evangelical churches outside prison. Others abandoned religious life altogether, after their release. The internal structures of the Evangelical Church remain, nevertheless, fully in place. More importantly, *El Centro de Rehabilitación* continued to fulfill its regulating/punitive function. *Trillos* and *mundanos* continue to feed an inmate pool labor that satisfies the needs of the community, when the state has ceased to provide resources for the most basic subsistence. Although "the heads of state", the *Prans*, have changed a few of times, the secular power also remains firmly in place, dictating the life of the prison, benefiting from the underground economy, and monopolizing (never uncontested) violence. That being said, it is important to acknowledge that, beyond the obvious fact of coercion and exploitation, this particular inmate order has also been successful containing the most brutal forms of violence that characterize other Venezuelan prisons.

I want briefly to conclude by reiterating my initial hypothesis: in Parahuachón, a social order has emerged from the utter lack of administration of justice on behalf of the State, which in turn has led to the creation of an autonomous structure whereby evangelicals function as a branch of a secular (*inmate*) power that delegates certain forms of punishment and other services to the congregation. Beyond its parodic or even carnivalesque dimension, this mechanism for administering life inside the prison entails a complex bureaucratic rationality that benefits and profits from the existing circumstances of the prison facility. Ultimately, it is the withdrawing of the State proper (as in the neoliberal model) which unleashes the forces that reproduce a "carceral-state-in-the-margins"; a "carceral-state-within-the-prison", along with different forms of exploitation and violence (Images 15.2, 15.3, 15.4, and 15.5).

Image 15.2 A pastor from one of the three churches overlooks Parahuachón after the religious service is completed. From that window, he can see an entire side of the facility, where many inmates gather to chat, play sports, or engage in diverse transactions. The now empty room holds precious objects: the congregation has been able to purchase musical instruments and a sound system. These are expensive possessions inside the prison, but no one dares to take them. *La rutina*, the carceral code, guaranties order; this is, a social structure where every infraction is punishable, sometimes even with death. (Foto LDG 2015)

Image 15.3 In the overcrowded prison of Parahuachón, space is a luxury and, of course, a sign of power. This cell houses a Pastor who earned his post through his *testimonio*: a proven record of bravery and probity in the eyes of other members of the congregation, but especially, in the eyes of the *Pran*. Hanging on the left side of the frame, the characteristic tie that all evangelicals wear to move around the prison. The dress code (a tie and a button-down shirt), along with the branding of the Bible, identifies the members of the congregation and separates them from the general inmate population. This identity generally protects them from the overt forms of violence in the prison, although no one is exempted from *la rutina*

Image 15.4 A solid iron gate guards the entrance of one of the churches of Parahuachón. *Gariteros* (look-outs), soldiers of the *Pran*, are posted outside. On the other side, a member of the congregation keeps the key to the lock. The border between both worlds is clearly demarcated, policed, and administered. An inmate might look for asylum inside the church, but it is impossible to bypass the control of the secular power. Evangelicals might choose to rescue certain prisoners by exiting the church and surrounding them with their bodies while branding a Bible. The *Pran* might or might not grant permission for the inmate to remain in the church and, in some cases, might demand that the offender be returned for punishment. For this reason, pastors will weigh carefully the privilege of saving an inmate's life. In one of our visits, such a situation occurred: a rather quiet commotion took over the prison, while discussions between the *Pran* and the pastor ensued. These conversations had a high level of formality, and every party involved evaluated carefully the cost/benefit of granting asylum or not

Image 15.5 After an impassionate, day-long conversation about religion and life in Parahuachón, a pastor stood in front of a large opening connecting two sides of The Tower. His voice turned unexpectedly thin. He seemed suddenly tired and uninspired, as he told me about his plans to "return to the world" (*suregreso al mundo*)—a phrase used by inmates to name the world awaiting outside the prison. His plan was joining another congregation, connected nevertheless to Parahuachón. The porosity of prison became obvious, with an oppressive twist: is one truly, finally out?

Notes

1. Names of actors and places have been changed. Dates have also been modified.
2. *Pran, Pram, or Principal* is the name given to the leader of a gang running a prison. The *Pran* is the ultimate Leviathan, as in the absolute Sovereign. He organizes the *causa* (the cause), a payment imposed on other prisoners for protection, as well as for the purchase of some communal goods. He has control of weapons, phones, and most businesses inside the facility. The *Pran* exerts his power through a government of sorts, called *el carro* (the car). The enforcing branch of this government is composed by well-armed men called *luceros* (stars). As we shall see, the Church also has a role in this regulatory and punishing system organized from within.

3. By the year 2010, the country had an inmate population of 34,270. See report of the Observatorio Venezolano de Prisiones at http://www.ove-prisiones.org/assets/informe-final-200-2010_ovp_fupad.pdf. See also the "Order of the Inter-American Court of Human Rights of September 6, 2012. Provisional Measures with Regard to Venezuela Matters of Certain Venezuelan Prisons Yare I and Yare II Capital Region Penitentiary Center" at http://corteidh.or.cr/docs/medidas/penitenciarioregion_se_05_ing.pdf
4. In 2007, the overall seizure of weapons in Venezuelan prisons reached 3825. The following year, 2148.
5. See Antillano (this volume) and Sepúlveda and Pojomovsky (this volume).
6. "(…) wherein powerful trafficking agents strive to establish a proxy state system wherever the state has effectively receded—complete with informal policing, popular justice, and local councils for holding neighborhood residents accountable to parastate authorities. Recently, scholarship has tracked the wholesale migration of such parastate networks into state prison systems" (Garces 2014: 251).
7. The gospels of Matthew, Mark, and Luke are referred to as the Synoptic Gospels because they include many of the same stories, often in a similar sequence and in similar wording. The narrative occurs near the end of the Synoptic Gospels (at Mark 11:15–19, 11:27–33, Matthew 21:12–17, 21:23–27 and Luke 19:45–48, 20:1–8) and near the start in the Gospel of John (at John 2:13–16). The Synoptic gospels' play of reiterating the same narrative history, albeit with slight twists, lends itself to textual and mythic re-adaptation.
8. The "malandro" in Venezuelan culture is slightly different than the Brazilian version. While in Portuguese, the notion is not necessarily emphasizing the criminal aspect of that identity, in our case, this feature is at the forefront. In the context of Venezuelan prisons, "el orden Malandro" entails a hierarchy, and precise codes that go beyond the confines of the prison. See also Antillano (this volume) and Sepúlveda and Pojomovsky (this volume).
9. The *Principales* (Principals) are the high-ranking members of el *carro* (the car, or organization that run the prison). There are no more of two of these, and they have the complete trust of the Pran.
10. Those who are not permanent members of the congregation and become prisoners of *El Centro de Rehabilitación*.

References

Agamben, G. (2000). *Remnants of Auschwitz: The witness and the archive*. New York: Zone Books.

Angel-Ajani, A. (2004). Expert witness: Notes toward revisiting the politics of listening. *Anthropology and Humanism, 29*, 133–144.

Bakhtin, M. (1984). *Rabelais and his world.* H. Iswolsky, Trans. Bloomington: Indiana University Press.

Behar, R. (1996). *The vulnerable observer: Anthropology that breaks your heart*. Boston: Beacon Press.

Frampton, M. L., Haney-López, I., & Simon, J. (2008). *After the war on crime: Race, democracy, and a new reconstruction*. New York: New York University Press.

Freston, P. (2001). *Evangelicals and politics in Asia, Africa, and Latin America*. Cambridge: Cambridge University Press.

Garces, C. (2014, July). Denuding surveillance at the carceral boundary. *South Atlantic Quarterly, 113*(3), 447–473.

Garland, D. (1990). *Punishment and modern society*. Chicago: Chicago University Press.

Giordano, P., Cernkovich, S. A., & Rudolph, J. (2002). Gender, crime, and desistance: Toward a theory of cognitive transformation. *American Journal of Sociology, 107*, 990–1064.

Hallett, M., & Johnson, B. (2014). The resurgence of religion in America's prisons. *Religion, 5*, 663–683.

Malkki, L. H. (1995). Refugees and exile: From "refugee studies" to the national order of things. *Annual Review of Anthropology, 24*, 495–523.

Melossi, D., & Pavarini, M. (1981). *The prison and the factory: Origins of the penitentiary system*. London: Macmillan Press.

Sanford, V., & Angel-Ajani, A. (2006). *Engaged observer: Anthropology, advocacy, and activism*. New Brunswick: Rutgers University Press.

Scheper-Hughes, N. (1992). *Death Without Weeping: The Violence of Everyday Life in Brazil*. Berkeley, CA: University of California Press.

Smilde, D. (2007). *Reason to believe: Cultural agency in Latin American evangelicalism*. Berkeley: University of California Press.

Smilde, D. (2013). Confrontando la Inseguridad: Estrategias de los Evangélicos. *Espacio Abierto Cuaderno Venezolano de Sociología, 22*(2), 245–263.

Smith, C. (2010). *Pentecostal power: Expressions, impact and faith of Latin American Pentecostalism*. Leiden: BRILL. Ebook Library. Web. 20 Dec 2014.
Steigenga, T. J. (2001). *The politics of the spirit: The political implications of pentecostalized religion in Costa Rica and Guatamala [i.e. Guatemala]*. Lanham: Lexington Books.
Sullivan, W. F. (2009). *Prison religion: Faith-based reform and the constitution*. Princeton: Princeton University Press.

16

Carceral Order, Mediation, and Representation: Fiction and Ethnography in a Venezuelan Prison

Chelina Sepúlveda and Iván Pojomovsky

We went to Peonía Prison[1] to carry out an ethnographic study about the informal organization of prisoners, the transformations into the carceral order, and its relationship with broader processes of social marginalization and exclusion.[2] We were supported by a collective of filmmakers[3] that worked with prisoners in Peonía and other prisons throughout Venezuela with the aim of creating films from the inmates' perspective. Our contact with these filmmakers encouraged us to experiment with visual anthropological methods, which gave us tools to attempt to create an ethnography that documents diverse perspectives on prison life.

Our approach, however, was experimental. In the beginning of our fieldwork in Peonía, we did not imagine that months later we would be involved in producing fictional films conceived and performed by the

C. Sepúlveda (✉)
Universidad Central de Venezuela, Caracas, Venezuela

Instituto de Estudios Avanzados, Baruta, Venezuela

I. Pojomovsky
Universidade Federal de Pernambuco, Recife, Brazil

S. Darke et al. (eds.), *Carceral Communities in Latin America*, Palgrave Studies in Prisons and Penology, https://doi.org/10.1007/978-3-030-61499-7_16

inmates. This emphasis on film production transformed our fieldwork and our theoretical orientation, placing at the center of our inquiry the problem of representation and its relationship with the configuration of the carceral order.

In this article, we draw on our field notes and employ visual ethnographic methods to analyze the carceral order. We worked alongside inmates to elaborate, produce, and stage a fiction film that they wrote, organized, and starred in. This process encouraged us to ask questions about *the work of representation*. Through the work of performance the subject, in this case, a group of inmates, produce themselves with the resources that their particular context (the prison) provide, objectifying their own position in a specific material and symbolic universe (the prison and the structural framework) (Bourdieu 1984). This was a way for the inmates to cope with precarious conditions and to face the tensions of representing the domination and oppression they undergo in the violent carceral world.

Following the work of inmates of Peonía's Prison to create fictional programs allowed us not only to address the work of representation from the perspective of the prisoners, but also to contribute to a debate concerning the methodology of creating fiction as part of ethnographic research. Here we raise the dilemmas posed by organizing and staging fictional accounts of the violence of the carceral order. For the prisoners with whom we worked, the production of the film series entailed not only their exposure to cinematographic training and perspective, but also a space of recognition and the possibility of repositioning themselves in the harsh world of the prison.

The Stage: Prison, Order, and *Rutina*

Peonía Prison is a penitentiary center whose internal regime—its organization and administration—is controlled by the inmates.[4] When we began our study, Peonía's population was 2500 inmates.[5] They were imprisoned in a facility built for 750 prisoners. This overcrowding is characteristic of Venezuela's prison system, which has expanded at a fast pace. Between 2013 and 2014, Venezuela's prison population grew to

50,000 inmates, an unprecedented high. This growth was a result of various factors, including the hardening of penal laws, particularly those associated with drug offenses; the establishment of procedures that allowed for expedited imprisonment; and the growth of the use of preventative detention. As a result, in 2008, the percentage of people incarcerated without being sentenced surpassed 60% of the prison population. In 2013, when we initiated this field research in Peonía Prison, of the 2500 inmates, 1800 were on trial and only 700 were serving sentences.[6]

The day we first visited the prison, Morgan was waiting to meet us to learn about our project and its aims. The audiovisual collective had arranged this morning meeting. Their introduction provided us entry. At that time, Morgan had been incarcerated for six years, and he was one of the most recognized and feared leaders among the prisoners at Peonía. He had a high-ranking position in the intensely hierarchical organization that dominates and manages life in the prison known as the *carro*[7] in the carceral world. Without his consent, it was worthless to obtain official permission to enter the prison. The goal of our visit that day was to secure Morgan's permission.

Once we passed the checkpoint at the entrance, we encountered another checkpoint inside the prison; there were other checkpoints in the corridor that led to our meeting place. They call these checkpoints *garitas*. In each one of these, inmates armed with different guns guarded the enclosure and sang[8] our arrival to the rest of the inmates.

We crossed the porch of the building that houses the cellblocks. Vendors were renting cell phones or selling drugs, which they unsuccessfully tried to hide from us. As soon as the introductions were made, Morgan excused his entourage of fellow inmates and offered us something to drink. He led us to a path that took us outside of the building. At each *garita*, inmates sang our departure.

After we crossed an area located behind the building, we came to a cafeteria that offered drinks and simple food. Morgan introduced us to the inmates in charge of the place and ordered sodas for everyone. In the style of both a politician and a good host, he pointed to a playground located on the other side of the area, which had been recently restored for children visiting inmates at Peonía Prison.

As if he were the leader of an association, he described and boasted about the efforts carried out by the inmates to improve conditions for the penitentiary center despite the institution's neglect. Other inmates regularly interrupted him for consultation or to make requests related to the internal life of the prison. Our conversation lasted until lunchtime. Despite our insistence, Morgan did not allow us to pay, nor did he pay. Later we learned that the restaurant was part of a string of shops and cafeterias spread throughout the prison and under the control of the *carro*'s leaders. They also control the drug traffic in its different scales and modalities.

After our conversation, Morgan accompanied us to the exit; there, a group of inmates were unloading lots of boxes from a truck that was parked at one of the enclosure's entrance. An inmate safeguarded the other side of the fence. Inside the building, a group of armed inmates guarded and supervised the operation, giving orders to another larger group without guns. Morgan noticed our curiosity and explained that the incoming goods were intended to replenish the prison's inventory. Without providing more explanation, he said goodbye.

Weeks later, we met some of the inmates that we observed unloading goods that day. They worked as forced labor in the framework of a unique system of discipline. In a carceral regime under the informal control of prisoners, control and moral subjection inside the prison is not produced through what Goffman (1970) characterized as a total institution,[9] but rather through a regulatory system that inmates call the *rutina,*[10] which works as an organizing principle for the life in prison.

We reencountered these inmates in an extremely unusual place reserved for those who break the *rutina,* which the inmates call the *Rehabilitation Center*. This Center, a jail inside the prison, forms part of the *rutina*'s discipline system. It is managed by an evangelist preacher[11] and run by leaders of the prison who have the power to judge and sentence.[12] The Rehabilitation Center was located in a precarious shack separated from the prison building by a fence built by inmates. A 60-square meter building without windows, the Rehabilitation Center had two indoor spaces inside it, a restroom without doors, eight bunk beds, and a television set. The preacher in charge informed us the day we met him that that the facility could hold between 20 and 100 inmates.

Supported by the audiovisual collective, we began to develop video courses at the Rehabilitation Center. There we met Pinto, a participant who, months later, became one of the leading actors of the film we helped to produce and a fervent promoter of the project. The hip-hop lyrics he wrote inspired him to create stories for the film. Pinto was confined in the Center for breaking an agreement over payment for drugs. There were, in fact, many roads to this double confinement. Some inmates we met were being punished for not contributing dues to what inmates called the *causa*. These dues needed to be paid weekly in order to sleep in the cellblocks. Other inmates were being punished for dishonoring bets, drug and alcohol abuse, or picking fights and engaging in other forms of violence.

The confinement period varied depending on the infraction committed, the capacity of the offender to pay off a debt, or the lenience that a *carro* leader might extend to an inmate. For example, Pinto remained there for several months. He was released and spent time in his regular cell, only to return to the Center intermittently, always for different reasons and different periods of time.

Discipline was not limited to confinement in the Center, but included a way of life and a framework of identity. Each inmate in the Center shaved his head. They were forbidden to leave the facility. They were forced to pray several times a day and to watch evangelical films with moral messages. In addition to participating in religious services, they had to carry out tasks that other inmates considered degrading,[13] such as collecting garbage, cleaning, painting the walls of the buildings, or transporting things and goods.

Morgan referred to the Center with pride, bragging that it was a form of discipline created under his government. He saw it as a modern way to administer punishment. Once he told us, in the propagandist tone he would use every time he referred to his management, that long ago in Peonía, and still today in other prisons, breaking the *rutina* meant cruel and severe punishment, even death to the offender. He recounted these atrocities and closed: "Here, on the contrary, we don't. Here we don't kill for nothing, here we control the speed. Here, we don't want to break or murder no one, but rather discipline."[14] Without knowing it, Morgan sounded like a Foucauldian parody, referencing the shift from punishment to confinement.

At Peonía, some transgressions were indeed punished by confinement to the Rehabilitation Center. We observed that transgressions related to economic debts were met with punishment in the Center given that confinement, not the offender's death, would ensure repayment. In addition, offenses of a moral nature, which involved transgressing symbolic obligations built into the prison's moral economy, were also punished by confinement to the Center (Fassin 2009; Karandinos et al. 2014).

In the context of the *rutina*, all exchanges and transactions are carried out in the context of strongly hierarchical relationships, which are characterized by oppression, dispossession, and exploitation. The *rutina* shapes a moral universe linked to a material base, with numerous branches: the control of weapons, which gives leaders the monopoly over violence; the control of all economic transactions (commerce, payments, and bets); and the forced appropriation of manpower as part of the discipline system. Far from a homogeneous order, the *rutina* is experienced and actualized in inmates' lives in diverse ways, according to the position they occupy in the highly hierarchical and differentiated order of the prison. Thus, a break with the *rutina* signaled, in some cases, the inability, or lack of resources and capital to compete and conduct oneself within the complex web of material and symbolic exchanges and transactions that shaped prison life.

It was in this space of the Rehabilitation Center where inmates who were relegated to the position of pariah within the prison order became excited by the idea of asserting themselves as movie stars and started to develop ideas for a film. The experience of dispossession, segregation, and violence that they suffered by occupying the most precarious and subordinated positions in the prison did not stop them from deploying all their resources and capacities in their own creative project.

Plot, Performance, and the Work of Representation

In his writing on the sociology of art, Becker (2008) proposes an approach to artistic work that highlights an analysis of the process of production. Instead of centering on objects, he suggests an approach to art that focuses scrutiny on the activities carried out by groups of people (artists, technicians, producers, publics) with a certain type of knowledge, a set of conventional resources, and ways of doing things. The activities involved in making art define, as a whole, what it can do (its symbolic effects, regardless of language and medium) as well as its uses (both by consumers and producers).

Drawing on this perspective, together with our field notes, we propose in this section to reconstruct the circumstances, views, and situations that converged in the creation of the film series. This confluence shaped the production and its meanings for the different parties involved. Given this insight, we focus here on the process of production rather than the final product.

Audiovisual training began some weeks after we initiated fieldwork. We started by screening some films produced by the audiovisual collective in other prisons. Despite the precarious conditions imposed by the prison setting, the screenings caught the attention of a sizable group of inmates, between 20 and 30, who sat on the floor and piled into a room far too small for the number of people in attendance. Produced and performed by inmates elsewhere, the stories generated excitement among Peonía's inmates. The videos recounted events of prison life. In the first video, after a riot, a commando of National Guards violently takes control of a prison and inmates defend themselves. In another film, after a rebellion, inmates manage to negotiate with the authorities to be moved to another prison. In the next, two rival gangs fight to control one cellblock. In another, rival gangs make a pact and together fight against the guards. The audience at Peonía enjoyed trying to recognize places or people. In another video, an inmate performs a hip-hop song, known as a *lírica* within Venezuelan hip-hop community's argot. The performance generated applauses and gestures of recognition. In the last film, a mother desperately attempts to appeal to the authorities to help her son, who lost the papers confirming his admission into a sentence reduction program when he was moved from one prison to another. The audience was deeply moved. The mother explains the situation to a female judge, who ignores her. The audience at Peonía reacted with indignation and several inmates, mimmicking guns with their hands, simulated shooting the screen.

Watching scene after scene, the audience of inmates expressed emotions and participated. They became part of the plot.

After these first experiences with audiovisual material produced in prisons, inmates had the opportunity to learn how to use a camera. They were asked to capture images of everyday life. When inmates themselves appeared on the screen was when the most enthusiasm was generated. They usually portrayed themselves as rappers or as thugs haranguing or encouraging their peers.

Despite the stereotypical nature of these representations, the performances were intense experiences for the inmates. Through these staging exercises (understood in Goffman's[15] sense), each inmate attempted to produce the best representation of himself in front of the others, recreating their image in a different context onscreen, although this was only an imaginary exercise. Often, the dynamics of prison life interrupted the activities organized in the Center. Frequently, the group would have to unload some goods arriving to the prison, collect trash heaps or debris, listen to sermons from the pastor or receive reprimands (muddled among insults and threats) from *carro* leaders.

During the first months, besides working with this group on video training, we dedicated much time to talking to leaders of the *carro*. Besides controlling access to weapons, drug trafficking, economic transactions, and relationships with outside agents (including us), they also aspired to maintain a monopoly over meaning. They tried to control what might be recognized, known, said, informed, or discussed about the prison.

Morgan himself informed us early on that nobody could talk about the *rutina* or attempt to understand it: "Whoever wants to understand it, goes crazy," he told us.[16] This censorship is not only a guiding principle, but works as part of a moral economy that renders collaboration with anyone outside prison life as suspicious. In an interview, a former prison leader who had been released warned us that the inmates would not talk to us: "That would mean to taint[17] the *rutina*". It was certainly the case that not all inmates agreed to talk to us, and those who did were careful with what they said. We understood that we did not have access to all spaces and interactions. Aware of these difficulties and concerned with gaining the principal leaders' trust, we attempted to understand different perspectives and create interactions that did not always prove fruitful for our purposes. It was the group at the Rehabilitation Center who offered us an exceptional view to understand the *rutina*.

After six months of visiting the prison, we experienced a meaningful shift in our work. For weeks, Pinto insisted on presenting us story lines for a film that he had generated with other inmates of the Center. Arriving at the Center, a group of roughly ten inmates waited to speak to us about the proposal. They told us a raucous story that involved the usual plots through which they enacted episodes of prison life. They seemed organized. They showed us notes and sang the songs that would accompany each scene. They showed us that they had the authorization of the prison officers responsible for cultural activities; these officers had allowed them to register participants. Some of the forms were already filled out, making clear that the inmates had been working for days on the proposal. They assured us they had the consent of all the *carro* leaders. It seemed pointless to try to alter the plot. From that day on, everything happened very quickly. From then on, the group devoted itself to the creative process without compromising their vision.

Just a week later, a group of nearly 100 prisoners was preparing to present a dress rehearsal to us at one of the terraces. Although most of inmates were from the Rehabilitation Center, some had been recruited from the main prison population. Hairstyles distinguished one group from the other. As props, they carried weapons of different types and calibers made of mud, tubes, wood, and other materials provided by the institution. Many people watched from various points around the prison, giving the scene an air of spectacle. Morgan watched with us from an improvised awning at one side of the field. Other leaders of the *carro* were also there.

Pinto was the designated storyteller. The central plot involved an event which occurred years ago in Peonía. Two rival gangs fought for control of the prison. One gang lived a dissolute, depraved life, full of excesses; the other (which would be the winner) lived an austere, measured, and productive life (alluding to the life of the *rutina*). The victors decided to forgive the losers and instead of eliminating them, they set out to teach them the virtues of the good life. At the end, the church unifies and redeems them. This outcome is preceded by a number of incidents. It all starts with Pinto's arrival to the prison after he kills the brother of the deputy of one of the gangs. The aggrieved deputy demands revenge; but his boss, moderate and just, reminds him of the prison principle according to which "the problems of the street are resolved on the street." However, Pinto's arrival at the prison generates tensions and sparks a brawl. The evangelist pastor intercedes to save his life. The rival gang of the aggrieved party protects Pinto and accepts him. Then comes the first confrontation between rival gangs. After a grenade explodes in the middle of a basketball game, the *cristianos*[18] collect the dead and wounded. To our astonishment, nearly one hundred prisoners participated in each scene.

Meanwhile, Morgan listened and watched the rehearsal attentively. It was obvious that he approved of the basic plot and supported the idea of the film with which, judging from his reactions, he was already familiar. This was not surprising given that the ideological tone of the narrative celebrated the *rutina* and elevated an episode that ensured his group's control of the prison as the foundational event of prison life. Moreover, blurring the boundary between audience and performer in the play, Morgan participated in the performance. He interrupted the rehearsal to guide actors. His judgments had nothing to do with the consistency of the plot, the quality of acting, the likelihood of the situation, nor the viability of the enterprise. He was concerned with how actions adhered to reality, to the codes of the *rutina*: "Pinto cannot arrive alone; someone has to receive him. That guy can't talk so much, if he is a boss. Pastors may not appear at that time, but at some other time. The basketball game can't happen unless the bosses approve. One boss has to call the other and they have to bet." In this way, the process of staging encouraged everyone to participate. Rather than addressing the plot and the acting, Morgan discussed with his peers the range of possible actions that could be taken in each scene of the play. It seemed almost like a scholarly exercise. In an exegetical manner, Morgan debated the rules that each scene would impose on the inmates' actions.

The day of the dress rehearsal, we realized that the process of producing the film offered a unique entry point to understand key questions of prison life. In the following months, we focused exclusively on this project. The audiovisual collective provided support to all the technical aspects related to the production and making of the film. Our role was to accompany prisoners in the process. Repeatedly and in different ways, we insisted, in vain, that the inmates should revise the plot, problematizing its violent character and its stereotypical characters. Each attempt at intervention strengthened their resolve to adhere to certain conventions. For instance, as a solution to the violence contained in the storyline, the group proposed using evangelic songs as background music, including a greater number of scenes in which pastors intervened, or making pastors preach a sermon after a shoot-out.

The film became a series after certain things happened which altered the cast: some actors were released from prison, transferred elsewhere, or punished. The serial format allowed for changes in each episode such as reassigning roles or dropping characters without altering the plot. Because of budget reasons, we were able to complete the filming of just the first of five chapters.[19]

The film series offered the inmates not only audiovisual training, but also recognition and the possibility of repositioning themselves within the social space of the prison.

Although the filming process involved a group of between 20 and 50 actors, the organizational tasks were assumed by a group of about 10 people. Pinto took on a leadership role and managed to generate great enthusiasm among his peers for the project. Overall, the inmates who played the roles of bosses in the story took on the traits of the people they mimicked.

In the weeks following the rehearsal, the group turned the story into a script, choosing locations, taking photographs, making props, creating sets, rehearsing, as well as engaging in the work of filming. They repeated, at each turn, the exegetical work that we observed the day of the rehearsal. Each scene generated discussions not about the aesthetic practices involved in their project, but rather how faithfully the film followed prison codes. Each discussion involved the deployment of a sort of prison wisdom. On one hand, it made manifest the prison rules; on the other, it outlined the dilemmas, difficulties and contradictions experienced by the people subjected to such rules.

Each stage of the process involved negotiation between the Center's inmates and prison leaders. The precise ways in which the *carro* participated in shaping the series was not always clear to us. Its intervention was obvious, because nothing could be done without its consent, but the *carro's* influence was never made explicit. After the general rehearsal, none of the leaders participated in the filmmaking process in overt ways. Some of the leaders explained they were prohibited from participating. Their faces could not appear in the film and they were not allowed to contribute to its production. Morgan explained that *carro* leaders could not abandon their responsibility to guard the checkpoints and cellblocks. Nevertheless, the *carro* did intervene in plot construction. When doubts and polemics arose over specific scenes and situations, prison leaders participated by resolving how things should turn out. Additionally, Pinto explained that every decision was made in consultation with *carro* leaders. Although they took care not to participate too openly, the *carro* seemed to use the film to shape its own representation. Thus, the production of the film generated a complex triad (participants, researchers and leaders) in which each group used the film tactically for its own agenda.

The filmmaking process provided insight into the *rutina* not only because of what was said and represented explicitly. The *mis en scene* simultaneously revealed and hid aspects of prison life. For inmates with whom we worked, for example, it was impossible to represent the exchanges and negotiations that *carro* leaders maintained with external agents (guards, stewards, merchants) (Antillano 2015), the economic transactions that secured the material basis of internal prison order, or the multiple forms of violence to which inmates were subjected.

For inmates, creating the film series offered a space of symbolic recognition and repositioning, albeit one that was precarious and fleeting within prison life. On one hand, it allowed inmates to disconnect momentarily from their pariah status, regain the possibility of moving freely within the physical space of the cells, and free themselves from the forced labor they had to perform as part of their punishment. Acting in the films also gave them the opportunity to let their hair grow in order to play the role of prison leaders. Paradoxically, the series granted them an escape from the *rutina* but only to celebrate it. They projected what they aspired to be through the film even while this involved deploying an act of symbolic violence; they aspired to be like those inside the prison who oppressed and dominated them.

Beyond the tensions and contradictions that shaped the final product of representation, the process of producing the film series illuminates how this group of artists and producers (the inmates with whom we worked) knew how to appropriate a set of tools (cameras, acting techniques, genres) and a certain language to imagine and develop its own representation within the limits (material and symbolic) imposed by the prison context.

Amid the instability, violence, dispossession and subjection that defined their prison experience, inmates asserted their imaginative and organizational capacity. They revealed their ability to compete for a different kind of capital and resources in the service of crafting their own representations. They reinscribed themselves, however imaginatively, within the symbolic and moral universe of the prison.

Fiction and Ethnography

Without planning, the process of making the film series took on aspects of *cinema vérité*, an approach developed by Jean Rouch which involves naturalistic techniques, typical of documentary filmmaking, as part of the framework of fictional strategies (Accolas and Wanono Gauthier 2012). But in the case we have analyzed here, the interplay of fiction and reality was not carried out in a controlled manner, through a narrative that structured the scenes and sequences. Instead, in this case, fiction and reality became enmeshed through the performances that the film project made possible.

In this case, fiction became a vehicle for ethnography, not only for its content, nor the creative process involved, but also the process of staging. The film series became a way to represent the *rutina*, not only because it displayed its components, but also because it staged the logic of its realization. The *rutina*, as a cultural repertoire, and moral and symbolic universe, is brought into being by the actors, much like a ritual. As non-linguistic phenomena the ritualized *rutina* creates and recreates reality through representation. Following Bourdieu's metaphor of the *feel for the game:*

The player, having deeply internalized the regularities of a game, does what he must do at the moment it is necessary, without needing to ask explicitly what is to be done. He does not need to know consciously what he does in order to do it and even less to raise explicitly the question (except in some critical situations) of knowing explicitly what other might do in return… (Bourdieu 1998, pp.166–167).

The process of producing the film series was in a way a representation of the *feel for the game* that in the prison context puts into practice, configures and, under certain conditions, transforms the order of the rutina. The disagreements generated by the film over how actors should negotiate the problems they faced in each scene made explicit the meaning and rules of the game. Through this process, inmates revealed what the *rutina* meant to them as they experienced it and what they hoped to achieve through it. At the same time, these performances revealed the dilemmas, difficulties and contradictions the inmates confronted while being subjected to the *rutina*. More than a parody, the story which this group of inmates created and performed became a way to make intelligible the prison order and the stark violence that sustains it.

Notes

1. Names of persons and places are fictional.
2. We thank Andreina Torres and Naomi Schiller for the translation and suggestions. This study is part of a larger research project initiated by Andrés Antillano, Iván Pojomovsky, Chelina Sepúlveda, Alberto Alvarado, Amarilis Hidalgo and Verónica Zubillaga. The fieldwork, which we completed between November 2012 and 2014, was conducted collectively, and included one or two prison visits per week. However, the views and opinions expressed in this article belong solely to the authors.
3. This collective of filmmakers and popular educators was the force behind the Popular School of Prison Communication, which offered training in audiovisual communication inside prisons across the country. The Ministry of Popular Power for Prison Service supported and funded this program.
4. An important strain of Latin American social science literature about prisons analyzes different forms of informal control by inmates and the

specific codes and hierarchies that constitute them. It also associates this retreat of government authority with the growth of the incarcerated population and conditions of overcrowding. For a review of this literature, see Biondi (2010), Dias and Salla (2013), Núñez (2007), Cerbini (2012), Darke (2013), Marques (2009). For a review on the Venezuelan case, see Antillano (2015).

5. This data was provided by the Ministry of Popular Power for the Prison Service.
6. For an overview of the politics of prisons in Venezuela and its effects on carceral order, see Antillano et al. (2015).
7. Inmates use the term *carro* to refer to the structure through which a group of inmates control and rule the life in the prison, exerting coercion and legitimacy. For an examination of the *carro* as a structure of power in the context of Venezuelan prisons under the control of inmates, see Antillano et al. (2015); Antillano (2015).
8. Inmates refer to the action of announcing arrivals, activities or other events that interrupt the prison's daily routine as "singing."
9. Other ethnographic work has asserted the inconsistency of the concept of *total institutions* in capturing the informal processes of control and the self-regulation of inmates. See Núñez (2007), Antillano (2015), Antillano (this volume).
10. Inmates refer to the conduct code that rules and organizes the life in the prison as the *rutina*.
11. For a description of the church and its role within Venezuelan prisons, see Duno-Gottberg (this volume).
12. For an exploration of how the *carro* functions as a form of management, regulation, and control in the context of the informal prison order, see Antillano (2015).
13. For further information regarding the inmates' moral conventions in the context of the *rutina*, see Antillano (2015).
14. Nevertheless, familiarizing ourselves with various histories led us to understand that the violence was not totally eliminated from the punishment system. Morgan told us a story about a young man who, after being caught stealing money, was shot in both legs. Seeing our horrified faces, Morgan clarified that the penalty was exacted not for the robbery itself, or because Morgan was the one aggrieved, but because the man denied his guilt.
15. Goffman (1997).

16. Perhaps it was not a limitation associated to our presence, but part of the nature of what Bourdieu (1998) calls the economy of symbolic goods, listing a series of principles that govern these types of exchanges. Among them, what he calls "the taboo of making things explicit. To say what it really is (…) is to destroy the exchange" (p.96). On the esoteric character that the prison confers the *rutina*, see: Antillano et al. (2015), Antillano (2015).
17. In prison slang *manchar* refers to the action of transgressing or dishonoring the *rutina*. *La mancha* was the term inmates used to refer to the effect of dishonoring on the prisoners' identity. For example: we carry a stain, or we are tainted, were common expressions among prisoners we met in the Rehabilitation Center.
18. *Cristianos* are the evangelical inmates.
19. The film project was not developed under the purview of the School of Penetentiary Communication, nor was it part of the official research project, which was supported by the Ministry of Popular Power for Prison Service. The film project had no dedicated funding. Filming was done using resources from the research project until they were exhausted.

References

Accolas, S., & Wanono Gauthier, N. (2012). Création et transmission en anthropologie visuelle. *Journal des anthropologues. Association française des anthropologues, 130–131*, 17–29.

Antillano, A. (2015). Cuando los presos mandan: control informal dentro de la cárcel venezolana. *Espacio Abierto, 24*(4), 16–39.

Antillano, A., Pojomovsky, I., Zubillaga, V., Sepúlveda, C., & Hanson, R. (2015). The Venezuelan prison: From neoliberalism to the Bolivarian revolution. *Crime, Law and Social Change, 65*(3), 195–211.

Becker, H. (2008). *Los mundos del arte: sociología del trabajo artístico*. Bernal: Universidad Nacional de Quilmes.

Biondi, K. (2010). *Junto e misturado: uma etnografia do PCC*. São Paulo: Editora Terceiro Nome.

Bourdieu, P. (1984). Espace social et genèse des "classes". *Actes de la Recherche en Sciences Sociales, 52*(52–53), 3–12.

Bourdieu, P. (1998). *Practical reason: On the theory of action*. Stanford: Stanford University Press.

Cerbini, F. (2012). *La casa de jabón: etnografía de una cárcel boliviana*. Barcelona: Bellaterra.

Darke, S. (2013). Inmate governance in Brazilian prisons. *The Howard Journal of Criminal Justice, 52*(3), 272–284.

Dias, C. N., & Salla, F. (2013). Organized crime in Brazilian prisons: The example of the PCC. *International Journal of Criminology and Sociology, 2*, 397–408.

Fassin, D. (2009). Les économies morales revisitées. *Annales. Histoire, Sciences Sociales,* 64e année(6), 1237–1266.

Goffman, E. (1970). *Internados: ensayos sobre la situación social de los enfermos mentales*. Buenos Aires: Amorrortu.

Goffman, E. (1997). *La presentación de la persona en la vida cotidiana*. Buenos Aires: Amorrortu.

Karandinos, G., Hart, L., Castrillo, F., & Bourgois, P. (2014). The moral economy of violence in the US Inner City. *Current Anthropology, 55*(1), 1–22.

Marques, A. J. (2009). *Crime, proceder, convívio-seguro: um experimento antropológico a partir derelações entre ladrões*. Doctoral dissertation, Universidade de São Paulo.

Núñez, J. (2007). Las carceles en la época del narcotrafico: una mirada etnográfica. *Nueva sociedad, 208*, 101–117.

17

Facing the First Command of Capital (PCC): Regarding Ethnography of Brazil's 'Biggest Prison Gang'

Karina Biondi

Destiny is written concurrently with the event, not prior to it. (Monod 1971a, 1971b: 184)[1]

Introduction

The Brazilian state of São Paulo plays host to 176 prisons and counting. These complexes hold more than 220,000 inmates, more than a third of the total number of prisoners in Brazil. This is among the primary reasons why the First Command of the Capital (PCC) is considered the largest prison gang in the country, since the collective of prisoners in question can be found in more than 90% of penal institutions in São Paulo. Since its emergence within the prison system in the early 1990s, the PCC has spread across the entirety of São Paulo's urban districts. But its reach also extends deep into other Brazilian cities and states.

K. Biondi (✉)
State University of Maranhão, São Luís, Brazil

S. Darke et al. (eds.), *Carceral Communities in Latin America*, Palgrave Studies in Prisons and Penology, https://doi.org/10.1007/978-3-030-61499-7_17

Throughout the 1990s and into the twenty-first century, the PCC's dramatic expansion has been concomitant with a simultaneous increase in inmate numbers and a sharp drop in state-wide homicide rates, a striking and counter-intuitive fact that was first observed within the prison system. In order to grasp the magnitude of these figures, in 1999, 117 violent deaths were recorded among an incarcerated population of 52,117, while in 2007 this figure had fallen to 11 violent deaths among 153,056 inmates. Later, there was also a decline in homicide rates in urban zones with a strong Command presence. Jardim Angela district, declared by the United Nations in 1996 to be the most violent district in the world, was once a neighborhood notorious for its violence, with murder rates comparable only to regions ravaged by civil war (97.97 homicides per 100,000 inhabitants). However, homicide rates in Jardim Angela began to decrease from 2002 forward, to a mere 16.88 per 100,000 by 2010.

State authorities often point to these statistics as evidence of the success obtained by public security policies. Some researchers endorse the discourse of the authorities, for instance, Carneiro (2010), who values the state's investment in policing and the increase in the number of arrests. Other studies question this narrative. For Manso (2012), the "success" of public security policies (investment in policing and intelligence services, increased incarceration, strengthening of the justice system, disarmament legislation) occurred at a time when the population had also begun to question the extent to which homicide was an acceptable option to deal with societal conflict. For studies based on empirical research, however, the main reason for the fall in the number of homicides has been the PCC (Biondi 2006, 2007; Dias 2005, 2011; Marques 2014; Feltran 2008, 2010; Hirata 2010; Telles and Hirata 2010; Willis 2015). From the beginning, the "PCC hypothesis" was widely criticized. If Manso (2012) writes that the PCC is the result and not the cause of the falling homicide rate in São Paulo, Carneiro (2010) attributes these prospects to an inversion of values, consistent with the profile of the researchers responsible for them, "a group that boasts strong social anti-control convictions", and that overestimates the actions of organized crime.

For the current author, it is important to take seriously what prisoners and residents from the areas once considered violent (i.e. those who could have killed, or those who might have died) say, do and think. These actors directly attribute the decrease in lethality to the arrival of the PCC. In a conversation during my field research, a woman was quite clear in this regard: "In the old days, every single day there was a corpse at my doorstep. Today, thanks to PCC, it doesn't happen anymore".

Although I have, at least since 2007, stressed a correlation between the PCC's growth and the contraction of homicides in São Paulo (Biondi 2007), the Command was not the focus of my attention at the beginning of my fieldwork in 2003. As we shall see, the question literally punctured and broke into my research. The social logic of what my informants had described, obligated considering new theoretical and methodological strategies to account for the phenomenon. Such research strategies, in turn, led me to reevaluate concepts that are frequently used across prisons studies and the social sciences more generally.

In this article, I shall summarize three phases of my research—first at undergraduate level, then at master's and doctorate levels—so as to problematize the nature of ethnographic "research subjects," and to demonstrate in practice the processes by which "research" and "subject" are simultaneously and mutually constituted in my own and any other realist account of the PCC.

First Phase: Adjusting the Focus from the Prison to the Prisoners

The prisons research started in 2004, at undergraduate level. Within the scope of Urban Anthropology, my initial goal was to carry out an ethnography of a prison facility. The image of a correctional institution I had in mind at the time was similar to what was depicted in the Brazilian film *Carandiru* (Babenco 2003) and the book that inspired it (Varella 2012), where physical abuse and sexual violence were part of the everyday routine. In the film, the abused inmate who sought to avoid such humiliations had no option but to slay the aggressor(s)—subsequently adding a count of murder to his sentence. Within this image, which is also related by many who were incarcerated in 1980s, inmates would take possession of any goods available to them—from a roll of toilet paper to the very space inside the cell—in order to sell them on the prison's underground economy. The inmate control of prison spaces ultimately pitted a wide variety of jail "gangs" against each other, which quickly devolved from territorial disputes into bloody and unstable wars inside the cellblocks.

Quite early in the research, though, I came to realize that such a scenario of either bidding or battling for space as depicted in the movie was inconceivable in a facility holding prisoners associated with the PCC. Moreover, I could not recognize in that prison anything resembling what Goffman (1962) had called a "total institution", even taking into account "secondary adjustments", perceived as central to the reproduction of prisons, asylums and the like. Wherever I looked, I witnessed the PCC in operation; in fact, the prisoner collective seemed to pervade every connection or tie established within the institution, from the ways in which yard cleaning, food distribution, toilet use and soccer games were organized, to the means of contact and communication between inmates and prison authorities. This is a form of self-regulation (or self-government) of the internal life of prisoners, like the cases registered in other contexts by Antillano (2017), Cerbini (2012), Darke (2018).

For instance, the water supply was subject to constant negotiation between the prison management and the "*brothers*," the term by which PCC members commonly refer to themselves. Soccer matches followed a singular ethic, according to which violent moves and profanity were avoided in order to ensure "peace among thieves". Among PCC *brothers*' everyday talk about their situation, they openly valorized prison escape, emphasizing the detainees' dissatisfaction with their situation of confinement and highlighting what they called "war against the system". According to the inmates, these two guidelines—peace among thieves and war against the police (Marques 2008: 289)—were the main reasons why they or anyone else should join the Command. As a result—they claimed—wars between rival factions, banal murders, extortion and sexual violence ceased to exist, and prisoners could not sufficiently praise the PCC's oversight in their new mode of coexistence behind bars.

While my original intention was to produce an ethnography of a penal institution, approaching it from the perspective of classical studies on institutions, the PCC's strong bearing on my material led me to focus instead on the way the organization ordered individual experiences of incarceration and established social patterns within that specific facility (Biondi 2006). This first phase of fieldwork was thus marked by a shift from the study of an institution to the assessment of a form of inmate self-governance that had already attained a hegemonic character in São Paulo prisons, but about which, up to that point, not much was known, and not nearly enough had been said.[2]

Second Phase: Where Is the PCC to Be Found?

In 2006, São Paulo witnessed a series of violent events that became known as the "PCC attacks" or the "second mega-rebellion". During the PCC's first mega-rebellion, in 2001, 29 prisons had risen up simultaneously (cf. Salla 2007: 82), making the PCC's presence and power within the penal system undeniable. This mega-rebellion, involving about 28,000 prisoners, was the first major action of the PCC. If by that time the authorities did not recognize its existence, it could no longer be denied after the 2006 revolt. Still, authorities continued to treat the PCC as a small group inside prison, isolated and under control. On the other side of the bars, however, the second mega-rebellion gave visibility to the PCC, showed its strength and contributed to its expansion into the vast majority of prisons. In short, it marked the PCC's consolidation in the prison system of São Paulo.

Although territorial disputes among gangs remained active during the first mega-rebellion, the hegemony of the PCC became especially notorious during the second mega-rebellion, both in the São Paulo prison system and in urban areas of the state. The second mega-rebellion enjoyed a much broader range and impact: 84 prison units rebelled, 299 public institutions were attacked, 17 bank branches were bombed, 42 police officers and prison guards were killed and 38 more were wounded.

With the exception of the first phase of my research, whose results had not been published when the second mega-rebellion occurred, there were no academic studies on the radical transformation that occurred in the prison over the past decade. In the days following the attacks, Sergio Adorno, coordinator of the main center of studies on violence in São Paulo, said in an interview that he was surprised at the PCC action and explained the reasons why he was not developing research in prisons:

> [W]hat happened was surprising. (…) The problem is that we do not know. We have little reliable information, analysis and research on organized crime in São Paulo. For many reasons. The main thing is that it is very difficult to do research in this area. To do it, you must enter into the carceral system, and this is difficult. We infer these things from what is reported in the press and doing research with young people in the periphery. (…) I did a lot of research in prisons about ten or 15 years ago and I used to enter the prison system very smoothly. At that time, it was unimaginable that a university professor could be kidnapped or attacked. Today is different. A person like me becomes a valuable bargaining chip (Colombo 2006).

Alba Zaluar, another expert in the study of violence and crime in Rio de Janeiro, regrets this gap: "My colleagues have never made a thorough study of organized crime in São Paulo" (Torres 2006). However, the wave of attacks in 2006, its size and the proportions it has achieved, boosted mobilization in the universities around the need to account for this phenomenon. This mobilization was condensed at the Organized Crime Dossier, launched by the Institute of Advanced Studies of University of São Paulo (Bosi 2007). One of the articles was written by Sergio Adorno, co-authored with Fernando Salla. Without revealing the means by which they conducted their research, the authors argue that the success of these events was guaranteed by the organizational structure of the PCC, "maintained by a hierarchical framework of 'employees', disciplined and obedient, able to execute orders unquestioningly" (p. 9).

In addition to boosting research on what was already taking place within the prisons for years, these attacks made clear that the Command's actions were no longer constrained by the limits of the institution analyzed in the previous phase of my work. The organization was no longer materially or practically confined to the insides of state prisons. This led me to expand my fieldwork at master's level to encompass the PCC's presence across multiple prison spaces (rather than studying in a single facility).

Heeding what I understood as the PCC's multi-locality, I extended my research to a number of prison units. In my second phase of fieldwork, I was surprised to learn that the Command's institutional reach did not depend exclusively on the positioning of *members*. I witnessed the PCC in action even in places where there was no single *brother*. Two occasions proved decisive in drawing my attention to this aspect. The first was during a conversation with an inmate. When asked about PCC's presence in institutions where young offenders serve custodial sentences (called FEBEMs[3]), his answer was blunt:

> What? A Junior PCC? No, there's no such thing.
> But then, aren't the guys inside the FEBEMs following any instructions from the Command?
> Well, they obey the Command, but minors aren't baptized [i.e. they are not accepted as members].

The second occasion was the inauguration of a Provisional Detention Center. The first group of prisoners to arrive at the new facility came from one of the few prisons under the control of a rival faction, the CBRC (Brazilian Revolutionary Crime Command). The second group, in turn, came from one of the units controlled by the Command, but that did not include any PCC *brothers*. When they first entered the facility, prisoners saw CBRC flags hoisted in the courtyard. They immediately refused to enter the pavilion and, after a brief confrontation, managed to, as they say, "bring the jail in to the PCC". Without a single *brother*, they organized among themselves "the maintenance,"[4] began to hold meetings with the director to negotiate the conditions under which their sentences would be served and, above all, without any ascendancy of one inmate over the other, managed to sustain the *Command's ethics* in their new prison environment. According to these prisoners, both the conquest of the prison and maintaining control of it as a PCC prison ensured that they would not be subjected to the existing ways of life of prisons controlled by rival gangs. They claimed that extortion, sexual abuse and physical violence were still common in prisons dominated by opposing factions. To keep the PCC there was, above all, to ensure their survival. A new ad hoc branch of the PCC was in so doing midwifed into existence. Only two months later would an affiliated *brother* be transferred into the unit. The reaction of those who had been in charge up to that point was: "Thank

God a brother has arrived. Here, take it. The responsibility is yours now. Enough of this pain in the neck!"

The possibility of the PCC making itself present in prison spaces (no longer in a single institution) without the presence of any *brothers*—that is, even in the complete absence of its members—became a central topic in my master's research (Biondi 2010, 2016). How was it possible to state that a jail would have been brought into the PCC, that a prison unit belonged to the Command, if no *brother* was in fact incarcerated there?

A description of how the PCC could constitute itself regardless of its members brought to the center of my argument the effects generated by the idea of *equality*, one of the four words that made up the PCC's celebrated yet highly misunderstood motto: Peace, Justice, Freedom and Equality. More than just a word symbolically added to its slogan, equality was a concept actively present in the prisoners' lives and in their reflections on their carceral experience. When deployed in practice, the concept introduced new tensions in the PCC wings, and extended across the entire capillary network of the PCC itself. As a result, existing power *foci* were often suppressed while new ones simultaneously emerged, an ever-present interplay of the formation and dissolution of hierarchies within the prisoner collective.

The first concept to prove inadequate to address the PCC indeed was "organized crime," which conveys the notion of an arrangement among individuals pursuing illicit activities. Approaching the PCC on a theoretical level meant at once to challenge the conceptual integrity and the application of "organized crime". In recent years, sociocultural anthropologists have made important contributions to overcome the limitations of such concepts as society, culture or group, understood as external forces shaping the individuals who make them up (Wagner 1974; Latour 2005; Strathern 1996; Toren 1996), and their proposals seemed quite suitable to perform this task. These authors refuse the appeal of any conceptual forms that emerge from transcendental tendencies in Western thought, any concept that acts like an external force, any concepts used by social scientists to provide explanation, because these concepts obscure the very relations that constitute human existence. Thus, they recommend following natives, focusing on actors' own reflections on their lives, and treating these reflections like a truly social theory. To do so, it is essential to avoid the introduction of any external explanation (any concepts that presuppose the existence of transcendent entities—whether "society," "culture," "language" or "group"—that are treated as priori entities that exist over and above individuals) for the phenomenon that is being described. It removes from the concepts any exterior power, any exterior force with the potency to shape an individual. The result is that the social is no more an explanation, but it becomes a thing to be explained, to be constituted.

So, an attempt to classify prisoners as either members or non-members of the PCC would end up reifying the group as an isolated or discrete entity, as a locatable, delimitable entity formed by a united cluster of members who are molded by forces understood as coercive and external to them. It would be to do violence to a complex system of relations put together by a quite diverse arrangement of actors who influence its shape. So instead of delimiting, and thus limiting, my object of study, I have moved beyond an approach to society as a group of individuals or some sort of transcendental force that provides its members with a frame within which to act and to know themselves.

However, by taking my interlocutors seriously and assigning centrality to their perceptions, I could see that they are not free of the transcendental tendencies in Western thought. But it appears, between them, as "PCC", "Crime", "Command". In other words, the people with whom I conducted my research consider the PCC an enduring force, or power, capable of exercising control over its participants. As I develop elsewhere (Biondi 2016), my challenge became to describe how the PCC's immanent production was materializing in parallel with the (equally immanent) construction of the PCC's transcendence, a force endowed with some degree of autonomy and capable of ensuring continuity to the organization. This "force" was responsible for bringing each member into the group as a result of his own attachment to this autonomous device, the PCC turning into an assemblage independent of any stable interpersonal or territorial ties or, in other words, a transcendence. My ethnographic purpose thus became an effort to describe not only the construction of this transcendence but also its effectiveness. Accordingly, I came to envision the transcendent without necessarily deeming it anterior or preeminent, that is, apprehending this external force while also appreciating its immanence and self-potency as both products and producers of a transcendent PCC. The double challenge was, then, to observe at the local and mundane instances, in the most subtle and casual relationships established between the parties: How did the production of this figure take place and to what extent did it act as an external element. In short, what I proposed was an immanent anthropology of a prisoners' collective construction of transcendence.

Covering the full range of levels on which the Command managed its informal policies, each imbued with the ideal of equality (i.e. in the base of the power relations and the war against the State, as described by Marques 2008), I noticed that immanence and transcendence, within the organization, were mutually sustained in a kind of continuous feedback loop. I could show how the PCC's immanence operated as an ever-evolving practice of emergence while producing a transcendent effect, and also, at the same time, how a PCC-transcendence existed only because it was based on the immanence that served as its guarantee. It was, therefore, not merely a matter of one establishing the other, but rather that they could only work together as a result of both of them, reciprocally and unceasingly, requiring and invoking each other.

This approach of the hierarchy in the Command was substantially different to that taken by a number of established prisons scholars. For Adorno and Salla (2007) the PCC was highly structured, constituted by "'employees', disciplined and obedient, able to execute orders unquestioningly" (p. 9). In my view, it was not a hierarchy that sustained the PCC, but rather the existence of a transcendence maintained by immanent forces. Of course, the absence of hierarchical structures does not mean that there is no hierarchy. Hierarchical manifestations appear, but they always encounter with the most important guiding principle of the PCC: equality. They do not crystallize. Dias (2011) also takes a different approach about to this question. She argues that there is a strong horizontal hierarchy in the PCC, commanded by a few members that occupy high positions in the PCC, disguised by its discourse on equality. For Dias, it is a perverse system in which a monopoly of violence based on arbitrary and authoritarian elements is exercised in the name of an alleged equality. In other words, people that say they live in equality are being deceived by a discourse made by those who intend to remain in power.

The distance between my argument and Dias's approach is the result of our differing theoretical and methodological approaches, in my case especially my fidelity (or perhaps radicalization) with respect to a feature of the anthropological discipline, as pointed by Lévi-Strauss in 1958: "While sociology seeks to advance the social science of the observer, anthropology seeks to advance that of what is observed" (Lévi-Strauss 1963: 363). While I try to avoid any external categories and thoughts (specially the moral assertions supported by state in assessing what is normal, good and correct) to describe the PCC's, Dias (2011) sees the organization through the lens of the State and describes it as a similar organization, with its hierarchy, operating modes, social division of labor and even a supposed claim to replace state democracy. However, the PCC has never suggested that it should be considered democratic according to state models.

This second phase of the research was therefore marked by a shift onto an analysis of a phenomenon that somehow did not match the sum of its parts and, therefore, was taking place even in the PCC's absence. Whereas the PCC's features led me to expand my research to several prisons, this new level of insertion allowed me to have contact with facilities that harbored no *brothers*, yet still belonged to the PCC. This phantom-like presence of the PCC even compelled me to abandon the ethnographic pursuit of multi-locality—according to which the PCC would be simultaneously active in several places—on behalf of an ethnographic approach that attempted to explore how everyday, mundane "micro-political" practices could generate something like "the PCC". In other words, distinct and often disarticulated social dynamics converged to produce the institutional birth and hegemony of the PCC.

Third Phase: The Movement in the Streets Hinges on the Prisons

For reasons beyond my control, my doctoral research (Biondi 2018) was not carried out according to the established standards for fieldwork. I had difficulties tracking down my old acquaintances, many of whom were incarcerated, while others had died. I spent much more time than expected attempting to gain some measure of trust from people still engaged in criminal activities. Sometimes, when I finally managed to approach someone, he was subsequently arrested and removed from my investigation. On other occasions, the social climate in the neighborhood where I was working would dramatically change overnight and my hosts would hastily send me away. It happened when, for example, police raids began to be made daily in the favela where I was and the residents associated my presence there with the police incursions. Even when I could finally settle somewhere, I ended up discovering that crucial developments related to that specific neighborhood were simultaneously taking place elsewhere, that is, there were several other people and places involved in those events that my gaze did not reach. It was usual that a *brother* from another neighborhood came to the place where I was doing my ethnography to discuss something that had started elsewhere. In these cases, my informants used their cell phones or moved between the neighborhoods involved, and I could not follow everything that was going on. Often the events continued to happen elsewhere, most often in several other places simultaneously, as more and more people got involved. All this compelled me to transit through different areas in pursuit of the elusive subject of my research. Caught up in this transition, I was faced with such disparate analytic situations that made my research seem impossibly disjointed, and made me feel incapable of scrutinizing or arranging them for the elaboration of a scholarly text.

The feeling I had was of sheer inability to narrate a consistent story. As much as I tried to perceive what was going on, I could never quite get a full picture. A nagging voice remained in my head that I was missing part of the story, that it was not being fully disclosed, that it was either poorly understood or the information was incomplete—all these anxieties stemming from my consternation at the poor quality of data gathered in a survey. This feeling of empirical desolation led me to search for alternative research methods; it triggered a series of twists and turns in my fieldwork procedures, and the new data, instead of filling the gaps that troubled me, only increased my repertoire of seemingly fragmentary material.

However (somewhat propitiously), at a certain point I realized that the way I saw things was not so distinct from the way my interlocutors also saw them. The difference, though, was that they were not obsessed with wholeness like I was and, therefore, did not perceive gaps or deficits whenever they happened to lose sight or track of something.

As a consequence, I began to pay more attention to one of the terms used, albeit rarely, by my interlocutors to refer to the PCC: "the movement". By approaching the PCC as a movement, I saw how the organization not only contains several movements, operating at distinct levels and speeds, heading in different directions, and displaying a diverse array of configurations and calibers, but that the movement brought together individuals, situations, telephones, personal relationships, ideas, struggles, lives, deaths, neighborhoods, business transactions and much else. There are no restrictions to what may constitute a movement, given that arrangements were always transactional and transitory. Moreover, the movement does not conform to spatial constraints or time intervals since they have neither a palpable origin nor an unequivocal end. Hence, the Command does not restrict its range to the span or scope of individual lives, not even of *brothers'* lives; it does not remain confined to any strongholds.

The heavy flow of simultaneous movements that constitute the PCC intersect, coexist, compete, pair up, strain and stretch one another. This creates a circumstance in which anyone transiting through one of its networks gets entangled in several movements, and is kept in a constant state of jumping back and forth between them. From each particular position occupied in the midst of that flow emerges a singular point of view. No perspective is identical to another: movements that are visible for some are concealed from others, and vice versa. Certain movements are inevitably kept out of sight, while others are ostensibly plain to see. This does not mean, however, that they are only fragmentarily or imperfectly graspable. For fragments only make sense against the backdrop of a whole they have supposedly integrated once and from which they might have issued or to which they are still subjected.

In contrast, far from being a natural unit ready to be apprehended, the PCC's movements are precisely what different perspectives are able to grasp of them. Their composition, layout and range depend thus on the viewpoint adopted. Furthermore, every time they occur, they retain the marks of the local conditions under which they occur and their variation takes place in accordance with these same conditions. The resulting variation is then called *rhythm*, the same name given to the very conditions that compose the movements and make them vary. Therefore, if they have no defined origin or end, it is because they turn out to be exactly what is construed on the basis of how these and other movements are regarded, or rather on the basis of their *situations*, which I defined as an arrangement of movements perceived from a particular point of view.

The difficulty in carrying out fieldwork during this phase of research was therefore due to the PCC's very mode of existence. While performing this research, I was led to set myself in motion too. From this position, I could not see exactly the same contours others were seeing, but I could still see the same way others were seeing. When I found myself inside the flow, moving about just as those I had been studying, I began to describe what I was able to glimpse from that position. Such description required the dislocation of a number of important concepts in the field of social sciences: territory, hierarchy, law, context. The third phase of my research was, therefore, clearly marked by a shift from the study of a transcendence connecting several participants to the investigation of a multitude of movements *in tune* with each other—and all of them in tune with that very transcendence, namely the PCC.

Final Remarks

The objectivity that had been planned in the first phase of my research had to be cast aside after all. As a result, notions of territory and context are strongly challenged by the idea of movement. What remains are perceptions of movements, rhythm variations and conformations of local conditions, all in a constant drift. The notion of hierarchy, in turn, gives rise to a dynamic of ideas, which exist only by finding expression within the movements revolving around them. These roaming bases, where more traditional concepts of hierarchy find absolutely no shelter, are equally deflective to the idea of law, to the modes of thought upholding it and to all that derives from it, along with all its semantic associates, such as norm, rule or code.

Whereas during the second phase of the research I made an effort to show that the PCC's very existence is contingent on its accomplishment; in the last phase I was led to broaden my perspective, realizing there is one PCC for each viewpoint aimed at it, and that all these viewpoints end up integrating the PCC into an assemblage of in-tune movement. Precisely because it took place in spaces outside the prison system and thus had to cope with the specific conditions of those spaces, I turned my attention to interactions I had not noticed while the research was being carried out inside the prison units.

As I have tried to explain, instead of applying some preexisting theoretical framework to the phenomenon under scrutiny, my endeavor was to rather let it point me towards another way of seeing the world. It is nonetheless important to stress that this very way of seeing the world, in turn, conditioned the way I carried out the research. At the same time, the way I approached it was linked to the developmental process of ethnographic research. In other words, while the field insertion entailed a reflection on the research subject, namely the PCC, my description of the PCC was inseparable from that particular mode of insertion. Hence, I draw attention to the coextensive character of the relationship between research and the subject, to their simultaneous and mutual inception and, finally, to the consequences of this conjugation in motion.

Throughout my fieldwork, the PCC brought me closer to something that Nietzsche had already proposed: an emphasis on the perspective and on the viewpoint, also stressed by Villela, who, inspired by the philosopher, advises not to "look beneath the perspectives for the way things really are", precisely because "things, beneath the perspective, are no way at all" (Villela 2004, p. 24).

In this chapter, I have tried to emphasize that the processes through which field research is executed generate ethnographic accounts that do not express exactly the researcher's representation of those subjects being studied, nor any hypothetical reality intrinsic to the phenomena under scrutiny. Contrarily, the texts produced on the basis of these ethnographies emerge from the researcher's relationship with his or her research subject and, therefore, constitute a singular point of view about the observed phenomenon. According to this perspective, ethnographic texts are, correspondingly, something very similar to what those people I have studied usually call situations, in other words, arrangements of movements such as they are perceived (and, with regard to texts, recorded) from a specific point of view.

Notes

1. Original in French: *Le destin s"écrit à mesure qu"il s"accomplit, pas avant.*
2. The PCC's presence in the media was relatively rare and the first book about it would only be written in 2004 by the journalist Josmar Jozino.
3. *FEBEM* (State Foundation for Minors" Welfare) was the old denomination for juvenile correctional centers managed by the São Paulo State Department of Justice. Their current denomination is *Fundação CASA* (Socio-Educational Center of Assistance for Adolescents).
4. In prison jargon, maintenance is the name given to a cell holding those prisoners, also called maintenance, responsible for the pavilion's internal management (comprising tasks such as food delivery, opening the cells, dispute resolution). They also operate as spokespersons between the detainees and the prison officials.

References

Adorno, S., & Salla, F. (2007). Criminalidade organizada nas prisões e os ataques do PCC. *Revista Estudos Avançados, 21*(61), 7–29. São Paulo: Instituto de Estudos Avançados da USP.

Antillano, A. (2017). When prisoners make the prison: Self-rule in Venezuelan prisons. *Prison Service Journal, 229*, 26–30.

Babenco, H. (2003). *Carandiru (film)*. São Paulo: Globo Filmes.

Biondi, K. (2006). Tecendo as tramas do significado: As facções prisionais enquanto organizações fundantes de padrões sociais. In M. P. Grossi, M. L. Heilborn, & L. Z. Machado (Eds.), *Antropologia e Direitos Humanos* (Vol. 4, pp. 303–350). Florianópolis: Nova Letra.

Biondi, K. (2007). Pesquisa em prisões: reflexões acerca da inserção em campo. In *Anais da I Reunião Equatorial de Antropologia. América equatorial: cultura na contemporaneidade*. Aracaju: ABA (1 CD-ROM).

Biondi, K. (2010). *Junto e Misturado: uma etnografia do PCC.* SãoPaulo: Terceiro Nome.
Biondi, K. (2016). *Sharing this walk: An ethnography of prison life and the PCC in Brazil.* Chapel Hill: University of North Carolina.
Biondi, K. (2018). *Proibido roubar na quebrada: território, hierarquia e lei no PCC.* São Paulo: Terceiro Nome.
Bosi, A. (Ed.). (2007). Dossiê crime organizado. *Revista Estudos Avançados,* Vol. 21(61). São Paulo: Instituto de Estudos Avançados da USP.
Carneiro, L. P. (2010). A Sedução do PCC. *Jornal Estado de São Paulo,* São Paulo, p. J5–J5, 02 de maio de 2010.
Cerbini, F. (2012). *La casa de Jabón: Etnografía de una cárcel Boliviana.* Barcelona: Edicions Bellaterra.
Colombo, S. (2006). Claro enigma. *Jornal Folha de São Paulo.* Caderno Mais, 21 de maio de 2006.
Darke, S. (2018). *Conviviality and survival: Co-producing Brazilian prison order.* London: Palgrave Macmillan.
Dias, C. C. N. (2005). *A igreja como refúgio e a bíblia como esconderijo?* Dissertação de Mestrado. Faculdade de Filosofia, Letras e Ciências Humanas da Universidade de São Paulo.
Dias, C. C. N. (2011). *Da pulverização ao monopólio da violência: expansão e consolidação do Primeiro Comando da Capital (PCC) no sistema carcerário paulista.* Tese de doutorado apresentada ao Programa de Pós-Graduação em Sociologia da Universidade de São Paulo.
Feltran, G. de S. (2008). *Fronteiras de tensão: Um estudo sobre política e violência nas periferias de São Paulo.* Campinas: Tese de Doutorado em Ciências Sociais, UNICAMP.
Feltran, G. de S. (2010). Crime e castigo na cidade: os repertórios da justiça e a questão do homicídio nas periferias de São Paulo. *Caderno CRH, 23*(58), 59–73.
Goffman, E. (1962). *Asylums.* Garden City: Anchor Books.
Hirata, D. V. (2010). *Sobreviver na adversidade: entre o mercado e a vida.* Tese de doutorado em Sociologia. Faculdade de Filosofia, Letras e Ciências Humanas da Universidade de São Paulo. São Paulo.
Jozino, J. (2004). *Cobras e Lagartos.* Rio de Janeiro: Objetiva.
Latour, B. (2005). *Reassembling the social: An introduction to actor-network- theory.* Oxford: Oxford University Press.
Lévi-Strauss, C. (1963). *Structural anthropology.* New York: Basic Books.

Manso, B. P. (2012). *Crescimento e queda dos homicídios em SP entre 1996 e 2010: Uma análise dos mecanismos de escolha homicida e das carreiras no crime*. Tese de doutorado em Ciências Políticas. Faculdade de Filosofia, Letras e Ciências Humanas da Universidade de São Paulo. São Paulo.
Marques, A. (2008). Faxina' e 'pilotagem': dispositivos (de guerra) políticos no seio da administração prisional. *Lugar comum - estudos de mídia, cultura e democracia (UFRJ), 25–26*, 283–290.
Marques, A. (2014). *Crime e proceder: um experimento antropológico*. São Paulo: Alameda.
Monod, J. (1971a). *Le hasard et la nécessité*. Paris: Éditions du Seuil.
Monod, J. (1971b). *Chance and necessity: An essay on the natural philosophy of modern biology*. Nova York: Alfred Knopf.
Salla, F. (2007). De Montoro a Lembo: as políticas penitenciárias em São Paulo. *Revista Brasileira de Segurança Pública*, ano 1, ed. 1, 72–90.
Strathern, M. (1996). 1989 debate: The concept of society is theoretically obsolete. The presentations: For the motion (1). In T. Ingold (Ed.), *Key debates in anthropology* (pp. 50–55). London: Routledge.
Telles, V. d. S., & Hirata, D. (2010). Ilegalismos e jogos de poder em São Paulo. *Tempo Social, 22*(2), 39–59.
Toren, C. (1996). 1989 debate: The concept of society is theoretically obsolete. The presentations: For the motion (1). In T. Ingold (Ed.), *Key debates in anthropology* (pp. 60–63). London: Routledge.
Torres, S. (2006). Crime organizado paulista é mais centralizado, vê estudiosa. Entrevista com Alba Zaluar. *Jornal Folha de São Paulo*, 15 de smaio de 2006.
Varella, D. (2012). *Lockdown: Inside Brazil's most dangerous prison*. London: Simon & Schuster.
Villela, J. M. (2004). *O povo em armas: violência e política no sertão de Pernambuco*. Rio de Janeiro: Relume Dumará.
Wagner, R. (1974). Are there social groups in the New Guinea highlands? In M. LEAF (Ed.), *Frontiers of anthropology. An introduction to anthropological thinking*. New York: Nostrand Company.
Willis, G. D. (2015). *The killing consensus: Police, organized crime, and the regulation of life and death in urban Brazil*. Berkeley: University of California Press.

18

Conclusion to Carceral Communities: Struggle and Carnival in Latin America's Carceral Worlds

Andrés Antillano and Luis Duno-Gottberg

Optics, and the Carnivalization of the Penal Order

> Prisoners from *La Modelo* prison in Barranquilla (Colombia) also experienced Carnival (…) For inmates, King Momo's festivity means freedom. (Colombia February 23rd 2020, www.Noticias.canalrcn.com)

> Inmates from a jail in Ecuador transformed the facility's courtyard into a swimming pool for the carnival. Local authorities denounced that the prisoners colluded with some officials to flood the patio with water. (Ecuador February 27th 2020, www.elcomercio.com)

A. Antillano (✉)
Universidad Central de Venezuela, Caracas, Venezuela

L. Duno-Gottberg
Rice University, Houston, TX, USA

S. Darke et al. (eds.), *Carceral Communities in Latin America*, Palgrave Studies in Prisons and Penology, https://doi.org/10.1007/978-3-030-61499-7_18

> The jail is pure carnival. In the Ezeiza prison, more than 200 women danced in the open air; "I haven't seen the sun for a long time," one of the inmates said. (Argentina March 21st 2011, www.lanacion.com)

The image of premodern penalty revolves around the chain-gang, men shackled together by iron collars on their necks, marching to their place of execution or imprisonment. A public spectacle, a traveling fair of criminals, led to the scaffold, or the promiscuous hodgepodge of people in the great confinement. The penal reformers of the eighteenth and nineteenth centuries, and later, the Latin American positivists of the late nineteenth and early twentieth centuries, coincide in their denunciation of the punishment institutions of the time: disease, vice, disorder, brutality, and degradation characterized a period that reason and science sought to overcome. This thesis is now canonical: the prison, as we know it, is the result of a sustained process of secularization, rationalization, and bureaucratization, directly connected to other "civilizing" and modernizing processes seeking to banish the chaos and promiscuity of the multitude, their affective excesses, and the spectacle of their atavism (Foucault 1978; Garland 1990; Pratt 2006). The new regime introduced different hierarchies and norms, transforming the old prison into a space of sanitized confinement, foreclosing undue contacts "inside" and, above all, any exchange with the "outside world."

Such is the picture of penalty prior to "punitive modernity" in a literature that, conceived for the European context, now seems insufficient or reductive for an enquiry of the Global South. The sheer promiscuity, the disruption of hierarchies, the confusion, the erasure of limits, the suspension of rules, or their substitution by unspeakable practices requires its own historical depth. The violence and transgression of Latin American prisons is related but not identical to the forces, the practices, and histories of European or Anglo-American prisons. Otherwise, the above atrocious and disturbing picture turns out to be a parody of itself; a vaudeville of cruelty and excess, a carnival of sorts, seen from the perspective of the Modern prison system, but also from a Eurocentric, voyeuristic perspective.

To think about Latin American prisons, we turn this teleological and self-confident view of penology on its head. In this reading, the coloniality of "the spectacle" thus becomes apparent: it responds to the peculiarities of Modernity in the Global South; to the reconfigurations of state power (particularly under neoliberal regimes); and to different forms of inmate agency that contest and negotiate authority in face of internal and external forces. The first step in this enquiry requires us to revisit the notion of carnival and the carnivalesque. Pratt, Laqueur, and Spierenburg have written about the carnivalesque spectacle of executions and corporal punishment in Europe, which continued well into the nineteenth century as public spectacles similar to popular fairs.[1] Here we ponder, nevertheless, a different angle of the carnivalesque, departing from Batjtin and then adopting a postcolonial optic to reveal the "grey zones[2]" of this so-called Second life of the people. He writes:

> As opposed to the official feast, one might say that carnival celebrated temporary liberation from the prevailing truth and from the established order; it marked the suspension of all hierarchical rank, privileges, norms, and prohibitions. Carnival was the true feast of time, the feast of becoming, change, and renewal. It was hostile to all that was immortalized and completed (Bakhtin 1981: 10).

Carnival is thus transgressive. It profanes the sacred. It usurps power and inverts authority. Norms and laws are suspended, giving way to a parallel world of indulgence and extravagance.[3] Whereas the Russian critic thought that these moments of sociability represented "the second life of the people, who for a time entered the utopian realm of community, freedom, equality and abundance", he also suggests that more than a rupture, this functions within the confines of power. It is, in the end, an ambivalent celebration: carnival was 'life itself, but shaped according to a certain pattern of play' (Bakhtin 1981: 7). Within our own argument, and as several chapters in this book suggest, the "prison carnivalesque" reinforces multiple forms oppression constituted in the wake of coloniality.

The anarchic, subversive practices of carnival were not only sanctioned but positively encouraged by elites and the authorities, *only* on special festive occasions. This served as a kind of "safety-valve", so that they could then return to their "normal" state of being obedient until the next feast came around. Revolutionary uprising would then be tamed by a burst of well-framed ("walled", like a prison, one could say) subversion. However, carnival is not merely a performance that dissipates subaltern forces, it is also a form of accumulation and potentiation of this energy: it is a productive form of economic and political accumulation.

Roberto DaMatta's classic, *Carnivals, Rogues, and Heroes: An Interpretation of the Brazilian Dilemma*, still sheds light into our understanding of ritual, subversion, and normalization. The dilemma between the highly authoritarian, hierarchal aspects of Brazilian society and the concurrent desire for equality and harmony in that society, is not strange to the contradictions and aspirations of the carceral world in Latin America: an ethos of communal life and struggle; solidarity and subversion in face of oppressive norms, coexists with authoritarianism and exploitative practices.

The carnivalesque inversion of the modern carceral world is at the core of this volume. Several chapters explore the subversion of state power within the prison, while revealing the reproduction of oppressive mechanisms of control and exploitation. Authors identify clashes between powers, formal or de facto; some of which take place *within* inmate rule—the government of the prisoners (Antillano, Ariza and Iturralde, Biondi, Duno-Gottberg, Fisher-Hoffman, Carter, Cerbini, Sepúlveda and Pojomovsky); or in face of State power, subversion, collusions, and pacts (Darke, Drybread, Macaulay). Some describe the inversion of hierarchies (Antillano, Sepúlveda and Pojomovosky, Biondi, Cerbini, Fisher-Hoffman), sacred experiences (Carter, Duno-Gottberg, Cerbini), and even parodies of the rehabilitation programs (Peirce, Weegels, Sepúlveda and Pojomovsky). Most insist on the porosity of confinement, depicting a prison with blurry limits, where the "inside" and the "outside" connect (Moore, Biondi).

Seen perhaps as archaic and anarchical, these practices and subjectivities defy the modernizing and secular rationality. Nevertheless, another order emerges, with its own rationality and often, mirroring the practices and processes of a Modern (inmate) state (Duno-Gottberg). This order regulates the internal life of prisoners in Venezuela (Antillano, Duno-Gottberg, Fischer-Hoffman, and Sepúlveda and Pojomovsky) and Brazilian (Biondi, Darke, Drybread). The violence of this model finds expression in the inmate reconfiguration and administration of space, as well as on their bodies (Ariza and Iturralde, Carter).

The carceral order in Latin America defies the notion of a foreclosed space, completely isolated from the exterior world. In several chapters, confinement reveals itself as porous. These prisons, are permeable to flows from and into the "outside world." Fluid and uncontrolled (Moore), this is an institution that defies the principle of total state control. In fact, these prisons spread out beyond its own walls (Biondi).

Institutionalized religion and spirituality are also transformed and replaced by the affect of a millenarian and apocalyptic religiosity or by magical rituals that seek to reshape and make sense of the experience of confinement (Carter, Cerbini, Duno-Gottberg). While this might seem counter to the ideals of normalization and rationalization of the secular penal model, Fisher-Hoffman, Sepúlveda, and Pojomovsky identify an arrangement of practices that reproduce inequalities of gender and race, or diverse forms of political subordinations and exploitation we have identified in the expansion of the Eurocentric Modern project.

Finally, an inversion of signs takes place in the order of representation of/in the carceral world: the abandonment of any attempt of redemption or resistance, in favor of the reaffirmation of the violent inmate order (Sepúlveda and Pojomovsky), the celebration of exclusion and despair (Carter), and the cynical conformation to the institutional discourse (Weegels).

This wide array of themes and images leads us to a grotesque and eccentric landscape, a monstrous mirror disfiguring and exaggerating the Modern prison project.

Mass media accounts of Latin American prisons are the result of a distorted perception; a vicarious consumption of the subaltern life, a spectacle of distant degradation, rather than the accurate result of immersive fieldwork committed to the culture, politics, and everyday life of inmates. Nevertheless, it is worth asking if the emergence of the "penal carnivalesque" in these ethnographies is an issue of optics. It might be, but in a very different sense. It is certainly not an invention. The ethnography strives for a faithful approach to each event; adding depth, detail, and context, while forcing ethical considerations and political engagement. It makes the invisible emerge, highlighting the paradoxical or contradictory nature of each narrative. The carnivalesque remains but not as spectacle, but as that complex interplay of forces; the subversion and restoration of power. What these chapters relate is the confirmation of grim tales of prison survivors; the routine brutality of intramural life.

Civilization and Barbarism: The Postcolonial Legacy of Latin American Prisons

How to understand this violent and treacherous world of Latin American prisons? Do these differences with respect to the larger Modern penitentiary project reveal the failures of Modernity in this territory? Is this "metaphysics of disorder" (Comaroff and Comaroff 2009), such widespread and uncontrolled "barbarism", just a sign of civilizational failure and backwardness? Such reading, rooted in different levels of exoticization and historical erasures, just reproduces under a not-so-subtle veil, the colonial paradigm. In this regard, Florence Bernault has warned us of such risk, in her discussion of African prisons; a case that resonates in other regions of the Global South:

> The degraded state of some contemporary African prisons might incite some commentators to think that African judicial systems have silently returned to pre-colonial archaic forms of punishment. At best, some might explain away the lack of improvement in the prison system as an effect of "underdevelopment", imagined as an indefinite standstill in the penal phase prior to the prison reform. Return or retardation: the threatening horizon of western orientalism only obscures the long-term maturation of the African penitentiary (Bernault 2003: 2).

Comaroff and Comaroff have shown that media images of crime and disorder from the Global South circulate deceivingly, suggesting that it is "*there*" where civilization ends, under the crushing violence of barbarism and abjection. Nevertheless, such reality not only has its equivalent in the Global North, but it is also a result of the insertion of the postcolonial periphery in the world order. Furthermore, the persistent domination, dispossession, and subordination to which these regions are subjected to by the centers of power also encompasses the underground and criminal economies on a world scale. In other words, more than isolated barbarism and backwardness, these expressions of "crime and disorder" speak to the continuation, in a different guise, of old colonial relations.

In the case of Latin American prisons, with their own share of brutality and chaos, irregular state control, and proliferation of violence, it is possible to trace the origin of their current configuration to the Colony and to the implantation of the metropolitan penal order in the region. Cuban novelist Alejo Carpentier offers a powerful image of the arrival Enlightenment and the ideas of the French Revolution in the New World, through the disembarkation of the printing press and the guillotine in the Caribbean. *El Siglo de las Luces* (*Explosion in a Cathedral*) (1962) shows these technologies, directly connected to order and terror, respectively, making way in the colonial world: "The guillotine had begun to form part of normal everyday life. Amongst the parsley and the marjoram, miniature guillotines were sold as ornaments, and many people took them home. Children exerted their ingenuity to construct little machines for decapitating cats."

The historiography on punishment during Colonial times shows the precarious nature of the early penal institutions, especially devoted to the subordination and control of the rebellious masses of Indigenous and African slaves. Ermila Troconiz de Veracoechea (1983) describes the hardship of criminal justice during the Colonial period in Venezuela, when prisons would unexpectedly collapse under the elements. Some prisoners, sentenced to capital punishment, would linger and die of natural death, waiting for an executioner who could never arrive, lost in the intricated roads of the remote province. Some prisoners would beg for a handout, stretching their hand through the prison's bars, in hope of completing their miserable diet. If the first modernizing attempts arrived with the Independence and Revolution, it did so with the paradoxes outlined by Alejo Carpentier above: the print press and the guillotine signaling both sides of that imported Modernity.

Starting in the 1830s, when the first penitentiaries began to be built on the continent, and during the next hundred years, all efforts sought to establish modern projects imported from Europe. From the late nineteenth century on, these where inspired by the new Positivist theories of criminology that dominated all debates in the field. These promised an alternative to the archaic Colonial model by introducing a new "rational" and "scientific" model of conceiving the penal order and its technologies (Del Olmo 1981; Salvatore and Aguirre 1996). The results differed however, from what it was expected. The incongruencies between the imported project and the actual practices responded more to local agendas and power structures than to the limitations of the Latin American ideologues. The implementation of European models was more mimicry than mimesis: it was not mere duplication, but rather, a "creative adoption" with the imprint of local customs and power relations. By embracing penal Modernity, Latin American elites found new ways to perpetuate practices of coercion and sustain their privileges. It was for this reason, perhaps, that the original projects were plagued by bitter disputes among intellectuals, power groups, and bureaucratic interest. These debates revolved around definitions of order, justice, and the nature of national projects (Salvatore and Aguirre 1996), rather than on the specific problems of operating prisons or controlling crime. At the disjunctive between narratives of Western modernity and on-the-ground local realities, brutal practices of oppression remained.

Even today, the planning and adoption of prison models is still conditioned by political, bureaucratic, and ideological interests, as well as by global trends, as shown by Hathazy (2016) in a discussion of rehabilitation programs in the Southern Cone. This was also the case of (failed) attempts to implement supermax prison models in Colombia (De Dardel and Söderstrom 2015). What we want to emphasize here is that new projects do not displace the previous "punitive repertoire", but they rather coexist. It even incorporates these new ideas and practices, to a realm that might contradict the principles prescribed by the imported doctrines, without disrupting local customs or the demands of the dominant elites.

These "creative adoptions" face insurmountable obstacles that limit their scope and, most of the time, wreck their purposes. Chronic budgetary shortages, legal loopholes, racist conceptions of society, or ideological prejudices (Salvatore and Aguirre, Op. Cit.) are other factors that lead to this configuration we have approached through the critical lenses of carnival. In the end, instead of real changes in the treatment of inmates, new projects serve more to reinforce and to cover up previous forms of punishments, structures of domination, or social, racial, and gender hierarchies (see also Fisher-Hofmann, this volume). In the end, the actual operation of this punitive system is be very different from the prescriptions by their European or North American ideologues. In fact, the postcolonial expressions of metropolitan punitive models assimilate, and even innovate in more effective and often brutal ways, to achieve greater control and plundering of the subaltern population.

The creation and expansion of prisons in the Global South faces similar challenges and tensions across the board, as seen in the case of Africa and India (Arnold 1994; Bernault 2003). These reveal themselves in the common traits and recurrent topics of our ethnographies: inmate stratification leading to "trusted prisoners", high levels of violence and degradation, overcrowding and extreme living conditions, weak control by the authorities, chronic lack of resources, and informality. Such features are not only persistent over time, going back to Colonial prisons[4]; but they are also present in other contexts of the Global South. This is perhaps the result of a tension between imported projects, difficult to implement in other contexts, and the persistence of local punitive practices, more adjusted to the particular power relations and economic conditions. In many ways, these initial or original conditions will determine the future of the prison project in the peripheries; sedimenting and institutionalizing certain practices and values—such as violence, racism, patrimonialism, authoritarianism, or the predominance of a moral discourse on crime (Darke 2018; Fisher-Hoffman, this volume). Furthermore, these "anomalies" can be understood as a result of the differences between the context of the origin of the model—the Liberal Europe of the mid-nineteenth and early twentieth centuries—and the context of reception—the "hybrid" (Salvatore and Aguirre) or "baroque" (Bolívar Echevarría) Modernity of postcolonial Latin America; the heteroclite and mestizo Modernity where multiple elements and temporalities overlap and openly clash.

We speculate that the expressions of State power in this peripheral carceral universe mirror, in this sense, the construction of nations in the postcolonial world. In the same way in which Modernity and nation states were imagined and deployed in Latin America as the result of external and brutal forces, along with resistance and negotiation, the State maintains a relationship of exteriority with subaltern groups within the nation, and within their carceral order. Domination does not operate by consensus, persuasion, or the subtle techniques of discipline and co-option that Foucault and others describe, but by pure and sheer violence and coercion, which lead to separation and exclusion (by race, social origin, religious beliefs, etc.). The thesis outlined by Guha in *Dominance without Hegemony* thus holds true here: the postcolonial state rests in the paradox of authoritarian control without hegemony.

The Economy of Dispossession and the Colonial Legacy of Confinement

A persistent legacy of the colonial model explains some aspects of the brutal and wretched nature of our prisons: the place occupied by peripheral countries in the world economic order as a supplier of raw materials, from the early Colonial times to the present.[5] Cheap and reliable commodities and labor, required strategies for population control by states and elites, trying to preserve their participation in international markets. From a Marxist inspired perspective, there are significant contributions for the understanding of the relationship between punishment and labor: the function of punishment in the regulation of labor markets; the exploitation of inmate labor; and the role of the prison in the making of the working class (Melossi and Pavarini 1980; Rusch and Kirchheimer 1984). The current role of the prison in regulating the surplus population is analyzed by Wacquant in this volume. (See also Wacquant 2001b, 2010; De Giorgi 2004, 2007).

Although the exploitation of prison labor and the extraction of rents did not have the same role in Latin America that it had in other colonial areas, such as Africa (see Bernault 2003),[6] it is possible to suspect a link between these prisons and the peripheral, dependent economy, since Colonial times, which rested on the control of labor and the export of raw materials. In fact, the inability of these economies to absorb large volumes of labor meant that the working population would chronically exceed the labor supply, with the constant risk of revolt and chronic civil war (see e.g. Izard 1991). Throughout its history, Latin American prisons have swallowed vast masses of ruined peasants, poor, unemployed workers and artisans, "*vagos y malentretenidos*" ("lazy and ill-restrained") who remain outside the contracted labor market. An additional problem in the early penal period, which continues well into the twentieth century, was the absence of a working-class proper, unlike in the case of European countries, where the prison is better understood in relation to the management of the workers, and as a way to face the social problems of the industrial society (see Salvatore and Aguirre).

A low demand for labor would reduce the support for rehabilitation and *correctionalism* programs, strongly associated with the tasks of disciplining the workforce. On the other hand, the subsistence economy and the acute levels of poverty among the most disadvantaged in countries dependent on exports of primary goods, has the effect of an even greater decrease in the living conditions of the inmate population (Rusch and Kirchheimer 1984). Finally, the unequal exchange between peripheral and metropolitan countries; the dispossession of the colonial and postcolonial world, and the spoliation by local elites (Galeano 1982), lead to chronic underfunding of the nation states. The end result is a permanent lag in the capacity to serve the poor population (as seen in the precarious social assistance systems in the region), and a greater emphasis on the abandonment of the surplus population, discarded and contained in the prison.

This role and weight of the world economy on the shaping of the penitentiary system in the postcolonial world is thus crucial to our understanding of this carnivalesque reality: the labor market, the living conditions of the poor, and the precarious state budgets might explain the differences between countries with a higher degree of dependence on exports of raw material and those that, such as Argentina, Chile, and Uruguay, advanced more into industrialization. This might also explain the importance given to correctionalist narratives in the latter, while the punitive dimension dominates the former.[7]

Finally, we must take note of the coincidence or timing of the crisis of the prison systems in the region, with the collapse of the import substitution model in the 1980s. The rise of Neoliberalism and its impact on the deindustrialization of Latin American economies is a key aspect on the production of this particularly brutal order. In any case, there is a wide field of research on the possible relationships between prison, criminal punishment, and the primary and extractivist economies.

Neoliberalism and the Prison Crisis in Latin America

The expansion of incarceration and overcrowding in Latin America coincides with the hegemony of Neoliberalism. Since the late 1980s, under the so-called "Washington Consensus", incarceration rates increased five-fold. Between 1992 (the year of the Carandirú massacre[8]) and the new century, the inmate population in Latin America increased by 100%; while just in the last two decades, it rose from 644,000 to 1,500,000 inmates (Nuñovero 2019). Such increment has been accompanied by continuous violence, massacres, and the emergence of gangs that dispute, and often manage to take control of the facilities.

This punitive turn materializes, to a degree, in the "War on Drugs", which peaked in this period. Its profound implications for the carceral order in the region were dire: militarization, criminalization of the poorest population (peasants, and youth from popular neighborhoods); high rates of arrests and prosecution; and increased severity in punishment contributed to the dramatic increase of the inmate population—of which, 15 to 50% would serve sentences related to drug offenses, depending on the country and year. The traditional place of Latin America in the production of commodities for the global market, and role of prisons in regulating its necessary labor come together once again. The former criminalized peonage in the sugar fields and tobacco plantations becomes, in time, the informal workers in the drug industry.

Several authors have discussed the connection between neoliberalism and punitivism (Cavadino and Dignan 2006; O'Malley 2009; Iturralde 2010; Brandariz and Sozzo 2014). This relationship has been understood by its cultural, ideological, and discursive dimensions, as the appeal to an individualistic ethos; the displacement of solidarity as a fundamental social principle; a moralistic discourse on crime; and the emphasis on security over other variables (Cavadino and Dignan 2006; Cheliotis 2013). From a "political economy" perspective, structural adjustments and deregulation generate a fragmented labor market, informality and exclusion; in short, a surplus population contained and regulated by neoliberal penalty (Wacquant, this volume, and 2003, 2010; De Giorgi 2004, 2007).

Beyond the disproportionate growth of the inmate population, Neoliberal reform had an impact on the internal functioning of prisons in the region. These policies generated significant distortions, and led to further deterioration of the material conditions of prisoners. Under such a model, the "rehabilitative ideal", along with the usual treatment programs, are discarded and replaced by sheer discipline and rigorous control, aiming at neutralization and retribution (Irwin and Owen 2004; Simon 2000). Although most of the ethnographies collected in this volume show the complete absence of rehabilitation programs, some research signals a different direction. The works of Peirce and Parker, in this volume, and Paul Hathazy (2016) for the Southern Cone, elsewhere, show the resurgence of the rehabilitative ideology in recent years.

Perhaps, the greatest effect of Neoliberalism on prison communities resides beyond the prison walls: the greatest impact is outside, in larger society and, more specifically, in the subaltern classes. The consequences in terms of exclusion, precariousness, and social fragmentation, makes it so that subsistence for the poor depends on the underground economy. In this realm, the prison plays an invigorating and regulatory role of illicit markets and criminal economies, as well as in diverse circuits of precarious labor.

Latin American prisons are thus filled by the marginalized youth from the *barrios* and *favelas* who in their confinement, often join criminal networks and illicit economies. Additionally, this transit through the penal system confers a significant reputation; a social and cultural capital of sorts that allows better navigation of the experience of exclusion. Unlike Wacquant's points regarding metropolitan countries (2001a, 2010), these prisons do not serve so much to contain and dissuade the huge surplus population (which, as Hathazy and Müller 2016, point out, due to its enormous size, exceeds the capacity of the penitentiary systems). Rather, in Latin America, prisons seem to act as an organizer and regulator of illicit markets and groups outside the law (see Biondi, this volume). One would even say that, in the same way in which the old prison fed the labor market by providing cheap labor for the formal economy (Melossi and Pavarini 1980; Hay 2001), the current penal system provides cheap labor for illegal markets in times of scarce and precarious work. These workers serve in multiple roles, including the supply of armed groups (at times, an army of sorts) to fight wars between criminal factions, or against the state.

Mass incarceration and heavy-handed policies become one of the pillars of the Neoliberal program, reinforcing and doubling social exclusion with criminal punishment (see Wacquant, this volume). Nevertheless, in a grotesque twist, or carnivalesque parody, the internal social order that results from mass incarceration is on many occasions very similar to the program and the ethos of Neoliberalism. This time, a penal Neoliberalism from below (Gago 2017): a de facto privatized prison, where the state hardly intervenes, while frequently the most rigorous discipline and the strictest control prevail but are exercised by the inmates themselves. This time, the carnival is, at least partially, in the hands of the inmates themselves. The prison utopia of the neoliberal project returns thus as a monstrous and disconcerting figure of agency from the margins.

However, the Post-Neoliberal projects that have come to power in the region did not necessarily reverse this trend. The case studies compiled here show that in spite of the so-called Pink Tide, Venezuela, Bolivia, Brazil, and Nicaragua not only continued with highly chaotic and ungovernable prison systems, but they also expanded the inmate population. Despite their initial attempts to replace the punitive policies of previous governments, the prison population continued to rise—even showing spectacular increases in its incarceration rate: El Salvador (411%), Ecuador (398%), Venezuela (302%), Brazil (221%), Nicaragua (219%). In the case of Bolivia, it has one of the highest prison overcrowding rates in the region, exceeding the installed capacity of its prison system by more than 200% (Nuñovero 2019).

This continuity of punitive policies between the Neoliberal regimes and progressive governments of the last two decades does not invalidate our thesis. It rather shows the limits of the transformations attempted; as well as the deep-rooted presence, or persistence, of the Neoliberal rationality. Post-Neoliberal governments were thus unable to overcome the colonial legacies, deepened by Neoliberal hegemony. The exclusion of the poor and the continued institutional violence, continued largely because these governments stayed tied to extractivist economic models, and the fluctuations of international markets. In fact, progressive policies, beyond the notable changes that they promoted, were often limited to a more equitable redistribution of the extraordinary income from the rise in commodity prices, without touching neither the dependence on these, nor the structural conditions that produce exclusion and poverty. In this context, mass incarceration remained an effective strategy to contain the poor who were kept out of both the labor market and the reach of redistributive policies.

A New Society of Captives

The work gathered in this volume shows a significant reshaping of social relationships among prisoners; but also, between them and diverse external actors. Such configuration challenges the idea of the prison as a space of hermetic and orderly confinement; already questioned in the early works of scholars such as Gresham M. Sykes. In a sense, this reality is foreshadowed by the history of Latin American penitentiaries. This body of research reveals a series of practices that dismantle the illusion of total state control. In fact, these ethnographies reveal the emergence of "new carceral communities", characterized by recurrent features: morganatic alliances between prison authorities and prisoners (Darke, Drybread, Ariza, and Iturralde); disputes and coalitions between judicial and administrative authorities and civil society actors (Macaulay); mutating relationships of power and authority among the prisoners themselves (Biondi, Cerbini, Duno-Gottberg, Sepúlveda and Pojomovsky, Fisher-Hoffman, Carter, Antillano); and unexpected exchanges between the prison and neighboring communities (Moore), or the irradiation of the prison into the larger society (Biondi).

These "new carceral communities" emerged in response to specific and traceable changes in the role of prisons during the past four decades. After the late 1970s, attempts to implement "decarceration" and the "dispersion" control mechanisms (see Cohen 1979), the following decade brought about harsh criminal prosecutions and punishment, leading to a violent process of re-incarceration. In the United States, this resulted in a massive inmate population, controlled through new punitive technologies and administrative models, among which privatization, and the supermax prisons and prison-warehouses are notorious.[9] Latin American attempts to replicate the model were few and unsuccessful: In Brazil, the construction of the Rehabilitation Center of Taubaté (known as the Piranhão prison), in 1985, not only signaled this new model of containment, but also its disastrous consequences: the Primeiro Comando da Capital, the famous criminal gang is said to have originated here (for Colombia, see De Dardel and Söderstrom 2015).

In Europe, the growth of the inmate population was less dramatic, and it even saw certain reduction in recent years. At the same time, this has been accompanied by the tightening of intermediate sanctions, diversion policies, managerialist approaches, impersonal techniques ("at-a-distance"); the development of specific strategies focalized on the control of immigrants; and more recently, soft (but efficient) forms to manage inmates (Ruggiero 2013; Crewe 2011; Liebling 2019).

Latin America engages this process of "reincarceration" under serious fiscal deficits; as a consequence of the debt crisis, the fall in commodity prices, and the general impact of all of this on state financing, under the guise of neoliberal adjustment programs. For several countries, this also coincides with the paradoxical effect of the dual transition to democracy and the expansion of free markets. In such juncture, with the loss of State legitimacy, and its inability to guarantee order, or even the most basic sustenance for the inmate population, the outcome is dire: an overcrowded and collapsed prison system, the rise in mass violence and slaughter, the deterioration in living conditions, and even the growing inability to govern prison (see, in this volume, Peirce, Ariza and Iturralde, Darke, Carter). In turn, the informal order of inmates was also overwhelmed by the flow of new prisoners in a context of scarcity, violence, and fierce competition for resources.

The breakdown of state power has led to "delegating" the control of many facilities to inmates (see, in this volume, Darke, Antillano, Biondi, Duno-Gottberg), who operate with diverse levels of autonomy. This might happen through agreement and negotiation with state representatives, or de facto. In this process of relative and problematic "autonomization", the State's role becomes that of a gatekeeper, enforcing the external custody of the facility; regulating the flows between the inside and the outside; or even playing the role of mediator, not only in face of the judicial bureaucracy, but also in relation to economic (illicit) fluxes. When the prison ceases to be, in Foucault's words, "the revenge against justice", the administration of confinement is reduced to the management of the Law in its most external form and, simultaneously, to regulating the flux of bodies and capital.

Paradoxically, along with the erosion of State power inside the prison, an increased concern about the carcereal becomes paramount, within a dramaturgy of power that seeks to capitalize on its visibility and political value. The prison now functions as a symbol condensing narratives about security, retribution, and morality amidst the collective anxiety and growing demands for a "strong hand" against crime and social disorder. This coexists with the agendas of actors from an increasingly fragmented bureaucratic field who dispute their political control over the penal system (see, in this volume, Peirce, Ariza and Iturralde, Macaulay. Also Hathazy 2016). Such disjointed choreographic movement, in which different actors within the state bureaucracy fight to control the jail, while behind the walls, other officials surrender their authority, reveals the complex dramaturgy of power for sure; but most importantly, it puts in evidence the fiction of the state. As political anthropology has insisted, the state is non-existent beyond an overall effect: it claims identity and unity through the management of loose aggregate of subjects—both state and non-state actors—responding to divergent agendas, heterogeneous interests and goals. In its darkest and most irrefutable extreme, the state dissolves into a chaotic multiplicity. This is, perhaps, a state ruled by King Momo.

The bureaucratic-authoritarian state of the old military dictatorships (O'Donnell 1975) now gives rise to a fragmentary state, incapable of governing over its population—neither by guaranteeing vital needs nor by controlling or preserving order. This is especially true with regards to the most excluded social groups, whose lives end up being ruled by actors and practices frequently situated at the fringes of legality: death squads, paramilitaries forces, vigilantism lynching, criminal groups (Campbell 2000; Gambetta 1993; Goldstein 2003; Huggins 1991; Marten 2007; Wilson and Lindsey 2009). These populations and their spaces become increasingly part of an interconnected network existing outside the old sovereignty of the state. The prison, with its multiple flows and the permanent renegotiation of sovereignty within it, is a locus of this redefinition of the role of the State in Latin America's fragmentary and unequal, but at the same time globalized, societies.

Previous forms of organization among prisoners, characterized by dispersion and overt competition over resources and opportunities; or the more stable smaller groups that provided protection against state representatives or other prisoners, have been displaced by new larger structures of self-government that monopolize power and even replace formal authorities in the maintenance of order and internal peace. This process of centralization is founded on coercion and strong control, and is quite different than the previous scenario of dispersion of informal power (Dias and Darke 2016). However, as the works collected in this volume and others point out (see Darke, Cerbini, Biondi, Sepúlveda and Pojomovsky, Duno-Gottberg, Antillano. See too Dias and Darke 2016), the power of these groups rests not only on force, but also on their ability to gain legitimacy by way of providing material and symbolic benefits to those under their rule; as well as by embodying and sustaining consensual values and goals. One would even say that the support of their "governed" population (resting on a cultural fabric and shared interests) is equally important as their own violent means of domination. Consequently, this power is much more effective and consensually respected than the power of the guardians, dependent on opportunistic transactions (Sykes 1974), on hard means of coercion (Dilulio 1987), or even on the new "soft" forms discussed in British penology (Crewe 2011; Liebling 2019).

Although the topic escapes the current analysis, a brief discussion on the pertinence of the notion of "prison gang" for the Latin-American case, seems necessary. Typical of the North American sociological tradition, it might be assimilated to the Brazilian case (see here the works of Darke and Bondi. Too Dias 2015; Dias and Darke 2016; Butler et al. 2018) and Honduras (see Carter), but it is more difficult to apply to other contexts. The council of delegates elected by inmates, in the San Pedro Penitentiary (Cerbini), *el carro* in the Venezuelan prisons (Duno-Gottberg, Fisher-Hoffman, Sepúlveda and Pojomovsky, Antillano); even figures such as the *chaveiro* or the *faxina*, in Brazil (Darke), display characteristics that distinguish them from the "prison gang" model. Beyond this conceptual discussion, there is an open field for research about the configurations and the conditions that generate such differences (See Hathazi and Muller 2016; Butler et al. 2018; Skarbek 2016).

The informal codes and practices regulating the conduct of prisoners also experienced significant changes in the last decades. The discussion on the social practices of inmates has the imprint of the early works of American sociology on incarceration, which introduced the term *prisoner code* to account for the values, rules, and prescriptions on the behavior in confinement. These studies agree that these codes have, as a central premise, non-cooperation with the authorities (Clemmer 1958); or they respond the "pains of imprisonment" (Sykes 1974). However, in Latin American prisons, the main source of tension is precisely the inability of authorities to offer security, maintain peace, or even to guarantee the basic minimums for subsistence. In this context, informal norms vary significantly, and aim at maintaining order, containing internal quarrels, promoting solidarity and subsistence mechanisms, reducing the uncertainty for a population abandoned to its fate, as shown by the authors in the book. Even in the symbolic order, be it religion (Duno-Gottberg), sorcery (Cerbini), or fictional narratives about life in prison (Sepúlveda and Pojomovsky), representation seeks to reinforce this task, through mechanisms that justify and communicate an internal social order.

To acknowledge the differences between the classical literature and our case studies should not lead to a vicarious "exoticization" of the Latin American carceral world. On the contrary, we ought to explore this specificity in its historical context, while keeping in mind the theoretical accumulation of the sociology of incarceration, as Hathazy and Müller have warned (Hathazy and Müller 2016). In fact, many of the dynamics that appear as exceptional from the European and North American perspective, but rather typical of Latin American prison, respond to categories already established by the literature on the subject—such as Goffman's developments on total institutions (see Antillano, this volume), or the idea of discipline by Foucault (Dias 2015). Nevertheless, the difference resides in that, in this case, they are "produced from below".

The reconfiguration of the links with the outside world is yet another important aspect to address. If what defines the nature of prison, is its enclosure, and its regulation of any exchanges with the outside world; that is because such ability amounts to the power to govern. Within the crisis of incarceration, we have been discussing, nevertheless, such total control becomes unsustainable. This is because inmates depend more and more on the exchanges with the outside, due to the decline in state capacity to provide the minimum requirements for subsistence. The expansion of confinement generated a significant effect on the extra carceral space, on those communities outside, from where the system fed its cells and the prisoners feed their needs. This porosity of the Latin American prison finds expression in, at least, three dimensions: first, in the relationship with the families during visits; second, in the interactions with the communities surrounding the penitentiary; and third, in the effects on the inmates' communities of origin.

The impact of carceral expansion on the families of inmates and other social networks is a field of growing academic interest. Comfort has written about "secondary prisonitazion" to describe such effect, which includes the experience of "visits", the role of the family during sentence time; and even the informal use that family members make of penitentiary institution to influence on their loved ones, or even leverage for own needs (Comfort 2007a, 2007b; Codd 2008. For Latin America see Pereyra Iraola 2017; Ferreccio 2015; Godoi 2015, 2016).

In addition to providing emotional support, connections with the "outside world", and serving as "modulator" of the experience of confinement, the family has, in the case of Latin America, a direct role in the subsistence of inmates. Given the collapse of state support mechanisms, and the renunciation to assume responsibilities for the well-being of inmates, families play a key role in the economic and material sustenance of their incarcerated relatives. In this role, it is usually the main, if not the sole source of basic goods (food, clothing, medicine, etc.), money, and illegal goods. In turn, this implies an economic, physical, emotional burden for families. In some cases, while assisting with the trafficking of illegal goods, relatives risk their own personal freedom (see Fontes and O'Neill 2019). This gives family members and visitors a central role in the prison economy, which conditions relationships, practices, and informal norms. On the other hand, family members are the main link to maintain communication with the outside world, be it with lawyers, employers, their neighbors and friends; or the criminal groups to which they belong. All of this allows the inmate to restore relations with the outside world that the prison intended to suspend. In sum, "*la visita*" (the visit), and in particular, the relatives and people close to the detainee, sustain the economy and the intramural subsistence. They are a vector and, at the same time a target, of the extended effects of the extramural prison, articulating an in/out flow of goods and relationships.

Along with mass incarceration, there is an expansion of the penitentiary system in the geography of each nation. This is a multiplication of facilities, which often move from urban centers to the peripheries, and to rural areas. This new prison geography comes with important consequences: First, it increases the pain of relatives, who must now travel long distances and make additional expenses to visit their loved ones (see Pereyra Iraola 2017; Godoi 2015). Second, it generates an unexpected economic revitalization, thanks to the new market created by the brand-new prison complexes, and their gigantic and continuous flow of visitors and officials (Moore, this volume; Silvestre 2014). In addition, whole neighborhoods that proliferate around the edge of this market and the relocation of relatives, prison workers, and ex-convicts, who decide to locate their residences in the shadows of the prison walls, are growing around the new establishments, causing suspicions and conflicts with the previous inhabitants (Silvestre 2014). The prison thus produces a new geography, remodels the urban space, gives rise to a robust local economy. The prison-rhizome expands its roots to the surrounding territory, rearranging life around it.

The third aspect to consider is the effect of imprisonment in the inmate's communities of origin. This occurs, on the one hand, as the effect of a kind of "secondary prisonitazion" (Comfort 2007a; Hathazy and Müller 2016), but this particular case, affecting peripheric areas and social groups. Prison thus redefines the social life of already impoverished communities in the region. Some of the consequences are destruction of the local productive force, due to the continuous flow of popular-class youth to jail; single mothers and dismembered families; erosion of social cohesion and breakdown of social networks; difficulties in the reception of returning ex-convicts; development of a tributary economy subjected to the rules of prisons, which expands the suffering of the sentence into the prisoner's family and community; and finally, the reproduction and perpetuation of social disadvantages and inequality (see, for the US, Kirk and Wakefield 2017).

On the other hand, the neighborhoods "replicate" the prison: practices and codes are copied, gangs of prison origin are exported to the society outside the walls. Crime is organized and regulated from the penitentiaries, and street criminal organizations are governed from a distance by heads of the prison gangs. The internal social order becomes a code with the power to expand, and become universal. The prison thus provides inmates, a knowledge and a set of relationships that are incorporated into new forms crime and alter life outside the walls (see Biondi, this volume, 2010; Dias and Darke 2016; Lessing 2017). Crime, illicit markets, criminal networks, change and organize themselves from inside prison; but equally important, prison irradiates as a culture and economy into the fabric of society.

Tied to a debate dating back to the middle of the last century, on the origin of the prison subculture, it is necessary to ask if the replication of the carceral community and codes can be simply understood as the export of the practices, codes, and structures of prison life into the world outside the walls. Or without denying the relevance of this process, should we rather look into conditions affecting simultaneously both spaces? There is certainly an isomorphism in both spaces. If this hypothesis holds true, the dynamics and trajectories would then flow in all directions, finding their most absolute condensation and monstrous realization in the prison. The carceral is thus the embodiment and consecration of this larger societal shift.

Notes

1. Thomas W. Laqueur, "Crowds, Carnival and the State in English Executions, 1604–1868", in A. L. Beier, David Cannadine, and James M. Rosenheim (Eds.) *The First Modern Society: Essays in English History in Honor of Lawrence Stone*, Cambridge University Press, Cambridge, 1989, pp.305–55. Pieter Spierenburg, *The Spectacle of Suffering: Executions and the Evolution of Repression: From a Preindustrial Metropolis to the European Experience*, Cambridge University Press, Cambridge, 1984.

2. The concept of the "Grey zone" might be productive in this exploration of shifting power relations and carnival in Latin American prisons. The original notion was coined by the Italian Holocaust survivor Primo Levi in his essay collection *The Drowned and the Saved* (1986). After acknowledging the human need to divide the social field into "us" and "them", Levi explains that such binary thinking is inadequate in the face of the complexity of life in the concentration camps: "(...) networks of human relationships inside the Lagers was not simple (...), it could not be reduced to the two blocs of victims and persecutors" (23). A key facet of Nazi practice, after all, was to attempt to turn victims into accomplices. The "grey zone" is thus inhabited mostly by victims who compromise and collaborate with their oppressors to varying degrees and with varying degrees of freedom of choice in exchange for preferential treatment. Levi insists that one should refrain from passing easy judgment on these morally ambiguous privileged prisoners.
3. "During carnival time life is subject only to its laws, that is, the laws of its own freedom. It has a universal spirit; it is a special condition of the entire world, of the world's revival and renewal, in which all take part." (Mikhail Bakhtin, *Rabelais and His World*).
4. In the context of the Cuban War of Independence, Latin America saw the creation of a model of confinement that anticipates the twentieth century concentration camp. General Valeriano Weyler was sent to crush the Cuban rebels by separating them from the civilians. His plan was to confine the latter to towns and forts controlled by Spanish troops. By the end of 1897, he had forced more than 300,000 men, women and children away from their land. He burned crops, preventing their replanting, and drove livestock away. The Spanish military made the countryside inhospitable and famine ensued. The "reconcentrados policy" took the lives of 150,000 to 400,000 people. See Jonathan Hyslop (2011) "The Invention of the Concentration Camp: Cuba, Southern Africa and the Philippines, 1896–1907", *South African Historical Journal*, 63, 2: 251–276.
5. Anibal Quijano's "*coloniality* of power" informs our understanding of Latin America's incarceration, a reality that is different but directly connected to the colonial systems of control of populations. In the case of the US, the continuity between the contemporary prison system and the long history of slavery has been explored by Michelle Alexander in *The*

New Jim Crow: Mass Incarceration in the Age of Colorblindness and Ruth Wilson Gilmore, *The Golden Gulag.*

6. Except precisely in the case of countries that maintained their colonial status, such as Puerto Rico (Santiago-Volles 1996).
7. There can be other motives for these structural differences, such as ideological narratives that prevail, as pointed out by Salvatore (1996), or disputes between bureaucratic and academic elites, as proposed by Hathazy (2016).
8. The "Carandiru massacre" occurred on Friday, October 2, 1992, in Carandiru Penitentiary in São Paulo, Brazil, when military police stormed the facility in response to a prison riot. Carandiru was closed in 2002, shortly after inmates coordinated simultaneous uprisings in 27 jails across São Paulo state during which thousands of visitors were held hostage (see Darke, this volume).
9. The United States Penitentiary Alcatraz Island, opened in 1934, has been considered a prototype and early standard for a supermax prison. David A. Ward, "Supermaximum Facilities", In: Carlson, Peter M.; Garrett, Judith Simon, *Prison and Jail Administration: Practice and Theory*, Jones and Bartlett Publishers, 1999. Cf. Chapter 35, p.252. The United States has both the world's largest prison population and the world's highest per capita incarceration rate.

References

Arnold, D. (1994). The colonial prison: Power, knowledge and penology in nineteenth-century India. In D. Arnold & D. Hardiman (Eds.), *Subaltern studies VIII: Essays in honour of Ranajit Guha* (pp. 148–184). New Delhi: Oxford University Press.

Bakhtin, M. (1981). *The dialogic imagination*. M. Holquist & C. Emerson, Trans. Austin: University of Texas Press.

Bernault, F. (2003). The politics of enclosure in colonial and post-colonial Africa. In F. Bernault (Ed.), *A history of prison and confinement in Africa* (pp. 1–54). Portsmouth: Heinemann.

Biondi, K. (2010). *Junto e Misturado: Uma Etnografia do PCC*. Sao Paulo: Terceiro Nome.

Brandariz, J. A., & Sozzo, M. (2014). *Beyond neoliberalism? A critical reading of the uses of this concept to think about contemporary transformations of penality.*

Paper presented in the European group for the study of deviance and social control 2014, annual conference, Liverpool.

Butler, M., Slade, G., & Dias, C. N. (2018). Self-governing prisons: Prison gangs in an international perspective. *Trends in Organized Crime*, 1–16.

Campbell, B. (2000). Death squads: Definition, problems and historical context. In B. Campbell & D. Bremmer (Eds.), *Death squads in global perspective. Murder with deniability* (pp. 1–27). London: Macmillan.

Cavadino, M., & Dignan, J. (2006). Penal policy and political economy. *Criminology and Criminal Justice, 6*(4), 435–456.

Cheliotis, L. K. (2013). Neoliberalism capitalism and middle-class punitiviness: Bringing Erich Fromm's materialistic psychoanalysis to penology. *Punishment and Society, 15*(3), 247–273.

Clemmer, D. (1958). *The prison community*. New York: Rinehart.

Codd, H. (2008). *In the shadow of prison. Families, imprisonment and criminal justice*. Portland: Willan Publishing.

Cohen, S. (1979). The Punitive City: Notes on dispersal of social control. *Contemporary Crises, 3*, 339–363.

Comaroff, J., & Comaroff, J. (2009). *Violencia y Ley en la Poscolonia: Una Reflexión sobre las Complicidades Norte-Sur*. Barcelona: Katz/CCCB.

Comfort, M. (2007a). *Doing time together. Love and family in the shadow of the prison*. Chicago: The University of Chicago Press.

Comfort, M. (2007b). Punishment beyond the legal offender. *The Annual Review of Law and Social Science, 3*, 271–296.

Crewe, B. (2011). Soft power in prison: Implication for staff-prisoner relationships, liberty and legitimacy. *European Journal of Criminology, 8*(6), 455–468.

Darke, S. (2018). *Conviviality and survival: Co-producing Brazilian prison order*. London: Palgrave Macmillan.

De Dardel, J., & Söderstrom, O. (2015). *The rise and fall of supermax: How the US prison model and ultra punitive penal police travelled to Colombia*. Neuchatel: Universite de Neuchatel.

De Giorgi, A. (2004). Neoliberalismo e Controle Penal na Europa e Nos Estados Unidos: A Caminho de uma Democracia Punitiva? *Vereda do direito*, (julio-diciembre), 29–42.

De Giorgi, A. (2007). Toward a political economy of post-Fordist punishment. *Critical Criminology, 15*, 243–265.

Del Olmo, R. (1981). *América Latina y su Criminología*. Mexico: Siglo XXI Editores.

Dias, C. N. (2015). A Produção da Disciplina pelo Encarceramento. *O Público e o Privado, 26*, 35–51.

Dias, C. N., & Darke, S. (2016). From dispersed to monopolized violence: Expansion and consolidation of Primeiro Comando da Capital's hegemony in São Paulo's prisons. *Crime, Law and Social Change, 65*, 213–225.

Dilulio, J. (1987). *Governing prisons: A comparative study of correctional management*. New York: Free Press.

Ferreccio, V. (2015). Familiares de Detenidos: Exploraciones en Torno a Prácticas de Equilibrio Institucional en las Prisiones de Santa Fe, Argentina. *Espacio Abierto, 24*(1), 113–145.

Fontes, A., & O'Neill, K. (2019). La Visita: Prisons and survival in Guatemala. *Journal of Latin American Studies, 51*(1), 85–107.

Foucault, M. (1978). *Vigilar y Castigar: Nacimiento de la Prisión* (3a ed.). Madrid: Siglo XXI.

Gago, V. (2017). *Neoliberalism from below: Popular pragmatics and baroque economies*. Durham: Duke University Press.

Galeano, E. (1982). *Las Venas Abiertas de América Latina*. Mexico: Siglo XXI.

Gambetta, D. (1993). *The Sicilian mafia. The business of private protection*. Harvard: Harvard University Press.

Garland, D. (1990). *Punishment and modern society: A study in social theory*. Chicago: University of Chicago Press.

Godoi, R. (2015). Vasos Comunicantes, Fluxos Penitenciários. Entre Dentro e Fora das Prisões de São Paulo. *Vivencia, 46*, 131–142.

Godoi, R. (2016). Intimacy and power: Body searches and intimate visits in the prison system of São Paulo, Brazil, *Champ pénal/Penal field* [En ligne], Vol. XIII |consultado el 13 de agosto 2020. http://journals.openedition.org/champpenal/9386; https://doi.org/10.4000/champpenal.9386.

Goldstein, D. (2003). "In our own hands": Lynching, justice, and the law in Bolivia. *American Ethnologist, 30*(1), 22–43.

Hathazy, P. (2016). Remaking the prisons of the market democracies: New experts, old guards and politics in the Carceral fields of Argentina and Chile. *Crime, Law and Social Change, 65*(3), 163–193.

Hathazy, P., & Müller, M. (2016). The rebirth of the prison in Latin America: Determinants, regimes and social effects. *Crime, Law and Social Change, 65*(3), 113–135.

Hay, D. (2001). Law and society in comparative perspective. In R. Salvatore, C. Aguirre, & G. Joseph (Eds.), *Crime and punishment in Latin America* (pp. 415–430). Durham: Duke University Press.

Huggins, M. (Ed.). (1991). *Vigilantism in modern Latin America: Essay of extralegal violence*. Westport: Praeger Publishers.

Irwin, J., & Owen, B. (2004). *The warehouse prison: Disposal of the new dangerous class*. Oxford: Oxford University Press.
Iturralde, M. (2010). *Castigo, Liberalismo Autoritario y Justicia Penal de Excepción*. Bogotá: Siglo del Hombre.
Izard, M. (1991). Vagos, Prófugos y Cuatreros Insurgencias Antiexcedentarias en la Venezuela Tardocolonial. *Boletín Americanista, 41*, 179–202.
Kirk, D., & Wakefield, S. (2017). Collateral consequences of punishment: A critical review and path forward. *Annual Review of Criminology, 1*, 174–191.
Lessing, B. (2017). Counterproductive punishment: How prison gangs undermine state authority. *Rationality and Society, 29*(3), 257–297.
Liebling, A. (2019). La Importancia Moral de la Autoridad: Por qué Debemos Interesarnos en el Trabajo y la Cultura del Personal Penitenciario? *I, V*, 15–40.
Marten, K. (2007). Warlordism in comparative perspective. *International Security, 31*(3), 41–73.
Melossi, D., & Pavarini, M. (1980). *Cárcel y Fábrica : Los Orígenes del Sistema Penitenciario Siglos, XVI–XIX*. México: Siglo XXI.
Nuñovero, L. (2019). *Cárceles en América Latina 2000–2019. Tendencias y Desafíos*. Lima: PUCP.
O'Donnell, G. (1975). *Reflexiones sobre las Tendencias Generales de Cambio del Estado Burocrático-Autoritario*. Buenos Aires: CEDES/ G.E. CLACSO, n 1.
O'Malley, P. (2009). *Neoliberalism and risk in criminology*. Legal studies research paper, 09/83.
Pereyra Iraola, V. (2017). (In)movilidades en Torno al Espacio Carcelario: Relaciones de Género y Gobernabilidad de las Cárceles Fenderales en Buenos Aires. *Revista Transporte y Territorio, 16*, 93–111.
Pratt, J. (2006). *Castigo y Civilización. Una Lectura Crítica sobre las Prisiones y los Regímenes Carcelarios*. Madrid: Gedisa.
Ruggiero, V. (2013). Punishment in Europe. A Critical Anatomy of Penal System. Basingstoke, Hampshire: Palgrave.
Rusch, G., & Kirchheimer, O. (1984). *Pena y Estructura Social*. Bogotá: Temis.
Salvatore, R. (1996). Revolutionary reform: Capitalist development, prison reform, and executive power in Mexico. In R. D. Salvatore & C. Aguirre (Eds.), *The birth of the penitentiary in Latin America: Essays on criminology, prison reform, and social control, 1830–1940* (New interpretations of Latin America series). Austin: University of Texas Press.
Salvatore, R. D., & and Aguirre, C. (Eds.). (1996). *The birth of the penitentiary in Latin America. Essays on criminology, prison reform, and social control,1830–1940*. Austin: University of Texas Press.

Santiago-Volles, K. (1996). 'Forcing them to work and punishing whoever resisted': Servile labor and penal servitude under colonialism in nineteenth-century Puerto Rico. In R. D. Salvatore & C. Aguirre (Eds.), *The birth of the penitentiary in Latin America: Essays on criminology, prison reform, and social control, 1830–1940* (New interpretations of Latin America series). Austin: University of Texas Press.

Silvestre, G. (2014). La Porosidad de la Prisión: Efectos de la Expansión del Sistema Penitenciario en el Estado de San Pablo. *Delito y Sociedad, 37*, 61–83.

Simon, J. (2000). The society of captives in the era of hyper-incarceration. *Theoretical Criminology, 4*(3), 283–308.

Skarbek, D. (2016). Covenants without the sword? Comparing prison self-governance globally. *American Political Science Review, 110*(4), 845–862.

Sykes, G. (1974). *The society of captives: A study of a maximum security prison*. Princeton: Princeton University Press.

Troconis, E. (1983). *Historia de las Carceles en Venezuela (1600–1890)*. Caracas: Acadamia Nacional de la Historia.

Wacquant, L. (2001a). Deadly simbiosis. When ghetto and prison meet and mesh. *Punishment and Society, 3*(1), 95–133.

Wacquant, L. (2001b). The penalisation of poverty and the rise of neoliberalism. *European Journal on Criminal Policy and Research, 9*(4), 401–412.

Wacquant, L. (2003). Toward a dictatorship over the poor? Notes on the penalization of poverty in Brazil. *Punishment and Society, 5*(2), 197–205.

Wacquant, L. (2010). *Castigar a los Pobres*. Barcelona: Gedisa.

Wilson, E., & Lindsey, T. (Eds.). (2009). *Government of the shadows. Parapolitcs and criminal sovereignty*. New York: Pluto Press.

Index[1]

[1] Note: Page numbers followed by 'n' refer to notes.

S. Darke et al. (eds.), *Carceral Communities in Latin America*, Palgrave Studies in Prisons and Penology, https://doi.org/10.1007/978-3-030-61499-7

The manufacturer's authorised representative in the EU is Springer
Nature Customer Service Centre GmbH, Europaplatz 3, 69115 Heidelberg,
Germany. If you have any concerns regarding our products, please
contact ProductSafety@springernature.com

Printed and bound by CPI Group (UK) Ltd, Croydon, CR0 4YY
22/09/2026
02220985-0001